D0339998

Policy and Politics in
France

Policy and Politics in Industrial States

A series edited by Douglas E. Ashford, Peter Katzenstein, and T. J. Pempel

Douglas E. Ashford

Policy and Politics in
France

Living with Uncertainty

Temple University Press

Philadelphia

Temple University Press, Philadelphia 19122
© 1982 by Temple University
Published 1982
Printed in the United States of America

Library of Congress Cataloging in Publication Data
Ashford, Douglas Elliott.
  Policy and politics in France.
  (Policy and politics in industrial states)
  Bibliography: p.
  Includes index.
  1. France—Politics and government—1958–
  2. France—Economic policy—1945–   .
  3. France—Social policy. I. Title. II. Series.
  JN2594.2.A82   320.944   82-5771
  ISBN 0-87722-261-4   AACR2
  ISBN 0-87722-262-2 (pbk.)

Contents

Editors' Preface

All industrial states face a tension between bureaucracy and democracy. Modern governments have found it increasingly difficult to formulate policies adequate to the complex tasks they undertake. At the same time the growing specialization and widening scope of government have led many to question whether it can still be controlled democratically. Policy and Politics in Industrial States explores how some of the major democracies have dealt with this dilemma.

Policy is a pattern of purposive action by which political institutions shape society. It typically involves a wide variety of efforts to address certain societal problems. Politics is also a much broader concept, involving the conflict and choices linking individuals and social forces to the political institutions that make policy. Comparative analysis of the interaction between policy and politics is an essential beginning in understanding how and why industrial states differ or converge in their responses to common problems.

The fact that the advanced industrial states are pursuing many similar aims such as increasing social well-being, reducing social conflict, and achieving higher levels of employment and economic productivity means neither that they will all do so in the same way nor that the relevance of politics to such behavior will always be the same. In looking at an array of problems common to all industrial states, the books in this series argue that policies are shaped primarily by the manner in which power is organized within each country. Thus, Britain, Japan, the United States, West Germany, Sweden, and France set distinctive priorities and follow distinctive policies designed to achieve them. In this respect the series dissents from the view that the nature of the problem faced is the most important feature in determining the politics surrounding efforts at its resolution. Taken to its logical extreme, this view supports the expectation that all states will pursue broadly similar goals in politically similar ways. Though this series will illustrate some important similarities among the policies of different countries, one of the key conclusions to which it points is the distinctive approach that each state takes in managing the problems it confronts.

A second important feature of the series is its sensitivity to the difficulties involved in evaluating policy success or failure. Goals are ambiguous and often contradictory from one area of policy to another; past precedents often shape present options. Conversely, adhering to choices made at an earlier time is often impossible or undesirable at a later period. Hence evaluation must transcend the application of simple economic or managerial criteria of rationality, efficiency, or effectiveness. What appears from such perspectives as irrational, inefficient, or ineffective is often, from a political standpoint, quite intelligible.

To facilitate comparison, the books in the series follow a common format. In each book, the first chapter introduces the reader to the country's political institutions and social forces, spells out how these are linked to form that country's distinctive configuration of power, and explores how that configuration can be expected to influence policy. A concluding chapter seeks to integrate the country argument developed in the first chapter with the subsequent policy analysis and provides more general observations about the ways in which the specific country findings fit into current debates about policy and politics.

The intervening six chapters provide policy cases designed to illustrate, extend, and refine the country argument. Each of the six policy analyses follows a common format. The first section analyzes the *context* of the policy problem: its historical roots, competing perceptions of the problem by major political and social groups, and its interdependence with other problems facing the country. The second section deals with the *agenda* set out for the problem: the pressures generating action and the explicit and implicit motives of important political actors, including the government's objectives. The third section deals with *process*: the formulation of the issue, its attempted resolution, and the instruments involved in policy implementation. The fourth and final section of analysis traces the *consequences* of policy for official objectives, for the power distribution in the issue area, for other policies, and for the country's capacity to make policy choices in the future. The element of arbitrariness such a schema introduces into the discussion of policy and politics is a price the series gladly pays in the interest of facilitating comparative analysis of policy and politics.

An important feature of these cases is the inclusion, for each policy problem, of selected readings drawn primarily from official policy documents, interpretations, or critiques of policy by different actors, and politically informed analysis. We have become persuaded that the actual language used in policy debates within each country provides an important clue to the relationship between that country's policy and its politics. Since appropriate readings are more widely available for Britain and the United States than for the non-English—speaking countries in the series, we have included somewhat more policy materials for these countries. In all instances, the readings are selected as illustration, rather than confirmation, of each book's argument.

Also distinctive of the series, and essential to its comparative approach, is the selection of common policy cases. Each volume analyzes at least one case involving intergovernmental problems: reform of the national bureaucracy or the interaction among national, regional, and local governments. Each also includes two cases dealing with economic problems: economic policy and labor-management relations. Lastly, each book includes at least two cases focusing on the relationship of individual citizens to the state, among them social welfare. Our choice is designed to provide a basis for cross-national and cross-issue comparison while being sufficiently flexible to make allowance for the idiosyncracies of the countries (and the authors). By using such a framework, we hope that these books will convey the richness and diversity of each country's efforts to solve major problems, as well as the similarities of the interaction between policy and politics in industrial states.

D. E. A.
P. J. K.
T. J. P.

Preface

The turbulence and intensity of French politics cannot help but create trepidation for anyone writing about the country. Nearly every writer on France, including many leading French citizens, have nothing but despair for French institutions and politics. The theme of this book is defined in a way that I hope will cause readers to reconsider the flood of criticism brought against French political achievements. The politics of French policymaking is an intriguing test of the more pessimistic arguments, because France has succeeded relatively well in a precarious world, even when striking out with highly nationalist measures and defying many Western democracies. The book is not intended to be an uncritical assessment of French policymaking, but does try to strike a balance between what French performance suggests must be some virtues in the French policy process, and the more well-known critiques of France.

There is less elaboration of the logic behind my analysis than some readers might wish for in this introductory book. The reason is quite simple. If uncertainty is the basic description by friend and foe within French politics, then perhaps it should be treated as a constant of French political life, rather than lamented. The policy analyses are the springboards from which we can begin to see how regularity and consistency is introduced into French politics despite its alleged excesses and weaknesses. In this limited sense, policymaking may be the bedrock of French politics and possibly a substitute for those more formal and reliable institutional relationships that most modern democracies have been able to develop. As I shall suggest in the Conclusion (see Chapter 8), there may even be positive advantages in having a loose connection between politics and policy, even though such weak institutional links may also expose basic democratic practices to greater risk. The ability to live and prosper with such ambiguous institutions may have its virtues, especially as the task of government expands with the modern welfare state.

In writing the book I have received the assistance of countless French politicians and administrators who patiently responded to a host of questions. I cannot acknowledge them all, and I hope that I have not betrayed their trust and cooperation. A number of French scholars and officials did read particular chapters of the book, and to them I am especially grateful: Louis Fougère, Bernard Gournay, Catherine Grémion, François Lagrange, Jean Padioleau, Guy Terny and Jean-Claude Thoenig. I have also been relentless in calling on many friends outside France who share my fascination with French politics: John Ambler, Suzanne Berger, Ann Corbett, Gary Freeman, David Goldey, Peter Hall, Jack Hayward, John Keeler, Martin Schain, and Vincent Wright. They all have added immeasurably to the coherence and balance of my thinking, and I hope I have done justice to their comments and reactions.

Several comments may help the reader. First, I have provided a list of abbreviations and frequently used them in the text because this is how the French themselves describe their governmental machinery. I have tried to avoid excessive use of French terms, but I do assume that the student will have a basic knowledge of French institutions and their names. Second, I have made a special effort to include in the references as many English writings as possible on French policies and policymaking. The references for Chapters 1 and 8 are all under General References, as well as some general government reports that are cited in several places in the book. I have doubts that the elitist character of French government exceeds that of most modern, complex governments, and so have made an effort to include notes on the many government reports that are available. Third, assuming that most undergraduate readers will not read French, I have tried to provide a balance of political views in the readings, especially so as to take into account the transition to a Socialist government.

Special thanks are due to the University of Manchester where my visit as Simon Professor provided time to write a first draft of the book. I should also like to thank Catherine Esser for helping with the translations. *Le Monde* kindly gave permission to reprint extended portions of a number of articles. The Royal Institute of Public Administration and Vincent Wright also gave permission to reprint parts of several articles from *Public Administration*. I am also indebted to the Cornell Center for International Studies, whose summer support has enabled me to return regularly to Europe.

Douglas E. Ashford

Ithaca, New York
December 1981

Abbreviations

AAE	Amicale des Algériens en Europe (1962)
ACOSS	Agence Centrale des Organismes de Securité Sociale (1967)
ADAP	Association pour le Développement des Associations de Progrés
AEE	Amicale pour l'Enseignement (1961)
AFPA	Association pour la Formation Professionelle des Adultes (1946)
AGIRC	Association Générale des Institutions de Retraites des Cadres (1947)
AGREF	Association Groupant les Plus Grandes Entreprises Fransçaises
AMEXA	Assurance Maladie des Exploitants Agricôles (1961)
ANACT	Agence Nationale pour l'Amélioration des Conditions de Travail
ANFPA	Association Nationale pour la Formation Professionelle des Adultes
ANPE	Agence Nationale pour l'Emploi (1967)
ARRCO	Association des Régimes de Retraites Complémentaires (1961)
ASA	Allocation Supplémentaire d'Attente (1974)
ASSEDIC	Association pour l'Emploi dans l'Industrie et le Commerce (1967)
ATOM	Mouvement d'Aide aux Travailleurs d'Outre-Mer (1965)
AVTS	Allocation aux Vieux Travailleurs Salariés

BAPSA   Budget Annexe des Prestations Sociales Agricôles
BAPSO   Budget Annexe des Prestations Sociales Obligatoires

CANAM   Caisse Nationale de l'Assurance Maladie
CANCAVA   Caisse Autonome Nationale de Compensation de l'Assurance Vieillesse Artisanale.
CDES   Commission d'Education Spéciale
CERES   Centre d'Etudes, de Recherches et d'Education Socialistes
CFDT   Confédération Française Démocratique du Travail (1964)
CFTC   Confédération Française des Travailleurs Chrétiens (1919)
CGC   Confédération Générale des Cadres (1944)
CGP   Commissariat Générale du Plan
CGPME   Confédération Générale des Petites et Moyennes Entreprises
CGT   Confédération Générale des Travail (1895)
CGT-FO   Confédération Générale Travail-Force Ouvrière
CIASI   Comité Interministériel d'Aménagement des Structures Industrielles
CIEMM   Centre d'Information et d'Etudes sur les Migrations Mediterranéens
CME   Commission de la Main d'Oeuvre Etrangère (1973)
CNAF   Caisse Nationale des Allocations Familiales
CNAV   Caisse Nationale de l'Assurance Vieillesse
CNLI   Commission Nationale pour le Logement des Immigrés
CNPF   Conseil National du Patronat Français
CODER   Commission de Développement Economique et Régionale
CODIS   Commission de Développement des Industries Stratégiques
COTOREP   Commission Technique d'Orientation et de Reclassement Professionel
CREDOC   Centre de Recherche pour l'Etude et l'Observation des Conditions de Vie

DATAR   Délégation d'Aménagement du Territoire et d'Action Régionale

DGRST   Délégation Générale à la Recherche Scientifique et Technique (1958)

FAF   Fonds d'Assurance Formation (1968)
FAL   Fonds d'Action Locale
FAS   Fonds d'Action Sociale pour les Travailleurs Migrants
FASTI   Fédération des Associations de Solidarité avec les Travailleurs Immigrés (1965)
FDES   Fonds de Développement Economique et Social
FECL   Fonds d'Equipement de Collectivités Locales
FEN   Fédération de l'Education Nationale (1948)
FGDS   Fédération de la Gauche Démocrate et Socialiste
FIAT   Fonds Intérministériels d'Aménagement du Territoire
FME   Fonds de Modernisation et de la l'Equipement
FNAFU   Fonds Nationale d'Aménagement Foncier et de l'Urbanisme
FNE   Fonds Nationale de l'Emploi (1963)
FNS   Fonds National de Solidarité (1956)
FNSEA   Fédération Nationale des Syndicats d'Exploitants Agricoles

GIP   Groupe Interministériel pour la Résorption de l'Habitat Insalubre (1970)
GISTI   Groupe d'Information et de Soutien aux Travailleurs Immigrés

IGAS   Inspection Générale des Affaires Sociales (1967)
INSEE   Institut National de la Stalistique et des Etudes Economiques

MDARM   Mouvement de Défense et d'Assistance des Rapatriés Musulmans
MODEF   Mouvement pour la Coordination et la Défense de l'Exploitation Familiale
MONATAR   Mouvement National des Travailleurs Agricoles et Ruraux
MRAP   Mouvement Contre le Racisme et pour l'Amitié entre les Peuples

ONI	Office National d'Immigration
ORGANIC	Organisation Autonome Nationale de l'Industrie et de Commerce
PCF	Parti Communiste Français
PS	Parti Socialiste
PSU	Parti Socialiste Unifié
RCB	Rationalisation des choix budgétaires
RI	Républicains Indépendants (Giscardian Party 1962–1978)
RPR	Rassemblement pour la République (Gaullist Party 1976–)
SFIO	Section Française de l'Internationale Ouvrière (Socialist Party 1920–1971)
SIVOM	Syndicat à Vocation Multiple
SMIC	Salaire Minimum Interprofessionel de Croissance (1972)
SONA-COTRA	Société Nationale de Construction de Logement pour les Travailleurs
SOUND-IATA	Soutien et Aide aux Travailleurs Africains (1963)
UCANSS	Union des Caisses Nationales de Securité Sociale
UCN	Union des Caisses Nationales (1968)
UDF	Union pour la Démocratie Francaise (Giscardian Party 1978–)
UDR	Union pour la Défense de la République (Gaullist Party 1968–1971)
UDVE	Union des Démocrates pour la Ve République (Gaullist Party 1967–1968)
UIMM	Union des Industries Métallurgiques et Minières
UNAPEI	Union Nationale des Associations de Parents d'Enfants Inadaptés
UNEDIC	Union Nationale Interprofessionnelle pour l'Emploi dans l'Industrie et le Commerce
UNR	Union pours la Nouvelle République (Gaullist Party 1958–1967)
URSSAF	Union pour le Recouvrement des Cotisations de Securite Sociale et d'Allocation Familiales (1967)

Policy and Politics in
France

1 The Policy Process and Institutional Uncertainty

In most of the comparisons between France and other modern democracies, France generally appears as an anomoly. Although the French Revolution left an indelible mark on the history of modern democracy, the country's erratic development over the nineteenth century and its resistance to change under the Third and Fourth Republics make France seem to be the model of how *not* to practice modern democratic government. The relapse of German and Italian democracies into fascism was such a dramatic instance of democratic failure that these two countries are often treated as exceptions in the historical development of modern democracy. On the northern periphery of Europe, Sweden and the other Scandinavian countries developed strong social democratic movements early in the century, and steadily progressed toward the modern welfare state. The bastion of democratic government seemed to be Britain, whose well-institutionalized democracy was successfully transplanted in North America. Espousing neither Anglo-Saxon political virtues nor Scandinavian social equity, France has always seemed to be Europe's temperamental child.

The standard view of France is perhaps best summarized by Thomson, who wrote one of the most influential histories of modern France. In his words, democracy and government were "two poles too far apart for the vital spark of democratic government to flash between them" (1958, p. 14). France seemed to be entangled in a dilemma of its own making, having insisted since Rousseau that somehow authority must be perfectly congruent with the popular will, while remaining vulnerable to political adventurers and heroic leaders because it could not build ideally democratic institutions.

The superficial evidence of instability is unmistakable. In the two centuries of struggle to achieve democratic government, there have been over a dozen constitutions and nearly every conceivable type of regime ranging from Napoleon's dictatorship to constitutional monarchy. Even when France seemed set on course, its political instability shocked the rest of Europe.

For nearly a decade the Third Republic (1871–1940) lived on the brink of disaster, and only a single vote (the Wallon amendment, by a little known prefect) rescued the democratic election of the president from monarchist designs. "The Republic was founded by a Monarchist assembly with a right-wing President and Government in power; on the motion of a Catholic lawyer who insisted that he was not asking for the Republic" (Thomson, p. 90). The turbulence of French politics seemed to devour ministers. The Third Republic had 104 cabinets in seventy years and the Fourth Republic (1946–58) had twenty-three cabinets with over 240 appointments (Dogan, 1979). The inventors of modern democracy seemed almost eager to debase participation. Under the Second Empire (1851–70) prefects were political agents. In one instance—when an election returned republicans—the prefect arranged to have the office and its electoral records burned (Chapman, 1955, p. 34). In the Third Republic election of 1881, the disparities between constituencies was so great that a million more persons voted for defeated candidates than for winning candidates (Zeldin, 1979, p. 27).

Obviously, such unfavorable conditions preoccupied the theorists and commentators on French political development. For one thing, the French have always been their own severest critics. Tocqueville's epic study of American democracy (1951) became the classic critique of France torn between the tyranny of the majority and autocratic rule. His book was widely praised at the time, but even an admiring John Stuart Mill observed that "from the scarcity of examples, his propositions even when derived from observation, have the air of being mere speculations" (P. Bradley in Introduction to Tocqueville, 1951, p. viii). Tocqueville's thoughts are the basis of one of the most severe of contemporary critiques by Crozier (1970) whose phrase "stalemate society" has become part of the French political vocabulary. An even more biting, if somewhat flamboyant, indictment has been made by a leading French politician, Alain Peyrefitte, whose book Le Mal Français (The French

Affliction) (1976) became an overnight bestseller. No event throughout French history seems to satisfy Peyrefitte, although Dumont (1979) wrote a fascinating refutation which indicates the dangers of uncritical historical interpretation. The effect of these much publicized and dramatic debates about the weaknesses of French democracy is that we lost sight of some of the remarkable accomplishments of French government, not the least of which is to have made steady progress toward a more prosperous and more equitable society under the Fifth Republic. There could hardly be a more appropriate vindication of the institutional achievements of the Fifth Republic than the victory of the Socialist Party in 1981.

French Politics Seen through the Policy Process

Unlike many studies of French politics, this study does not take the fragility of French democracy and the weakness of French political institutions as a starting point. A policy approach relies much less on abstract theories about success and failure and more on how well the policy process responds to major social, economic, and political issues. More abstract economic or social theories derive arbitrary standards of performance from their assumptions, whether or not these are relevant to political and institutional realities. France may have fallen short of many reasonable expectations in bringing about social change and may not have achieved the political stability of much of Europe and North America, but to attribute such generalized failings to policymakers may underestimate the complexity of modern government. A major purpose of this volume, then, is to underscore the intricacy of many policy choices confronting France over the past two decades. Seen through the policy process, French politics has not been the dismal failure that many of its own critics assert. Given the bewildering array of social and political forces brought to bear on French (and any other) government, one might even claim that France has had considerable success.

Assessing French politics through the political conflicts of real choices leads to very different conclusions. For one thing, French leaders are asked to accept higher risks than most Western democratic leaders have experienced. For over a century, France has had a multiparty system that imposed enormous demands on the patience and ingenuity of party leaders and caused endless conflict over electoral alliances. Even if one survives an unpredictable and often unjust electoral system, there is then the bickering over forming a coalition government and the scramble for ministerial power. Once in office, the executive is surrounded by numerous quasi-autonomous bodies designed to curb national authority and review his decisions. While it is possible to use an elaborate and well-institutionalized system of administrative law to circumvent democratic control, it is also true that civil servants have their vested interests in the system and their own ways of resisting change. The intricacy of the party system and the unreliability of parliament mean that a leader can rarely depend on more conventional ways of passing legislation. If one concentrates on how difficult it is to produce collective decisions in France, much less implement them in a society acutely aware of its individual rights, one is more likely to sympathize with French leaders than to criticize them. The problem was succinctly stated by one of many frustrated prime ministers of the Fourth Republic, Herriot, "You are condemned to live together."

The policy process in democratic countries is essentially a procedure to link popular demands and preferences to collective, and ultimately governmental, decisions. In the pursuit of more quantitative and behavioral approaches to politics, our discipline has often oversimplified the politics of making the critical connection between demands and performance. Without becoming immersed in disciplinary quarrels, the overall effect has been to neglect the role of political and administrative institutions in making such a connection. Oddly enough, French political science pioneered the study of electoral sociology in the 1930s in an effort to understand the curiosities of French political behavior, but their work—and subsequent efforts by American political science—has done little to penetrate or explain the institutional constraints and uncertainties of French politics. On the contrary, the French seem to have a genius for maximizing political ambiguity. The institutional uncertainties abound in the electoral and party systems, the lawmaking process, and the administrative system. The poorly defined relationships of the president, prime minister and parliament have produced reams of constitutional speculation. A policy approach to French politics concentrates on how these uncertainties affect French capabilities to make collective decisions.

As argued throughout the series, it is difficult to put a policy process in perspective without comparison. Indeed, this may explain why so many French critics of the system fail to see that the stability and effectiveness they perceive (and sometimes exaggerate) in Britain, the United States, or Sweden are purchased by imposing other kinds of limitations on performance, and even on the manifestation of democratic values. The constitution of the Fifth Republic is itself a revealing illustration. The most important author of the 1958 constitution, Michel Debré, clearly envied the discipline of British parliament and parties, the authority of the British prime minister, and the apparent ease with which British civil servants implemented ministerial desires. One perceptive observer of French politics suggests there has been a longstanding effort "to import and to adapt the British model as the French misunderstood it" (Hayward, 1973, p. 2). As we shall see in the policy analyses to follow, French ministers are regularly deterred by considerations that would be easily swept aside in Britain, or would seldom arise in Sweden. There is a certain naiveté in thinking that if only institutional uncertainty would disappear, there would then be few problems reconciling democratic values with the realities of governance. A policy approach suggests the opposite. If institutional ambiguities were removed, there might be little democracy as we understand it in the West.

The general result is that the writing on the politics of policymaking in France presents curious contradictions. On the one hand, French critics feel that the policy process—and in particular the administration—produced an overcentralized and arbitrary state, but they provide little specific details on how the necessary reforms might be achieved. This book differs from the French interpretation of the country's ills in suggesting that the rapid transformation of policy problems and procedures over the past two decades may have had the unintended and constructive effect of making the French people aware of some fundamental institutional weaknesses of their political system. France is still in the very early days of the Socialists' rule, but the opposition victory of 1981 presents us with a fascinating test of whether the weaknesses perceived by many French critics were linked to the long period of Gaullist rule and their alleged manipulation of the administration, or if France suffers from a deeper institutional problem of persuasively linking political demands and preferences to policymaking. As I shall argue in more detail in the Conclusion (see Chapter 8), whichever interpretation is correct, over the first twenty years of the Fifth Republic, policymaking has often been at the center of partisan and electoral controversy. As such, policies have had more direct influence on French politics than in many modern democracies where policymaking is more carefully sheltered from competitive politics.

From the perspective of more general theories about policy and politics, France is also an elusive and difficult case. The aim of all the books in this series is to show how policy plays an increasingly important role in modern democracies, and may even be a more important causal factor in explaining the performance of political systems than are elections, party politics, or legislatures. If we take the general systems model of politics—most clearly elaborated by Easton (1965)—as the prevailing view, it is fairly clear why France does not meet the conventional expectations of political scientists. In the Eastonian system (which has, in turn, stimulated a great deal of highly aggregated research on systems as a whole), "inputs" are assumed to have a reasonably clear and direct link to "outputs." Generally speaking, the "black box" of government and administration serves only to translate what are thought to be reasonably clear demands and preferences into what are thought to be appropriate and satisfying performance. Not only was the logical simplicity of the Eastonian model attractive, but it readily accommodated the prevailing behavioral methods of recent political science which used the individual, studied through surveys and direct observation, as the basic unit of analysis.

Nearly any approach to politics through the policy process is likely to differ from the abstract preoccupations of systems analysis. First, a great deal of the behavior within complex policy processes cannot be attributed to any single individual, but takes place under the umbrella of accumulated legislation, and within the protected confines of an administration that is necessarily protected from many daily concerns of political actors. Second, governments embody general principles and objectives in constitutions, individual rights, and judicial standards that are, in the short term at least, not open to political manipulation. There are collective constraints that affect the capacity and procedures within the black box. Third, a great deal of more recent writing on the development of the welfare state suggests that the input-output relationship is not a simple causal link and probably never was. Policymakers make complicated trade-offs of rewards and benefits in the policy process. Administrators pursue their self-interest and often have vested interests in particular clienteles. Even on the "input" side of politics, parties have internal conflicts and rivalries, and elections have distorting effects on the expression of preferences, so that a perfect translation of demands into performance is probably impossible. Thus, both the principles and practice of democratic politics suggest that the policy process is highly discretionary, and that the aggregation of individual attitudes and values is, at best, an approximation.

When I refer to the macrotheories of politics throughout the book, I shall be referring to more general approaches to the study of politics that do not provide the concepts or methods by which we might penetrate the underlying tensions and diversity of the policy process and, in turn, its effects on both performance and the aggregation of demands. Although macrotheories and their behavioral elaborations raise many interesting questions about political participation and elections, they do not provide tools to define the pervasive and continuing influence of government itself. Essentially, the study of the politics of policy starts where the abstract theories leave off; that is, we are concerned with how political influence is exercised within governments and through bureaucratic procedures. The causal links are often reversed and, particularly with the growth of government, often rooted in mutual dependence between actors within government or administration.

In most democratic systems, there are fairly well-defined and stable institutions that serve both as filters for the aggregation of such influence and as agencies to set general priorities and goals. France is a particularly instructive illustration of the importance of policymaking precisely because the institutional constraints generated by strong parties, an effective legislature, and a delineated executive are poorly defined. An approach to France through systems analysis is almost certain to be baffling because institutional uncertainties deprive the analyst of the most commonly observed structures used to study the balancing of "inputs" and "outputs." Generally speaking, the French critics are unpersuasive because, as we shall see in the policy analyses to follow, they cannot separate what may be the more general problems of democratic governance from the alleged political ills of France. Many of the same complaints are echoed in Washington, London, and Tokyo, and a comparative analysis should help unravel the shared and the unique problems of a country. At the other extreme, the systems model is so abstract that it does not help us identify how politics is used within the policy process. An abstract model necessarily applies such a rarified concept of politics that the politics of policymaking simply falls through its sieve.

For purposes of this volume, I have devised an intermediate approach which is intended to capture the intuitive, if untestable, wisdom of the French critics while avoiding the abstract level of much political science. To do so, I am asking a fairly simple question that is ignored by both the critics and the theorists. If we consider the institutionalized behavior which links demands to performance a hallmark of the policy process in democratic systems, how has France sustained the legitimacy of a policy process that has existed for so long with less institutionalized restraint than found in most modern democracies? Will the analysis of the politics of policymaking in France enable us to see more clearly how political and institutional constraints, contrary to the critics' view, are indeed imposed? And will the policy analyses also help us see that even with weak institutions, there is an institutionalized relationship between "inputs" and "outputs" that helps find an acceptable balance within the political system? These issues will be discussed in the Conclusion (see Chapter 8), but a preliminary task is to specify the nature of institutional uncertainty in France.

Institutional Uncertainty and French Policymaking

The political and historical development of every democratic system has a continuing impact on the policymaking process. In approaches to politics that place more emphasis on broad societal characteristics, such as social stratification or religious differences as they relate to politics, the policy process is given less importance. In the formative years of most modern democracies, aligning intensely held social differences with politics and policy was a major problem. The historical sequence of reconciling such resistance to change with the requirements of majority rule and free elections varies greatly from country to country. The diversity of this process is perhaps the true genius of democratic government. From this slow process evolves the mediating institutional framework which makes collective decisions possible. To understand the importance of policymaking in France and its relation to French institutional development, one must understand that building acceptable procedures and rules to share the risks and costs of collective authority was a particularly difficult task.

There is a large political science literature dealing with uncertainty as it affects individuals in elections and voting. Less has been written about uncertainty as it relates to the role of institutions in reconciling popular demands and governmental performance. Because the central theme of the book is institutional uncertainty, it is important to define the phrase. Essentially, I am referring to the transformation of highly diverse and constantly changing individual expectations to the working of government. Elections and parties are obviously not the only way in which such aggregation and reconciliation takes place. To have a democratic government means to have accumulated a body of law and procedures, a shared understanding about individual and collective rights, and a developed set of legislative and executive rules for sharing in the exercise of power once parties and elections have expressed popular preferences. Where the combination of these expectations is well-defined and widely shared, one can speak of institutional certainty, meaning that law, rights, and collective authority as vested in government are clearly understood. The basic theme of the book is that the institutional reconciliation of these problems has not progressed as rapidly in France as in most democratic countries.

The phrase "institutional uncertainty" is used to differentiate the particular organizational and legal problems of establishing effective government from the broader concept of legitimacy. One can find many regimes, especially in the Third World, that unquestionably have the overwhelming support of their citizens as individuals, but do not have a clear understanding of how choices and expectations may be reconciled in an orderly way. Saudi Arabia and Iran clearly have legitimate governments, but in neither case would we think that they have institutional stability. Institutional stability implies more than widely shared beliefs concerning the use of collective authority. For democratic governance, it also implies that alternation of parties, definitions of executive and legislative roles, and checks on the use of collective authority by both political and administrative actors are clearly established. Not surprisingly, as the role of government expands—as it clearly has in every advanced welfare state over the past generation—the possibilities of institutional instability increase. It is perhaps fair to say (though it is a broad historical generalization) that the Fifth Republic was born out of institutional instability. By 1958, most of Europe knew how to make decisions that, in effect, greatly expanded the role of government. Without diminishing the progress that had been made under the Fourth Republic (1946–58), by European and North American standards the nature of governance itself remained ambiguous in France.

In most democratic countries, we can detect a critical period when a series of fundamental decisions were made on how to relate popular government to the necessities of collective authority. While the democratic institutions that emerged from these transitional moments in history have undergone continual change, a deeply held consensus was formed—usually in the formative years of the new democracies—as to how institutions might exercise collective authority. Even where we find similar social cleavages and economic interests, the democratic compromise often took different shape. In the United States, for example, the federalist debates provided the ground rules for the sharing of power between the federal government and the states, in ways that the Founding Fathers thought would best preserve individual rights and protect minority interests. In Britain, an aristocracy seized upon the common law to restrain an unreasonable monarchy, and devised cabinet government. In effect, parliamentary and cabinet rule acquired all the powers of a monarchy, and became the sole guardian of democratic legitimacy. For late modernizers such as Germany, Italy, and Japan, the process was more erratic and the institutional groundwork of democracy less well-established. The fragility of democratic government in these countries is in no small measure due to the understandable tendency to rely more heavily on old institutions, the traditional bureaucracy, and even predemocratic values in order to make the transition more rapidly.

France falls midway between the early democratic revolutions—where the central issues were clearly seen—and the later transitions—where there was little time to engage in the extended debates and accumulation of experience that permits each democracy to find its own solution to the compromise between democratic values and collective authority. France had a very clear concept of democracy at a relatively early stage in its political development, but great difficulty translating the concept into institutional form. In the rapidly shifting balance of forces during the Revolution (Godechot, 1968), the country drifted toward chaos and turned to a strong man, Napoleon, who seemed capable of solving nearly all the institutional dilemmas that were sapping French strength and vitality. Indeed, the Napoleonic period is probably the most intense period of institution-building among Western societies. The nearest equivalent is perhaps the Meiji restoration period in late nineteenth-century Japan (Pempel, 1981). In hardly more than a decade, France acquired a supreme legal advisory body, the Council of State; a number of highly trained administrative bodies or *grands corps*, each with their designated duties, privileges and rules (see Chapter 2); a rigidly hierarchical educational structure capped off by the French Academy whose special task was (and remains) to purify the French language; and a carefully designed territorial structure under prefects (provincial governors) who were personally selected by the Emperor, who called them *"mes petits empereurs"* "my small emperors" (see Chapter 3). Napoleon, distrustful of the common law, also set in motion the systematic codification of the rules and procedures governing every aspect of French life. These codes are the basis of administrative law in France, covering nearly every topic from social security to urban development. While most of the French people worshipped their hero, the political dilemma is fairly obvious. Democracy languished while a modern institutional and administrative structure was superimposed on the society.

The effects of this critical period in the development of French democracy can hardly be underestimated and, in many ways, is still at the root of contemporary disputes over the nature of collective authority in France. For one thing, France acquired an elaborate and top-heavy administrative system, no doubt far more elaborate than needed for what was then a peasant society. In Kessleman's terms (1970), France was "overinstitutionalized." The system of rules, procedures, and laws governing the relationship between popular government and authoritative decisons was intricate and easily appeared arbitrary. In their daily lives most French having inspired democratic governments, found themselves confronted with inefficient and unresponsive institutions. The intensity and duration of institutional uncertainty obscures the fact that, compared to much of Europe, political participation progressed over the nineteenth century despite the numerous shifts from constitutional monarchy to republic to empire. In 1830, there were more voters in France than in Britain. Under the Third Republic, universal male suffrage was unencumbered by the property qualifications that were still common in Europe. Nonetheless, France had "big government" well before the rest of Europe. In 1830, for example, the Ministry of the Interior had 200,000 employees when the British Home Office was only an informal collection of a few dozen clerks.

Putting aside much of the historical detail that made the administrative system the key to French institutional development, it became almost inevitable that those who find government lacking in some respect would find the administration the cause of their problems. Indeed, because the top-heavy and intricate administrative structure was the institutional framework for the state, they could hardly find anything else to blame. Other countries seemed to have more flexible and less oppressive mediating institutions, often built on principles that could more easily accomodate change and adjust to new demands. British administrative practice was based on the common law, which appeared to have pragmatic and tested solutions for every dilemma and need (Ashford, 1981b). The Americans developed a system of intergovernmental bargaining among the states and federal government which was a strong decentralizing force on the society. Despite the relapse into fascist rule, Germany had the idea of the *Rechstaat*, or legal state, to guide them through the complexities of modern government (Dyson, 1980). Of course, the French often failed to see that each of these institutional compromises imposed other uncertainties and costs on politics and society. Thus, France had made the administrative state the central issue in the institutional compromise between democracy and collective authority. The fact that it was uniformly condemned from all quarters is quite possibly the best clue to its importance. In a policy study, it is also important to see that the reasons for blaming the administrative structure for all of France's ills varied a great deal.

The popularity of the most outspoken critics—led by Michel Crozier and elaborated in his widely acclaimed work on the "stalemate society" (1970)—easily overshadows the other two forces which, in many ways, were no less alarmed that French institutions seemed to work poorly. There were, first, those in power—the Gaullists—who had little choice but to use the existing administration in 1958 when propelled into office by the Algerian crisis. While it is natural, in a democracy, to criticize those in office, it is often forgotten that many of the Gaullist leaders were no less content with French administration than were the less inhibited critics outside government. In 1945, de Gaulle had given the task of creating a new body of general administrators (*administrateurs civils*) to his most trusted lieutenant, Debré, who organized the National School of Administration (ENA) with the express purpose of neutralizing the influence of the old, specialized *grands corps* (see Chapter 2). If de Gaulle relied excessively on the technical expertise of the higher civil servants in the early years of the Fifth Republic, it was in part because France was threatened with becoming technically and economically deficient in a rapidly modernizing Europe (see Chapter 4). As we shall see in the policy analyses to follow, the Gaullists were often disappointed when they did depend on highly technocratic solutions to policy problems. De Gaulle had no option to counter administrative power except an appeal to political parties, most of whom initially distrusted his intentions. To de Gaulle the "regime of parties" meant the Fourth Republic that had brought France to the brink of civil war over Algeria and had neglected French military and economic strength in a precarious world. But at the root of the dilemma is the fact that the administration attracts many of the best minds of France who understand how government works. By 1980, there was much less doubt that government could be run without depending on the administration. In fact, the Socialist government of Mitterrand in 1981 was quickly dubbed the "republic of the professors" and his cabinet was full of elite administrators. Even the National Assembly, elected in the euphoria of a Socialist victory, found that nearly 60 percent of the new deputies were former civil servants (*Figaro*, July 21, 1981).

A second group—easily treated as peripheral to the argument over French institutions—is the administrative elite itself. While it is fairly easy to demonstrate the inefficiency and heavyhandedness of the bureaucracy in any modern welfare state, it is much more difficult to show how bureaucracy will be replaced. The dissatisfaction with French institutions that seemed to spring from all quarters in the 1960s often failed to see how vulnerable the civil service was and how many internal divisions compromised their effective power over decisions. Whether real or imagined, the "failure" of the Fourth Republic fell just as heavily on the shoulders of top civil servants as on the leaders of the endless party squabbles that eroded the authority of the Fourth Republic. De Gaulle's determination to modernize the French economy and to restore effective government was as much a threat to the administration as it was to the undecided political parties. As the cases will show in more detail, the elite civil servants did not at all agree on how to use their new opportunities. There was, for example, a bitter internecine struggle within the Ministry of Infrastructure (now the Ministry of the Environment and Quality of Life) between the older, rurally based *grands corps*, the *génie rural* or rural services, and the more technically advanced *ponts et chaussées* or civil engineers (Thoenig, 1974). The reforms of local and regional government, in 1964, generated a severe split within the elite prefectoral corps, the chief administrators of the French departments (Grémion, 1979; see Chapter 3). In the early 1960s, the prestigious Council of State, an elite of the most talented administrative lawyers of France, was in open conflict with de Gaulle; the president even tried to impose new rules to curb their powers over administrative law. While many of the complaints over the power of the administration are justified, they were by no means unique to France in the 1960s. Nearly every democratic government was undergoing a process of self-examination about reconciling administrative power with the expanding role of government.

For the critics themselves, the dependence of French political institutions on administrative power was, of course, conceived in more sophisticated terms than simply a stalemate. In his early work on French administration, Crozier (1964) had developed a general theory about French behavior, based on the idea that the French are predisposed to avoid face-to-face conflict. In his interpretation, conflict avoidance produced cycles of neglect and spasms of rapid adjustment that resulted in further centralization and bureaucratization of French life. Unable to work together in harmony, the French depended on administration while simultaneously resenting it. Essentially, the argument is based on the inability of the French to handle the ambiguities of power, which has a long tradition in the field of social psychology. The Crozier group became strong critics of French administration, but it is important to see that their theory was not designed specifically to challenge bureaucracy. The theory is not constructed from general statements about French institutions, but is a description of national character intended to explain collective behavior in many contexts. The administration was only its most obvious target. Without concentrating on its methodological problems (Borricaud, 1970), it is by no means obvious why such a theory is more appropriate to the administration than to the family, the firm, a political party, or any other group in French society.

The appeal of the stalemate hypothesis is derived, in part, from the time when it was conceived. In the early years of de Gaulle's rule the Fifth Republic was pursuing Jacobin ideals (the group in the Revolution advocating strong central control) with the greatest determination, though—as we shall see—without uniform success. As Frears noted some years ago (1972), the theory gained recognition because it fit with prevailing ideas in social science where France always appeared as a curious exception. Insofar as most political science models placed a premium on equilibrium and stability, France was doomed to be the awkward case. But some French scholars, less well-known in English, questioned whether French behavior and institutions were indeed as curious as they appeared when contrasted with Anglo-Saxon democracy. For example, Georges Lavau noted (quoted in Frears, 1972, p. 39), "in the final analysis it is extremely doubtful whether French political society has a significantly lower level of consensus than the United States, the United Kingdom, the Netherlands, or Belgium." In a policy framework, much of the protest and even violent behavior of the French may be attributed to institutional uncertainties. The Gaullists were reduced to a minority party in the 1981 elections precisely because they were never able to reconcile their Jacobin ideals with the complexity of modern government. As several authors have suggested (Waterman, 1969; Wright, 1978), the fragility of French institutions may be no more than a reflection of the uncertainties of French politics policymaking.

Policy Change under a Dominant Party

France did not escape more general political and administrative uncertainty over the past two decades, but neither did any modern welfare state in the search for ways to reconcile a vastly expanded public sector with democratic governance. But to place the development of French institutions in a policy context, one needs a finer tool than a general theory of personality. Since 1958, the French policy process has gone through three important transitions, each of which helps explain the strengths and weaknesses of French policy and politics and, more generally, French institutional development. The transformations correspond roughly to the presidencies of de Gaulle (1958–69), Georges Pompidou (1969–74), and Valery Giscard d'Estaing (1974–81), culminating in the Socialist victory of Mitterrand in 1981. Roughly distinguished, the three periods represent, first, the foundation of the Fifth Republic and the decade needed to restructure political parties and to restore policy effectiveness to government. In a policy perspective, the second period was, in many ways, the most crucial; it was under Pompidou that the Gaullists became an organized party and began to see the enormous social costs of a decade of rapid economic and industrial growth. Under Giscard, a third period began with the ambitious aim of making France into a liberal society along nineteenth century lines. As the voters decided in 1981, his task was perhaps the most hopeless because France had never been a typically liberal society. These transformations correspond to the agenda, process, and consequences of the policy process described in the following chapters.

In more conventional political analysis, there is less need to differentiate the internal transformations of politics and policy. For example, the long period of Gaullist rule from 1958 to 1974 has often been considered a "dominant party" system in relation to electoral and legislative politics, in some ways similar to the long periods of Liberal Democratic rule in Japan or Social Democratic rule in Sweden. But the political relationship within French government, how parties may or may not affect policy decisions, and entire range of issues confronting government are very different from one country to another. Although the treatment of the policy process to follow is chronological, this in no way implies that the relation of policy politics within any given period always has uniform implications. For those less concerned with the relation of performance to politics, the "dominant party" scheme satisfactorily describes the basic structure of partisan politics, but it also blurs important differences between periods that were essentially produced by policy choices and, in turn, affected the political and institutional assumptions of the Fifth Republic.

The institutional uncertainties facing de Gaulle and his collaborators from 1958 to 1969 are easily underestimated, in part because a president who proclaims "me or chaos" is almost certain to stimulate disapproval, and in part because his immense influence allowed him to overcome objections to his Jacobin policies. But from a policy perspective, it is important to remember that de Gaulle, for all his determination, did not know himself how the new constitution would work in practice. As Wright has written (1978, p. 23), the new constitution tried to fuse parliamentary power with an independent executive and "in the resulting lengthy text confusion competed with contradiction and ambiguity and obscurity." The president's role was described in lofty terms that suited de Gaulle's vision of France. The president "sees that the Constitution is respected, ensures by his arbitration the regular functioning of the organs of government and the continuity of the State" (ARTICLE 5). A number of basic decisions were reserved for the legislature but, reversing the American federal formula, those not specified revert to the executive. The president can select and dismiss his prime minister but, contrary to the formalism often attributed to France, the relation between the prime minister and the president is unclear, as is the relation of the prime minister to the legislature (Debré, 1974).

The power to dismiss a prime minister at will is, in fact, a double edged weapon in the reality of political life. All the recent presidents of France have had doubts about their prime ministers, but none have used this power until circumstances were such that the change would not reflect on the judgment and influence of the president himself. De Gaulle had doubts about Pompidou from the mid-1960s, but he waited until the May 1968 demonstrations provided a pretext for dropping him. As president, Pompidou decided within a year that the appointment of his flamboyant and popular prime minister, Chaban-Delmas, threatened to overshadow his office, but he did nothing until a tax scandal weakened Chaban in 1972. There were constant rumors that Giscard would dismiss his resolute prime minister, Barre, whose economic liberalism was showing small results, but he did nothing. One can easily exaggerate the ease with which formal rules can be translated into effective policy control.

To further buttress executive control over the legislature, ministers are not allowed to hold seats in parliament, but deputies and senators are elected along with their substitutes (*suppléants*) so that the political risk of joining a cabinet is reduced. On leaving the cabinet, the minister's substitute simply retires from the scene and a by-election reinstates the original holder. There are restrictions on parliament's budgetary powers (if no budget is agreed to by the end of the year, the previous year's budget automatically comes into effect), and even greater limits on parliament's ability to initiate legislation. Oddly enough, de Gaulle retained the Senate from the Fourth Republic although it has always housed the cautious champions of traditional middle-class France that de Gaulle despised. A Constitutional Council was formed to deliberate on constitutional issues, only to become the battleground for enraged legislators when de Gaulle attempted more high-handed decisions. Thus, the Constitution of the Fifth Republic by no means granted the executive unqualified powers. Many of the political crises of the early Gaullist period were actually conflicts focusing on such undecided institutional issues.

In a policy study, it is perhaps more important to grasp the state of mind of those taking high office. De Gaulle resigned from office in 1946 an embittered man. Except for a small clique of the "faithful," he took no open part in French politics for over a decade and even refused to endorse the feeble band of Gaullists surviving in office in the Fourth Republic. The "faithful" were mostly persons who had followed him into exile in London in 1940, or had supported him in the Resistance (Pilleul, ed., 1979). There were, to be sure, the Gaullist "barons," men such as Michel Debré, Olivier Guichard and Jacques Chaban-Delmas, who were authoritative voices within the party, but all these men (de Gaulle distrusted women in high office and never appointed one to the Elysée) were instinctively responsive to de Gaulle's views and needs. However autocratic de Gaulle was, governance was almost too easy. In the midst of numerous policy crises, the situation was not appropriate to make enormous institutional experiments. Under de Gaulle's austere style of leadership (no smoking, and only the most polite controversy in cabinet meetings), there was litle disposition to deal with the complexities of policymaking. Though it enraged the opposition, de Gaulle relied heavily on technocrats and experts; many of them, such as Jacques Rueff, reported privately to him. Their advice was often wrong or only momentarily successful.

De Gaulle was the only president who could transcend institutional constraints. He could even define institutions to suit himself, as he did with the doubtfully constitutional device of unilaterally having a referendum on an amendment providing for direct presidential election in 1962. But the period of unrestrained power was fairly short. The Gaullists knew that they could seldom resort to emergency powers once the Algerian revolution ended. In 1963, de Gaulle was forced against his will to make a generous settlement in a serious mining strike. The 1962 legislative elections were by no means a clean sweep for the party. Their electoral fortunes did not improve in the 1967 legislative elections. In 1962, the Communists, de Gaulle's bitter foes, regained their normal 20 percent support from the electorate; in 1967, their representation in the Assembly soared to 73 seats. The inflationary aftermath of the Algerian war plus the economic, military, and industrial spending to assure French *grandeur* forced the 1962 Stabilization Plan and created doubts among leading Gaullists. The 1968 student rebellion and subsequent general strike completely upset de Gaulle's plans. In his combat with traditional France, de Gaulle designed the 1969 referendum to refashion both the Senate and the regional governments to suit his desires. Unable to rule the society he inspired, he resigned immediately upon its defeat. The material progress and political prestige of France reached new heights under de Gaulle but, paradoxically, he left the Fifth Republic with a number of unresolved institutional problems. As Hoffman writes, de Gaulle wanted "to escape from the boredom of bourgeoise society" (1974, p. 246) and often "dwarfed and distorted his own institutions" (p. 240). His inspiration and will power set France on a new course, but he did little to solve the institutional complexities of modern government.

For this reason, Pompidou's presidency is in many ways the critical transition in construction of the elaborate governing apparatus to deal more systematically with the intricacies of policymaking in a rapidly modernizing France. Pompidou was one of the few "barons" not associated with de Gaulle during the war, but was sent to him after the French liberation when de Gaulle asked an aid to find him "someone who could write." A graduate of the elite Ecole Normale Supérieure (top administrative school for education), Pompidou developed close contacts with French business and finance during the "years in the wilderness." When asked to reenter government as prime minister in 1962, he was an officer of Rothschild's Bank, but had remained one of de Gaulle's personal advisers. A clever, articulate man, Pompidou—unlike de Gaulle—did not progress through the discipline of the army and had no special claim on French patriotism. He was the first president of the Fifth Republic who had to live by his wits and was intimately familiar with the rough-and-tumble of daily politics. Moreover, he inherited all of de Gaulle's unfinished institutional chores.

First, de Gaulle's impatience with party squabbles meant that the Gaullists had never organized a modern political party, a task which fell on Pompidou as the 1967 elections approached. There is more than a little irony that Pompidou's mastery of party politics, as well as the magnificent speech he gave before the party congress in 1967, triggered de Gaulle's suspicion of his prime minister (Decaumont, 1979), but even before 1969, the "regime of parties" was beginning to overtake France and Pompidou was the president to complete this adjustment. Second, it fell to Pompidou to heal the wounds of the 1968 demonstrations and strikes. Under crisis conditions, he forced businessmen to take their social responsibilities more seriously and gave labor unions a measure of political power. Group politics could no longer be brushed aside. Pompidou candidly admitted that France had a "bastard" set of political institutions (Decaumont, p. 16). He set out to construct more effective policy coordination between the Elysée and the Matignon, increased the visibility of the planning process, and helped launch (with severe misgivings) new social reforms under the slogan, the "New Society." The "barons" remained key figures, but were increasingly divided over Pompidou's intentions and were challenged by a younger generation of political leaders.

Above all, Pompidou saw that the ambiguities surrounding the mandates of the president and prime minister must be reconciled if France were not to risk a paralyzing split were these two offices in open conflict. His proposal to give each office the same term (five years) died, as Pompidou said, "in the Sinai war" when the Middle Eastern crisis forced postponement of the necessary constitutional referendum. In 1972, the Socialists and Communists agreed on a common program and, in the 1973 legislative elections, the Left regained its losses from the disgrace of the 1968 demonstrations. Pompidou inherited all the problems of complex government that de Gaulle found boring or trivial. The final historical irony was Pompidou's premature and tragic death which ushered in the new regime of Giscard who, in turn, would reduce the Gaullists to a minor party. Nor had the process of linking policy and politics been entirely successful. In its later years, Pompidou's government was rocked with scandals and handicapped by the president's prolonged illness. Giscard seemed a reasonable compromise, though a mere 200,000 votes could have given Mitterrand his victory in 1974. In a curious way, Pompidou did more to construct an effective, modern government than de Gaulle, but the French people had not yet decided what they wanted to do with it. In 1974, the institutional uncertainties of France often seemed no less than in 1969, but the important change was that France had by then assembled a more competent, integrated policy machinery.

Giscard's presidency (1974–81) was at once the most daring and the most disappointing (Frears, 1981). A brilliant financial expert of aristocratic background, his meteoric rise in French politics was itself, in part, a function of the Gaullist need to attract Center voters. In 1962, he became the youngest Minister of Finance in French history and, thereafter, he played a subtle game of keeping distance from the Gaullists, while gradually assembling the factional parties of the Center into the Republican Party. In the 1965 presidential elections, an attractive centrist candidate, Lecanuet, demonstrated that the Center might displace the Gaullists when votes attracted by Lecanuet deprived de Gaulle of a victory on the first round. Giscard's electoral slogan for the 1978 legislative elections, "change without risk," is perhaps the best clue to his defeat, both as an effective president and as a popular leader. Like the Gaullists, he played on fears of a Left government, but unlike the Gaullists, he wanted to make radical changes in the French economy and society. For example, in his early years of office he pressed for reform of archaic laws on divorce and abortion. He hoped to resurrect a benign form of classic liberalism, hardly appropriate for France or any advanced industrial society (Giscard d'Estaing, 1978).

His dilemma in building an acceptable alternative to the Left shows the importance of the policy process in modern democracies. Dependent on Gaullist votes in the legislature and often in open warfare with the new Gaullist leader, Jacques Chirac, Giscard's reforms regularly set off intense controversies within government that eroded his credibility, while compromises with his conservative supporters made him look ineffective. More important, the elaborate policy process became his preferred way of befriending supporters and, to a greater extent than ever before, government was infiltrated with presidential friends (Agnès, 1980). Many had feared a split between Left and Right, between the presidency and premiership, but the ironical outcome was that, in dividing power, even the Right and the Center could not agree on national policies. In 1976, the tense relationship between the president and the ambitious young prime minister, Chirac, became an open fight; Chirac resigned in anger. Later in 1976, Chirac—already a deputy from Corrèzze—ran against the president's handpicked candidate for mayor of Paris and won. From his influential retreat in the Paris Hotel de Ville, Chirac launched new broadsides against the president.

But the important policy effect can be seen in Giscard's unprecedented manipulation of the policy machinery of govenment. De Gaulle had been determined, but he left policy implementation and many routine decisions to his trusted staff. Pompidou was a true political animal, but he was able and willing to manipulate political forces outside the policy process. Giscard seemed unable to assemble the broad, centrist political backing that he claimed could save France, but he conducted the policy process in even more manipulative and arbitrary ways. The cabinet was increasingly filled with his personal friends. His new prime minister, Barre, an able and dedicated civil servant, was politically colorless. No post in the far-flung network of stage agencies seemed immune to Giscard's personal and confidential influence. Even the Gaullists found the "new monarchy" uncomfortable as Giscard's economic, military, and foreign policies appeared to compromise French *grandeur*. The Socialists saw the unaccountability and insulation of high-level policymaking as a new "decadence." Possibly the most balanced criticism came from a high official, Bloch-Lainé, not unsympathetic with Giscard's aim of building liberal foundations for French democracy, who wrote that in practice Giscard's rule was only "neo-Jacobinism," arbitrary decisionmaking in guise of reform (*Le Monde*, January 23, 1981).

The overall result is that, in many ways, the first twenty years of the Fifth Republic were no less uncertain than the politically turbulent years of the Fourth Republic, but for very different reasons. The Fourth Republic never decided how to link policy and politics. In the drama of rapidly changing ministers and cabinets (eighteen prime ministers in twelve years), the working life of government depended even more on civil servants than in the Fifth Republic (see Dogan, 1979). Under all four presidents of the Fifth Republic, the relationship of policy and politics changed radically because, in their various ways, each of them sought ways to fill the gap between policy and politics. From a policy perspective, their enormous task was no less than to create an accountable and responsive policy process amidst great political and institutional uncertainty. All four presidents have had distinct styles and approaches to policymaking, in many respects more dramatically different than those in governments with more competitive party systems, such as Britain, where strong societal and elite consensus has insulated the policy process from politics (Ashford, 1981b) or West Germany, where strong organizations outside government persisted throughout electoral and political change.

French Society and Politics: Living with Diversity

Institutional achievements must be measured against the complexity and intensity of the issues confronting a society. By this measure, the accomplishments of the Fifth Republic are among the more impressive in Western Europe. Converting social change into effective policies is not nearly as simple or uniform a process as often assumed in more abstract comparisons. Part of the aim of this book and others in the series is to uncover how democratic governments respond to changing needs and preferences. From such a perspective, there are few countries in Europe where societal change generated more uncertainty about the use of collective authority. For different reasons, both de Gaulle and his critics emphasized the institutional and political weaknesses of France. But even if we discount partisan self-interest, each policy problem mobilized a diverse and conflicting set of demands that often neutralized effective action. Thus, as Crozier and other critics suggest, France may have been a stalemate society because it was virtually impossible to assemble such a variety of interests, preferences, and demands in an orderly way. What the stalemate hypothesis leaves out is that constructing an acceptable and legitimate way of transforming social diversity into effective government is no easy matter.

There are dangers of being seriously misled in comparing nineteenth century France, and even the Third Republic, with a prosperous and expansive contemporary France. The crises of France a century or more ago may ignore how intractible many social problems were. For example, in 1850, only half the French population spoke standardized French. At the turn of the century, nearly half the population was still supported by agriculture. But, compared to much of Europe and Japan, the social and industrial shocks of nineteenth century France produced less social change. France remained a fragmented and self-reliant society. In the 1911 census, half the farmers had holdings of less than five hectares (about ten acres), half the labor force worked in establishments employing less than five persons, and nearly half of the persons in the industrial sector of the economy classified themselves as *patrons* (employers), rather than employees (Marceau, 1977, p. 13). In a nation that was still fighting powerful antidemocratic elements within the society, bringing order to such a small-scale society would have required immense political skill and patience.

Though apparent under the Fourth Republic, the Fifth Republic felt the full force of demographic change and all of its consequent demands for new services and benefits. The French population increased nearly twice as much in the twenty years following the Second World War as in the previous century. Although the postwar baby boom declined by the early 1960s, the Fifth Republic inherited a huge demand for new schools, teachers, and for educational opportunity generally. In 1963–64, there were nearly 70 percent more primary school students than the immediate postwar level, and *lycée* (secondary) enrollment had trebled (Vaughan et. al., 1980, p. 191). The number of university students doubled under the Fourth Republic (180,000 in 1958), but it more than quadrupled in the following twenty years (820,000 in 1978) (Gagnon, 1981). Combined with inadequate facilities and diminishing career prospects, this fantastic increase in the university population was a basic cause of the 1968 demonstrations.

Over the 1960s, the unbalanced demographic composition of the population generated a dual burden. In addition to the increased birthrate, which most French welcomed after generations of population stagnation, there were large increases in the elderly population. From 1860 to 1946, the French population had grown by only three million persons: one fundamental reason why the Third Republic could easily neglect welfare reforms. But the demographic vise worked so that in recent years the active population actually decreased, which meant that smaller numbers of people had to support both more children and more aged (Marceau, 1977, p. 26). In 1974, an active population of approximately 21.2 million persons was supporting 10.1 million retired (*Cahiers Français*, 1977, p. 11) while the state steadily increased the value of pensions and other benefits. As we shall see (in Chapter 6), from 1975 to 1980 the rate of increase of French welfare benefits was nearly three times the growth rate of the economy, despite the financial strains of the oil crisis and economic dislocation.

The rapid growth of the economy and its social repercussions are perhaps most visible in the changing occupational structure of France. Between 1960 and 1970, 1.3 million persons left agricultural employment, and an additional million were expected to leave between 1970 and 1980 (Planning Commission, 1976). Over the 1970s, the French economy was absorbing about 180,000 persons per year from agriculture. Farming employed nearly a fourth of the French population in 1960; by 1980, it supported only a tenth of the population. While government pursued many other expensive policies from 1960 to 1976, the Ministry of Agriculture budget nearly doubled (Keeler, 1981, p. 147) in order to soften the transition to a fully urban, industrial society. The policy implications are even more intricate because in France, as in much of Europe and North America, the highly productive agricultural sector (about a tenth of France's farmers account for 45 percent of production) left thousands of politically disgruntled farmers on marginal holdings.

Without doubt the most dislocating social effect of rapid social and economic change was the production of not only a larger, but a more differentiated industrial working class. As in most democracies, the industrial transformation of the past generation did not produce the class struggle so long predicted by Marxists, but instead confronted government, business, and unions with a diverse and demanding set of needs. As one French sociologist, Mendras, wrote (1979, p. 38), "The bourgeois and proletarian classes of today are mere shadows of themselves as they existed at the turn of the century, especially at the cultural level, but their power struggles still end up organized along the same lines, even if the weapons, territories and tactical stakes have greatly changed." Laurence Wylie (1957) wrote a classic study of the traditional village of southern France where priest, primary school teacher, and Communist militant carried on their genial, but intense, struggle isolated from much of the French society. When he visited Roussillon and Chanzeau a decade later (1963, pp. 159–234), he could barely recognize them. Between 1949 and 1962, the French gross national product (GNP) doubled and household incomes increased 130 percent. By the Fifth Republic, the traditional middle-class indulgences, though diluted by commercialization, were widely available.

But progress did not necessarily simplify the policy process and, in many ways, it greatly complicated policy and politics. Both the Gaullist Right and the Socialist and Communist Left were slow to devise new solutions, while the social transformation had diverse and subtle effects on political life. As in most advanced industrial societies, the most visible effect was the rapid growth of white-collar employment, which doubled over the 1960s. Between 1960 and 1970, nearly a million persons were added to service industries and half a million to commerce (Planning Commission, 1976). But the aggregate changes do not convey the host of policy problems. For example, while the total labor force was growing, the number of self-employed was diminishing by nearly two million persons. The small shopkeeper, grocer, and craftsman were gradually disappearing, though certainly not as fast as the Gaullists hoped. In 1975, there were still over 300,000 firms with less than ten employees, but they employed only 8 percent of wage earners (*Cahiers Français*, 1977). The 47,500 middle-sized firms employing between ten and 500 persons, the basis for the powerful Confederation of Small and Middle-sized Firms (CGPME), still provided 45 percent of the jobs. About 1,300 large industries (over 500 employees) accounted for 47 percent of employment, organized in the French Employers Association (CNPF). In fact, the overall industrial structure of France changed relatively little in the decades leading up to the Fifth Republic (Berger and Piore, 1980, p. 95). As a result, government was confronted with all the complexities of an advanced industrial society while retaining many characteristics of a more traditional, small-scale society. As we shall see (Chapters 4 and 5), these divisions weakened the labor movement, confused industrial policy, and complicated wage policy.

For many reasons, the alleged strength of the Fifth Republic must be measured against the enormous social needs of a rapidly changing society, as well as the weaknesses of the Fourth Republic. In 1960s, nearly ten million persons moved into larger towns and cities (Ashford, 1981a) where the basic services of water, sewerage, roads, and housing were badly deficient. The endless battle between mayors and administration over urban growth and investment (see Chapter 3) resulted from the desparate struggle to accommodate this flood of persons into urban life. At the same time, the country was obligated to resettle about 1.3 million French Algerians in France, many of whom had never seen their motherland. Most chose to settle in the south of France where economic expansion offered jobs and the climate was congenial, but they also became a perpetually disgruntled and sometimes violent minority who felt betrayed by de Gaulle. In addition, there was the growing flow of immigrant workers into France, especially the Paris region, to do many of the menial chores that the French rejected in their prosperity. By the late 1960s, when the social and economic costs of a large immigrant population was becoming apparent, there were about 200,000 foreign workers arriving each year (see Chapter 7).

Thus, the social context of policymaking under the Fifth Republic is replete with urgent requirements to rebuild the policy process in order to meet the problems of rapid social and economic change. Many of these urgencies were created by the Gaullists themselves, whose nationalist ambitions presupposed a stronger France. The result was that the relationship of social forces and social differences to French politics became more ambiguous than in the past. The deep social cleavages between Catholic secular forces, urban and rural France, and industrial and agrarian interests could no longer be easily played against each other. The theme of "two

Frances" (D. Johnson, 1978) has a long and often persuasive history in the analysis of French politics and society and is recast in Crozier's theory of a stalemate society. But the forces of change unleashed under the Fourth Republic and pressed even more urgently under the Fifth Republic made a spontaneous polarization of French society around political choices more difficult. The political extremes of both the Right and Left could less easily polarize issues because the issues themselves were often more complex and because French society could not be readily dichotomized around them. Unrestrained partisan politics was no longer automatically transformed into a persuasive popular appeal. Although the French people could rally to their hero, de Gaulle, during the crisis of 1958, French parties went through a prolonged and tortuous metamorphosis in the 1960s and early 1970s. In the course of this transformation, the Gaullists became the engineers of their own destruction, and the Socialists learned the value of moderation.

Parties and Elections: One Step Backward, Two Steps Forward

However gloomy the political predictions about France may have been in recent years, the French people never failed to demonstrate the vitality of their democratic convictions. In a period when many democracies have seen voter interest and electoral support eroding, the French continued to participate in elections at record levels. In Britain and the United States, for example, turnout in major elections has steadily declined for nearly twenty years. In contrast, in the second ballot of the 1974 presidential election, a contest between Giscard and the Socialist candidate, Mitterrand, 87.5 percent of the eligible voters appeared at the polls. French enthusiasm for elections is all the more remarkable because there is usually a seriously contested election every year, even though the term of the president is seven years and the term of the National Assembly is five years. With almost equal vigor, the French also fight elections for departmental councils, municipalities, and a host of functional bodies such as labor tribunals (*prud'hommes*), factory councils (*comités d'entreprise*), and social security advisory boards (Laroque, 1953). Although the Gaullists remained the dominant party within the governing coalition until 1974, they were acutely aware of electoral pressures. In this fundamental sense, one might argue that democratic politics were never more vigorous than under the Fifth Republic.

Popular interest in elections is perhaps even more surprising because the electoral process, as with many French institutions, is so unpredictable. Five different national election procedures were tried out in the Third Republic and two in the Fourth Republic. The multiparty structure has always required two ballots: the first round of voting to try to narrow down the field of candidates, and the second to make the final selection. The National Assembly is composed of 470 deputies from single-member districts throughout metropolitan France (a varying number are also elected from overseas constituencies) who are elected under a plurality system. Of the 264 Senators, the 69 from more populous departments are elected by proportional representation, and the remaining under the two ballot system and indirect voting system that greatly favors rural France. Local or communal elections are organized around lists with a different system for large cities and small communes. Departmental councils are indirectly elected. There are many inequities in the electoral system (Cotteret et al., 1960), but it is designed to try to bring some order out of the diverse and intense political convictions of the French people and to discipline parties.

In countries considered more stable democracies, such as Britain, the electoral and party influence steadily progressed over the nineteenth century. Though parties often disputed increased suffrage and were realigned as socialist parties arose, the institutional canvas on which mass parties painted their designs changed much less. This orderly process seldom obtained in France. Since the Revolution, the aim was to devise a "one and indivisible republic" which would somehow instantly convert popular will into authority. In doing so, the French always seemed to be their own worst enemies because they could neither unite behind two or three major parties nor decide on a fair electoral system. On the contrary, factional parties and electoral manipulation prevailed. De Gaulle was determined to bring more discipline to French parties and, with Debré, turned to single-member constituencies with a plurality system for deputies in hopes of subduing French appetites for electoral and party fragmentation. For all the problems with the policy process, this was perhaps his greatest failure. Among the variety of institutional uncertainties under the Fifth Republic, the most important were undoubtedly those surrounding democratic representation itself.

Throughout most of the Third, Fourth, and Fifth Republics, France was ruled by coalitions of parties such as Clemenceau's Bloc Nationale in 1919, Eduard Herriot's Cartel des Gauches in 1924, and Blum's Popular Front in 1936. Leaders seldom hesitated to arrange electoral laws to be disadvantageous to their opponents. Changes in 1951 under the Fourth Republic were openly designed to exclude the extreme parties of the Left and Right, the Communists, and the Gaullists. De Gaulle hoped that his more stringent electoral system of 1958 would eliminate the Communists, though its actual effect was to demolish the remnants of several reactionary party factions on the extreme right (Criddle, 1975). His writing of the municipal election law in 1964 (see Chapter 3) was also intended to obstruct the Socialists and Communists but, like most of these efforts, it failed to do so.

Our image of the Gaullists as the dominant party throughout the 1960s may underestimate how insecure they felt and how much energy they lavished on electoral competition. For one thing, when they came to power in 1958, the loosely organized party had languished for a decade. In electoral terms, their victory was not all that impressive for they obtained only a fifth of the votes, no more than they had in 1951 at the nadir of the Gaullist Party (see Table 1-1). In the 1962 legislative elections they had only 44 percent of the vote, although de Gaulle could still call on his masterful handling of the French army uprising in Algeria to enhance his image. In the 1965 presidential election, de Gaulle was visibly humiliated when the energetic leader of a centrist party, Lecanuet (later an ally of Giscard), forced a second ballot. In the 1967 legislative elections, twenty-five crucial seats were won by only 500 votes (Bon, 1978, p. 180). One French electoral expert has calculated that had a mere 100,000 votes been properly redistributed, the Gaullists could have lost the election. Thus, the image of the Gaullists as sweeping effortlessly into office and ruthlessly overriding opposition needs careful evaluation.

Closer to the truth, the Gaullists were always threatened with becoming a fringe party of the Right, just the Communists have always been threatened with becoming the fringe party of a militant

TABLE 1-1   Percentage of Votes Cast for Major Parties in
                 Legislative Elections, 1958–81

Party	1958	1962	1967	1968	1973	1978 1st	1978 2nd	1981 1st	1981 2nd
Communist	19	22	23	20	21	21	19	18	7
Socialist*	16	13	19	17	21	23	28	37	49
Gaullist	21	32	32	37	37	23	26	20	22
Center†	11	19	14	10	13	22	23	17	18

Sources: For 1958–73, Frédéric Bon, Les Elections en France; Histoire et Sociologie (Paris: Seuil, 1978), Annexes, pp. 198–210. For 1978, L'Année Politique, 1978, p. 485. For 1981, Le Monde, June 25, 1981. Percentages rounded to nearest whole number.

Note: Percentages for 1958–73 are for first ballot only.

*"Socialist" includes four different groupings over the time period, with the present Socialist Party appearing in 1971. Prior to 1971, only the largest Socialist group is given.

†Center voting is very complex, starting with the old MRP or Catholic voters of 1958 and evolving through numerous party factions to become mainly Republican voters by 1978.

socialist left. The Gaullists had no natural social base. As noted above, many of their policies were explicitly designed to neutralize, if not demolish, the cautious bourgeoisie of traditional France whom de Gaulle (with some justification) blamed for the humiliating defeat in World War II and the confusion of the Fourth Republic. With the possible exception of the Communists, party organization in France has always been weak, but in 1958 the old parties of the Fourth Republic still had some territorial strongholds, while the Gaullists initially had none. They were a party of "barons,": strong, dedicated followers of de Gaulle who wanted a Jacobin republic. Though this does not differ in most French parties, Hoffman notes the party had no clear platform (1974, p. 217). "Gaullism is a stance, not a doctrine; an attitude, not a coherent set of dogmas; a style without much substance—beyond the service of France and French grandeur, itself never defined in content, only by context." The curious thing about their amorphous and vague appeal to French nationalism is that the party was ideally suited to adapt to greater internal and external strains on France in the 1960s, but the ideological amalgam was no clearer than in other parties.

The relation of party politics to the policy process in France differs from most European democracies in important respects. The British Member of Parliament is strongly rooted in his or her constituency and has high political status, but is effectively disciplined by Parliament so that British parties are clearly distinguished from the "parliamentary party." Though in practice, British MPs have only marginal influence over policy decisions, it appears that Debré hoped to transplant British party discipline in the Fifth Republic by forming party groups within the National Assembly. In contrast, representatives in the German Federal Republic are virtually unknown to the voters of their constituencies, while they are also effectively disciplined in the Bundestag. The French politican is a rather different amalgam of characteristics for, on the one hand, he or she usually has strong local roots, in part because national party organizations are weak except for the Communists, and in part because the deputy or senator is expected to help bring tangible benefits to the constituency. Because the French representative can rely on neither a strong party organization nor a strong legislature, he or she becomes more of a political entrepreneur than in many other democracies. Rather like American congressmen, an aspiring politician climbs the political ladder slowly from municipal office, to departmental council, and eventually to national office. The important difference, again quite contrary to the legalistic image of France, is that elected officers are accumulated (*cumul des mandats*) and provide a local network (*réseau*). In some cases, such as the Gaullist Chaban-Delmas in Bordeaux, (Lagroye, 1973) or the Socialist Mauroy in Lille, a powerful regional power base is organized that can have major influence in the party (see Chapter 3). About three-fourths of the Deputies and a remarkable ninety percent of the Senators accumulate elected offices to maximize their local influence, but their national significance in the policy process is probably no greater than the modest role assigned most elected officials in modern democracies.

Although it is easy to criticize French party politics for its disorganization and isolation from the policy process, the system does enable representatives to bring benefits to their constituents, and the rewards (including a generous salary of about $50,000 plus expenses) are substantial. The conversion of party politics into effective government is encouraged by the furious pace of elections.

As might be expected in a multiparty system, it is critically important that candidates from the same coalition do not run against each other in the same constituency. There is nothing more deadly in French politics than a three-cornered contest (see Chapsal and Lancelot, 1975). French electoral sociology is replete with instances where Gaullists and Republicans, or Socialists and Communists, have lost by refusing to withdraw on the second round of elections. Pompidou's success in building a Gaullist Party in the 1960s depended heavily on his control of the crucial negotiations between the first and second ballots. Mitterrand's determination to sustain the alliance with the Communists, despite their often bitter differences, was based on the fact that were the two parties to fight each other in the second round of elections, neither would have a chance because a plurality would most go to a candidate from the Center or Right. The curious effect is that while politics remain heavily localized in France, elections provide an essential discipline and national focus. In unforeseen ways, democratic politics remains the driving force of French politics.

There are certain advantages in a multi-party system and in parties that are not immutably wedded to fixed positions. Given the pace of change in France in recent years, flexibility was essential, and it was the intransigence of Communist Party policy that made it seem unable to govern. Possibly the best evidence of the kaleidioscopic nature of French parties and elections is simply their rapidly evolving names. The Gaullists have changed their name no less than five times (see Wright, 1978, p. 138), which is why for purposes of this book they will be referred to as simply the "Gaullist Party." What I shall call the "Republican Party" under Giscard has never been a party in the accepted sense, but a collection of local dignitaries aligned with Giscard and loosely organized around local clubs. Until the 1971 Epinay Congress of the Socialist Party, socialists were divided among remnants of the Fourth Republic's SFIO; a new, more social democratic group, the PSU; a militant and strongly Marxist organization of militants, CERES; and various factional parties of the radical left. All of these groups retained their identity and leaders within the Socialist Party. It was Mitterrand's masterful orchestration of such rivalries, not to mention his patience with the ideological and strategic permutations of the Communist Party, that finally won him the presidency. If one reads a full account of his patience and endurance, often mixed with adroit reversals (see R. W. Johnson, 1981), one cannot help feeling he has more than earned his prize.

Just as the French distrust of parties handicapped their ability to build strong institutions, so also it made for weak parties that could not translate popular support into policy with confidence. The exercise of power is itself a disciplinary experience, but as Wright points out (1978, p. 145) the Gaullist Party went through several difficult metamorphases while in power. The historical Gaullists were personnally bound to *le général* and predominanted in the early years of the Fifth Republic. There were also the post-war idealists and reformers who rallied to the party in hopes of building a strong France, many of them the early graduates of the National School of Administration (ENA) (see Chapter 2). Then followed the changes introduced by Pompidou who at first wanted the party to appeal to moderate voters, and who was later confronted with a more united Left. Most recently, we have seen the full transfer of power within the party, not always accomplished with the tidiness and discretion of more disciplined parties, as Chirac tried to resurrect an image of a strong, nationalist party to neutralize the growing strength of the Republicans under Giscard.

While the Gaullists were wrestling with the problems to be discussed, there were severe internal party conflicts. De Gaulle was loyal to progressive elements of his party dating from the Resistance, and two Gaullist militants of distinct socialist leanings, Vallon and Capitant, were kept within the party's umbrella. Moreover, these men had real influence in advancing their ideas about labor participation and profit sharing (see Chapter 5). Decaumont (1979, p. 14) notes that differences over enlarged participation sowed the seeds of distrust between de Gaulle and Pompidou, his prime minister, as early as 1966, and this is confirmed by Debré (Andrews and Hoffman, 1980, p. 339). The irony is that de Gaulle's distaste for party politics made him dependent on Pompidou for the organization of a stronger party machine over the 1960s, and Pompidou's firm leadership in the 1967 Lille party congress clearly offended *le général*.

Internal party strife continued under the Pompidou presidency (1969–74). Pompidou's prime minister, Chaban-Delmas, conducted a Kennedy-style campaign for his proposals to build a "New

Society" which caused deep suspicions among Gaullist stalwarts. A month after Chaban-Delmas' cool reception at a meeting of the party's National Council in 1970, the president publicly expressed his disapproval in a press conference when he stated, "I attach more importance to the individual in society than to society itself." When Chaban-Delmas said that he had "not abandoned regionalism" in September 1970, the president noted a month later that the department was the keystone of local government. The intricate plan of Chirac and the party secretary, Juillet, to undermine a too progressive Chaban-Delmas, is now part of French political folklore. In 1974, Chaban announced his candidacy for the presidency, only to learn that the Gaullist parliamentary leaders, organized by Chirac and Pierre Juillet, had voted not to support him. Episodes of this kind could be multiplied, but the point is that the Gaullist Party was a conglomerate with an uncertain social base and was often distracted by bitter internal fighting. The presumably strong governments of de Gaulle and later Pompidou were constantly distracted by these internal party conflicts, many of which affected basic policy choices.

Despite the weaknesses of the French legislature, the Gaullists were acutely aware of popular support and of the necessity to maintain a majority coalition in the Assembly. Indeed, the strong, partisan objections to their strength needs to be balanced against their constant electoral concerns. As shown in Table 1-1, their electoral support in 1958 was barely more than that of the Communists. Over the 1960s, they were only able to increase their vote by about 10 percent, hardly an overwhelming gain for a party enjoying all the patronage and benefits of government for a decade. If the Communist Party had not badly miscalculated the May 1968 demonstrations, the decline that appears in the 1970s might have begun earlier. Not the least of the ironies of the May demonstrations was that the crisis provided another surge of nationalist feeling to reinforce the Gaullists at their weakest moment. They only had absolute majority from 1968 to 1973 but by then the party was starting to decline.

Since 1970, as happened in the many democratic regimes, parliamentary security produced more severe internal party strife. Pompidou knew they could not survive without "an opening to the left," meaning an appeal to the small center parties. Increasingly the party turned to the small shopkeepers, artisans, and professions who had regarded their party with skepticism, and whom many leading Gaullists considered the cause of French economic and social backwardness. Pompidou included more Center party figures in his cabinet, and created a cabinet post for small industry and commerce. The champions of big business found themselves approving the *loi Royer* in 1973, the law that gave new protection to small entrepreneurs and merchants. But the appeal to the center was, and remains, extremely risky, for the center voters can easily move their support to other parties. This is precisely the strategy which Giscard d'Estaing so skillfully developed over the 1960s; it won him the presidency in 1974 and lost him the presidency in 1981.

Giscard himself was a product of center politics, though until he was president he never took an active party role. In the cabinets of the early 1960s, he represented the traditional *bourgeosie* and held the influential post of minister of finance. Leaving the ministry in 1966, he began to assemble a loosely knit party of provincial leaders (*notables*) who had always distrusted the Gaullists' Jacobin ideas. In politics it is often difficult to know whether one's ostensible friends might be a greater threat than one's avowed enemies. The Gaullist leaders saw that Giscard's philosophical distance from power only concealed a greater menace to their power than did the despised Communists. They needed the Republicans, and several Republican leaders were in the cabinet throughout the 1960s and 1970s. But Giscard's vague appeals to a new liberalism were an anathema to Jacobin thinking. When Giscard proposed that voters might choose the "yes but" option in the 1965 presidential elections ("yes" for a strong government, and "but" for the liberal approach), de Gaulle's frosty reply was that "One cannot govern with buts."

Giscard's unforgivable offense was to oppose de Gaulle in the 1969 referendum which, as we have seen, led to de Gaulle's resignation. Giscard, of course, was playing a very crafty game which rested on using the roughly 10 percent of Centrist votes to gain control over the hardcore Gaullist vote of about 20 percent. Although the Gaullist vote held up in the 1973 legislative elections, the single-member districts they had instituted to punish small parties took its toll on them. Their Assembly group was cut by over a 100 deputies (see Table 1-2). In the 1974 presidential election, the

TABLE 1-2   Membership of Major Party Groups in the
National Assembly, 1958–81

Party	1958	1962	1967	1968	1973	1978	1981
Communist	10	41	73	34	73	86	44
Socialist and Radical	83	106	121	57	102	115	283
Center*	182	91	85	94	119	123	61
Gaullist	207	233	200	293	183	154	83

Source: *Le Monde*, June 23, 1981. There is a total number of seats for metropolitan France which changes slightly between elections and was 488 in 1981. Some small groups are omitted.

*Center includes the changing variety of small parties, but by 1978 and 1981 these are allied with the Republican Party.

Gaullists turned to one of their most progressive leaders, Chaban-Delmas, to run against Giscard and Mitterrand, but Chaban-Delmas' poor showing on the first ballot (a mere 15 percent) forced withdrawal to save the Republic from Socialism (Mitterrand had 43 percent). After sixteen years of rule, the proud Gaullists were humbled. At his inauguration, Giscard pronounced "From this day will date a new era in French politics," something which few old Gaullists could doubt as they watched their new leader, Chirac, become prime minister to a president who had helped destroy their party. Ironically, they were defeated by the same fears of the Left which their party had so assiduously cultivated since 1958.

But was the regime really new or were the old high-handed habits of the Gaullists only cloaked in a new rhetoric? True, many of the social reforms were long overdue but, by 1974, French society had moved so far toward being a mass, liberated society that the obvious changes often seemed condescending. In short order, Giscard canceled plans for an atrocious *autoroute* along the left bank of the Seine, lowered the voting age to eighteen, provided birth control assistance, liberalized abortion, and divorce laws. There was even a minister for women, the high-spirited Françoise Giroud, who later wrote a book (1977) on the absurdities of high-level political life. There was a flurry of major reports: Guichard on local government (see Chapter 3); Sudreau on industrial reorganization (see Chapter 4); Haby on education; Merault on incomes policy; and Peyrefitte on justice. Giscard himself visited prisons, toured immigrant tenements, and even dropped into village cafes. For a brief spell everything seemed in movement but, as the pressures and complications of policymaking increased, the reformist urges subsided into what the French called the "new monarchy."

The abrupt change from popular innovator to pensive recluse made it more apparent that Giscard was dealing largely in images. After the quarrelsome break with his Gaullist prime minister, Chirac, in 1976, the president became less and less accessible and surrounded himself with a small circle of select friends (Agnès, 1980). The new, colorless prime minister, Barre, never tried to overshadow the President, and the president's directives to Barre— the annual "letter to the Prime Minister"—had an unavoidable royalist tinge. In the rough-and-tumble setting of French politics, Giscard's musings about the "year 2000" sounded more like a distracted monarch out of touch with his subjects than a reformist president of a country under seige with problems of energy, inflation, and unemployment. The reforms that struck at the roots of French society were often abandoned under pressure from the Gaullists in the coalition: the land tax bill of 1975 was rejected, and the excess profits tax law of 1978 was amended into a shambles. Local reform was quietly shunted aside as the 1977 local elections approached (see Chapter 3), and judicial reform became a threatening law that the Socialists were quick to repeal.

The French people recalled that in 1967 Giscard had criticized de Gaulle for the "solitary exercise of power" (Chapsal and Lancelot, 1975, pp. 588–89), but Giscard's pensive superiority appeared even more remote than de Gaulle's lofty approach. The Gaullist party was badly torn from within over the costs of participation in Giscard's government. The president's speech, suggesting a defense policy suited for "all azimuths", sounded like the death knoll for their cherished independent defense force and possibly an approach to reentry into NATO which they detested. On his return from the United States, Giscard's observation that the entry of the Left into French government would not necessarily block the working of French institutions sent shock waves through the Right. Under pressure from his party and outraged over Giscard's refusal to share power with him, from 1976 Chirac launched a virulent campaign against the Republicans, even though the Gaullists had no option but to support Giscard in the government. Perhaps the curious spectacle of the Right locked in internecine warfare persuaded French voters that the Left could be no worse and, in 1981, the Socialists came to power.

The French socialist movement has a long history in France, composed of long periods of decline and disaster interspersed with moments of glory. It would be easy to attribute Socialist failures to the Right, considering the long road to power from the Fourth Republic to 1981; however, the Right often seemed to be their own worst enemies, a characteristic that, as we have seen, is by no means confined to the Left. As R. W. Johnson (1981, p. viii) points out, hopes for equality after the Revolution were displaced by Napoleon's Empire. The few months that a Socialist leader, Louis Blanc, came to power in the Second Republic (1848–51) were disastrous: during the "nine week wonder" of the Paris Commune (1871), the main Socialist spokesman was in jail, and Léon Blum's Popular Front rescued the Third Republic in 1936 only to make little impact as the war approached. Socialist infighting was, as Johnson notes (1981, p. ix), "seized upon by external audiences with an enthusiasm almost devoid of discrimination," but the light that the Left seemed able to shed on French problems was dim indeed.

Although the various schemes of the Right to exclude Socialists and Communists from power were often successful, until the 1970s the Left never seemed able to govern. The split of the International Socialist Movement in 1920 left the Socialists a rump party (SFIO) and produced a Communist Party totally subordinated to Moscow. As on the Right, the bitter differences between the competing parties of the Left were hopelessly exacerbated by their respective leaders. Although there was a Socialist minister in 1891, and many more since, the Left never became a credible alternative for voters; nor could they make useful alliances with a strong labor movement, as did most socialist movements in Europe, because it too was divided around fiercely held ideological lines (see Chapter 6). Indeed, until the 1960s the old Socialist party, the SFIO, was more rural than urban. Of 40,000 Socialist local councilors elected in 1965, only 1,800 came from towns and cities of over 9,000 persons (Wilson, 1971, p. 178). The two urban fiefdoms, Lille and Marseilles, were led by aging leaders, Mollet and Defferre, who could barely tolerate each other except to condemn Communists.

Mitterrand observed this dismal situation for many years before joining the Socialist Party in 1971. At times a minister in the Fourth

Republic, his main advantage over his Socialist rivals seems to have been that he learned patience and understood the byzantine struggles of the Left. Even his own career was a history of miserable failure and disappointment that would have long since defeated a man lacking his single-minded conviction that the Left must be united. Relegated to obscurity in 1958, he was the victim of a controversial assassination attempt that many thought had been staged. With little organized support but his "superclub" of dedicated followers, he managed to win the presidential nomination in 1965 only after the efforts of Deferre to create a "federation" of the non-Communist Left (FGDS) failed. In 1967, he managed to get a dozen members of his coterie elected to the Assembly, but in the 1968 reversal at the polls all of them were defeated. Losing his almost frigid composure after de Gaulle's resignation in 1969, his hasty claim to the presidency shocked French sensibilities and probably cost him the nomination. After laboring for years, the Socialist Party united at the Epinay Congress of 1971 and suffered through a year of dogged negotiations with the Communist Party to form the Common Program in 1972. His long struggle to unite the Left was achieved by the 1974 presidential election, but he lost by a mere 200,000 votes. The Communists then abandoned the Program in late 1977 on the eve of the 1978 legislative elections. A solitary and pensive figure, in many ways surprisingly similar to de Gaulle, he overcame these defeats to undo his image as a perpetual loser in French politics. There is perhaps no better illustration of the conviction and fortitude so crucial to successful leadership amidst the uncertainties of French politics.

One might reasonably ask what hope propelled the Left and Mitterrand during the many years of isolation. To some extent, the conventional approach of political science through parties and elections has given us a rather distorted image of the possibilities of the Left. We forget that in the 1965 presidential elections, Mitterrand claimed 45 percent of the votes on the second ballot, ample encouragement for a person who obviously thrives on a steady political diet. Cooperation with the Communists has a much longer history than the much publicized Common Program of 1972. In both the 1965 local elections and the 1965 presidential contest, there was substantial, if informal, Socialist-Communist cooperation to avoid the pitfalls of winner-take-all contests. In the 1973 legislative elections, the Socialist Party nearly doubled its strength in the Assembly (see Table 1-2) and, in 1978, the combined vote of the Left finally exceeded the Right, despite the failure of the Common Program. The possibility of victory had realistically existed since the decline of Gaullist popularity and unity from 1969 (see R. W. Johnson, 1981, pp. 80-102). A leader was needed who could perform the extraordinary feat of living with the Communists, while also attracting a portion of the undecided Center voters.

For obvious reasons, the Communist Party (PCF) enters less frequently into a policy analysis of French politics than do the other parties. Nonetheless, they are a crucial element of internal politics. In the quadilateral party structure that emerged under the Gaullists, their grip on 20 percent of the electorate (see Table 1-1) was a constant electoral consideration of the ruling parties. The historic importance of the 1981 presidential election is the failure of the Gaullist efforts to have isolated the party for the previous thirty years. But playing on fears of Communist subservience to Moscow inadvertently gave them considerable negative influence in many spheres of decisionmaking. Nor were they by any means totally excluded. As we shall see, the Communists or their union, the CGT, were active participants on numerous issues. The intricate network of administrative bargaining often directly involved Communist groups in planning consultation (Chapter 4), in social security agencies (Chapter 6), in a wide range of industrial relations problems (Chapter 5), and in local government (Chapter 3). In fact, contrary to an analysis based on national partisan politics, the policy perspective shows that the Communists have been heavily engaged in French policymaking for many years. Ironically, their fervent claim to French nationalism and their commitment to a strongly centralized state, if often disputed by the Right, actually resulted in the Communists support of the Right on many issues. Given the uncertainties of French politics, one takes help where one can get it.

The agonies of the PCF under the Fifth Republic, as it emerged from its ghetto existence in French politics and tried to shed its Stalinist image, are endless (Kreigel, 1972). Political ambitions may tear apart the democratic parties, but the Communists are torn apart by their own militant dogmatism. First, the party is based on the 200,000 or more well-trained and disciplined militants who run party and factory cells. If anything, they are even more suspicious of compromise with Socialists than with their leaders. Every experiment with electoral alliances set off furious internal debates. Second, leaving the ghetto jeopardized the Party's grip on working class votes. Many experts think that when the Socialists won nearly a third of the working class votes in 1973, the 1972 Common Program was already doomed. Third, there are no more bitter enemies than ideological adversaries. Any cooperation with Socialists threatened the Marxist purity and preeminence on which the Party existed. Only in 1976 did the PCF decide that the "dictatorship of the proletariat" was no longer the centerpiece of Party doctrine. Lastly, as in years past, the Party reeled before the excesses of the Soviet Union, such as the Czechslovakian invasion, the Polish crisis, and the Afghan occupation.

Throughout all these internal struggles, one must remember that there was, and remains, no greater threat to the Communists than a strong Socialist Party. Mitterrand's unwavering determination to forge an electoral alliance with the Communists is only equaled by Communist uncertainty over whether they wanted one. The Communists' retreat from the Common Program in September 1977 was clearly designed to sow discord among the Socialists, which it did, and to rescue the Party from the surge of Socialist popularity. As R. W. Johnson points out (1981, p. 182), the 1978 legislative elections were probably the point of no return. Socialist gains were larger than Communist gains, but by then the Communists could only withdraw electoral support by betraying the hopes of the Left, completely shattering their Party and condemning themselves to another generation in the ghetto. Mitterrand's composure and determination eventually overcame Communist vituperation and duplicity. In the 1981 presidential election, the Communist vote slumped to its lowest point in the Fifth Republic, and Communist representation in the Assembly was nearly halved (see Table 1-2). Socialist patience and cunning accomplished what Gaullist hostility and scorn could not do.

Our interest in these intense party struggles is different from more conventional party and electoral analysis which emphasizes the dominance of the Gaullists. In policy terms the dominant party system has not been as influential as it may appear in terms of national partisan differences and electoral outcomes. Dominant

Gaullism disturbed many French and foreign observers, but it was not dominant for very long. In 1969, it faced the complications of competitive party politics and failed. By 1973, it was defensive Gaullism; in 1974, it was surpassed by Giscard's centrist strategy. And as Bourricaud, a leading French sociologist, pointed out (*Figaro*, June 25, 1981), Giscard's ineffectual liberalism provided the themes for a Socialist victory in 1981. However much we admire competitive politics, for nearly a decade into the Fifth Republic the Left was so badly divided that it was not a credible alternative. In fact, internal fights and leadership struggles on both the Left and Right weakened parties as potential instruments of policy formation. As I shall elaborate in the Conclusion (see Chapter 8), the policy process itself provided a focus and a coherence to party politics that leaders, parties, and the French people seemed unable or unwilling to construct. We shall turn next to the reinforcement and elaboration of policymaking in France which, if it developed a life of its own, was essential to French social, economic, and political development.

Policymaking and Administrative Politics

The politics of policymaking in France is rooted in the integral relationship between administration and politics in the French policy process. The main reason why France never fit the abstract political science models is that administration has a crucial role, not simply in the conduct of government and the execution of public policy, but in defining the very concept of French sovereignty and statehood. Both Gaullists and Socialists were accused of using Jacobin excesses in manipulating the administration, but no responsible party has ever suggested dissolving the administrative state that exists within the French state. Critics of French society and politics, such as Crozier and others, have claimed that administrative power is at the foot of French ills. As I have argued above, this position does not account for significant failures or spectacular successes of French policymaking. Perhaps the most important demonstration that the administration is not simply an albatross around the neck of policymakers is that the new Socialist government of 1981 took office with relatively little friction and was quickly staffed with top civil servants, many of them from its own ranks.

To acquire a perspective on the problem, it is helpful to recall that over the 1960s and even into the 1970s, many European governments were preoccupied with the alleged inefficiency, disloyalty, and excess power of administration. The French "disease" may not come from French germs. In Britain, Prime Minister Wilson was deeply distrustful of the higher civil service and assembled, as have most prime ministers, a coterie of personal friends and advisers, anticipating Giscard's personal style of rule after 1974. Prime Minister Heath was openly contemptuous of bureaucracy and his design, if not his efforts, aimed at radically reducing the power of Whitehall (Ashford, 1981b, pp. 74–80). More recently, the finely tuned system of administrative penetration of Swedish policymaking has broken down after having dominated policy process in ways that French civil servants never thought possible (Anton, 1980). Considering the reverse problem, the Social Democratic government of West Germany took office in 1969, deeply troubled as to how a weak national administration would implement its decisions. Several elaborate studies were done on bureaucratic reliability and effectiveness (Mayntz and Scharpf, 1975). To put the French administrative state in perspective, one must recognize that every modern democracy has encountered perplexing problems of how to guide and, if it is still possible, to control the power of the bureaucracy.

The ostensible ease with which politics and administration and, in turn, the decisionmaking hierarchy, are distinguished in Anglo-Saxon countries has not spared their leaders from the problems of guiding a vastly expanded governmental structure. In some ways, it has left them even less well-prepared than France to cope with the unforeseen complexities of policymaking in the modern welfare state. Political science itself has tended to assume that governmental processes are a "black box" that somehow operates with mechanical precision. However much they may dislike a top-heavy and centralized administrative state, the French have never had such illusions and are skillful in harnessing bureaucracy to political objectives. Less considered is the possibility that France's long experience with an influential and centralized administrative system may have actually left her better prepared to deal with the intricacies of modern government. French concern with the effective meshing of political and administrative decisionmaking may be a great advantage not only to government, but to the protection of democratic values against bureaucratic zeal.

In trying to understand the French controversy over administrative power, it is important to know that it has been the target of reformers: the Left and the Gaullists. The administration may have influence, but this implies neither that they always get their way nor that they are partisan. The severe indictment of Birnbaum (1977) seems less compelling now that a Socialist government occupies office with its own quotient of elite civil servants. As happens frequently with doctrinaire approaches to complex problems, the arguments of the liberal reformers and Leftist critics were oddly alike (see Chapter 2), though they had very different "solutions." The Leftist critics felt that a socially representative civil service would be a more responsive and efficient civil service. Their main complaint, and an oddly contradictory argument, was that the Right was using the administration "to parachute" top civil servants into political office.

Putting aside the sociological absurdity of the argument, many Socialists and Communists at lower levels of the system (they controlled three-fourths of the large cities after 1977) worked congenially with the same administrative elite that served Gaullists in Paris, using the same system to extend their influence and eventually to climb the political ladder to national office. Indeed, from a more dispassionate perspective, one might observe that the past decade or so—when the Left was confined to local office—was excellent preparation for governing the state after 1981. The inner contradictions of the liberal position are some ways even greater. How does one simultaneously create autonomy and coordination in a complex government? How can government do more while enjoying less interdependence among the functions and decisions of administration? Both liberal and Marxist arguments claim with alarming naiveté that if administration were, in some sense, ideally organized, politicians would have no problems.

The French administrative system was not perfectly suited to Gaullist, Giscardian, or Socialist designs. There were enormous conflicts over planning objectives (see Chapter 4), the reorganization of the Ministry of Infrastructure (Thoenig, 1974), and regional and local reforms (Grémion, 1979). On the other hand, some important reforms—such as the reorganization of the Ministry of

Agriculture under Pisani (Tavernier, 1967)—went smoothly and turned out to be effective. But a simple balance sheet of successes and failures does not capture the more subtle transformation of administrative politics in France under the Fifth Republic. As I argued for Britain (Ashford, 1981b), to understand how a policy process changes in relation to its administrative underpinnings, one must first grasp the particular relationships governing the use of political and administrative influence. The political-administrative interface differs in every democratic country.

At the pinnacle of the policy process, administrative politics focuses on the president's office, the Elysée, and the prime minister's office, the Matignon. Contrary to its imposing external facade, the Elysée is a modest installation compared to the residences of most heads of state. The president's office operated on a small budget of about two million francs during most of the 1960s, and increased to about six million under Giscard (Massot, 1977, p. 159). While there is obviously no minister or high civil servant who does not quickly respond to requests from the Elysée, the professional staff itself is also small—thirty-three persons in 1976 with 146 secretaries and technicians. For all the prestige of the presidency, the reality of its operations are probably closer to Cohen's description (1980, p. 81), "One does not command within the entourage of the President." As I have described, there are distinct differences in how each president has selected his staff, how his personal style affected their duties, and how his priorities were communicated to ministers and their civil servants, but the president of France does not have an immediately subordinate policy staff that can begin to follow all the problems of government.

Of course, a great deal of high-level gossip and rumor surrounds the lives of persons working within the Elysée and it hardly seems surprising that any president would select discreet, loyal advisers. Some of them, such as Foccart, de Gaulle's foreign policy advisor throughout his presidency, had immense influence, and performed a number of highly delicate missions. The key official in the Elysée is the secretary general of the presidency. These officials have enjoyed long tenure of office and special relationships with the president (Wright, 1978, p. 65). Their power arises from the nature of power in any complex system: control of information and access to the president. They have been labeled "surreptitious prime ministers." But as Massot (1979, p. 183) points out, they never preside at meetings when a politician is present and, as Suleiman writes (Rose and Sulieman, eds., 1980, p. 129), their job is to organize the information network leading to the Elysée, not to give orders to ministers.

For a number of reasons, the mutual dependence between the Elysée and Matignon is the core of the policy process, and reflects much of the uncertainty and informality that characterizes the entire French system. The rise of the Socialist Party generated immense speculation about how a conservative president might select a prime minister were there a left-wing Assembly. In 1978 and 1981, alarm was expressed over the dangers of the bicephalous executive because of the virtual impossibility of splitting the operations and priorities of the two offices. Among the many informalities affecting high-level decisionmaking in France, the role and duties of the prime minister are the least defined. Appointed by the president, the prime minister "presents" his program to the Assembly, but varying periods have elapsed before prime ministers felt obliged to do so. There are no indications in the constitution as to what would transpire, if anything, were the Assembly to reject such a program. Two prime ministers were dismissed at the height of their influence, possibly because their popularity threatened to overshadow the president. This is indicative of the political delicacy surrounding the roles of president and prime minister. Pompidou, in de Gaulle's lofty phrase, was "put in reserve" in 1968 after having achieved the largest electoral victory that the party had known; Chaban-Delmas was dismissed in 1972 shortly after he received a massive vote of confidence for his "New Society" program. The greatest risk to a prime minister is too much success. On the other hand, one of Pompidou's prime ministers, Messmer, had never held elected office.

The crucible of top-level policymaking is the Council of Ministers, where the shared executive activity of the Elysée and Matignon converges. If anything, the policymaking activity of Elysée and Matignon has increasingly overlapped in recent years, as Decaumont (1979) points out in his excellent study of Pompidou's presidency. The most common coordinating device to prepare and to implement policy is the interministerial committee. The number varies with the needs of government, but there are usually about twenty-five or thirty of such committees actively preparing policy materials and following major government decisions. Either the president or the prime minister presides over the key interministerial committees, although the relevant technical advisors from the Elysée often attend. Some deal with continuing problems of importance, such as the work of DATAR (the regional planning agency). Some are formed for more specific objectives, such as the group of interested ministers assembled in 1969 to formulate the "Plan Calcul," a strategy for developing the French computer industry, or to prepare a law of major political importance, such as the Paris regional statute of 1975. There are, in addition, numerous high-level committees attached to specific ministries, such as the High Committee on the Environment under DATAR (Massot, p. 221), or the interministerial committees that administer the numerous special public investment funds (see Chapter 4). No modern government could function without such elaborate coordinating and planning activity. Whatever their activity, their work serves to bind the Elysée and the Matignon into a single policy apparatus. Ultimately no important orders can be issued without both presidential and prime ministerial signatures.

The importance of interministerial committees in the policy process is not so much their formal administrative role, as their evolving and dynamic character in dealing with the intricacies of modern government. Massot (pp. 223–24) gives a good example. In 1959, an interministerial committee was formed for manpower training and several years later was linked to the prime minister's office through a special delegate. When a major manpower training law was passed in 1966, an interministerial committee was formed as well as a National Council on Manpower Training to represent interested parties outside government. Soon afterwards, the expanding activity spawned a secretary general attached to the Ministry of Education and a president for a special fund. In a third stage from 1971, a special tax for manpower training was leveled on employers and the concept of training was enlarged to include continuing education. At this point, a secretary general of professional training was created and attached to the prime minister's office (actually Jacques Delors, later to become Mitterrand's minister of finance). In the fourth and most recent change, training was redirected under Giscard to respond to unemployment problems, and linked more directly to the Ministry of Labor. The illustration underscores the informality and flexibility of high-level committees in French government. Their role is much less a performance of formal administrative duties than a molding of major programs to changing needs.

Despite the constitutional subordination of the prime minister to the president, close observers of French government are almost uniformly persuaded that the office is in no sense readily excluded from the policy process (Massot, p. 181; Decaumont, p. 117; de Baecque, 1976; and Cohen, 1980). On the contrary, the prime minister is the president's main channel to ministers, the Assembly, and the administration. The prime minister has a large staff of about 2,000 persons, of whom roughly 500 are involved in top-level decisions (Massot, p. 174). The remainder are occupied with key support activities such as DATAR, national research priorities (DGRST), the national printing office (Documentation Française), the *Journel Officiel*, and the direction of the Civil Service. Thus, as Massot describes in detail (pp. 181–204), the prime minister's office is not only the main executive arm of government and the overall director of the administration, but also has critical policy functions in developing new initiatives in areas such as nuclear energy, women's rights, offshore pollution, and many others. In the 1981 Socialist Government, the prime minister was given primary responsibility for a complex decentralization policy (see Chapter 3) and for a large nationalization program (see Chapter 4).

Like the secretary general of the presidency, the secretary general of the government under the prime minister is a key official, and the two must work as a team. From 1946 to 1976, only five persons held the office; one of them, M. Donnedieu de Vabres held it for ten years between 1964 and 1974 (Massot, p. 187). But the effective power of the prime minister originates in the essential functions of his office: organizing the work of the government and its ministers; preparing detailed papers and reports for cabinet meetings and pursuing the implementation of cabinet decisions; drafting laws and orders in cooperation with ministers and following their course through the legislature; and, finally, transmitting to ministers and all other government agencies the orders and priorities of the Elysée. Another indication of Giscard's "monarchial" tendencies was his decision to issue cabinet minutes under his own name rather than the prime minister's.

The changing structure of the cabinet is one of the best keys to understanding the flexibility *within* French government despite the prolonged period of rule from the Right (see Table 1-3). The four presidents of the Fifth Republic clearly had very different concepts of how to organize government, how to make compromises between their political strategies and the policy process, and how to pursue their priorities at the highest levels of decisionmaking. Compared to many cabinet systems of Europe, French cabinet structure has evolved rapidly, another reflection of the institutional uncertainty of French politics. While Britain, for example, has tried superministries, too, the basic organization of the cabinet, the differentiation of ministers, and their links to the policy precepts changed very little in recent years. In West Germany, proposals to expand the cabinet and to increase ministerial policy capabilities were rejected as incompatible with the strong bureaucratic grip on the policy machinery (Mayntz and Scharpf, 1980, p. 150). In contrast, there are numerous degrees of freedom in organizing the French cabinet, and presidents have freely used this flexibility.

There are no formal rules binding the president and prime minister in organizing the cabinet, but political realities cannot be ignored. As elsewhere, the cabinet is primarily composed of ministers in charge of a large department of government. Most governments in the Fifth Republic have had about thirty members, but Mitterrand's 1981 government of forty-four persons was an interesting and significant departure. As in most countries, all ministerial ranks are not included in the working cabinet, usually about half the ministers of the Government. In 1981, there were nine regular Socialist ministers, five "superministers" or ministers of state who also controlled departments, and three ministers with specific missions (*ministres délégués*) attached to the prime minister's office. There have been three or four ministers of state in most governments since 1958. They are usually persons close to the president and they handle problems of high priority. For example, de Gaulle's 1959 government had ministers of state for foreign affairs, research, the european community, and culture (de Gaulle's close confidant, André Malraux). In 1974, Giscard made his confidant and political hatchet man, Poniatowski, the sole ministre délégué; this was an obvious rebuff to the Gaullists as their decline became apparent. Under the 1976 Barre government, an even more

TABLE 1-3   **Major Transformations of the Cabinet, 1959–81**

Cabinet Positions	De Gaulle/ Debré (1959)	De Gaulle/ Pompidou (1968)	Pompidou/ Chaban-Delmas (1970)	Giscard/ Chirac (1974)	Giscard/ Barre (1976)	Mitterrand/ Mauroy (1981)
Ministers of State	4	4	3	1	3	5
Ministers	15	12	13	14	13	21
Delegated Ministers*	1	2	2	—	1	8
Secretaries of State†	4	8	14	19	16	7
Secretaries of State to PM	2	4	4	5	2	2
Total	26	30	36	39	35	43

Sources: For 1959–74, *L'Année Politique*, pp. 6, 375, 416, and 331. For 1976, *Le Monde*, August 29–30, 1976. For 1981, *Le Monde*, June 24, 1981.

*In all cases, delegated ministers are under the prime minister except in 1981, when five were under ministers.

†From 1970, secretaries of state begin to lose their autonomous status. In 1970, eight are assigned to tasks under ministers; in 1970, ten; in 1976, twelve; and in 1981, all seven.

delicate political maneuver was tried: three ministers of state represented the three elements of Giscard's coalition (a Gaullist, Guichard; a Centrist, Lecanuet; and a Republican, Poniatowski). As will be elaborated further in the Conclusion (see Chapter 8), the task of constructing a democratic consensus never ends in France.

The differentiation of ministerial ranks is used to overcome political uncertainties and to define policy priorities. The Socialist government, for example, had three delegated ministers under the prime minister for women, parliamentary relations, and administration. To add to the confusion, there are also secretaries of state who have less status and, in recent years, are most often attached to the prime minister or to a ministry. The most dramatic change in their use was under Pompidou's presidency. In 1969, he appointed nineteen secretaries of state; many of them were paired with Republican politicians as Pompidou searched for an "opening to the left" and tried to consolidate his party. In an effort to create the image of a more sleek government in 1974, Giscard appointed fifteen ministers, but added nineteen secretaries of state to boost his centrist strategy.

Selecting a cabinet is a delicate political act in any democratic country but, with a weak legislature in France, balancing political and policy considerations demands great skill. Possibly the most ambitious attempt was the 1981 Mitterrand government where five ministers of state each had departmental responsibilities and each represented a major element of the Left: the minister of the interior, Deferre, represented the older socialist generation and had fought off Communists in his Marseilles feifdom for thirty years; the minister of commerce, Michel Jobert, was an independent progressive and a former secretary general of the presidency who had the foresight to vote for Mitterrand in 1974; the minister of transportation, Fitterman, was the senior Communist among four in the government; the minister of the plan and regional development, Rocard, was Mitterand's leading rival for the presidency and headed the more cautious, social democratic group within the Party (PSU); and the minister for research and technology, Chevènement, led the militant left-wing group (CERES) within the party. After struggling fifteen years to unite the Left, each week Mitterrand still faced the same political groups around the cabinet table.

Each minister has his or her own staff or *cabinet* of about thirty persons, a characteristic that sharply differentiates high levels of French policymaking from most European countries. A British minister, for example, has only a small personal staff for political business, and for policy purposes is totally reliant on the permanent secretary and other civil servants. In both Germany and Sweden, bureaucratic influence also reaches to the peak of government (Anton, 1980; Mayntz and Scharpf, 1975). Because a ministerial cabinet is heavily composed of high civil servants, much of the criticism of the administrative state within French government rests on the alleged abuse of administrative power by ministerial cabinets. But Suleiman's careful study (1974) indicates that such criticism may not correspond to the realities of French administration. More important, the ministerial cabinets may give ministers leverage over the policy process in ways that escape many contemporary democracies. True, the ministerial cabinets are largely composed of top civil servants from the elite *grands corps* who, in turn, control the highest levels of the civil service (see Chapter 2), but an intricate mixture of administrative and political roles is by no means unique to France.

The ministerial cabinet provides the minister with his private "think tank," with his own resources in the formulation of policies, and with a personally responsible staff to help unravel the complications of implementing policies in an ever-expanding and more complex state machinery.

Contrary to the image of French government as an arbitrary machine which manipulates the levers of power, the ministerial cabinet gives ministers an innovative and experimental capacity that is badly needed in the modern welfare state. The ambiguities created by the changing shape of the cabinet and by the latitude given ministers in organizing their own work may increase institutional uncertainties at high levels of government, but exercising these powers is seldom a tranquil affair. As we shall see in more detail in Chapter 2, there is real tension between the highly trained technical experts of the higher civil service and the general administrators and, in turn, between top civil servants and politicians.

Compared to Britain, France has been able to adjust with relative ease to many problems of the modern welfare state that do not neatly fit the traditional functional compartments of government. Throughout Europe, the policy process has become much less a task of simple command, than one of how to assemble information, maintain lateral coordination among interdependent programs, and reach lower levels of government across the increasingly remote distances between policymakers and those who actually implement policies. The task is, then, to rearrange and reorganize the highest levels of government to reflect new needs and priorities in the era of the welfare state. Possibly the best example of the French capacity to adjust the structure of government to new needs and priorities in the era of the welfare state is the Planning Commissariat, which has taken on a number of guises as planning objectives have evolved over the past thirty years (see Chapter 4). The ability of the French to reorient the planning process and to involve thousands of persons in the consultation process for each plan has been studied, and often envied, by most European countries. Similarly, the regional planning agency (DATAR) has gone through several metamorphoses as the political and administrative aims of regional development have changed. Another organization rescued from bureaucratic oblivion by Barre is the Centre d'Etude des Revenus et des Couts (CERC), an agency now producing high quality income and wage studies. De Gaulle and his successors placed a high priority on industrial, technical, and social research. The DGRST and the National Scientific Research Council (CNRS) have been generously funded. Although linked to the Ministry of Finance, the official agency for economic forecasting and economic research (INSEE) is among the most accomplished in Europe and publishes a wide variety of highly specialized economic analyses. Under the Fifth Republic, ample resources were also allocated to the official printing office (Documentation Française) and the quality and amount of reports, investigations, and basic information compare favorably with any European country. Indeed, one expert on British government (Birch, 1980, p. 165) thinks the volume of factual material is substantially superior to the publishing effort of British government.

The organization of advisory activity displays particular characteristics in France. The 900 or more advisory committees of British government operate behind the same veil of secrecy that restricts all policy debate in Britain. The Swedish rely on highly elaborate but largely administrative Royal Commissions to formulate major new policies. Some of them have lasted a decade or more before proposals emerge. All such activity is open to charges of corporate influence (policy formation by the clients of government and without full public discussion). Oddly enough, a presumably more remote and arbitrary French government seems to go out of its way to provide access and even institutionalized protection for both clients and critics. At the pinnacle of government there is the Economic and Social Council, a constitutionally established national advisory body composed of members appointed by all the major pressure groups. While it has no formal powers, its reports and advice are excellent and many of them will be cited in the policy analyses to follow. The entire system of administrative law provides another check, and a citizen or a group can launch a complaint against government, using a form found in every post office. If not settled at lower levels, important cases eventually ascend through the administrative courts to arrive at the Conseil d'Etat, the national administrative court whose decisions are binding on the entire government. The highly articulated administrative system also makes auditing procedures more significant than in many European countries. The annual reports of the Cour des Comptes, the audit agency and itself an elite administrative group, is a handy checklist of official transgressions and excesses. However much one may object to the policies and priorities of the Fifth Republic, one can hardly argue that French officials are isolated behind bureaucratic walls.

Pressure groups have an important role in the French policy process, but have many structural features of French politics. De Gaulle's initial intentions toward pressure groups were similar to the distance he hoped to keep between the legislature and the executive but have been steadily eroded over the past two decades. There are, first, the elaborately organized Chambers of Commerce, Agriculture, and Trades, whose impressive offices and assembly rooms can be seen in nearly every sizeable town. Unlike professional associations in most Anglo-Saxon countries, the three national associations have a semipublic existence, extracting both privileges and subsidies from the public budget for their services to the state and to communities. Official state support for the Chambers of Commerce is a major bone of contention of the National Employers Association (CNPF), which feels—with some justification—that it is the more dynamic and responsible organization. One reason for the weakness of the trade union movement is that it, too, is split. Divided into three parts, a Communist (CGT), an independent socialist (CFDT), and a more traditionally social democratic (FO) union, labor pressure groups are swept along in a whirlwind of ideological, partisan, and industrial combat which will be described in more detail in Chapter 5.

Those who feel that the Gaullist or later versions of the Fifth Republic operated without restraint should read the saga of endless concessions to agricultural pressure groups, although the privileged position of farm groups is by no means unique to France. The National Federation of Unions of Agricultural Producers (FNSEA) has 30,000 local offices and 600,000 members (Wright, 1970, p. 187). As one might expect, there are smaller farm organization for Communists (MODEF) and Socialists (MONATAR), as well as a direct action group, Paysans-Travailleurs, most often engaged in the seizure and dumping of cheap Italian wine. Like the elected and administrative officials, farmers successfully exploit the territorial organization of France to maximize their influence over the formation and implementation of agricultural policies. One careful student of French agricultural politics writes, "At the departmental level each FNSEA enjoys exclusive access to a parallel network of councils and commissions that deal with everything from prices and tax policy to the administration of disaster relief" (Keeler, 1981, p. 154). In addition to paying the generous agricultural subsidies common in Europe and North America, the government also relies on the FNSEA to organize training courses, rural youth programs, and land consolidation schemes. Given the magnitude of farm problems (Sokoloff, 1980), it is not too surprising that the government welcomed assistance.

Pressure groups impose similar, if not as highly organized, constraints on policies that affect education and social security (see Chapter 6). The National Federation for Education (FEN) has a membership of 540,000, involving three-fourths of all teaching and school administrative staff (Wright, 1980, p. 191). Within the FEN, which has been increasingly torn by internal fights over educational reform, the National Union of Primary Teachers (SNI) enlists 90 percent of its eligible members. The teacher unions were an important contributor to Mitterrand's victory in 1981. Busily occupied with new reforms, the government did not welcome the SNI demand that all state aid to private (including Catholic) schools be withdrawn. The ministers of education quickly replied that the group should leave national policies of the government.

There are no simple measures of the impact of pressure groups on official policies but, in France—as in most advanced welfare states—there are conflicting tendencies. On the one hand, citizens are increasingly aware of their right to organize. In France, for example, the Mouvement Verte or ecologist group has been most successful; they took nearly 10 percent of the votes in the 1974 presidential election. The law of 1901 which established the right to form associations is regarded as a basic liberty. Some years ago the Conseil d'Etat (1972) was asked to make an inventory of groups registered under the 1901 law on public organizations, which include every conceivable variety of organization from the Comédie Française to the giant public investment bank, the Caisse des Dépôts. The inquiry was exhausted by the time the study reached 3000 groups registered under the law. When one of Giscard's reforms threatened to restrict group activity, there was even an association (ADAP) formed to protect associations (Le Monde, April 22, 1980)! Of course, the vitality of group activity in France does not mean that all the political clubs, movements, and associations have a direct impact on public policy, but it does mean that French policymakers must be aware of the risks of encroaching on organized interests. Indeed, given the weaknesses of political parties and the legislature, groups may acquire more effective influence and provide more essential service than groups in more stable systems.

The effect creates a peculiar form of pluralism in French policy process. More stable executives, such as Britain, and more self-assured legislatures, such as in the United States, have other ways of consulting special interests and meeting their demands as policies change. French groups have little stability: in part, because the groups themselves undergo significant transformations over time and are often linked to an unstable party structure. Groups cannot rely on political parties to achieve their aims, nor does parliament have the power to protect their interests. Thus, the relationships between groups and policymaking is, in some ways, more direct than in the Anglo-Saxon parliamentary model, but not nearly as stable as the hierarchically organized labor and industrial interests of Germany. Falling between the stools of stabilizing group interests around the political process, as in Britain or the United States, or forming reliable group expression outside the formal process of government, as in Germany, French officials work very hard to devise ways to aggregate interests in both the formulation and implementation of policy. If this process were purposefully undertaken to exclude others or to monopolize access to government, it might be considered a form of corporate influence. Linking groups to the policy process falls very heavily on the executive and the administration because other institutions, either formal or informal, are unable to integrate so many interests. As will be elaborated in the Conclusion (see Chapter 8) this is one of the intriguing ways in which French government must work very hard in order to stand still.

Democratic Institutions and French Policymaking

In the policy process of most modern democracies, parliament is a critical link in relating policy to public demands and to group interests. The weak legislature of the Fifth Republic has evolved partly from its initial design and partly as a result of the multiparty structure. There is wide agreement among French constitutional experts that de Gaulle wanted to create a parliamentary regime without parliamentary sovereignty. The major transformations of presidential power since 1958, which I have outlined above, were the price paid for the ambiguities intentionally introduced over political restraint over the policy process by de Gaulle's insistence on a strong and autonomous executive. The paradoxical result was that, for twenty years, the Fifth Republic experimented with other ways to link public preferences to the policy process and to integrate group activity with policymaking.

The checks on the National Assembly and Senate are elaborate: no minister may hold an elected office (but the *suppléant* protects a place in a constituency); constitutionally, the Assembly may meet no more than five and a half months a year; lawmaking powers are sharply differentiated from "regulatory" and executive powers (art. 34); the president establishes the Assembly agenda; the Assembly can have only six committees or *commissions* which are aligned with party strengths and thereby weakened; a Deputy or Senator cannot propose a bill appropriating funds without permission; and even the procedural rules of the legislature must be approved by the Constitutional Council. The parliaments of nearly every modern democracy are overloaded, but the French legislature can justifiably feel particularly grieved. In the spring session of 1975, for example, the legislature raced through 106 government bills, twenty-two private bills and twenty-eight treaty approvals (Wright, 1980, p. 116). In the crucial budget debates, which is one of the few meaningful encounters between the executive and the legislature in modern democracies, there is barely time to debate whole department budgets for more than a day. Of course, French deputies and senators are not alone among democratic representatives in trying to digest fifty pounds of budget documents in a month or so.

There are three main ways by which the Assembly can disapprove a government decision, but each entails high risks. First, a tenth of the deputies can propose a motion of censure, but having done so they cannot again support such a motion for a year. With the minority opposition generally limited to a third or so of the seats, the opposition is effectively limited to three or four censure motions each year. Only favorable votes for censure are counted in achieving the absolute majority needed for censure, so that all abstaining deputies are assumed to be supporting the government. Between 1959 and 1978, there were only twenty-five censure motions, only one of which was carried (1962). Second, a prime minister can "engage the responsibility of the government" (ART. 49) for a bill, essentially making a particular proposal a motion of confidence. If there is no motion of censure, the text is automatically adopted. Third, the prime minister submits his program to the Assembly, but no one knows what would happen if the Assembly were ungracious enough to reject it. Under a multiparty system, a government's program cannot be a strong statement. Most often the "program" is no more than a vague declaration of intent, sometimes not presented to the Assembly for several months, and sometimes given a note of urgency by declaring it "an engagement" of governmental responsibility (Massot 1979, pp. 68–72).

However, one can exaggerate the importance of direct partisan control in any Western parliamentary democracy. As policymaking has become more complex, most parliaments have become primarily a device to aggregate electoral preferences, and, as we have seen, French presidents and prime ministers take elections very seriously. The power to dismiss a government is not a very useful policy instrument. Even in Britain, the "mother of parliaments", it is easily hedged to suit partisan convenience (see Ashford, 1981b). For all the opprobrium heaped on the Fifth Republic's leverage over parliament, there have been only five formal dissolutions of the Assembly since the Third Republic (1877, 1955, 1962, 1968, and 1981). The Assembly is obviously the bulwark of the democratic process, but the combination of presidential rule and parliamentary sovereignty has always been ambiguous. Of the eight prime ministers in the Fifth Republic, five were not even in the popularly elected branch of the legislature when chosen. After becoming prime minister in 1962, Pompidou did not even run for office until 1967 (see Massot, pp. 66-67). The disdain for parliamentary control over policy is clear, but the more difficult question is whether logrolling in the American legislature or forceful party discipline in the British parliament are, in any sense, more sensitive to either democratic values or policy needs.

If one looks more closely at some major policy decisions, there is ample evidence that both the Assembly and the Senate do have influence even though the president and prime minister escape their direct control. Giscard's bill for a capital gains tax was hacked to death by amendments in the Assembly. In 1975, a mild proposal for a small land tax was riddled with 500 amendments. Bills to reorganize local government have been regularly withdrawn or amended into impotence by the legislature (see Chapter 3). Deputies and senators effectively defend their political self-interests. More important, as the presidential regime and party structure has evolved over the past twenty years, the Assembly and Senate have become more respected and more influential actors in the policy process. The Senate debate on nuclear energy policies in May 1975, for example, is widely regarded to have been important in reshaping policy. The budget reports of Senator Bonnefous on waste could not be ignored and his 1977 report on anomolies of nationalized industries policy was influential. The increasing intensity of partisan politics itself helped restore parliamentary prestige, and when Mitterrand took office in 1981, he pledged to reinforce this trend.

The policy process is always a subtle blend of learning from the past and preparing for the future. The genius of democratic government has been to discover numerous institutional alternatives to link collective authority to the exercise of power. The particular French compromise has not always been satisfactory but the policy analyses to follow will suggest that France has often been criticized for the wrong reasons. As a mobilizer of opinion and organizer of the opposition, French democratic institutions remain intact. Jacobin instincts have been curbed. By 1969, it was clear that Gaullist *grandeur* quickly wilted when transplanted, and by the 1973 legislative elections the Gaullist Party was in severe disarray. Under the first three presidents of the Fifth Republic, the presidential regime was increasingly subject to party and parliamentary pressures. Whatever de Gaulle's shortcomings, Giscard's efforts to rule from the serene heights of the Elysée looked manipulative and self-serving. The basic institutions of the Fifth Republic were accepted by the public over its first decade, not a bad record in a world replete with failures in institution-building. By 1981, 84 per cent of the French population thought French institutions were working well or well enough (*L'Express*, February 21, 1981). Indeed, they had sufficient confidence to elect a Socialist government three months later, perhaps the ultimate tribute to the success, however unintended, of the conservative coalition that had governed for twenty-three years.

There are, of course, disturbing uncertainties to be found in every democratic system of government. They would be more troubling if it were not that every experiment in modern government that tries to eliminate such uncertainties has ended in authoritarian rule, chaos, or both. The French policy process, as will be elaborated in the following chapters, displays surprising capabilities, many of which escape more abstract models of politics and are ignored by the more vociferous critics of French government. First, the intricate mixture of executive power, administrative self-interest, and partisan pressures in decisionmaking kept pluralist politics alive. Naturally, the uncertainties and ommissions of pluralist decisionmaking sat very uncomfortably on the couch of presidential rule, as any American president can testify. But the result was a slow, incrementalist form of policymaking. As will be argued in more detail in the Conclusion (see Chapter 8), given the complexities of policymaking in advanced welfare states, incremental decisionmaking may not only be a preferable approach to policymaking for practical reasons, but it may be the only approach that can combine the essentials of democratic rule with modern government.

Second, contrary to the image of France as a legalistic and arbitrary monolith, the policy process is an awesome collection of informalities. The interlocking roles of president and prime minister are only vaguely defined, and their evolving relationship is played out against the background of changing policy priorities and strategies. Political capabilities to restructure the peak organizations of French policymaking and the rivalries among elite administrative groups cast doubt on the pessimistic views of French critics. Even the constitutional subordination of the prime minister and cabinet to the president must be exercised with a sense of political realities. From a policy perspective, these uncertainties may have encouraged French leaders to be more cautious and more thorough in designing new policies. One can, of course, find single decisions of importance—such as the Concorde—where highly technical forecasts were incorrect, but these decisions are hardly a test of institutional viability and are, by no means, confined to France. As has been elaborated in many theoretical works on decision processes, the problem is much more one of knowing how right or wrong one might be as external conditions change, and designing the necessary self-correcting machinery to keep the ship of state on course.

Third, the policy analyses will show that despite, and possibly because of, the incrementalism and informality of the French policy process, enormous political, social, and economic changes took place in France over the past twenty years. There is a tireless, experimental quality about French policymaking that eludes more formal models of politics and has been largely ignored by French critics. Democracies endowed with more stable institutions have often marveled at the ingenuity of French policymaking, but few operated under similar institutional uncertainties. The profound nature of uncertainty may have been a stimulus for more careful consideration of policy options and procedures. Coming to a climax with the Socialist victory in 1981, the highly politicized policy process of the Fifth Republic may be its greatest strength.

2   Administrative Reform: Compromising with Necessity

Administrative politics has been a major French preoccupation for several centuries. For this reason, the raging controversies over administrative reform and administrative power surrounding the Fifth Republic are hardly new. Indeed, the persistence of the debate is perhaps the best clue to the importance of administrative politics in the French policy process; it may even imply that the administration is, to some extent, a scapegoat for other French problems. It is by no means obvious that French civil servants have more influence, or are more devious, than those following their bureaucratic self-interest in other modern democracies (see Reading 2-1). The German concept of the state is deeply rooted in the bureaucracy as the guardian of public law and order (Dyson, 1980). Modern Japan emerged from a feudal past under the careful guidance of an administrative class (Pempel, 1981). Sweden developed an intricate policy process whose fulcrum is the consultative and bargaining process within the bureaucracy (Anton, 1980). Reading only the critics of French administration, one might form the erroneous opinion that only France has a recalcitrant, inefficient, or manipulative civil service.

A counterargument can be made that French civil servants have shown remarkable adaptivity as the regimes of the nineteenth and twentieth century created institutional uncertainties. The argument is not that political instability justifies administrative excesses, but that under conditions of instability bureaucrats will naturally follow their own self-interest. Historically, France looked to its administration for continuity in times of stress. It is at least an open question of some complexity whether politicians did a better job in guiding

65

civil servants than civil servants may have done in serving the French state. The bureaucratic tradition of France is one of the oldest in Europe; it traces its modern origins to the eighteenth century, when many European countries were still barely unified. France was then the most powerful country in Europe, and the original justifications were military, not civil. Modern warfare demanded better logistics, engineering, and organization. The first "modern" administrative elite corps, the *ponts et chaussées*, were trained at the Ecole Polytechnique as skilled military engineers. The elite group of administrative legal experts concentrated in the Council of state can trace its origins to monarchist efforts to assemble a workable bureaucracy.

Napoleon needed a strong army and a stable administration to embark on imperial wars; he created the prefects, whom he dubbed his *petits empéreurs*, whom he often favored over even his leading generals. After 1814, when France was left in a shambles by Napoleonic adventures, the administration was vital to the country's reconstruction and for the organization of payment of war debts to Britain. Still a primarily peasant society, France did not need an administration with initiative, but it badly needed one intent on law and order to unify the new country. From roughly the July Monarchy (1830) onwards, however, the bureaucracy began to diversify: its earlier concentration in the Ministry of Interior, which supervised everything from relations with the Catholic Church to agriculture, began to split off into new specialized ministries.

France did not embark on intensive modernization of industry, commerce, and banking until the Second Empire (1852–70). The Emperor Napoleon III initially used the bureaucracy in ruthless ways and his early rule established the reputation of French administration as overbearing and arbitrary. But the dilemma of a bureaucracy in a highly developed society—political realities versus the pursuit of policy aims—began to appear before the end of Napoleon III's rule. Even so, the occupation of northern France in the Franco-Prussian War, the debts and destruction of war, and the intense power struggle in the early years of the Third Republic (1871–77) meant that France needed its officials more than ever before. Although the political instability of the Third Republic helped restore administrative powers, major reforms of education, commerce, and relations with the Catholic Church demanded administrative skill and support. Republican rulers were by no means always content with their officials, but the groundwork for republican institutions could never have been layed without effective administrators. Then, as now, there were severe critics of the administration (Chardon for example), but France needed the continuity and security of a strong administration.

Context

Given the struggle to establish democratic government in France, it is hard to imagine France succeeding without a competent administration. Of course, the bureaucracy extracted concessions for the services to the state, but in doing so the administrative system also developed weaknesses that could be exploited. Administrators are divided into roughly twenty *grands corps* which are ranked in order of their prestige and influence. The most important are the *corps diplomatique*, the *inspecteurs des finances*, the *préfets*, the legal experts or *conseilleurs d'état*, and the engineers or *ponts et chaussées*. The *grands corps* roughly correspond to the major ministries, in these cases to the Ministry of Foreign Affairs; the Ministry of Finance (since 1978, divided into two parts); the final court of administrative law or the Conseil d'Etat; the Ministry of the Interior; and the Ministry of the Environment. Thus, each has its particular preserve from which to seek national influence and to influence policies through friends in other ministries, or *cabinets*, and by using both the field administration and those on detached service to agencies outside government.

Several features of this system make it almost impossible to reform (see Reading 2-2). First, each *corps* has its own source of revenues (often the vestiges of fees charged for administrative services), its own publications, and its own alumni association. The members enthusiastically attend annual conferences and are in close touch with their colleagues. Second, the high levels of competence of elite civil servants and the advantages of the state in producing the best trained technicians and scientists give top civil servants immense prestige, both inside and outside government. Legal experts for other ministries, for example, are usually members of the elite legal corps organized around the Conseil d'Etat and are needed throughout government. Likewise, the highly trained engineers from the Ecole des Mines are in high demand in nationalized industries, private firms, and banking. The result is that administrators integrate a wide variety of activity that is not within the direct scope of civil servants in other countries. Of course, civil servants, in turn, have access to information and inside knowledge.

The origins of the elite administrators of France display most of the social and educational biases found in every advanced industrial society. Indeed, France has an elaborate educational hierarchy with the top administrative schools at the pinnacle (Suleiman, 1974 and 1978). The French situation is similar to the Britain one where it has also been difficult to persuade talented young people to enter the private sector. As we shall see, eventually the Gaullists had doubts about the system because the attractions of loyal administrative service conflicted with Gaullist hopes of creating new incentives for more entrepreneurial behavior. The expansion of the welfare state also generated numerous routine and professional positions that did not appeal to the ambitious *fonctionnaire*. The social services do not provide particularly glamorous jobs, and the late development of the welfare state in France did not encourage the most able civil servants to pursue positions in social welfare.

While the heavy hand of French administration is more visible and can be more obstrutive than the administration in many modern democracies, in some respects France no longer deserves the reputation of an overadministered country. But unlike most countries, the civil servants are part of an ostensibly unified system that makes them more visible and can create the illusion both inside and outside of France that the system should, therefore, be more easily controlled, redirected, and evaluated. Curious as it may seem, the difficulties in achieving these aims provide the rationale for the main critique of the bureaucracy by leaders of both the extreme Right and extreme Left. Though he is certainly not an orthodox Gaullist, Crozier's critique of the administration echoed political doubts (1964). Administrative influence expanded as part of a self-fulfilling prophecy. The attack failed to note, however, that the most rapid growth of French bureaucracy in the 1960s was in areas where France had been deficient (education, welfare, communication) and which were essential to rapid social change. The administration could hardly avoid the attack of the Left on Gaullist government, for officials have no choice but to support new policies. But there were no serious dislocations in the installation of the Socialist government in 1981 and, as we shall see, the Mitterrand cabinet had no difficulty finding an ample supply of willing and eager civil servants to pursue its policies.

The French administration is more properly assessed in relation to the growth of administrative services in other welfare states. Compared to many European countries, France does not have a large bureaucracy. In 1980 there were just under two million full-time civil servants, excluding the military (*Cahiers Francais*, 1980, p. 27). Even if the several hundred thousand temporary civil servants are added, as well as the roughly half million employees of local government, the figure compares favorably with Britain where, in 1980, national government employed about 700,000 persons and local government employed 2.5 million. The rate of growth in the French civil service has been fairly constant over the past twenty years; it increased most rapidly from the late 1950s into the early 1960s (about 47 percent between 1956 and 1967), and then it actually tapered off from 1968 to 1978 (a 40 percent increase). These figures do not exceed the rate of growth in most modern welfare states and, for France, much of the growth is in the Ministry of Education, which nearly doubled in size between 1956 and 1967 (teachers are national employees), and almost doubled again between 1968 and 1978.

The more political controversies center, of course, on the higher civil service. The first controversy focuses on detached service, which enables members of the elite *grands corps* to move from ministerial cabinets to public corporations and back to their "home" ministries. Suleiman (1974, pp. 245–46) found that about a third of the *conseilleurs d'état* are working in other jobs, and three-fourths of the *inspecteurs des finances* are scattered about the government. In the course of these moves, prominent members acquire access to policymaking in many parts of government. Weighing the overall effect on policymaking is difficult. On the one hand, they remain loyal to their initial elite group and "home" ministry and, thereby, may obstruct change. On the other hand, they become effective mobilizers of opinion within government and provide essential communication and coordination in complex policy decisions.

The second controversy is, in many ways, even more difficult to resolve. Critics of the higher civil service regard detached service as a form of unaccountable government and a way by which politicians can manipulate leading civil servants. There is undeniable evidence that many top civil servants have used the network and loyal service to acquire political office. The difficulty with this criticism is that, in an age of complex government, it is hard to imagine a system which would reliably insulate political and administrative decisions. To the extent that the French system elevates influential civil servants to elected office, they become visible and accountable to their constituencies. The threat that the impartiality and neutrality of administration may suffer needs to be evaluated in relation to other political systems. There are frequent complaints from both Conservative and Labour ministries in Britain that they cannot extract ideas and support from their top civil servants. In American politics, about 4000 top administrative positions are political and change with each government, meaning additional dislocation and discouragement for top levels of the bureaucracy. The French tendency to politicize the higher civil service is not unique to France, nor is the French "solution" to the difficulties of finding effective top-level officials completely without compensating features.

The result is that the purpose of administrative reform was never clear in France. There were the common experiments with broadening the social base of recruitment, adding more managerial courses in civil service courses, and encouraging young recruits to work in less rewarding ministries. Even if one could define the aim of such reform in manageable terms, the interdependence of governmental decisions and the pressing needs of political leaders make the laborious task of any fundamental reform unattractive. Perhaps there is a lesson to be learned from more stable political systems such as Britain and the United States, where apprehension over the effectiveness and accountability of the higher civil service rarely produced clear-cut results. But, as we shall see, the changing political objectives of the governments of the Fifth Republic and the politicization of the higher civil service may have made top administrators more sensitive to the aims of government and the political demands of their masters than are civil servants in countries that embarked on ambitious reformist plans.

Agenda

Much of the criticism of French administration is geared to the earliest Gaullist period. Given the political exigencies of the Algerian revolution, de Gaulle had little choice but to rely on the bureaucracy to carry on the normal functions of government. Paradoxically, there were few parties in France who were *more* critical of the higher civil service than the leading Gaullist barons but, at the same time, they were forced to rely on them. Their suspicions are rooted in the Vichy period and the French failure to resist the Nazis. For example, when France collapsed in 1940, a hundred prefects met to pledge their loyalty to the Vichy regime. After the liberation, de Gaulle directed his close adviser, Debré, to organize a new National School of Administration (ENA) to help create a more loyal and effective civil service. As in the case of parliamentary reform, Debré looked to the ostensibly well-disciplined British higher civil service as a model.

There could have been no greater threat to the old elite administrative groups, the *grands corps*—each protected by special privileges and fortified within their own ministries—than the proposed body of general purpose administrators (*administrateurs civiles*) combining administrative and managerial talents. But the old elite groups were under no immediate threat because it would take twenty years for the new breed of civil servant to reach the higher ranks. More important, ENA could not succeed without the support of the old civil service and the cooperation of the ministeries. The top graduates of ENA were understandably envious of the status of the old bureaucracy; the *grands corps*, in turn, could resist promotion of general administrators to key posts. As it worked out, ENA graduates still needed to complete their training in the *grandes écoles*, so the task of seducing the new type of civil servants was not that difficult. We shall, of course, never know what might have happened had de Gaulle not resigned in 1946; he might have helped pave the way for the "ENArques." Left to their own devices, like any good administrators, they followed their best interests.

One of the historical ironies of the early Gaullist reforms of French administration was that they returned to power in 1958, precisely the moment when the products of the ENA were rising to important positions in the administration. The new Gaullist government inherited all the problems of their early reforms. The most difficult obstacle to reforming administration in France, or any other democracy, is that a decade or more is needed for new selection, training, and promotion to have effects. But a decade of acculturation in the French administrative system—no doubt coupled with the ineffectiveness of the Fourth Republic—meant that the ENA graduates unmistakably displayed the elitist qualities of the other *grands corps*. The new school tried to be territorially and socially representative of France, and the new "general purpose" administrators achieved many distinctions but, in the final analysis, they behaved much like their predecessors in the other elite corps (see Reading 2-2).

In any event, the middle of the Algerian war was not an auspicious moment to continue the reforms de Gaulle had begun in 1945. Indeed, those who are quick to criticize de Gaulle and Pompidou for their manipulation of the civil service often fail to note that change was virtually impossible in the early years of the Fifth Republic. As noted in Chapter 1, the Gaullists had little or no grassroots support and no direct involvement in government for over a decade. Although there have been a series of minister delegates for administrative reform attached to the prime minister's office, a global reform was impossible. Since the resignation of Debré as prime minister in 1962, who was the most determined of the Gaullist leaders to reform the machinery and procedures of government, no prime minister felt willing or able to combat the entire system. Even so, the appointment of Pompidou as prime minister testifies to de Gaulle readiness to disregard administrative traditions. Pompidou's contacts and skills were in the world of banking and commerce, not in the internal bureaucratic world of government.

Unlike British parties whose adversarial motives seize issues for whatever political advantage may appear, the Gaullists were much more subtle in expressing their doubts about the administration. They knew that such a massive organization could not be changed by a frontal attack and, as in many other policy choices, decided to attack those aspects of the problem most relevant to their objectives. Primary among these aims was to have a reliable and effective administrative machine extend to the cities and regions, where rapid change was essential to Gaullist industrial and economic goals. As Grémion (1979) has documented so well, the first reforms of 1964 were to assemble effective policy machinery at the departmental and regional levels. Gaullist motives were, of course, connected to their grass-roots weaknesses, and their efforts to stream-line territorial administration met with severe resistance from the prefectoral corps.

Relying heavily on tested comrades to supervise the government, de Gaulle was particularly vulnerable to charges of excessive reliance on technocrats. But we should also remember that this was a frequent charge brought against many democratic governments in the 1960s. Even so, de Gaulle's cabinet, and most of those to follow in the Fifth Republic, was one third or more directly appointed high civil servants (Birnbaum, 1977). However, the distinction between technocrat and policymaker at high levels of government is, at best, ambiguous. Many of the trusted civil servants had been so intimately connected with de Gaulle in the Fourth Republic or during the Algerian crisis that it is misleading to think of them as conventional technocrats. One should also recall that the constitution made the direct appointment of ministers from outside parliament a legal option. The charges of technocracy merged with the general discontent with complex government as it began to appear in the 1960s. Unlike confidential advisers or anonymous experts, civil servants who acquired political status were visible and accepted political risks. Nor did the growing politicization of the high civil service go uncriticized by more conventional officials (Bloch-Lainé, 1976; Reading 2-2) Many resented the growing practice of parachuting direct appointments from ministerial cabinets into electoral contests. One by no means negligible qualification was also that technocratic ideas were often inadequate. Perhaps the most revealing case is J.-M. Jeanneny, industrial policies were a mixed success, whose reform of social security (see Chapter 6) was only a temporary palliative, and whose political career ended in 1969 when his master plan for the 1969 referendum was defeated, which led to de Gualle's resignation. One might ask if political leaders needed friends of this kind!

Process

In the second major transition of the Fifth Republic under Pompidou, many problems of administrative reform broached in the early Gaullist years came home to roost. Again, the bewildering mixture of political and administrative aims was found. Pompidou had indicated the new trend through his earlier efforts to invigorate and broaden the Gaullist Party. Lacking a strong local organization, the rising new generation of young civil servants—many of them inspired by de Gaulle—were a natural source of new talent and support. Increasingly, the bright young men from ENA and the other *grandes ecoles* sought out junior positions in ministerial cabinets from which they could leapfrog into political jobs and eventually seek elected office. All this contributed, of course, to an interpenetrating network of administrative and political interests at the highest policy levels. One of the persons who most successfully launched himself in this way was Jacques Chirac, the model of a politically ambitious civil servant.

Starting as an "ENArque," he was first a member of the elite *grands corps* of auditors, the Cour des Comptes; then he spent several years as a chargé in Pompidou's ministerial cabinet in the early 1960s. In 1967, he launched a political career and was elected deputy from Corrèze. After serving under three prime ministers between 1968 and 1974, he became prime minister and leader of the Gaullist Party in 1974. Perhaps a more typical case is Jerome Monod. He left ENA and the Cour des Comptes to become an assistant in Debré's ministerial cabinet in 1959. After spending most of the 1960s rising within the regional development agency (DATAR), he shifted to become director of Chirac's ministerial cabinet in 1975. His political career was fully confirmed when he became secretary general (chief administrative officer) of the Gaullist party in 1976.

The politicization of the higher civil service reached full bloom under President Pompidou and, in turn, had important repercussions on demands for administrative reform. Within this struggle at the highest levels, the competition and rivalries of the *grands corps* continued. One of its manifestations was the movement to rationalize administration, an experiment that went on in different forms in most European governments at the time. Like the British under Heath, who barely disguised his dismay over bureaucracy, the French experimented with modern budgeting methods and were susceptible to the idea that fiscal and financial management could be made highly rational. In the late 1960s, an enthusiastic group of high civil servants established a project to rationalize the budget (*rationalisation des choix budgétaires* or RCB) within the Ministry of Finance. As so often happens when France, or any other modern government, undertakes structural change, the attack on old administrative habits was easily dispersed. The new group was the spearhead of some talented engineers and microeconomists of the *ponts et chaussées* who saw an opportunity to gain turf in the Ministry of Finance at the expense of the less quantitatively trained *inspecteurs des finances*.

There was an additional subplot, for the RCB group was loosely tied to the Planning Commission, to regional planners of DATAR (Delégation d'Aménagement du Territorie et d'Action Régionale) and to rivalries between the Planning Commission and the Ministry of Finance (Ashford, 1977). The aim of RCB was to experiment with the application of cost-benefit studies to specific programs. Like many notions about rationalizing government, it could not achieve a grip on the policy process before economic conditions changed so drastically that the effort was wasted. More important, like nearly every direct attack on entrenched bureaucracies, it was easily deflected by the Ministry of Finance (mostly by discreetly giving it too much to do) and was eventually discouraged by Giscard himself (as minister of finance). He correctly saw that a radically new budgeting system would jeopardize the Ministry's crucial role in bargaining (*arbitrage*) among ministerial budgets (see Chapter 4).

The third, and in many ways most important, transition under Pompidou was the search for ways to integrate ENA with the administrative system. Pompidou inherited the problem from the early Gaullist years, though his own practice of encouraging ambitions young civil servants to enter politics probably exacerbated the problem. The 1968 demonstrations triggered growing discontent within ENA and, even before the strikes, it was clear that the new administrative group was unhappy about its prospects. Some ENA students joined the demonstrations and a few even refused to take high status appointments in the elite administrative groups after graduation. From the government's viewpoint, there were increasing doubts over the success of the ENA venture and fears that the students were too academic and not well-grounded in the actual practices of government. After the May 1968 strikes, the president appointed a blue-ribbon committee under Bloch-Lainé (see Reading 2-2) to study the malaise of the school and its relation to the *grands corps*.

Bloch-Lainé was well known for his reservations about the increased politicization of the civil service; he had twice refused ministerial office (Bloch-Lainé, 1976). In many ways, he was a dedicated civil servant on the British model but he, too, participated in the many influential political clubs that abound in Paris. In any event, he found that the draconian solution to excessive ambition and infighting in the civil service—abolishing the *grands corps*—would not materially help. His hope was that competition could be confined to professional standards, and that more applied training in ENA would help promote meritocratic practices. The ENA crisis was only one of many awaiting Pompidou's presidency, but the issue of the administrative state persisted. The most coherent reply came from Pierre Racine, another trusted civil servant close to the Gaullists, who was appointed director of ENA to work out a new compromise. Racine's analysis (see Reading 2-3) is sensitive to the intricacies of French administration and one of the clearest expositions of the dilemmas facing administrative reform in France. As he argues, there is no simple way of separating the dual role of the elite *grands corps*. The entire concept of the French state rests on their quasi-autonomous role in fulfilling their functions for the state as guardians of the law and public interest, while also being the most expert advisers of government.

As most European and North American democracies have learned, there are no simple ways to transform a complex administrative system, nor, once one begins to study alternatives, are there many attractive options. In Pompidou's last year, the Bouvard Report (see Reading 2-4) pointed the direction for the future. Rejecting the search for "rational" solutions, Bouvard saw that training, recruitment, and cirriculum are unlikely to alter the perception of administrative self-interest within government. Bouvard goes to the heart of the matter; the control of budgets. He raises important questions that have plagued every modern democracy: how fiscal power can be best integrated with the rapidly expanding functions of government in the welfare state, and how an increasingly elaborate array of administrative interests may defend their programs and privileges as government grows. The French Ministry of Finance had long been recognized as the "superstructure" of French administration, and its elite *inspecteurs des finances* are among the most influential at all levels of government (see

Chapter 3). As Bouvard argued, within the Ministry, the Directions of Forecasting (*Prévision*), Budgeting, and Taxation (who carry on their own rivalries) can easily block policy change in any part of the administration.

Consequences

As we have seen, French politics is inextricably linked to French administration. France is by no means unique in not finding simple solutions to the inefficiency and complexity of modern government, though many scholarly and partisan critics often sound as though France were the only confused country. The moral may well be that politics and administration cannot be neatly compartmentalized. The distinction of France may be that it never pretended that this could be done. Nonetheless, the administrative system adjusted to a variety of demands and needs during the Fifth Republic. Possibly the best demonstration of its versatility is the ease of transition to the Socialist government under Mitterrand. His cabinet is heavily peppered with members of the *grands corps*, including a talented financial expert, Jacques Delors, as minister of finance, who had served under the Gaullists. There is no evidence that the Left has experienced bureaucratic resistance to their plans.

If the French prefer to avoid utopian goals, the risk of their pragmatic approach is basically political rather than bureaucratic. The Giscardian regime, the third phase in the development of the Fifth Republic, exposed a new kind of threat. Appointing bright civil servants to political positions is one issue, but infiltrating government to place loyal, personal friends in numerous key posts is another. The "monarchial" tendencies of Giscard (see Reading 2-5) alarmed even the Gaullists. In earlier forms of political-administrative interaction, the network served to restrain personal rule and the rivalries of administrators could not be simply overridden. Giscard's tactic was removal of even these cumbersome checks. In effect, the best guarantee against administrative abuse— administrative conflict itself—was short-circuited.

While there may be no panacea for administrative reform, each country must work out its own solution within the context of political-administrative exchange. The French are no exception. On the one hand, there is the appeal of bringing the public sector closer to the private sector by closer collaboration with businessmen and industrialists (see Reading 2-6). In a country where top administrators are regularly placed on detached service with large public corporations, nationalized industries, and with a variety of mixed public-private contractual projects (see Chapters 3 and 4), France is probably among the more skilled administrative systems in blending entrepreneurial and administrative talents. On the other hand, the possibility of making civil servants more responsive to public opinion remains important and has formed part of the Socialist critique of the civil service (see Reading 2-7). Part of the Socialist position, which also influences their labor relations policies (see Chapter 5), is to have more self-management (*autogestion*) within the civil service, though even if worked out in satisfactory ways, such a reform would not alter the hectic pace of decisionmaking at high levels of government. In many respects, the precise definition of administrative procedures in the French administrative codes, the elaborate system of administrative courts, and the internecine warfare among the *grands corps* remain the best protection against administrative excesses.

In the final analysis, the best restraint on bureaucracy is that even in an age of advanced techniques and information systems, it makes mistakes. Some of them are trivial but revealing. For example, Giscard asked one of his ministers to redraft the divorce law, which was about to go before parliament, in readable language (*L'Année Politique*, 1975). Some are serious. France was late in developing a modern highway system, in part because administrative experts connected to the nationalized railways were so successful in monopolizing transportation investments. While hardly a distinguishing feature of French policy, the social security system is a maze of overlapping benefits, funds, and programs (see Chapter 6). A massive program to consolidate communes failed (see Chapter 3). Thus, calculating the efficiency of administration is not easy and there are many blotches on the record of the higher civil service. What may differentiate France is that the intricate pattern of interlocking political and administrative decisionmaking may give democratically elected officials a chance to learn from these errors.

Two decades of preoccupation with administrative reform throughout Europe and North America have not produced dramatic global reforms, but the French tactic has penetrated the outer defenses of bureaucratic power.

Unlike the partially autonomous structures of Germany or Sweden, the politicization of French administration produces both sensitivities and skills that may be less apparent where bureaucracies are more easily insulated from political demands and political incentives. There is no reason to bar administrators from elected office nor does their personal security differ markedly from lawyers whose practices can be guarded by partners, or businessmen whose interests can be protected by trusts. It is somewhat ironical that after two decades of criticism from the Left (and elsewhere) about the interlocking nature of politics and administration in France, nearly three-fifths of the newly elected Socialist National Assembly in 1981 were civil servants—in part because of Socialist strength among teachers who are national employees (*Figaro*, July 21, 1981).

Thus, a major institutional uncertainty of French politics and policy is precisely that French administrators are so openly dependent on politicians. The threat to democratic government is not so much that civil servants may be elected to office, where they inevitably accept the same risks as those of all elected officials. Much more threatening, particularly with the growth of government in the modern welfare state, is the possibility of elected officials not knowing, and not being able to find out, what kind of influence the administrative system actually exercises. Poorly defined political and administrative boundaries may stimulate the search for new ways of organizing the network of political and administrative influence at high levels of government. From this perspective, French leaders acquire office knowing that they must manipulate an intricate system, and are clearly concerned that the bureaucracy responds to new policy priorities and departures.

But a highly politicized administrative system also creates certain vulnerabilities for the political system. There are, of course, the possibilities of confidential abuse and scandal, but these weaknesses barely distinguish France from most modern governments. Paradoxically, the growing use of political incentives in controlling the administration may undermine the historic strengths of French administration, its technical competence, and its dedication to public service. Many felt that, under Giscard, the increased concentration of the network around the Elysée has begun to transform the entire upper level of French administration into an easily manipu-

lated and purposeless body of presidential sycophants. Even the
Socialists were accused of "neo-Jacobin" tendencies when the new
government promptly removed a number of high officials on taking
office in 1981. Patronage and favoritism are part of every administrative system, but once a country converts its entire policy machinery to purely partisan ends, the foundations of democratic life are
threatened.

Readings

2-1. THE POLITICIZATION OF THE FRENCH CIVIL SERVICE*

*A major and continuing debate between the governing majority
and the parties of the Left has been the political attachments of the
higher civil service. Vincent Wright notes that these charges are by no
means new in the history of French politics and administration and
that, indeed, it would be difficult to organize a government without
considering the interface between political and administrative responsibilities. As he points out, there is little reason to think that the
Socialists or Communists would behave differently were they to come
to power.*

In some respects, the power of the civil service may have decreased during the Fifth Republic.

It can be argued that with a stronger political Executive the
power of the civil service should, logically, decline. The argument
appears to be strengthened when one considers that for the first
time, the government can now depend on a disciplined majority in
the National Assembly. Certainly, the influence of civil servants
within Parliament, often open and outrageous during the Fourth
Republic, has decreased and become much more discreet.

Observers have also pointed out that, in some respects, successive Gaullist Governments have tried to limit State intervention.

*Vincent Wright, "Politics and Administration under the Fifth Republic," *Political
Studies*, no. 22 (1972), pp. 44–65 (selections). Footnotes have been deleted.

The notion of the interventionist, 'dirigiste' and protectionist State was weakened under the 'neo-liberal' influence of Pompidou as Prime Minister, Giscard d'Estaing as Finance Minister, and Albin Chalandon as Minister of Housing and Equipment. The State continues to intervene massively in the economic domain (investment grants, regional incentives, loans to declining industries) but it is increasingly leaving the management of the economy to the private sector. The growth of the *sociétés d'économie mixte* is an indication of State willingness to intervene in the economy but the organization and functioning of these *sociétés* underlines the willingness of the State to leave a great deal of initiative to the private sector.

Not only is the Executive apparently intent on limiting the scope of State activity and hence the potential power of the civil service, it has also shown a determination to control the administration more closely. Indeed, the Constitution of the Fifth Republic was the first to recognize the place—a subservient one—of the French administrative machine. Debré's thinking on administrative reform involved not only the exaltation of technical expertise and a denunciation of 'politics': it was also greatly concerned with the need to subordinate the administration to the will of the Executive; and with the army rebellious, the police resentful and the colonial civil service mutinous, this was scarcely surprising. Amongst the measures taken were the 1959 revision of the civil service statute and the 1964 decree on the personnel of the O.R.T.F. which gave the Government greater control over personnel and reduced the influence of the unions, limitations were placed on the right of State employees to strike, ministerial control over the nationalized industries was tightened, and the activities of such bodies as the Association du corps préfectoral were seriously limited.

Constraints upon civil service power remain very strong.

It is a platitude worth repeating that the civil service has constant need of others in order to ensure the creation, drafting and execution of policies. It is not merely a question of calling on outside groups to 'legitimize' administrative decisions. The needs go much deeper.

The growth of pressure group activity since the war; the forging of new, close and more subtle links between the groups and the administration and the permeation of the civil service into nearly all sectors of French society have increased the potential power of the administration in some respects. But they may have also seriously reduced it. As 'audience, advisors and clients', the group are 'the foremost participants in the process of bargaining over government policy, and instrumentalities for the enforcement of its rulings'. Some groups 'colonize' and dominate certain parts of the administration; this was made clear in the 1959 Rueff Report and the more recent report of the *Conseil de Impôts.* There have been constant examples of determined pressure groups wrecking the plans of the 'technocrats': the miners during their great strike, the lorry drivers, the small shop-keepers of Nicoud, the peasants who are largely responsible for the frequent changes in French agricultural policies, the liberal professions who have protected their outrageous tax privileges with great success, the education lobby, spearheaded by the powerful Société des agrégés, which has sabotaged many of the University reforms of Edgar Faure. The administrations with all the good will in the world (and it is not always apparent), appears helpless to combat the excessive privileges of certain groups. Other groups are agencies of the Executive's will. Generally, however, the groups and the administration have a symbiotic relationship. Henry Ehrmann, the foremost student of pressure groups in France, detects a change in the attitudes of civil servants in recent years; he refers to the greater pragmatism which prevails and which has 'led many civil servants to take a less exalted view of their rôle as infallible arbiters. In their contacts with interest groups they seek to conform to a new image of a representative bureaucracy which reflects better than hitherto the society in which they act'. This state of affairs does not conform very neatly with the technocratic model presented by critics of the régime.

The need to weaken the position of the parties was a piece of Gaullist dogma. But the parties were strong only in the minds of the Gaullists. One of the basic problems of the Fourth Republic was that the parties were not strong enough or, at least were not strong enough in the Right and the Centre. With the exception of the Communist Party (which played no part in Government after May 1947) and possibly the Socialist Party, the parliamentary parties of the Fourth Republic were weak, ill-disciplined and incoherent groups of independent-minded and constituency-oriented Deputies. Instead of introducing aggregated (and therefore generally compromise) demands into the system, they tended to become the spokesmen, and prisoners, of all the disparate and often contradictory elements which composed their electorate. Demands were, therefore, specific and generally more extreme. Paradoxically, the founders of the Fifth Republic should have been concerned with strengthening the parties, in order to construct useful and effective buffers between the administration and the interests. Ironically, this 'antiparty' régime has given birth to parties of the Right which are, for the first time, reasonably coherent and disciplined. But the parties, as such, are kept, or keep themselves, free from 'entanglement' with the civil service.

The Executive is less cut off from opinion than the critics contend. First, the Government not only has at its disposal the traditional means of testing opinion—the reports of the Prefects and of the *services des renseignements généraux*: opinion polls are frequently published in the main newspapers, and polls are now regularly commissioned by the Ministry of the Interior to test opinion on specific issues. Second, as already noted, the tentacles of the civil service reach out into nearly all areas of French society: the Government is thus guaranteed a constant flow of information. Finally, the Fifth Republic lives in an atmosphere of electoral tension. Since the beginning of 1958, political fever has been maintained by five general elections, six referenda, two presidential elections, senatorial and departmental elections every three years, and municipal elections every six years. And each electoral consultation is considered to be politically 'decisive'. What better circumstances in which to exact concessions?

The policies of the Fifth Republic display little more 'coherence' than those of the Fourth. In certain ministries, there has been great instability of personnel (the portfolio of Education, for example, has changed hands eleven times since May 1958) and, as already seen, in organization. The declared policy of 'ouverture et continuité' may be an excellent political ploy but it does little to decrease the uncertainty which presently surrounds decision-making. What political attitude should a Prefect adopt in a régime in which the enemies of yesterday become the allies of today and possibly the Ministers of tomorrow? The Fifth Republic, for all its good intentions, has learnt that ultimately all decisions are 'political'.

2-2. AN EVALUATION OF ADMINISTRATIVE REFORM OPTIONS*

The participation of many ENA students in the May 1968 demonstrations led to a major reevaluation of the School, its recruitment, teaching, and placement. Central to the students' concerns was the more favorable treatment given certain grands corps. *In his report to the Prime Minister, Bloch-Lainé, himself a member of the elite financial inspection corps, explains why merging the* grands corps *with the mass of government employees is unacceptable. He also discusses why qualifying exams* (concours) *and privileged mobility and pay of some higher civil servants should be preserved.*

The Distinction between Corps and Services

1. The principle today retained in the higher civil service would be the pure and simple assimilation of the *grands corps* with the services. This would be an inflammatory obstacle to personnel mobility. Belonging to a corps, the civil servant could not leave without suffering career disadvantages; each corps would be the privileged supplier of a service or a ministry; the system would thus constrain the movement of personnel.

This interpretation has been contested. The distinction between corps and services, which has been presented as a novelty, has been recognized in law for some time. The *grands corps* have an interministerial vocation. The interministerial character of the civil administrators (ENA graduates) has been declared in numerous statutes since 1945, and has been solemnly reaffirmed by the 1964 reforms. The Commission itself will formulate some propositions to further accentuate the interministerial character of the recruitment of subprefects.

On the whole, for the majority of the Commission, it is neither possible nor desirable to disassociate in all cases the fact of belonging to a *corps* and the vocation of specific positions. The missions confided to administrative services have a specific character: if they do not presuppose specialized training, at least they presume certain abilities acquired through constant practice, that is to say, throughout an organized career. In this respect, the *corps* of civil

*Prime Minister, *Rapport de la Commission d'Etude des Problèmes de l'Ecole Nationale d'Administration*, Paris, Documentation Française (Supplement to Notes et Etudes Documentaires), 1969 (selections).

servants serve as support. Without proposing an entirely new and coherent organization of the higher civil service, it would appear difficult to renounce such support. Certainly it is essential that the *grands corps* be largely open, that the channels between them be multiplied by detachments for temporary service, by field service, and through other means. But to mutilate or destroy them would run the risk of creating general confusion, with heavy consequences.

On the other hand, the minority and the majority of the Commission agree in proposing a greater specificity for the ENA. Without opposing the desire to differentiate training to support a unity of a corps having a universal vocation, one should note the two divergent exigencies thus expressed. Such uncertainty leads us to avoid initiating a radical change in the structure of the *corps* and to maintain a certain degree of identity between corps and the services.

2. The suggestions made concerning remunerations also evoke certain reservations. In effect, it is proposed to "link the principal remuneration to the situation of the *corps*, with supplementary advantages linked to responsibilities and to achievement as determined at the level of the services". In principal, such is already the situation. Experience shows, however, that this does not overcome the grave irritating problem of existing disparities in remuneration, reflected in the unequal shares between rich ministries and poor ministries. If it is a question of standardizing pay scales by a rigorous statutory control among the *corps*, such changes in pay scale could be achieved by uniform grading so that compensation (*indiciaries*) becomes homogeneous, but this does not seem a realistic aim to accomplish in a single blow.

For the rest, one can also ask whether it is opportune to establish a system in which all the careers offered to former pupils of the ENA would be perfectly "calibrated". This would make little allowance for the effect of responsibilities and individual qualities manifested in the course of a career. There is a certain paradox in underlining the advantages of private sector methods, where success and failure sanction great disparities, while proposing at the same time what one could call guaranteed careers.

Belonging to a *corps* seems definitively less determinant than appointment to a ministry or a service. If the solution of a single *corps* were chosen, nothing would be changed concerning the actual pay inequalities, and the administration's resistance to personnel mobility would hardly be overcome. The Commission has been led, by its desire for efficiency, to focus its research on a field other than the juridical distinctions.

Criticisms of the Qualifying Examination

If it is opportune to deconsecrate the qualifying examinations (*concours*) and just to condemn them insofar as they forever protect the privileged, an exact measure of its real consequences must still be taken and more risky procedures of selection must not be substituted for them.

No one is unaware of the imperfections of the qualifying examination: rapid as the progress in testing can be, it will never completely eliminate the artificiality of a classification made with the aid of more or less scholarly criteria without regarding the qualities and disposition of the candidate. It is also true that these risks are aggravated when selection leads directly and permanently to professional positions: it remains a sort of wager on one's aptitude to fulfill certain functions. These functions often require qualities very different from those which can be tested.

Nevertheless, the value of the selective classification upon leaving the ENA cannot be denied. Even if the *grands corps* do close their doors to many qualified candidates, they have, in a general way, attracted many students who are among the best. The examinations undergone in the course of training at the ENA are not limited to evaluating intellectual talent; they can also reveal character traits which can offer a fairly solid test of future performance. If the recruitment for the *grands corps* were as unsure as many contend, this would soon change the recruitment of pupils to ENA.

The majority of members of the Commission agree that it is perilous to renounce the many advantages offered by the qualifying examination without firm guarantees: by its objectivity, by the nature of its tests and trials, this mode of selection has given chances for social mobility to generations of Frenchmen who, despite differences in personality and required knowledge, are foreign to the thinking and habits of the higher civil service to which they aspire. The ranking of students at the time of leaving the ENA—if it is obviously imperfect, and if it must at any price lose its apocalyptic aspects—preserves a certain equity which no other system can assure.

The idea of standardizing the selection of candidates for the high civil service is attractive. Under this system, juries would decide on the first position of ENA graduates, would arbitrate at the time of the second appointment, and would even decide eventually on access to certain positions. The Commission does not ignore the advantages to personalizing the selection process and adapting its criteria. But it cannot ignore certain grave risks of politicization or of personal influence, which would be introduced under this system and against which the qualifying examination has been a precaution. The propositions formulated by the partisans of radical reform do not appear to the Commission to be sufficiently precise on the guarantee of the future objectivity of selection.

For these reasons, a majority of Commission members continue to favor a single qualifying examination, while preferring to manage its use and to mitigate its harmful effects.

The Abolition of "Privileged Channels"

The essential cause of the current malaise should be sought in the quasi monopoly of members of the *grands corps* over positions of high responsibility in the administration. The existence of privileged channels, or more exactly of "reserved sectors", discourages highly qualified candidates, interferes with the normal progression of career patterns, and accentuates excessive compartmentalization. Thus, a major obstacle is raised to the establishment of the coherent employment policy for high civil servants.

The Commission has been led to revise this analysis on certain points. In effect, it seems to the Commission that there is a tendency to overestimate the "predestination" from which members of the *grands corps* benefit. Certainly, the initial advantage derived from belonging to these corps cannot be denied. Throughout one's career, this constitutes a favorable "initial prejudice." However, studies which the Commission has conducted, comparing the careers of ENA students who graduate from the same class, show that the determination is far from being absolute, and that the exercise of responsibilities and different functions can modify the original conditions to a great extent, leading to unexpected career outcomes. It is advisable to increase the flexibility of the system, but not to repudiate it. Finally, it is necessary to remember that the ENA is not yet twenty-five years old and that the civil administrators trained in it are only now arriving at the required age to exercise functions of high responsibility. Many among them, moreover, already hold such positions, the number of which is frequently underestimated.

The disadvantages of a systematic hiving off of the *grands corps* are very real. In the view of the Commission, correction is needed. The detachment of members of the *grands corps* to fill positions of qualified civil administrators should be instituted with care. This practice can, at times, respond to the legitimate concern to promote a candidate less distinguished by this original position. In this case, one can also see the usefulness of a reform or a profound transformation of the services. But, if practiced too often, it cannot be justified.

These diverse considerations have led a majority of the Commission, finally, to prefer the definite advantages derived from reinforcement of the civil administrators (the ENA system) over the insufficiently calculated risks of measures attacking the other corps.

2-3. PROBLEMS OF IMPLEMENTING ADMINISTRATIVE REFORM*

Following the inquiry into problems of placement and morale at ENA, the Director, Pierre Racine, prepared an evaluation. In one of the first frank discussions of the increasing politicization of the French higher civil service, Racine acknowledges the demoralizing effect of careerism and the erosion of civil service dedication. He sees no way that ambitious ENA graduates can be dissuaded from seeking rapid promotion through ministerial cabinet positions, but considers this a threat to professional conduct.

A General Appointment Policy for Civil Servants of the Corps and Ministries Recruited through the ENA

Despite the intentions of the authors of the 1945 reform, there has been no general appointment policy applied to civil servants graduated from the National School of Administration which constitute, along with the engineers of the technical *grands corps*, the

---

*Pierre Racine, *Rapport sur le réforme de l'Ecole Nationale d'Administration*, January 1970, mimeographed (selections).

framework of French administration. It is not a question of imagining a policy which would correspond to an abstract conception of the administration: this policy should be inspired by a general view, but also rests on a general knowledge of particular situations and concrete problems in each administration, notably of the ministries which encounter different situations—the Finance Ministry, all the technical ministries, the large social ministries, including National Education, and the small ministries.

In the establishment of this policy, neither is it a question of finding a uniformity of conditions for all the agents of these corps and ministries, which would not correspond to diverse functions, but rather to pursue two fundamental objectives:

—To give comparable positions to civil servants during their first ten years of service.

—To establish a greater equality of opportunity for the ultimate attainment of high positions of responsibility.

Thus understood, contrary to what many ENA students believe, the problem cannot be reduced to that of clarifying the relationship among the three *grands corps* and the civil administrators (ENA graduates). The problem is broader than this. In effect, it is a question of clarifying the place of the diverse corps in the administration, and the relationship of the corps to one another; of determining the role of civil administrators in the technical ministries; of reinforcing the weaker ministries; of assuring a real mobility of personnel; and of exchanges between the corps as well as between central administration and the provincial services.

This policy must be inspired exclusively by the general interest of the state and by the requirements of the administration, and not based on the advantages to be gained by certain corps members, no matter how brilliant.

For clarity of exposition, we will examine successively the following problems:

—The role of the *grands corps* in the administration today and the conditions of their functioning.

—The situation of the civil administrators (ENA graduates), their relationship with the *grands corps*, their place in the various administrations and, in particular, in the technical ministries.

The Role of the Three Grands Corps in the Government and Their Work

The *grands corps* of the Council of State, the Court of Accounts, and the Financial Inspection Corps constitute one of the most original characteristics of the French administration. The place that they occupy in the administration is, in large measure, the result of history and tradition rather than the result of a theoretical conception. They have played, and they continue to play, an essential role in two respects: first, as distinct administrative bodies and, secondly, because of the extensive functions their members fulfill individually in most sectors of the administration and often in industry.

At the present time the state could not do without the assistance of the *grands corps*, but it must be frankly admitted that the conception of their role by certain members, and the practices which have developed in past years pose grave problems which should be debated openly and impartially.

We will therefore examine, in turn, the normal and beneficial contribution of the *grands corps* to the functioning of the administration, as well as the deviations and excesses.

—The normal and beneficial contribution of these corps to the functioning of the administration and of the state.

This contribution is threefold:

a) First of all, the *grands corps* have an important function of their own, to counsel and judge for the Council State, to audit for the Court of Accounts, and to inspect for the general inspection of finances.

These functions constitute their *raison d'être*, which they must therefore fulfill exclusively and give priority.

b) Various individual tasks are assigned to members because of their independence, the quality of their preparation both inside and outside their corps, and due to their broad perspective resulting from varied nonspecialized experience.

In this way, members who are often called upon to assist in interministerial cabinets which need their qualifications contribute to the conduct of government, as well as to the smooth functioning of the administration as a whole. Thus, they are engaged in multiple activities, often of an exceptional or temporary nature, many of which involve conceptualization: special studies, inquiries, reform commissions, formulation of the Plan, regional planning (DATAR), organizations for reflection or synthesis, technical assistance abroad, teaching assignments, and juridical or financial advice. Members are particularly well-suited to act as arbitrators because of their recognized impartiality as well as their independent status and broad perspective. Where the government wishes, they also render an important service before decisions are made by clarifying opposing viewpoints and factual situations involving administrative rivalries, working conditions in public enterprises, and labor conflicts in the private sector, for example. The flexibility of organization in the *grand corps* gives their members the opportunity to pursue such tasks without detracting from the fulfillment of their primary duties.

c) Finally, the government has a practice of calling upon members not only to exercise responsibilities within the administration but also to serve in other organizations whose higher positions are nominated.

If a reasonable equilibrium had been maintained among these three activities, few problems would have occurred in the central administrations or at the ENA. However, in certain cases, current trends take on aspects of a real deviation, and entail certain abuses which are increasingly detrimental to maintaining administrative cohesion.

The three *grands corps* are more and more considered to be the surest means of rapidly acquiring high administrative positions under particularly privileged conditions. For many graduates of ENA, entry into the *grands corps* represents only a waiting period of four years, because this is the minimum period of apprenticeship that the corps impose on their recruits.

After this apprenticeship is served, they immediately seek positions in the ministries, in the diverse autonomous organizations which are dependent on them, or even other *grands corps*—notably in a prefectoral or diplomatic corps, the nationalized sector or large private enterprises.

The concern to get ahead thus becomes the primary motivation for these graduates, consequently demoralizing those who continue to believe that a high civil servant can usefully serve in any part of the administration.

This tendency is particularly marked in the financial inspection corps, but is also spreading to the Council of State and to the Court of Accounts. It is encouraged by two phenomena, the first of which has already been mentioned:

The policy of overrecruitment and of excessive temporary detachment practiced by the *grands corps* conflicts with demands made on them by ministries or by their own members.

To be entirely objective, it should be recognized that the excessive number of recruits can be attributed, to a certain extent, to the ENA itself which, to placate its students, each year asks that the number of positions designated by the *grands corps* be as high as possible. To achieve temporary satisfaction for each graduating class, the effects of excessive detachments and the inequities between civil administrators and the *grands corps* are aggravated from year to year.

The ministerial cabinets are old and durable institutions of French administration and the ministers could not do without the assistance of personal collaborators, but it must be recalled that with the ministerial continuity resulting from the Fifth Republic's general institutional stability, the cabinets play even more significant role than heretofore. It has sometimes been the case that these cabinets become a screen between the minister and his administration, but such is not our problem today. What is at stake is the frankly excessive influence cabinet members have in deciding nominations to high administrative posts. By observing certain spectacular careers, many young civil servants (a large number of whom belong to the *grands corps*) consider entry into these corps, followed by service in a ministerial cabinet, as the normal springboard for their careers. Too many nominations under these conditions, involving young civil servants who lack the necessary experience, have thus contributed to the development of a sometimes cynical careerism, whose principal effect is to undermine the morale of civil servants, who do not benefit from these privileged channels. The gravity of the present situation is that these practices are solidifying into a system which even claims as its justification that an essential mission of the *grands corps* is to constitute a natural reservoir of talent upon which the government can draw to fill responsible positions. This conception has been dubbed the "fish pond" (*vivier*) theory.

While it appears acceptable to choose from the *grands corps* some of the high officials for the central administration and related organizations, this unique theory must be considered doubly inacceptable:

—First of all, from the point of view of good administrations, because the *raison d'être* of each corps lies only in the continued exercise of the primary functions for which it was created. A corps cannot be justified by other means, but should only contribute within reason to other tasks in the general interest, taking into account the legitimate aspiration of other categories of officials at the same level.

—Socially and politically, neither can one accept this conception which leads in practice—if not in the avowed intentions of its authors—to the creation within the higher civil service of two classes of officials, one of whom benefits from advantages and privileges often derived less from their individual merit than from their belonging to a certain *grands corps*.

When objections are raised to this state of affairs and to the conception which seeks to justify it, the contention is made that to abolish such practices is to "kill" these corps. Nothing is further from the truth. The motivation of the reform is to end the disparities which demoralize the administration, and to reestablish more equitable conditions in favor of all officials with the same qualifications.

To refuse to examine this problem frankly and objectively is to voluntarily close one's eyes to an unhealthy situation, aggravated each year by the burgeoning number of promotions which compromise the efficient functioning of the ministries in the short term—government's principal means of action. Therefore, it is essential to examine the role and work of the *grand corps* in the administration as a whole.

Two of the *grands corps*, the Council of State and the Court of Accounts, regularly fulfill their traditional missions. Without a doubt, they could be constrained by the government to fulfill them more vigorously and in closer adherence to the administration's policy, while at the same time conserving their autonomy. This is the case with the Council of State, for example, whose efficiency would be substantially increased if it participated not only in the discussion of texts, but in their elaboration, in close cooperation with the responsible departments. At the same time, the broad view of problems afforded by the performance of such multiple administrative and juridical activities makes it an invaluable instrument for the study of administrative reform.

The financial inspection corps certainly still practices its traditional tour of inspection. The corps is particularly rigorous regarding its young members who are obliged to pursue these tours during the four years following their entry in the corps. Thereafter, inspection tours are organized, often in a selective manner, in order to deal with specific problems or for the benefit of the administration. But no one can contest the fact that for different reasons—the principal one being the excessive policy of temporary detachment of its members for other tasks—the Financial Inspectorate no longer conducts a *systematic inspection* of the administration's finances. This must be regretted particularly since the growing magnitude of state and local intervention in the economy, industry, public works, and regional policy makes such an inspection even more essential. The use of modern information systems, notably computerization, should permit the Financial Inspectorate to exercise a more comprehensive and efficient auditing without, moreover, requiring it to abandon its traditional "tour" which retains its value for the apprenticeship of young inspectors as well as for the maintenance of administrative vigilance in its departments.

Without intending to offend, it must be said that it is aberrant for a corps, however prestigious, to become identified in the minds of its members and especially of its latest entrants, as existing solely to be used in rapidly climbing the administrative career ladder.

2–4. A PROPOSAL FOR A MINISTRY OF ADMINISTRATIVE REFORM*

Although the prime minister has usually had a minister of state assigned to administrative reform, there were no significant structural changes since World War II. In this reading, a deputy proposes that the prime minister take control from the Ministry of Finance, whose

*Bouvard Report, 1974, "Fonction Publique et Réformes Adminstratives," Assemblée Nationale, Commission des lois Constitutionnelles, *Journel Officiel* (Avis sur le loi de finances pour 1974), no. 685, session 1973–1974, pp. 1–51 (selections; footnotes deleted).

detailed and cumbersome budgetary procedures have blocked every effort to build a more accountable administration. In general, he argues that neither ministers nor civil servants will favor administrative reform so long as the powerful director of the budget in the Ministry of Finance can so easily manipulate their budgets.

Institutional Constraints and Practices

Administrative rules and practices, reinforced by jurisprudence, prevent the flexibile and united action necessary to accomplish reforms. Two particular obstacles must be examined: the compartmentalization embodied in the higher civil service's statute, and the rigid and cumbersome budgetary and accounting procedures which result in a veritable dictatorship by the Ministry of Finance.

The Compartmentalization of the Statute and the Departments

The higher civil service's statute blocks administrative reform in two ways: it impedes the free movement of personnel, and presents an obstacle to their recruitment. The statute does not allow the most efficient assignment of personnel:

— Its decreed conditions for review and advancement fail to reward the most highly qualified.
— The multiplicity of specific statutes linked to structural compartmentalization block the organization of multidisciplinary work groups.

The recruitment of specialists needed by the administration to participate in its reform is prohibited by the statute:

— The administrative pay scale, including its supplementary provisions, is unfavorable to attracting specialists such as consulting engineers or computer specialists.

If included in the corps, they would not be able to participate in many stimulating activities which might otherwise lead them to forego the advantages of the private sector.

— The higher civil servants' quasi monopoly of access to top administrative posts does not permit the recruitment of businessmen experienced in dealing with problems of organization and management.

The autonomy of each minister presents a particularly difficult obstacle to surmount, both in terms of promulgating an interministerial reform and of introducing new management techniques.

Procedures of interministerial coordination appear to lack effectiveness:

—Efforts to integrate administrative departments lead to results which are more apparent than real.

—According to these procedures, the ministers concerned are organized into interministerial commissions. An example is the commission presided over by M Iehlé regarding administrative devolution (*déconcentration*).

—In the end, these efforts only confirm decisions made by each individual minister; for example, the extremely important devolution of responsibilities implemented in the Ministry of Infrastructure was almost completely controlled from start to finish by its minister, and resulted in the reinforcement of the ministry's provincial administration as a whole.

—The approval of structural reform by Council of Ministers appears to be only a formality.

Each minister is, in effect, master of his own house.

—The rules of the Council of State grant him full autonomy in the organization of his activities.

—The *grands corps* which make up his administration fully support him whenever the ministry's autonomy is under attack.

It should be noted that the extensive compartmentalization of each ministry's activities often presents a great obstacle to the minister himself.

The Rigorousness of Budgetary and Accounting Procedures

The French administration is organized in such a way that the Ministry of Finance exercises a veritable dictatorship over the administration as a whole.

The conditions governing the use of funds are embodied in particularly rigid rules which make managerial flexibility nearly impossible.

Funds are distributed in set categories:

— Parliament examines funding by category and by ministry.

—On the other hand, in relations between the Ministry of Finance and the spending ministries, the accepted unit of negotiation remains the budgetary chapter.

Budgetary utilization is strictly regulated.

—Transfers from one budgetary chapter to another are strictly limited by detailed budgetary rules.

—Funds must be used within the year.

Under these conditions, there is no room for flexibility.

—The distinction between budgetary credits for operating expenses, transfers, and investment does not allow the formulation of alternative solutions.

—This distinction also works against calculating amortization which is necessary to audit results.

—The procedure of program authorizations and payments only partially facilitates the establishment of long-range plans.

A priori financial controls paralyze any initiative.

Preliminary financial controls by the public auditors or by the paymasters (*trésoriers-payeurs généraux*) within a decentralized framework frequently amounts to the control of opportunity.

—At all levels the public accountants constrain initiative through an array of detailed rules.

—Under these conditions, the desire to achieve results is often overridden by the necessity to follow accepted procedures.

—This situation is especially detrimental to the development of both management by objective and to the delegation of responsibilities.

Thus, under the pretense of assuring that the employment of funds conforms to parliamentary decisions, controls and auditing procedures actually undermine efficient budgetary utilization. The nation's elected representatives, responsible for the wise appropriation of public monies, must denounce continuing this system.

The Ministry of Finance accepts only those reforms which maintain its power.

The high quality and considerable scope of this ministry's activities become doubly significant due to rules embodied in French administration.

Because of the close cooperation between the prime minister and the minister of finance, the latter is particularly well-placed to assure the perpetuation of the present system despite reform efforts.

In addition, the Organization and Management Office (*le Service*

Central d'Organisation et Méthodes) is improperly attached to the Finance Ministry's Budget Department.

No other country in the world is afflicted by the ascendancy of such a financial apparatus. As Michel Debré once said, "France is ruled by its accountant."

The obstacles elaborated above must become the object of reforms:

—Political will is dependent upon those in power, notably upon the support they find in parliement.

—The remarkable tool which the administrative bodies represent could be put to use in the service of reforms rather than fighting against them. This is, first and foremost, management problem.

—The prime minister, whose coordinating role is essential, must affirm his authority to override the ministry of finance.

2-5. THE POLITICAL MANIPULATION OF THE ADMINISTRATION*

By 1980, many felt that the adroit manipulation of the administration by Giscard had created a government within government. Yves Agnès provides the names of dozens of persons in key posts who were personally loyal to the President. However, he also points out that no important party wishes to change the system because each can use it for his own interests. A "spoils system" serves all political interests, and makes a travesty of standard administrative practices.

The Disparity

Is all this [the packing of government positions by loyal Giscardians] shocking? In any case, the political class has reacted very mildly to the systematic installation of a "Giscardian state." The Left—and, in particular, the Communist Party—has criticized the manipulation of the media. As for others, they take heart against their bad luck. The supporters of Chirac are enraged but keep quiet, probably out of fear that their own past excesses would be cited. The Socialists, who were long ago ousted from positions of authority, have had time to digest their eviction. The Socialist Party

*Yves Agnès, "L'Etat-Giscard," *Le Monde Dimanche*, March 2, 1980 (selections).

concedes that nominations to high posts is at the government's discretion. At most, sectarian interpretation of texts and, above all, Giscardian "hypocrisy" are decried: however, measures are enacted without fuss, in contradiction with official claims.

But the most feared step is taking charge of filling the lower bureaucratic echelons, in particular the regional and departmental field services of the different administrations. Today this is called "selective assignment" (*fontionnalisation de l'emploi*). A confidential report dated April 1973, prepared by a group headed by Henry Krieg (general inspector of the administration) cleared the way for the present measures. The report analyzed the causes of bureaucratic sclerosis. "Factors of a statutory nature still resist and block change," the report notes, "such as the conceptions of *grands corps* and career, the propriety of rank, confusion between grade and position, geographical mobility and sectorial insufficiencies, the difficulty of interchange between centrally and provincially trained administrative *grands corps*, the administrative and technical *grands corps*." In order to rejuvenate and energize administrative officials and to give flexibility to the system, selective assignment was proposed. Under this system, one is no longer named, for example, departmental director of agriculture because one has attained the necessary rank, but rather assigned provisionally by dipping into the much larger pool of all high civil servants.

Spoils System

How can one fail to welcome the intention to attack administrative sclerosis after all that has been written and said concerning one of the major defects of our system? But at the same time, how can one fail to recognize that the government's nomination of this group of high civil servants could result in a few years with a veritable political criss-crossing of France? And this is precisely the Giscardian paradox: the disparity between official liberal discourse and authoritarian practice.

This practice has already been adopted, for example, in the postal and telecommunications service, and for "academic inspectors" in national education—who have become directors of the departmental education services—and is being studied by several ministries. The new practice calls into question the dominant conception of the civil service and even the notion of public service, which should not be confused with allegiance to a party. Labor unions were not fooled and greeted the report of Gérard Longuet, U.D.F. deputy from the Meuse, with apprehension during the discussion of the 1980 civil service budget in the National Assembly. They were right. M. Longuet borrowed the philosophy of the Krieg report and wrote: "The administration is at the nation's disposition to conceive and implement the policy defined by the Executive, within the Republic's legal framework. The chief executive must be able to name to a responsible post the civil servant whose competence and authority he deems as suitable."

In this way, we have already introduced a system analogous to the American "spoils system," whereby the federal administration is reshuffled with each presidential change. But the administrative organization of the United States—with its fifty states—is not comparable to French centralization, where such a conception gives greater cause for alarm. However there is no doubt that such is the president's objective—even though, as usual, he is trying to obscure it. In his reply to Ivan Levai at a June 14, 1978, press conference, he affirmed: "For each position I look for 'the best', and one has only to examine all the nominations made in the course of the last few years to see that my idea has been that in each instance we nominate the best. I do not know if the best share a political preference. . . "

The facts are there. The "best" are Giscardians! In private, the president does not hide his intentions.

2-6. THE NEED TO INCREASE EXTERNAL
INFLUENCE ON THE ADMINISTRATION*

Possibly more than most countries, the French administrative system provides a relatively small elite with virtually unchallenged powers over government, public corporations, and even a number of private industries. Lombard voices a frequently-heard complaint that the small elite is neither well-trained nor fairly selected for these choice positions. Given the diversity of French administration itself, he argues that more external recruitment would help democratize and vitalize an administration that depends too heavily on its political control of many facets of French life.

*François Lombard, "Pour une overture de l'administration française," Le Monde, August 20–21, 1978 (selections).

The legislative elections have shed light on an interesting pardox: on the one hand, the French people have manifested their dissatisfaction with the present system, the "French affliction" (*le mal français*) and the "stalled society" (*la société bloquée*), characterized by an omnipotent administration; on the other hand, they have sent as their representatives to the National Assembly an increasing number of civil servants—accounting for nearly 48 percent of newly elected deputies. Two factors can explain this pheonomenon: the cooperation of school friends or fellow graduates within the political parties, especially the majority parties; and the complementarity between an administrative and political career, whereby a public official has sufficient time to prepare a campaign. In fact, two types of civil servants have been elected: teachers, especially of the Socialist Party, who are close to their electors by virtue of their teaching functions; and, mainly in the majority parties, high civil servants who are often quite young, and the "cadets" of the regime.

Civil servants' quest for power results in an excessive concentration (*cumul des mandats*) of functions and responsibilities, sources of obstruction and discontent. Without fundamental change, this situation could lead to an eventual social explosion. Only a real opening up of the system to external influences, difficult to accomplish in the absence of a political will to change, can give the present system the transfusion necessary for its survival.

An Excessive Concentration of Powers

Ostensibly, the French administrative system embodies all virtues: an objective selection of the best officials based on merit, job security, and many opportunities for career advancement. In reality, the objectivity of the selection process is entirely relative: "merit" is differentially distributed at the National School of Administration (ENA) according to whether the student is Parisian or provincial; if his or her parents are wealthy or not; or whether his or her father was a financial inspector, minister, or diplomat. Of course, heredity may play a role, but the process of selection gives more room to other methods.

Source of Blockages and Discontent

The concentration of administrative and economic powers in the hands of high officials in public enterprises results from the widespread recourse to leaders "parachuted in" by the administration. The choice of economic leaders has often been dictated as much by political and administrative considerations as by competency. Contrary to the conclusion of François de Combret, advisor to the president, who recently wrote that "for the most part, high civil servants do not have the experience necessary to undertake the overhaul (*redeploiement*) of our nations' industrial apparatus," it is not unusual to find administrative officials placed at the head of a public enterprise employing over ten thousand people. They inevitably have a hard time introducing management systems in these industries, rewarding creativity, and strengthening competition in the private sector. At the same time, competent and experienced personnel see themselves brushed aside for consideration for positions of leadership; this results in an inefficient utilization of human resources and a deterioration in social relations, notably at the executive level, where once latent discontent is now becoming manifest.

Many Frenchmen hope to control this system, but at the last minute—more out of fear of Communism than from a preference for change—vote for the majority. If effective change does not reduce the concentration of powers and open the administration to outside influences, the movement of executives toward the Socialist Party will continue to grow. A series of reforms are essential. Frenchmen will no longer let themselves be duped by technocratic discourses and other books on the "French affliction" which often serve as pretexts for inaction.

The Necessity to Increase External Influences on the Administration

The institutional rules of the French administration, established following World War II, must be adapted to our competitive industrial society. The broad outlines of this policy should be the following:

To establish more systematic exchange between the public and private sectors. Is it acceptable that a civil administrator can be assigned to a leading position in a public enterprise after serving in a nationalized bank, while, on the other hand, it is almost impossible for a top executive of this same bank to work in the administration? This could be accomplished using a limited contract or on a permanent basis through a regular external recruitment drive.

In areas of administration closely related to the private sector, such as the corps of commerical councilors, a significant number of positions should be reserved for qualified personnel from the private sector who are experienced in international business dealings. Sometimes external candidates expose the deficiencies of new civil servants who arrive at the Ministry of Industry without serious interests in international commerce, but solely because of their class ranking.

—Avoid sclerosis in the administrative structure through the practice of distributing the greater part of positions in the *grands corps* at the time of graduation; external recruitment should account for nearly half of these positions, with entrants chosen for their competency and experience, not their political connections.

—Replace the ENA and its relatively narrow course of study with several schools adapted to the requirements of each career (financial inspection, diplomacy, commerce) and introduce diverse training and ways of thinking.

—Better inform young people concerning administrative careers and allow selected students to serve internships in different administrative departments, as is done elsewhere (for example, summer internships at the White House).

—Finally, combat the administrative spirit which, with some justification, haunts ambitious university and secondary school students. Too often they are told, "Outside the ENA, nothing."

More than ever before, we are in the process of creating a nation of civil servants. One means of escaping from the "French affliction" lies precisely in increasing the value of industry, research, and innovation.

We do not wish to question the principles which have made French administration among the most honest and competent in the world, but to propose certain reforms. The extension of recruitment to external personnel is a way to include diverse experience in the higher civil service. Other measures might be undertaken but would involve a more fundamental sociological analysis. Management of the public domain must not become the privilege of a few. The rejuvenation of personnel through an exchange between the private and public sectors should allow us to end the "French affliction" from within and to qualify the *de facto* monopoly of a minority.

2-7. SOCIALIST PROPOSALS FOR ADMINISTRATIVE REFORM*

After their break from the Communists in late 1977, the Socialists made self-management (autogestion) a more important part of their election platform, extending it even to administrative reform. The parties of the Left have not advocated massive structural change in the civil service which is, in many ways, more essential to their aims than to the Right. In this essay, the national secretary for the public sector, Michel Charzat, explains how the Socialists would like more responsive and more responsible administration of the public sector to be achieved by more planning, more open information policies, and more citizen participation in a decentralized government.

Building a New Conception of Service

Restoration of the idea of public service as an expression of the will to serve others; affirmation of the state's role within the framework of a growing and fundamentally altered economy; and finally, specification of functional criteria for an enlarged, democratized, and more autonomous public sector—these constitute a single purpose: democracy.

For socialists, there is no question of forging a new concept of public service in the administration unless two necessary conditions are met.

The first depends on restoration of the legitimacy of one state; respect for individual equality before a responsive administration; procedural simplicity; and administrative neutrality. The second condition is to establish medium and long-term planning by responsible men and women who will democratically decide how to break through all forms of giantism and centralization.

But there is no need to wait for necessarily profound political transformations to conceive new ways to adopt public administra-

*Michel Charzat, "Rénover le service public," *Le Monde*, August 23, 1980 (selections).

tion to public service, such as the growing force of *autogestion*. Having established the deterioration in the public sector and analyzed its causes, the Socialist Party intends—beginning this November—to propose a new conception of public service.

From this perspective, I will indicate four areas for reflection.

Management in the Service of the Public

The notions of profit, productivity, and social utility must be disassociated. No one contests the fact that the search for financial equilibrium constitutes an element of good management, but it should not be the sole objective. Planning should adopt a new orientation to management, in particular a global and decentralized appreciation of social utility (*rentabilité sociale*).

Concerning prices of goods and services produced in the public sector, two principles should be applied: given the global financial choice which rests on political decisions, it is a question, on the one hand, of satisfying the greatest possible number of users, on the other hand, of favoring those whose need is greatest. While awaiting an optimal and fair income redistribution, a general equilibrium achieved by marginal price adjustments can only reproduce present inequalities. In commercial products, the criterion of quality—frequently overlooked in public commerce which equates value with sales—should be applied. These objectives do not imply free services, which could be a source of inequalities, but rather the extension of services to fill new needs (culture, health, information).

A Clarification of the Rules of the Game

The organizations which manage public services should be "transparent" and furnish complete information to the public, who could then reinforce their control over them. Such organizations should not wait for a public demand to be expressed, but should actively seek out the needs of a public, long unaccustomed to expressing itself.

Public services should also play an important role in providing more general information to the population. Information procedures should be simplified and information should be accessible, in dispersed locations, to everyone.

A Rearrangement of the Relations between Central and Local Powers

A new mode of governance, a new sharing of tasks between the state and local governments, and between citizens and institutionalized powers, must be sought. Breaking away from administratively imposed uniformity, the public service should be localized as much as possible. Its renovated management should facilitate a better circulation of studies and information, which is a primary condition for the achievement of maximum social utility and the individual right to know.

An Instrument of New Democracy

Nevertheless, it is essential to avoid benefitting the well-off through these measures: the public administration must not, by its management, constitute an element of discrimination and social compartmentalization. In this perspective, the direct intervention of workers and users in administrative management should be encouraged. These initiatives will not only permit the administration to become the "common good," as democratic socialism implies, but more immediately will bring to an end the waste of the popular capabilities and bureaucratic sclerosis.

The public service—a democratic conquest and aspiration—must be defended with firm and united resolve in the interests of a larger unity. In effect, service constitutes a legacy of the Left on which two generations have lived and continued to live. But, at the same time, it is important to explore ways of rehabilitating and transforming service. For us Socialists, self-management must give public service a new content, and give the power of the Left a second chance.

3 Local and Regional Reform: Territorial Compromises

Few reforms send more tremors through the fabric of French political institutions than proposals to restructure local, departmental (provincial), or regional government. As in most countries, areas of localized power are closely associated with the organization of political parties, the mobilization of elections, and the implementation of public policy at lower levels of government. If any of these delicate areas were well stabilized in France, the many proposals to reform French local and regional government might have caused less controversy. They might also have been more successful if other dependent interests were clearer as to how their concerns might have been affected by reform. As in the other cases discussed in the book, change has been a gradual and hotly disputed process.

Like every modern democracy, France had little choice in adjusting its complex intergovernmental system to the new needs of the welfare state. What distinguishes France is that at no time could reforms be introduced without consideration of the bewildering array of demands of both local and national political actors. Compared to most of Europe, this has been a laborious and intricate process. Sweden, for example, put a royal commission to work and, a few years later, emerged with a consolidation of local government from about 1,200 units to 270 units with very little controversy. In Britain, the process of global reform went ahead with the approval of local governments and over 1,400 units were transformed into about 450 by exercising the strong powers of Parliament (see Ashford, 1982). The ease with which such fundamental reforms can be designed and implemented is one of the best clues to a highly centralized policy process. On any such scale, France would surely be among the least successful but, at the same time, the entire network of central-local relations has undergone immense change over the past twenty years.

Heated debate over local and regional reform in France is by no means new. It was one of the major issues dividing the Revolution which was eager to wipe out the regional identity of the French provinces; it eventually gave way to the Jacobin group whose concern for a "one and indivisible Republic" still permeates reform efforts. Early in the nineteenth century, Tocqueville's classic study of American pluralism (1951) was an eloquent statement of French discontent with local government. The modern system originates with Napoleon's institution of prefects, who he called his *petits empereurs* (small emporers). Like many chief executives throughout French history, Napoleon took a personal interest in their selection and frequently consulted them. During the Second Empire (1851–70) there was a furious debate over decentralization (Basdevant-Gaudemet, 1973) which helped mobilize the republican forces that finally came into their own with the Third Republic (1871–1940). Deprived of both local and national influence for most of the nineteenth century, the republican forces considered local government the bulwark of democratic rule. Thus, for many decades France has lived with a basic contradiction between its Jacobin tradition and local democratic convictions. As in other policy problems, the demands that de Gaulle and his successors were to make on France could not avoid this historic controversy.

Context

The decentralization debate has continued for two hundred years and shows few signs of abating. For many critics of Jacobin tendencies, decentralization was the root cause of French conservatism and lethargy. For the champions of regional movements, decentralization seemed the essential reform to launch a new kind of democracy (Gourevitch, 1981). A close look at the historical record suggests a different interpretation. In fact, for all its complexity and caution, the system has shown remarkable adaptive capacities as the social and economic needs of France evolved, and as the French charged through the various regimes of the nineteenth century. There has always been an evolving relationship between the state-appointed prefects and the elected mayors of the communes. The attack on centralized authority is not new in France, but the built-in capacities for change may be underestimated even though they may not be as apparent as in federal systems or in more stable unitary systems. There are also certain pitfalls in projecting the problems and practices of much simpler nineteenth century states onto the complexity of the policy process in the twentieth century. The communes, departments, and, more recently, the regions have always been imbedded in the institutional fabric of France (Ashford, 1982).

First, France has always had a unified administrative system reaching down to the departmental or provincial level. Many of the discontents over the administrative system inevitably slipped over into a criticism of local intervention by prefects and other national agents at the departmental and regional levels. Indeed, the common Anglo-Saxon phrase "local government" makes little sense in France, while its phrase, the *collectivités locales* is almost untranslatable. The job of field administrators is to see that the "small republics" remain harmonious with the state. To accomplish this, prefects have a threefold role: representation of the state, expressed in their rulings on administrative law and procedures; representation of the Ministry of the Interior, found in their supervision of elections, budgets, and communal proceedings; and executive agency for the departmental and communal councils. If this latter duty often appears subordinate to their functions for the central government, we should also remember that their multiple role incorporates the divided interests and cross-pressures that appear frequently in the organization of the French policy process (P. Grémion, 1976).

Second, the communes were (and are) proud of being "small republics" and, as de Gaulle learned to his dismay, they can mobilize considerable influence in the policy process. For all the opprobrium heaped on the prefects, many studies have shown that the successful prefect must work cooperatively with the communes. Indeed, the tendency for prefects to become the hostages of their areas helps explain the "waltz of the prefects," whereby large numbers are reassigned every few years. Another reason, of course, is that national politicians like to have familiar officials running important areas of the country. Being a prefect is a precarious job, although most of them are part of the elite administrative group, the prefectoral corps (see Reading 3-1). From the earliest democratic experiments of the nineteenth century, electoral defeat has often condemned a prefect to assignment at one of the outlying departments of France. The Fifth Republic was no exception. When Mitterrand came to power, thirty-five prefects were reassigned, and eight prefects who were closely aligned with Giscard went into retirement. Defferre, the Socialist Minister of the Interior, appointed the former regional prefect of his Marseilles fiefdom to the prestigious position of prefect of Paris, and the former departmental prefect from his area to be prefect of police. The desire to have reliable colleagues in key positions hardly distinguishes the Right from the Left in any democratic country.

Third, the intricate links between the 36,000 communes of France and the field administraton tends to take on a life of its own. From mutual dependence has grown what Thoenig (1975 and 1978) calls the "honeycomb" or intricate interface between political and administrative actors throughout the hierachy that links localities to national government (see Reading 3-3). Contrary to the criticism of arbitrary national rule over localities, the honeycomb suggests that the state can be, as de Gaulle often was, defeated with relative ease in its efforts to direct local priorities. In France, the locally elected can also run for office in elections at higher levels and accumulate elected office (*cumul des mandats*). Accumulation of office is a powerful tool that can be used to moderate administrative excess, to block reform efforts, and to propel local leaders into national office. About nine-tenths of the senators hold one or more local offices, and roughly three-fourths of deputies hold local offices (Léotard Report, 1979). Giscard gave up his efforts to limit the *cumul* and the Socialists hope, at least, to separate regional council presidents from other elected offices. In the early months of their rule, a number of regional council presidents who held national office resigned in favor of local representatives who would have more time for regional matters. Whether this curious device to aggrandize political influence through the local government system will disappear remains to be seen but, in the past, it has provided a tool to influence administrative decisions and to block global reform.

Lastly, the critics of the dispersed local government system overlook the fact that none of the more technocratic or Jacobin reform

proposals worked very well. As we shall see, the laboriously constructed proposals of 1968 (Fouchet reform) and 1971 (Albin Marcellin reform) to consolidate the overarticulated system failed mis-
erably. From a policy perspective, immense effort was expended to
accomplish very little. At the same time, the Gaullists and their
successors were (and are) under great pressure to acquire local
assistance and cooperation for a wide variety of social and economic
policies. For the Gaullists in particular, plans to modernize French
industry and to accomodate millions of new urban dwellers made
local support essential. Over the 1960s and 1970s, roughly ten
million persons moved to larger towns and cities; next to Japan, this
was one of the largest urban migrations in the postwar period. De
Gaulle could not achieve his other policy aims without help from
the communes but, as we shall see, he could barely live with them.

An approach to local and regional reforms through the policy
process does not suggest that Paris is insulated against local needs
and demands. Unlike much of Europe, massive reform of central-
local relationships by national initiatives was ruled out. In many
respects, the reorganization of French local government is much
closer to the diffuse, incremental transformation of American
federal-local relationships, both in terms of the intermixture of
political and administrative actors, and in terms of the differentiated, and sometimes arbitrary, efforts of national agencies to impose specific requirements and conditions on local government.
Nor were the changes that occurred achieved without real concessions by national government. Billions of francs have been spent to
develop declining regions of France and to placate regional
nationalist sentiments. If some of the policies seem arbitrary, we
should remember that Britain simply brushed aside regional demands when they no longer served the partisan interests of national
leaders (Ashford, 1981a). Perhaps closer to the truth, the complexity of modern government needs diverse links to lower levels of
government and cannot achieve the aims of the welfare state without the local adjustments essential to most services.

The local government system is another example which shows
how misleading are the formalities of French government. There is
an apparent symmetry and order to the system of twenty-two regions (including Paris), the ninety-four departments, and the
36,000 communes, which cannot be translated easily into the reali-

ties of modern urban problems and policies. The wide variation in size and resources provide some idea of the complications of shaping policies which affect the local government system. Nine-tenths of the communes have a population under 2,000 persons and include about one quarter of the total population. At the other extreme, the thirty-nine communes of over a 100,000 persons include over half the total population. Unable to force through a global reform, the central policy task was to devise a differentiated strategy enabling such divergent local units to respond to the social and economic priorities.

Mutual dependence between local and national government is reinforced by taxation and budgetary considerations. While the communes are responsible for a smaller portion of public spending than in many other European countries—about one fourth of all public spending, or 155 billion francs in 1977—they have a crucial role in developing public works. About two-thirds of all public investment involves local government; this is much higher than in most European countries (Ashford, 1980). During a period of rapid economic and industrial expansion, the communes and departments are vitally important to national policy aims. Control is imposed through the controversial *tutelle*, or supervisory powers, of the prefect and through an intricate system of negotiating investment loans (see Reading 3-2). Until the Socialist reforms of 1981, prefects exercised *a priori* control over local budgets, although the communes could vote their own levels of taxation. For the thousands of small communes, these controls were not oppressive for they could not manage their affairs, but for the large cities and towns—mostly under the control of the Left—the prefect was an oppressive creature. Needless to say, the complex pattern of compromise and bargaining between communes and prefects helped generate the intricate pattern of intrigue and complicity of central-local policymaking (P. Grémion, 1976).

Agenda

Of the three phases in the evolution of policy and politics in the Fifth Republic, the earliest Guallist period was, in many ways, the most difficult. The Gaullist Party had very weak local roots and, for a decade, had existed by hovering on the fringes of parliament as a small clique. De Gaulle may have been impressive when national crises occurred, but he was not a grass-roots politician in any sense and only learned some of these skills as the threat from the Left grew over the 1960s. Unlike nearly all their competitors, the Gaullists had few local strongholds comparable to the Socialist bastions in Lille and Marseilles. At the same time, as described in Chapter 2, the Gaullists were not satisfied with the administrative system, and viewed the pattern of central-local relations—so often riddled with collusion between the field administration and local politicians—as one of the causes of French weakness. About the only major concession de Gaulle made in the new constitution was to preserve the Senate, often called the "grande maison des communes," because of the concentration of locally elected senators. Ironically, it was.the Senate, and its reform, that were the cause of his downfall in 1969.

With so few political resources, the Gaullists had little choice but to follow the dispersed and multiple attack on a major policy problem that characterized so many policy initiatives. The large industrial and commerical centers were fundamental to the economic regeneration of France. De Gaulle initially gave the problem of bringing coherence to the local government system to his trusted confidant and first prime minister, Debré. His first effort was an attempt to create a more flexible and responsive field administration which, of course, brought him into direct conflict not only with elite prefectoral corps, but with the many other elite administrative groups entrenched in the regional and departmental services of the major ministries. Decrees could launch these changes, but could not guarantee compliance.

In 1959, for example, all regional offices of the ministries were ordered to adopt the same regional boundaries and, in 1964, in the early stages of regional reform, these offices were ordered to work under a single executive, a regional prefect. Whatever may have been the Jacobin motives for these early changes, they were stubbornly resisted by the prefectoral corps (see Reading 3-1), who saw the region as a threat to their historic power at the departmental level, and who feared that increasing the responsibilities of field officers of other ministries could only lead to their decline (C. Grémion, 1979). There was even a comical situation in one region where the departmental prefects refused to agree on a central location, so regional meetings rotated from one departmental office to another for several years.

But the aims of the Fifth Republic gave a special urgency to reform and temporarily lifted the political stalemate that had frustrated repeated reform attempts. There had been thirty-four proposals for regional reform during the Third Republic (Mény, 1974, p. 177). Thus, it is hard to argue that the Gaullists were only responding in order to further their immediate self-interest. Modernization of local, departmental, and regional government was in many ways a prerequisite to accomplishment of their other aims, and the needs were more or less self-evident. First, the overly complex and ineffective communes system of (then) 37,000 communes needed consolidation. Second, the highly complex ways of transferring resources to localities and of sharing of national and local tax burdens had to be simplified. Third, any national government intent on social and economic change would have needed some way to coordinate activity among and within the ninety-four departments.

But, as so often happens in the politics of policymaking, important departures were often made when political motives coincided with administrative needs. In this respect, even the determined political leadership of the Gaullist government was no different from that of earlier French regimes or of other democratic countries. What differs is that the Gaullists, like most French governments throughout the Fourth Republic, were firmly committed to the exclusion of Communists from policymaking and, if possible, to the elimination of the party. With this in mind, the local election law was revised in 1964 with the intention of making it more difficult for the Left to win municipal council elections. The PCF had suffered badly in the 1962 legislative elections because of its division over Algeria, and the Gaullists hoped to exploit the opportunity to add to Communist losses in the local elections. The new local election law forbade the restructuring of local council candidate lists between the first and second ballots in communes of over 30,000. In a party system where every party receives a minority of votes, unless parties forge coalitions before the election, they can be completely excluded from the second ballot.

But very early in the Fifth Republic, the Gaullists learned that their national popularity was not easily transformed into local support. On the contrary, their efforts at electoral manipulation may have had a backlash and, in the 1965 local elections, the PCF extended its control of cities over 30,000 persons from 25 to 34 cities. As we have seen in Chapter 1, in the 1967 legislative elections, the Communists regained their normal strength in the National Assembly. Moreover, the 1965 local elections served as a proving ground for electoral alliances between the Socialists and the Communists. Contrary to the intentions, local elections were teaching the Left how to live together.

Swallowing their disappointment, the Gaullists looked for more effective organization of local government. Three devices were tried, all of which eventually gave way to the pressure of local politics. In 1963, de Gaulle established the Délégation d'Aménagement du Territoire (DATAR) under another Gaullist stalwart, Guichard. DATAR was to work with the Planning Commission to disaggregate the national development plans to the regional level, and to act as a stimulus for new, modernizing elites at the local level. In fact, the notion of strengthened regional agencies to promote industrial and commercial development had their origins in the Fourth Republic when Pierre Mendès-France encouraged the formation of development committees (*comités d'expansion*) in the regions. DATAR and its regional administrative agencies (CODER or Commissions de développement économique et régionale) were meant to push for the modernization of France. The proposal not only met with the suspicion of the prefectoral corps and the local notables, but was opposed within government by the Ministry of Finance (then under a bright and ambitious young *inspecteur des finances* named Giscard d'Estaing) who felt that the Planning Commission and DATAR were the leading edge of uncontrollable spending and therefore, a threat to the plan for stabilizing the French economy (see Chapter 4). One of the early acts of the new Prime Minister, Pompidou, was to break the deadlock within the central government by working out a compromise whereby the Ministry of Finance would exercise its usual budgetary and auditing powers within the CODER while giving some control over development projects to DATAR and the Planning Commission.

The second major device to promote urban development among the communes was the search for new ways of encouraging the consolidation of the overarticulated system. The first device could hardly be called an innovation. Since 1890, France had had a way of forming unions (*syndicats*) of communes to provide services over larger areas. Until 1959, these were confined to single-purpose unions of communes for such things as water supply, buses, and so on. The Debré government extended this practice to multipurpose unions (SIVOMs or Syndicats intermunicipals à vocation multiple). By 1975, there were about 1,703 SIVOMs grouping over 16,000 communes and involving over nineteen million people (Ministry of Infrastructure, 1976, p. 15). The main reasons the SIVOMs grew was that the state provided lower interest rates for their loans for public works and, as it turned out, mayors found the SIVOMs a useful device for rejecting more thorough forms of consolidation pressed on them by Paris and the prefects. The political and social prestige of the mayor is such that even an allegedly arbitrary regime was cautious in approaching consolidation. Plans were made over 1967 and 1968 to compel the communes to merge (under a minister of interior who was forced to resign by the May 1968 strikes). Such global reforms were quickly disowned once the Gaullists realized that they were unable to force change at the local level. Thus, the Gaullists' second strategy to force change had to be abandoned (see Reading 3-2).

As in every highly industrial country, the large metropolitan areas were a major problem because more housing, industrial sites, and transportation were needed in a relatively short time. In 1966 the government, still living in the atmosphere of the unbridled power of the early Gaullist years, forced four large cities (Bordeaux, Lille, Lyon, and Strasbourg) to form metropolitan agencies (*communautés urbaines*) that would merge the suburban and central-city communes. Because one of the Gaullist "barons," Chaban-Delmas, was (and is) mayor of Bordeaux, a larger authority was more easily established for his area. But the struggle to consolidate Lyon, a fiercely independent regional city, dragged on in the courts for several years. Thereafter, five additional metropolitan areas were added, but on a voluntary basis, and an effort to persuade Nantes to reorganize was dropped because of local resistance. Like the election reform, the Gaullists proved to be poor political strategists. Given the limitations of land in many old French cities, the enlarged urban authorites incorporated working class suburbs, and voters of the Left increased their control over urban development. Even the Gaullist leader, Chaban-Delmas, eventually made his peace with the Socialist communes that became part of his urban political stronghold.

The agenda for local-level reorganization and reform was set by the mid-1960s, but the Gaullists had made some serious political blunders. The initial plans for regional administrative agencies that were meant to override local rivalries and resistance were soon bogged down in internal governmental controversies. The program for forceful consolidation of the communes had to be abandoned, and the metropolitan authorities actually enlarged the powers of more progressive communes over the urban development. The Gaullists learned an important political lesson from their early efforts. A frontal attack, which could easily be put in motion in Britain and Sweden, would not work in France. Moreover, as the Left gathered strength, it saw that arbitrary reforms would only provide ammunition for the Socialists and Communists, their most dreaded enemies. As the process of change continued in the late 1960s, Pompidou changed tactics and methods.

Process

As outlined in Chapter 1, Pompidou was a pragmatist. Important trends can be detected that occurred while he was still prime minister. After ascending to the presidency in 1969, major changes occurred, particularly in the reconstruction of the relations between national and local government. Pompidou came from rural France; he was much more comfortable than de Gaulle with the complicity and diversions of local politics. He was also intent on building a strong Gaullist Party and knew this could not be achieved without local strongholds. Pompidou fashioned the compromise between the 1968 strikers and the government: experience taught him that the pace of change in France would have to decrease. No doubt his most important lesson in local politics before he took office was the failure of de Gaulle's 1969 referendum which tried to breach the notables' national bastion, the Senate, while reforming the regions at the same time. Pompidou learned early in his presidency that one cannot do open battle on two fronts. He had expressed doubts about the wisdom of linking two major reforms (Senate and regions) in the 1969 referendum (Bodiguel et. al., 1970), as had other trusted advisors to De Gaulle.

In any event, the referendum rejected constitutional change and made a hero of the centrist president of the Senate, Alain Poher, who was instrumental in mobilizing the notables against the reforms. One of the reasons the old guard Gaullist leaders have never trusted Giscard d 'Estaing is that he, too, came out against the referendum, and used the Gaullist attack on local politicians to mobilize the centrist coalition that would eventually carry him to the presidency. But in the adjustment of policies on local and regional reform, the important change was that Pompidou, the new president in 1969, saw that the effort to eliminate the commune as the basic unit of local government would not work and that the Gaullists, if they were to survive, would have to soften their aims in order to develop grass-roots strength to withstand growing unity of the Left.

In his inaugural speech, the new president left little doubt about the shift in policy when he observed that "the French remain profoundly attached to their municipal life, and the commune constitutes the first and living expression of this collective confidence which finds its expression in national unity" (Bunel and Meunier, 1972, p. 14). His affirmation of the new direction was dramatized by the selection of Chaban-Delmas, one of the few Gaullist leaders to have a firm local power base located in Bordeaux (Lagroye, 1976), as his prime minister. The most revealing change was Pompidou's insistence that Gaullist deputies run in the local elections in 1971. Among 172 Gaullist deputies, 157 ran for local office in 1971. But the unmistakable political lesson was that the Left, which had been working toward electoral cooperation for some years, could defeat the Right by dominating local offices. In 1971, Communist control was extended to forty-five large towns and cities, and the Left—even before the Common Program of 1972—was able to run united lists of Socialist and Communist candidates in eighty-four large towns and cities. Like all politicians, Pompidou wanted more than anything else to be reelected in 1975 and needed to unite the growing factions within the Gaullist Party. To do this, he had to substantially change the process of local government reformation.

Because the local reform policies, like most policies in France, had multiple objectives and methods, the emergence of a more cautious policy is hard to detect. First, in 1971, Pompidou allowed a second effort to press for consolidation of communes to continue under the Minister of the Interior, Marcellin, but he also permitted the National Assembly and the Senate to nullify all the strong provisions of the law. After several years of laborious consultation with communes, the prefects were only able to find about 3,500 communes where consolidation could occur voluntarily, and of these only about a thousand were ever completed. This accounts for reduction of the number of communes from roughly 37,000 to the present number of 36,000; this was no small accomplishment given the resistance to change, but it was hardly a massive reform.

Pompidou also found the efforts of his energetic and popular prime minister to build stronger regional agencies troublesome. Few sensitive observers of French politics failed to notice that a month after Chaban-Delmas asserted that he had "not abandoned regionalism" in late 1970, Pompidou noted in a speech at Lyon that the importance of the department could not be neglected. The shift in policy reflected Pompidou's traditional style of government, but it was also part of the ever-present power struggle within the Gaullist Party, and the president's own design to establish firm control of the party. The more liberal prime minister, Chaban-Delmas, soon lost control of regional development policy, and an old guard Gaullist, Frey, brought this responsibility within the president's office. Perhaps the best indication of the president's conciliatory attitude toward the communes and departments was that the regional reform of 1972, which converted the CODER into public authorities (*établissements publiques*) with advisory regional councils, was unobtrusively acheived.

In hopes of combining more liberal economic policies with the Gaullist Jacobin views, Chaban-Delmas pressed reforms leading to better economic coordination or *concertation* (see Chapter 4). Part of this policy was to seek new ways of inducing the communes and departments to enter into contracts with administrative agencies for development purposes (see Reading 3-2). The financial and fiscal basis of French local government had barely changed a century or more ago, and the rapid growth of cities over the 1960s resulted in pressing needs for more public works, industrial infrastructure, housing, and transportation in French cities. Though more conservative Gaullists suspected that *concertation* might diminish central control of the economy and budget, Chaban-Delmas launched a program for developmental contracts for middle-sized cities— another way, of course, to demonstrate Gaullist support for the grass-roots and to compete with the growing organization of the Left in cities and towns. Indeed, the cumbersome and inefficient procedures of government lending to cities was a major grievance of mayors, and it never failed to arise whenever government undertook other reforms.

The finances of local and regional reform policy had been studied for many years (see Ashford, 1980), but the administrative system had consistently failed to adapt new procedures (see Reading 3-2). The Bourrel report in 1965 was a scathing attack on administrative inefficiency in administering municipal loans. For the Sixth Plan (see Chapter 4), a special study group had been assembled on urban investment and another damning attack was made on the Ministry of Finance and the service ministries. The new prime minister wanted to allow communes to group their investment needs (*globalisation des investissements*) and to link them to contractual arrangements between the state and the localities. While Pompidou shared conservative Gaullist opinion that these new devices would weaken national supervision, he skillfully turned the reform to good political use. The contracts for the larger cities were soon supplemented with contracts for small cities and villages, then for depopulated areas, and eventually even for special urban projects for immigrant workers (see Chapter 7) and expensive cultural projects. In this way, the politics of compromise and partisan advantage eroded the most determined efforts to dislodge the complex network linking the territorial system to Paris.

Nonetheless, Pompidou was persuaded that a way must be found to modernize the outmoded and complex French local government system. If not for his premature death in 1974, it is likely that his adept manipulation of politics and administration would have brought important changes. The groundwork was laid with a Commission on Decentralization under the Gaullist leader, Peyrefitte (see Reading 3-3). Among other appalling inefficiencies, the report described the preparation in a small town in the Jura region fifty pounds of documents with 766 signatures at a cost of 200,000 francs in order to get permission to build a small addition to their school. As in Britain, inefficiency was the main Gaullist objection to cumbersome local government. The important departure of the Peyrefitte Report (1974) was the recognition that unless there was a radical redefinition of national and local responsibilities, the combination of national rivalries, administrative resistance, and local intrigue with officials would again disarm the most determined efforts of the Jacobin modernizers. Pompidou told several friends that local reform was a primary aim for his second "septennat," but he died the day after the report was submitted.

Consequences

Of all the policy problems discussed in this book, the interlocking decisionmaking process of French local and regional reform reveals the complexity of French policymaking. On the one hand, the power of state relentlessly returns to the issue of local and regional reform, reformulates the problem, and points the way toward new, but always marginal, adjustment to meet national objectives. On the other hand, the political-administrative framework of the state is constantly vulnerable to the mobilizing capacities of the communes and the local politicians. One might easily consider the outcome a monumental "nondecision" if it were not that the intricate process of mutual accomodation between the optimal and the possible solutions was being defined in concrete ways. France responded to most of the problems of rapid urbanization despite the overarticulated structure of communal government, while the local politicians regularly extracted concessions from Paris in the form of local investments subsidies, local tax privileges, and, above all, protection of local political access to the policy process. Both preserved their dignity while contributing to the solution of national problems. Much the same continued under Giscard and similar forms of mutual accomodation are apparent in the Socialist reforms.

There was also remarkable continuity between the local reform policies launched by Giscard and the preparations made by Pompidou. In his rather magisterial annual "Letter to the Prime Minister" of January 1975, in which the president outlined the major reforms of the coming year (most of which never appear), the new president raised the necessity of reexamining local government. Later in the year, he appointed the Commission on the Development of Local Responsibilities under the Gaullist leader, Guichard (see Reading 3-4). A sign of the changing tactic was that the commission of eleven members included seven mayors and three prominent regional councilors.

Given the dispersed and incremental nature of French policy-making, the Guichard Report (*Vivre Ensemble, 1976*) is an outspoken and original review of the problems of French local government. The Commission decribes the communes as "institutions without realities," (p. 27) and outlines how new fiscal and financial powers might be given to them. The issue of consolidation is skirted by suggesting voluntary ways of creating "federations of communes," but even this mild reform alarmed the mayors. With an eye to the local reforms forthcoming from the Left, the Commission felt that that the *tutelle* should be "banished" (p. 104) but is appropriately vague about the specific guarantees to be given to the communes. There are frank discussions of the future of contractual agreements (including an open admission that the Ministry of Finance had never liked them); the development of a local civil service with privileges and security comparable to the national administration; the reorganization of local taxes; and measures to strengthen the departmental councils. Most of these proposals reappear under Mitterrand in 1981. The report incorporates Guichard's intimate knowledge of French local affairs, beginning with his work in DATAR in 1963, and is a diplomatic mixture of incentives and cajolery to induce the mayors to recognize the radical changes in French government and society.

But similar to the fate of the British Royal Commission on the Constitution, the Guichard Report appeared at a bad time. By 1976, the old guard Gaullists were intensely suspicious of Giscard's motives and methods, and there was little chance of getting their enthusiastic support after Chirac, Giscard's first prime minister, resigned in July 1976. By the mid-1970s, the common front of the Socialists and Communists, despite continual outbursts of bad temper, was working well for electoral purposes. The Left made important gains in the 1976 elections for departmental councils, and the coalition of Gaullists and Republicans faced the prospect of large losses in the 1977 local elections and the 1978 National Assembly elections. These fears were justified, for the Left constructed united lists of candidates in nine-tenths of the communes in 1977, and took control of 154 of the 221 cities over 30,000 persons. As a result of the fight between Giscard and Chirac over the future of the Gaullist-Republican coalition, Chirac resigned as prime minister in August 1976, only to run for mayor of Paris and win against a handpicked Republican candidate. Like his predecessors, Giscard was learning about local politics the hard way. With national elections planned for 1978 and the presidential election looming ahead for 1981, 1976 was not a good year to upset mayors. Indeed, after his defeat in 1981, Giscard pointed to the 1976 canton elections (departmental councils) as the turning point in the effective electoral cooperation on the Right.

Like many Giscardian reforms, the effort was soon dispersed into several pieces of involved, if not very successful, legislation to strike a new deal with the communes. With great pomp and ceremony, Giscard assembled government leaders in late 1977 to announce his new strategy, and gave the hardworking new prime minister, Barre, another "mission." A special office was established in the Ministry of Interior to mobilize support from the mayors, and an energetic official, Bécam, somewhat frantically rushed about the countryside "consulting" the mayors. A voluntary survey of mayors was launched (later published as the Aubert Report, 1978) and, like most surveys, it told policymakers what they already knew. Everyone could agree that the local government system was ridiculously complex and inefficient, but no one could agree on how to change it. Out of this enormous effort to mobilize support emerged a battery of legislation, misnamed the *loi Bonnet*, after the minister of the interior, who had actually assumed his office after most of the measures were drafted.

The complexities of the new proposals confirmed that, no matter who ruled France, designing a new local government system would be a protracted and risky business. The main bill involved a series of intricate provisions devolving more powers (*compétences*) on the communes. There were excellent reports from both the Senate (Report de Tinguy) and the National Assembly (Report Voisin) which made explicit the tax and budgetary concessions that the mayors wanted as the price of reform. In the tumultuous legislative sessions that extended over 1979 and 1980, the government was frequently outvoted and, on more than one occasion, the allegedly powerful minister of the interior pleaded for the restoration of essential parts of the bill. By this time, the Gaullists and the Republicans could barely conceal their hostilities, while the Socialists and Communists took every opportunity to offer amendments to augment local powers in order to embarrass the government and to call on their formidable array of local support. In this debate, as in many other policy debates, the Senate distinguished itself for the quality of its suggestions and reaffirmed that, despite the best Gaullist efforts to subdue *la grande maison des communes*, it remained a powerful national lobby for local interests.

The most controversial elements of the reform were in separate bills. The president wistfully hoped to limit the number of elected offices that one could hold. After nearly two years of direct consultation with the party leaders by Barre, the reform was quietly dropped. Another major grievance of the mayors, particularly those in smaller cities and towns, was that they had to pay fees (*primes*) (see Reading 3-5) for national administrative service when making plans for public works or designing projects that needed public loans. To avoid the direct imposition of these charges, which are divided among the *grands corps* and can increase the incomes of high officials (in a rapidly developing region one *inspecteur des finances* was rumored to recieve 50,000 francs a month for simply signing loan applications), the government agreed that a small precentage of the operational transfer to localities would be retained and would be distributed by national government. Space prohibits outlining the severe reversals of government aims in trying to modernize local taxes (Ashford, 1980a). Suffice it to say that improvements in the base and distribution of direct local taxation were only purchased by Paris taking major responsibility for inflationary increases that reportedly cost the Ministry of Finance several billion francs.

When the Socialists took power in 1981, a new and no less complex process of local reform was again launched. For the Socialist mayor of Marseilles and the new minister of the interior, Defferre, the new decentralization proposals were the climax of a lifetime of struggle under the Right and became one of the highest priorities of the Mitterrand government. But the old intricacies were not to disappear effortlessly. The first phase of the *loi Defferre* was dramatic. The prefects were abolished along with their *a priori* controls and replaced with Commissaires de la République whose role is similar to chief executive for the communes. There will be only *a posteriori* budgetary controls, but there will also be an elaborate system of new auditing officials under the elite Cour des Comptes. Departmental and regional councils will be directly elected starting with the coming local elections of 1983, for which the parties of the right and left were already organizing in 1981. The *loi Defferre* is of course a major bid for the continued local support for the Socialists which did so much to mobilize their power in the local elections of 1971 and 1977.

As might be expected, all the opposition parties bitterly fought the *loi Defferre* even though it was basically a *loi-cadre* or general law whose full implementation rests on a number of laws to come (Richard Report, 1981). The first is a new law on the powers of the local councils which will be an acid test of Mitterand's ability to persuade ministers to give up their powers. There is then a law reforming local tax powers which may take several years and a law creating a local civil service, in some ways the most radical of the Defferre reforms because it might destroy the uniform administrative system that France has known since Napoleon (see Chapter 2). Perhaps the most innovative aspect of the reforms is to give regional and departmental councils a larger voice in economic and social policies, an objective strongly urged by the Socialists' trade union allies, the CFDT (see Reading 3-6). After an extended challenge by the Senate (Giraud Report, 1981) and a challenge in the Constitutional Council, local reform became the first major structural change accomplished by the Socialists, though it will take many years to implement it fully.

As the Pisani Report (see Reading 3-6) suggests, the Socialists have an additional and easily conflicting commitment to the strengthening of regional government. The minister for planning, Rocard, has a difficult decision; he must assure that the limited resources available for regional programs are used effectively, and he is under increased pressure to decentralize decisionmaking. The new government has promised new two-year regional plans, but there have been complaints from the CFDT, a strong government supporter, that the government is not giving sufficient powers to the regional social and economic committees, and not fulfilling left-wing hopes for increased economic self-management through regional planning. For example, one amendment to the *loi Defferre* placed restrictions on how much aid to local firms could be given from public funds. Thus, even the more energetic efforts toward decentralization by the Socialist government do not escape the difficult political choices of balancing party interests, national and local preferences, and, ultimately, the relative status of the various tiers of the local government system. Many of the more ambitious elements of the initial Socialist plan for decentralization (Socialist Party, 1980) have already been modified.

Given the ambiguities of national political institutions, the communes and the departments help fill the void between performance and political demands and social preferences. Local politicians are motivated to enter into national policymaking, and both parties and elections encourage them to do so. It is instructive that even the early reforms of the Mitterrand government did not escape the same charges of Jacobin centralized decisionmaking that had been used for so many years against the Gaullists and Giscardians. One might argue that the realities of French politics and the aims of the state confront each other more directly, if in a rather disorderly way, through central-local politics than through the national policy process (see Ashford 1981a). The struggle to define the nature of institutionalized power continues in the process of local and regional reform just as it does in many other policy proposals. Indeed, were it not for the checks of national policymaking provided by communal and departmental politics, the Fifth Republic might not have weathered its first two decades as well as it has. By their capacity to enter into policymaking and produce accomodation between national and local interests, the communes may have again fulfilled their historic role of rallying to preserve the Republic.

Readings

3-1. ON REORGANIZING THE PREFECTS*

Using a pseudonym, a high civil servant wrote the following article castigating the selection and training of prefects. He suggests how

*Philippe de Quinsac, "Préfets, mais quels préfets?," *Revue Politique et Parlementaire* 73, no. 819 (1971): 33–46 (selections).

ENA should be reformed in order to give specialized training for specific administrative tasks, while paying more attention to retraining civil servants and to mid-career courses for those selected for top positions. His essay is important because it reveals how the adaptation of the prefectoral corps to the needs of a complex society presents the administrative elite with insurmountable problems. A continuous process of administrative training would destroy the present system of selecting grands corps *members on graduation from elite civil service schools and would, thereby, break the grip of the* grands corps *on French administration. For this reason, any substantial reform of territorial administration implies a complete reorganization of the entire civil service system.*

The present recruitment of the prefectoral corps at the underprefect (*sous-préfet*) level relies entirely on the National School of Administration (ENA). The method of listing capabilities as they correspond to an examination of qualifications is no longer used. We believe that it is advisable to return to such a system, whether based on an internal competition, open to prefectoral administrative personnel, or through the creation of a competition of students similar to the Ministry of Foreign Affairs.

It would seem desirable, in any case, that *internal promotion* be developed among the executive offices of the ministry. Of course, this problem is well understood by ENA itself.

ENA was created to democratize the higher civil service, but its effort to break the caste spirit seems to have failed. Never has the autonomy of the *grands corps* in relation to the whole administration been more marked. Never have these *corps*—the Financial Inspection, Council of State, Court of Accounts and Diplomacy—been more power-hungry; today, as never before they push their members towards the top administrative and governmental posts—not to mention big business. Nor is the democratization of recruitment anything but an illusion. The ENA's high civil service examination is, in the end, a failure; among successful candidates, one finds as many sons of high civil servants and business leaders as prior to 1945. Even more serious, the creation of the ENA and its guiding principles are in direct opposition to the *democratic conception of access to top posts—internal competition at all levels.* Even if one were to democratize applications for the ENA examinations (*concours*), the desired end would not be attained. The issue is not only to give an opportunity to young people from modest backgrounds at the beginning of their careers, but to offer the possibility of advancement to all, at all stages of their administrative careers. The present conception of ENA and of the *grands corps* which it "supplies" can only end in the creation of technocratic mandarins; this is, in the long run, dangerous for the administration and for the state to the extent that it divides the administrative elite from the rest of the civil service. In the prefectoral corps, more than elsewhere, the dangers of this type of recruitment are confirmed.

Clearly, ENA must continue to exist. But to fulfill its true vocation as outlined by some of its creators, it must be reformed in a different way than recommended by the Bloch-Lainé Commission.

It should be pointed out that the present method (inspired by the Polytechnique School's traditions), whereby ranking on the final examination determines the candidate's assignment and entire career, is unjust and dangerous. A boy who dreamed all his life of one day becoming a diplomat will be assigned as a civil administrator to the Veterans' Administration, not as an attaché to the Foreign Affairs or as a consul, because he is ranked twenty-fifth and not eighteenth on the list. By the same token, a young man hoping to someday join the prefectoral corps may find the only available position is at the Ministry of Infrastructure, for which he is unprepared—because its financial and administrative problems are determined by the technical nature of the ministry. As for the mobility to move civil administrators from one ministry to another, and from the central administration to the provinces, it will only make sense when it is uniformly applied—that is, when the mobility applies to all the corps, including the Financial Inspectors and the Council of State. Without a policy of unrestricted mobility which might end after ten years of administrative service at the maximum, we believe that a *return to competition by corps* is necessary. The ENA would thus become a school of applied studies where students would meet, work together, and prepare for their future collaboration, but knowing from the first day to which corps or ministry they would eventually be assigned.

Specifically this would entail: a separate competitive examination for each *grands corps*, including the prefectoral corps, and a single examination for civil administrators; an internship of two years at ENA (renamed the School of Applied Studies) where different sections would be reestablished for: the corps of Financial Inspectors; the Court of Accounts and Financial Administration; the Council of State and Administrative Tribunals; the Prefectoral Administration and the general administrative inspectors; Foreign Affairs; and corps of civil administrators. But these reforms would not, in themselves, be enough, because ENA has other missions. It is surprising that, during a period when continuous job training (*la formation permanente*) becomes an imperative, there is no "Institute for Retraining Administrators." This should be one of the essential functions of ENA, which could offer in-service training in the course of a career, as well as possibilities for transferring from one administrative division to another. Finally, ENA should fill a gap in the French high administration, becoming a true "Staff College" (or, better, a "Marshalls' School") where, between the ages of thirty and forty, top administrators would receive training and undergo a selection complementary to their original training and selection at ENA.

A School of Applied Studies for successful young candidates at the qualifying examination, a permanent "recycling center" for high civil servants, and a Staff College for the administration—this triple effort would give ENA a far greater importance and usefulness than it currently has. It would become a dynamic *center for the permanent education of high civil servants of the French administration* and not just a nursery school—not to say the incubator—of an aristocracy incapable of surmounting its own problems or achieving internal unity.

It is evident that questions concerning the prefectoral corps can hardly be evoked without, at the same time, evoking the numerous problems facing the French administration. It is in the framework of a profound reform outlined above that the transformation of the prefectoral *corps* should be achieved. This *grands corps* is better suited than any other to help provincial France adapt to the modern world during the last thirty years of the twentieth century. It is well qualified for this task insofar as it constitutes a reserve of administrators capable of synthesizing and conceptualizing—rarer and more precious than technicians at a time when leading private enterprises are evolving from an outdated "Taylorism" [mechanical concept of organization work] toward a neo-fayollisme [flexible work organization], substituting organizational innovation and decentralization for the more structured and concentrated administrative activity. It remains advisable that the *corps* adapt itself so as to avoid the double risk of technocracy and politicization, and remain what it always was, which was its basic excellence: the administration by concertation, of the dialogue between men and the state, and of the progressive and reasonable adaptation of local structures to the great changes in history.

3-2. CENTRAL-LOCAL TAX AND SUBSIDY PROBLEMS*

The movement of over ten million persons to larger towns and cities over the 1960s meant that localities were hardpressed to provide new services, and to build new facilities and housing. At the same time, an archaic local tax system was undergoing reorganization and aroused intense controversy between national officials and the communes. In a very thorough report from the Economic and Social Council under a study group of Grossman, the entire episode is recounted along with the numerous misunderstandings that inflamed the mayors. In fact, the tax system was being reformed using an outdated system because the mayors themselves could not agree on a new system of dividing tax revenues or the new national transfer (VRTS). The curious effect was that the transfer kept growing much faster than it would have had the tax remained in local hands while local direct (property) taxes provided a smaller and smaller proportion of local revenues.

Local Finances

The responsibility for financing public works never ceases to pose serious problems for French local government. Local resources and the means by which they can be secured are limited; at the same time, communes and departments must give financial priority to their operating expenses, estimated at up to 80 percent of the ordinary budget for a city of 20,000 to 50,000 inhabitants.

*Grossman Report, "Les possibilités offertes aux collectivités locales en matière de ressources financières externes (subventions et emprunts)," *Avis et Rapports du Conseil Economique et Social*, Paris, Imprimerie Nationale, July 31, 1973 (selections).

In local finances, as in the administration, we find ourselves in an intermediary phase where new needs arise before means can be found to satisfy them.

In particular, it should be stressed that without the vagaries of current regulations, the localities could find sizeable resources within the urban tax system which would meet the financial needs of public works.

Leaving aside certain supplemental financial sources, the revenues available to local governments consist of the product of local direct taxes levied on their areas and the new revenues allocated to them by the state since the reform of the old local indirect taxes. Since these resources are insufficient to allow complete self-financing of their public works expenditures, local governments have recourse to substantial external resources, in the form of subsidies and loans.

Local governments' tax collection has not kept pace with increasing demands. The ordinance of January 7, 1959, should have reformed the system of direct local taxation, but ten years passed before implementation and, taking into account the delays caused by the revision of property values and indirect taxes, the effects of the modernization of direct local taxation will not be felt for several more years.

In the meantime, the old system of increasing rates (additional *centimes*)—itself a vestige of the "four veils" (the tax system of the Revolutionary period)—and its archaic, complex, and unjust effects are maintained.

The abolition of the local salary tax by the law of January 6, 1966, which extended the scope of the T.V.A. (value-added tax), deprived departments and communes of their other source of revenue. It was originally anticipated that roughly 85 percent to 100 percent of the product of the tax on salaries would be distributed to the local governments.

Following this, the law of October 9, 1968, put the entire product of this tax at the disposal of local budgets but, shortly afterwards, the tax was abolished. Since January 1, 1969, local governments receive—according to the same criteria as formerly used in the calculation and redistribution of the salary tax—an "allocation of the local salary tax" (VRTS), consisting of a levy on state revenues.

Compared with the local tax, the VRTS represents an improvement insofar as it reduces the disparity between growing cities, but those with little commercial activity are pitted against center cities and suburban dormitory towns.

It is interesting to analyze in greater detail the mechanism for attribution of the VRTS for two reasons: on the one hand, originally intended as a stopgap substitute for the local tax, it has gradually increased in fiscal importance and now appears as an initiative designed to satisfy, in the form of a global subsidy, the demands of certain local elected officials. On the other hand, its division among competing parties is made on the basis of new criteria, which necessitated rethinking the problem of local finances; these criteria should also serve as the basis for the distribution of the global subsidy instituted by a March 1972 decree.

While the proceeds from the local tax rose in 1967 to 6,175 million (about $1.5 billion), 7,253 million (about $1.8 billion) were distributed in 1968 as supplementary local revenues, representing an increase of 17 percent far above the rate of increase of the old local tax in the last years of its existence. Thereafter, the VRTS attained (one billion francs equals about $250 million):

8.2 billion in 1969, a rate of increase of 13 percent.
9.3 billion in 1970, a rate of increase of 13 percent.
10.7 billion in 1971, a rate of increase of 15 percent.
12.2 billion in 1972, a rate of increase of 14 percent.
14.0 billion in 1973, a rate of increase of 14 percent.

The opinion of the Constitutional Commission on the proposed Finances Act for 1973 emphasizes "that the sum distributed this year, 12.2 billion francs, represents a 3.1 billion bonus for local governments in comparison with the formula used prior to 1968."

The division of this total amount among various competing parties is based theoretically on two overriding principles: first, the proportion granted will vary in direct proportion to the local tax contribution as measured by the local taxes paid by households, in other words, according to the property tax; and second, a small part is reserved for redistribution to attenuate in communes' financial disparities, based on a minimum per capita allocation. In fact, a twenty year transition period was forecast for the progressive substitution of the new criteria for the old system.

The formula adopted to give local governments supplementary revenue has not escaped criticism: if the evaluation of salaried income seems a satisfactory base by which to vary additional revenues, the fictive character of the tax base (because the amount of the VRTS is determined each year as a function of what the tax on salaries would have produced were it still levied) regrettably recalls the "fictional principles" determining the local direct taxes whose archaic character has been frequently denounced.

In addition, certain cities with growing economies protest that the global resource is linked to the overall growth rate instead of to local growth, while the least favored communes complain that its redistribution compensates inadequately for inequalities observed under the old local tax structure.

However, despite its disadvantages, the VRTS appears to be a compromise between the contradictory demands made by local officials concerned about maintaining their autonomy; they want free use of their resources but, at the same time, are aware of the administrative, technical, and economic difficulties caused by increasing tax rates in their constituencies. To the extent that the VRTS is viewed by them as a portion of state taxes, intended to give local governments the capacity to meet new responsibilities, it is regarded as satisfactory.

3-3. THE LOCAL AND DEPARTMENTAL NETWORK*

The work of Crozier and his students developed a new theory of stagnation and ineffectiveness within the network of relationships that link the departments and communes to national government and its goals. Essentially, these scholars argue that the intricate pattern of interdependence between elected and administrative officials at many levels of government leads both to resist change and modernization at the local level. An intricate pattern of "complicity" is created between local mayor and officials, among the various administrative services at the department and region, and vertically between those elected to higher office and ministerial officials. Many of the early reform

*Peyrefitte Report, *Décentraliser les responsabilités*, Paris, Documentation Française, 1975. From the essay of Michel Crozier and Jean-Claude Thoenig, "L'Importance du système politico-administratif territorial," pp. 1–38 (selections).

efforts hoped to break this unproductive relationship, but its resilience and influence exceed the power of national government itself.

System is not used here to conform to current fashion but, on the contrary, to demonstrate a fundamental phenomenon which, unfortunately, is as often misunderstood by local officials as by successive Parisian reformers.

The politico-administrative system is composed of a number of administrative services, representative bodies, groups, and associations, all of which are independent of one another—general councils, prefectures, ministry field services, municipalities, chambers of commerce (and also of agriculture and artisans), federations of employers' trade associations, as well as worker and agricultural unions. Regularly instituted measures to promote coordination are ineffective, with each unit complaining about the jealously guarded isolation of the other units, the excessive compartmentalization, and a general lack of communication. However, despite coordination and communications problems, the behavior of the various units and their members are as interdependent as if they were engaged in playing the same game. Despite the game of protection and noncommunication, the game unites all the players. If central efforts at coordination are resisted by local actors, this is not because they do not know one another, or are too far apart, it is because they are part of a system with other forms of coordination which, although semiconscious, are for that reason all the more effective.

It is in this way that the relations between local elected officials (mayors and general councilors) and civil servants who head the state administration's field services (prefects, subprefects, division heads, tax collectors, and so on) reveal a powerful interdependence between them. Elected representatives declare themselves hostile to civil servants who, in turn, criticize the elected officials. But, at the same time, both groups are united by a profound complicity. A good elected official has the ear of his department's civil servants and a good civil servant knows how to listen to those elected from his constituency. Their activities are complementary, and are not incomprehensible if one considers how they are coupled. The elected representative must take the initiative, but he will allow an initiative thought desirable by the civil servant provided that, firstly, the latter allows him to profit from it and, secondly, the civil servant takes into account the elected official's needs and desires. The subtlety of this relationship can result in misunderstandings and difficulties in communication, and its complexity does not facilitate the coordination hoped for by the technocrats. But there does exist an interdependence. To understand the resulting decisions, it is more important to understand the partners' relationship with one another than the *a priori* preferences which each brings to that relationship.

Between bureaucrats and notables [local dignitaries] there develops a complicity based on shared experience, complementary interests, and identical values—a complicity durable enough to resist the test of divergent roles and interests. It is thus that elected officials as well as civil servants accept as legitimate certain forms such as the general (national) interest. Similarly, each group shows itself extremely understanding regarding the electoral preoccupations of local elected officials. This relationship of "conflictual complicity" which exists between bureaucrats and notables is found at various territorial levels: between mayors and officials of the Ministry of Infrastructure, tax collectors, or subprefects at the local level, and between general councilors and prefects or ministerial division heads at the departmental level.

These relationships take on the character of a system most clearly when official decisionmaking is examined. All observations show that in reality, no official makes a unilateral decision. Decisions are arrived at through a compromise which is acceptable to other interested officials, and are the indispensable preliminary to any decision, whether it be within the administrative services or among the territorial divisions. The characteristic of this politico-administrative system is that it obeys a "particularistic general rule," which can be observed through officials' institutional differences or partisan orientations.

To conclude, the tacit or informal rule is close to the following: no compromise—and therefore no decision—is directly negotiated between the parties directly concerned. It operates through the intervention of an individual or group which is not a part of the specific institutional milieu. Functions of integration and coordination are fulfilled by an actor whose activity and source of legitimacy are different in nature from that of the parties he integrates or

coordinates. The coordinator even tends to impose his precon-
ceived solution; he takes into account the involved interests, but
imposes his solution without real negotiation with the concerned
parties. Its success is more likely if it is elaborated in the guise of
another rationalization: technical imperatives, "local traditions,"
or the general interest.

3-4. THE GUICHARD REPORT ON SMOTHERING LOCAL DEMOCRACY*

*President Giscard d'Estaing continued the Gaullist efforts to
reorganize local government, but in a more conciliatory way. He
appointed a blue-ribbon committee under a prominent Gaullist
leader who had long experience with local problems, Olivier
Guichard, to look for new solutions. His report to the President is a
remarkably candid account of how local governments feel oppressed
by national government. In this section he elaborates how the functional expansion of the French state has virtually excluded communes
from many new activities, while simultaneously imposing a wide
variety of new controls on them. His account is especially interesting
because he discards many of the Jacobin concerns that had occupied
hardline Gaullists in the past, particularly in criticizing the* tutelle.
*Even so, the mayors found his report threatening and with the
approaching legislative elections of 1978 the President decided to
pursue a piece-meal strategy and avoid direct clash with the communes.*

The Inflated State

Today's state has absorbed into itself almost all administrative
substance. From the point of view of local responsibilities, this
situation is obviously unhealthy and detrimental to both administrative efficiency and the state's dignity.

In effect, the state is mired in everyday life. It is more and more
often called upon to manage the daily lives of the French population: education, housing, health, and soon. The state itself, or its

*Guichard Report, *Vivre Ensemble* (A Report to the President), Paris, Documentation Française, 1976, pp. 23–27.

intermediaries, dispenses a whole range of favors. To this end, it sets up detailed regulations to which its civil servants become fervently attached.

Thus overburdened, the state often has neither sufficient time nor energy to play the role expected of it by the public: to set overall policy priorities, to establish the rules of social life, and to enforce them. But on the other hand, it has encroached on the normal role of local governments.

Having become too massive, the state was bound to fragment. This occurred in two ways: through the development of its own services, and the rapid multiplication of public institutions.

For local governments, for the citizen, where is the state? It is everywhere—it is the tax collector, teacher, school supervisor, public works engineer, and agricultural extension agent. Its scope is immense. Each administration follows a sectorial policy, providing regulations and financial support as well as privileged access to power networks to ensure its influence.

The state has also multiplied the number of public institutions. These institutions, in their various forms, often bypass the traditional administration and do not share the latter's sense of obligation to local governments.

At the same time, the state (congratulating itself on its flexible evolution) has even stripped itself of a number of its former responsibilities, granting these to private organizations along with corresponding budgetary resources and regulatory powers.

Undoubtedly the state is still a weapon of overall control. However, this control is often lax or ineffective when confronting institutions indifferent to the state or to local concerns. A strange dialogue ensues: the state must endow new institutions with resources in order for them to pursue the public interest, and their autonomy is guaranteed by their legal status. Thus, the state is open to criticism for actions it does not control.

In the same way, the state is burdened with the disadvantages of centralization of responsibilities, without enjoying the advantages of unity. This is the main point: everything is centralized, but there is no center—or rather, there are as many centers as there are services. Public affairs management becomes rigid and compartmentalized due to centralization.

Smothered Local Democracy

The continued growth of the state has left no room for the development of local responsibilities. The division of responsibilities has become confused, generating inequalities and conflicts. Local governments have become the agents of ministerial policies. Charged with overseeing and managing public construction and public services for the state, they are unable to pursue local policies adapted to local problems. Because of unequal means and extremely diverse local situations, inequities result from the application of a uniform state policy.

In short, local democracy—as conceived under the Third Republic (and retained under successive regimes)—has been largely emptied of its former substance.

Excessive Control

General confusion as to the financial "rules of the game" makes excessive control even more irritating to localities. Although the state can, to its credit, point to the considerable lessening of its juridical and budgetary control over local government, local officials protest that financial and technical *tutelle* constraining them have never been more heavy-handed.

The financial *tutelle* is exercised, above all, through the mechanism of the subsidy, which must be obtained in order to gain access to loans at privileged rates. The quest for subsidies, it must be admitted, is humiliating. Like individuals, local government never gains the upper hand in this area.

The technical *tutelle*, by means of subsidies—but also by the development of norms and procedures—never refrains from asking for the most subtle details. Moreover, it is a bizarre system that authorizes localities to engage and pay state engineers to construct public works, while these same state agents are charged with controlling their "clients." The entire system leads to a malaise in the relationship between citizens and the administration.

The citizen is not ungrateful. But he is indifferent to decisions made without his participation. Elected leaders certainly contribute to them but mainly from anonymous higher levels. The state rarely explains its reasons and cloaks its decisions in esoteric language. Thus, the citizen often feels that he is given what he does not want and denied what he asks for: for example, an extravagent sports facility is built when he may have preferred a more modest, but well-staffed and well-maintained, facility.

3-5. HOW MUTUAL ADVANTAGE REINFORCES THE CENTRAL-LOCAL NETWORK*

Based on a system of fees and honorarie (primes) collected by royal servants several hundred years ago, all the grands corps still have the right to certain income as a percentage of their total services of various kinds. For example, highway and and auto inspectors share a fund derived from a small percentage of auto registration fees. The most fiercely attacked charges are those made on communes for technical services of rural and public works engineers. In 1973, these obligatory honoraria amounted to $12 million for engineers alone and, at higher ranks of the corps, can double a person's salary. Such systems of mutual advantage make it virtually impossible to break the grip of the grands corps and, in turn, provide the basis for a symbiotic relationship with the communes who need their help. In the following article, Michèle Champenois provides one of the few descriptions of efforts to reform honoraria and to eliminate the inequities they create.

It is a taboo subject. One cannot speak of it without irritating those directly involved: the rural engineers and, especially, public works engineers (*ponts ets chaussées*). How can the system of supplementary remunerations for state engineers—who receive honoraria for city projects in addition to their official salaries—be reformed? René Martin, former president of the Public Works Division of the Council of State, was asked this quesiton.

Charged by then prime minister Jacques Chirac to propose ways to "break the link existing between certain technical corps' remuneration and the work and studies done at the expense of the localities," M. Martin delivered his report in December 1975. Since then, no decision has been taken. Modifications of the system—not a far-reaching reform—have been prepared. But it is unlikely that they will be applied in the near future. Along with a certain "ethical" reform of the system, M. Martin proposed, in effect, an in-

---

*Michèle Champenois, "Les ingénieurs de l'Etat, mercenaires des communes," *Le Monde*, April 16, 1977 (selections).

crease in the rates of fees, badly received at the time of antiinflationary struggle.

But this sensitive dossier could reappear on another occasion. Raymond Barre has, in effect, asked a task force presided by M. Lassy, to reflect on certain structural causes of inflation . . . such as the percentage remuneration of numerous public and private professions: notaries, real estate agents, ship-brokers, architects, consulting firms, and the state's technical agents. But is does not seem, at the present time, that there is a real desire to highlight these anomalies and arouse the discontent of one or another corps.

Far from proposing the suppression of this special system, M. Martin concluded that the system could only be partially reformed in order to attenuate some of its vices. For him and for other authorities, it would be impossible to abolish these privileges without provoking a revolt of the affected engineers for whom supplementary payments represent on average a third of their income and much more in certain cases. Nor could these payments be integrated into their "normal" salaries without provoking a chain reaction on the part of other categories of high civil servants. A deadlock now exists. The engineers are even less prepared to renounce their honoraria while other corps benefit from special advantages which are not the object of reform or even clarification.

If this system is more often criticized than other percentage-based remuneration plans (for example, the general paymasters and postmasters receive a percentage on public bonds issued, and mortgage registrars benefit from an appropriation on certain taxes), it is because the system of remunerating the technical corps involves very large sums and, particularly, because it reflects directly on the already difficult and ambiguous relations between the state and local governments.

Aside from departmental highway maintenance, which is part of the obligatory duties of the public works service, all the projects and studies requested by the departments and communes, as well as the maintenance of local roads, entail the distribution of honoraria. The intervention of state services is not obligatory—it is requested by a meeting of the municipal council and submitted for (rarely refused) prefectoral approval. Each year local government pays into the departmental treasury the honoraria calculated according to a digressive scale: 4 percent for projects less than 20,000 francs, 3 percent between 20,000 and 200,000 francs, 2 percent between 200,000 and 1 million francs, and 1 percent for any over this amount.

Hierarchical inequalities exist in addition to geographical inequities. The departmental assistance fund (allowing for national equalization among departments) is distributed on an essentially hierarchical scale ranging from an index of 4 for a foreman to 80 for a chief public works engineer. Although very unequal, this "sharing of the pie" with all technical personnel, no matter how far removed from the corps itself, guarantees a certain solidarity. For construction work completed in 1973 and paid for in 1975, according to M. Martin, the average remuneration was: 51,000 francs (about $9,000) for a head engineer, 37,000 francs (about $6,000) for a regional public works engineer, 26,000 francs (about $4,500) for a departmental public works engineer, 5000 francs ($900) for a technical assistant and 3,000 francs ($500) for a foreman. On the average, for a first-class general engineer, these honoraria represent 28 percent of his income and 41 percent at high ranks, thereby almost doubling his base salary.

Before distributing the assistance fund according to the hierarchical schedule, the departmental public works director can appropriate up to 10 percent of the total amount in order to "correct anomalies" and distribute bonuses at his discretion, which those affected call "feeding one's friends."

Under this system everyone has certain advantages. The state gains because highly qualified engineers and technicians are not tempted to enter the private sector for better pay. The cities and localities have competent services conveniently at their disposal which are not too costly; the honoraria represent on average 2 to 2.5 percent of project cost, whereas private consulting firms would take 7 percent. Finally, the engineers themselves claim that this money is not stolen. They point to the evening municipal council meetings they must attend and to the overtime hours they give in order to complete local projects. Besides giving the administration topnotch technical services, the supplementary work of the engineers (according to their main union), provides "respect, moral authority, and material satisfaction." They hope for clear "rules of the game" accepted by all. They agree that the system should be modified but not abolished—at least, not unless they are offered a financial compensation. The circle is closed.

3-6. THE SOCIALIST DEBATE OVER REGIONS AND DEPARTMENTS*

The debate within the Socialist party over whether regions or departments should have a stronger role continued a what has been a controversy within France since the Revolution. Much the same debate took place over the Gaullist local reforms of 1964. The briefing documents prepared by a Socialist policy advisor, Edgar Pisani, generated a new debate within the Party over how centralized planning to achieve socialist economic goals might be reconciled with decentralized local government. In a way that is not totally dissimilar to controversies within the Gaullist party in the 1960s, Pisani hopes that more democratic departmental and regional councils will make more centralized planning acceptable. His ambiguous proposals to consolidate communes were no more acceptable than those in the Guichard Report.

All the rights that the Constitution and the present organic law do not reserve specifically to the state hereafter belong to local government.

Through the deliberations of their elected councils, the localities regulate their own affairs. The law defines the conditions under which localities participate in the prerogatives of the state. The autonomy of local government is guaranteed by the following:

—The right granted to localities to refer to constitutional courts any law abrogating their autonomy.
—The right granted to all localities including citizens or their associations, to refer to administrative courts any act of government, its administration, or of another locality undermining its autonomy.

Respect for the law and the expression of national unity and national will is assured to the localities by appeal to administrative courts, and can be instigated by the following:

*Edgar Pisani, *Rapport*, Socialist Party, mimeo, Paris, 1977 (selections).

—A legal officer assigned in the department.

—Other localities whose powers extend to the locality concerned.

—Citizens or associations established in the locality.

Before pursuing an appeal, the legal officer has the right, through a formal and duly justified procedure, to ask the accused official to reconsider his decision.

These decisions of localities are not subject to any other control nor any other supervision.

The National Plan adopted by Parliament sets general objectives and imposes discipline on all. But it cannot override the localities' decisions within the domain of their competence.

The local governments are involved in the elaboration of the National Plan. Respecting the National Plan, each collectivity adopts a plan and programs which defines the objectives it proposes to achieve and the efforts which it will devote to their attainment.

At any time during the three months following adoption of the present law, the departmental councils may propose an organization taking into account territorial and demographic realities as well as the will of inhabitants and of their elected councils.

On the proposition of a National Commission, consisting of senators and deputies and presided over by a councilor of state, a decree of the council of state will be adopted listing the municipalities, the definition of their circumscriptions, and their rank.

In the above specified conditions, the municipalities receive prerogatives formerly exercised by the state's departmental services, as well as those formerly granted to the communes or their groupings for public services, public works, and conditions affecting the quality of life. Communal and municipal elections take place on the same day every six years.

At its initiative or upon the demand of ten percent of its voters, a council may organize a referendum on any subject of communal concern. Municipal councils may do this to determine essential planning options.

In the three months following its installation, each communal council and each municipal council deliberates on a "Charter of Democratic Participation and Self-Management." This charter defines the conditions under which citizens and their associations participate in local life and responsibilities. The delegations of power voted by a council in this way are its responsibility. The "Charter of Democratic Participation and Self-Management" defines, in particular, the duties of councils, mayors, and presidents, and of communal and municipal administrations for informing the public.

To coordinate their actions, to implement tasks of common interest, to permit them to progressively and harmoniously assume the newly delegated tasks, the municipalities of one department may constitute an intermunicipal union with multiple functions (*syndicat intermunicipal à vocation multiple*). This public establishment is administered by the departmental council. The representation of each municipal council is based on the size of its population. The council elects an executive commission and a president.

The region is an autonomous local government. By direct universal suffrage, it elects an assembly which designates the executive president. The assembly receives the advice of a regional committee representing localities and cultural, social, economic interests within its area. By its deliberations, the assembly decides on the problems of the region. It adopts the budget and votes on tax rates.

The region is the seat of the commissaire of the Republic. In the region, he represents the entire government and has authority over the totality of the state's administrative services.

The region is the privileged level for national planning. It contributes as much to its elaboration as to its implementation. It does this through studies, organizing coordination, and by offering assistance.

It is at the regional level and with its participation that:
—Research, higher education, and adult education are organized.
—Regional policies for employment, transportation, and tourism are defined.
—Public credit institutions are decentralized to benefit localities as well as economic activities.
—Sanitation and social services, both public and private, are coordinated.
—Participation of the localities in the definition of the policies of large national enterprises (transportation, energy, communications) is organized.
—The coherence of major investments is assured.

On the advice of a committee, the assembly develops the following:

—A long-term and a medium-term plan of development.

—A cultural and information charter.

The regional assembly distributes the whole of the resources aimed at mitigating territorial inequalities within its area. It does this according to a redistribution schedule established in the framework of planning.

4 Economic Policy: Desperation or Design?

The rapid growth of the French economy over the past twenty years has created an impression of a vigorous, competitive, capitalist France. In fact, French leaders have been plagued with fears that French industry and commerce would be unable to withstand the forces of a more competitive world economy. French writing on the economy is filled with alarm over growing American investment in France in the 1960s, and later with apprehension that more competitive German and Japanese firms will make France their main market. Stoleru, a champion of an invigorated French economy under the Gaullists, noted that, in 1966, a fourth of American European investment was in France, which amounted to over 1.5 billion dollars by the end of 1964 (1969, p. 30). Though France is one of the strongest economies of Europe, for years French economic policymakers have lived with the spector of France becoming an economic colony of more modern competitors.

The apprehensions of French economic policymakers become more intelligible when we take into account the institutional uncertainties that they faced under both the Fourth and Fifth Republics. If the tones became more strident after 1958, it is partly because of de Gaulle's own determination to make France both a military and industrial power. The vulnerabilities of the French economy were by no means imagined, but the difficulties of transforming the economy introduced numerous political and social problems; for one thing, in attacking French conservative economic practices, the Gaullists were also attacking their natural allies. Nonetheless, from 1962 to 1968 the economy grew at 6 percent a year. Even after the dislocations and social costs of the 1968 strikes (see Chapters 5 and

6), the economy bounced back to grow at almost 7 percent a year until the oil crisis. Again, the economy responded to the oil crisis and reached almost 5 percent growth in 1976 and, even during the ensuing depression of the world economy, sustained growth at about 2 percent a year (Stoffaës, 1978, p. 209). In 1980, France was one of the strongest economies of Western Europe. The gross national product had in fact increased by 136 percent since 1960 (CERC, 1979, p. 15). If things were going so well, one might reasonably ask what leaders were so worried about.

The simple answer is that there was little in French history to reassure them that France would be equal to the challenge from abroad while also meeting internal demand. France was never a strong economic power in the nineteenth century and many Frenchmen seemed to like it that way. A keen political observer of French society, André Siegfried, wrote, in 1931, of the superiority of a self-sufficient agrarian economy and of the damaging effects of imposing a world economic order on France. Until 1850, about two-thirds of the French population still found its living in agriculture and, as late as 1930, a third of the French people were still peasant farmers. Successively burdened with the war debts of Napoleon, the Franco-Prussian War, and World War I, the French developed a fiscal conservatism appropriate to the debtor nation. Since 1892, France had been protected with stiff tariffs and an income tax passed by the Chamber of Deputies in 1909, which was quickly struck down by the Senate. Until the late 1930s, the national budget was kept in strict equilibrium. Although government spending grew slightly faster than the national product, the French had never wanted government to intervene forcefully in the economy (André and Delorme, 1978, p. 45).

Context

French economic conservatism meant not only that the economy grew slowly in the past, but also that industrial development appeared relatively late. At the same time, conservative habits had protected France from many of the economic shocks that spread across Europe early in the century. As a self-contained, agrarian economy France did not feel the full force of the 1920s depression until fairly late in its cycle. In 1932, when unemployment was nearly 6 million in Germany and 4 million in Britain, France had only

300,000 unemployed. With a heavily controlled and heavily protected economy, the French economic advisors counseled conservatism from Poincaré in the 1920s until the dawn of the Fifth
Republic itself. Indeed, one of the chief architects of French economic policy for over forty years, Jacques Rueff (1972), was clearly
proud of France's continued self-reliance and self-sufficiency in
what was, and often still is, regarded as a world full of unreliable
economic partners. Only under the threat of a fascist revolt did
France turn to inflationary policies in 1936 under the Socialist prime
minister, Blum, but even these hasty efforts were soon overtaken
by the war and made no deep imprint on French economic conservatism.

State intervention in the economy began under the rigor of the
Nazi occupation of France and with the desparate efforts of Vichy
France to meet German demands while feeding and clothing the
French people. There is a bitter reminiscence in Gruson's detailed
account (1968) of how planning information was first assembled
from the statistics kept during the occupation, where one can find
detailed records of each type of pasta being rationed among the
French people. Under the pressure of war, the French began to
learn about planning. The *comités d'organisation* organized by the
Vichy regime began an industrial census, elaborated food production plans, rationed raw materials, governed working conditions
and wages, and determined prices.

The Liberation of France and inclusion of the Left brought an
important change in official reluctance to intervene in the economy.
First, the government nationalized a number of basic services (railroads, electricity, and gas), the Bank of France (the main public
bank), and one large auto firm, Renault, as a result of its collaboration with the Vichy regime. Second, there was immense war damage and a Ministry of Reconstruction was organized under an
energetic advocate of public works and public planning, Claudius-
Petit. His ministry later became the Ministry of Infrastructure and
the main advocate of public sector investment planning, which, as
we have seen in other situations, is concerned with public works and
local investment. It is also the bastion of an elite administrative
corps, the *ponts et chaussées*, who became a formidable force in the
expansion of French planning efforts. Third, with the arrival of the
Cold War in 1947 the United States decided to provide massive

economic aid to free Europe. To receive the funds for France the first of dozens of special funds was organized, the Fonds de Modernisation de et l'Equipement or FME, which later became the funnel to inject public money into economic and industrial development projects.

By far the most important decision, at this early state of building the machinery of economic policymaking, was the formation of the Planning Commission (Commission Générale du Plan, or CGP). The early planning operation brought together a fascinating collection of top French economists, and their leader, Jean Monnet, had a central role in the economic reconstruction of both France and Europe as a whole. Many of the young planners and economists drawn into the CGP gave it a strange complexion of highly technocratic planning combined with the mystique of the Resistance and Gaullist dedication to build a strong France (Gruson, 1971). But Monnet's initial aims were more mundane to rebuild heavy industry and the industrial infrastructure needed to restore French economic power (Cohen, 1977). Nonetheless, there followed from 1947 to the present a series of national plans, each adjusting to new economic goals and each incorporating somewhat more refined and ambitious techniques than the previous one (see Table 4-1). Indeed, the changing character of planning itself is an important clue to the changing economic strategy of French leaders as well as to the institutional constraints that each government saw as potential obstacles to French economic prosperity.

The CGP is itself one of the major sources of institutional uncertainty in the postwar development of French government. There have been numerous studies to uncover its particular secret of success, and even more detailed studies to try to determine whether it was successful at all (Shonfield, 1965; Cohen, 1977; Hayward and Watson, eds., 1975). With a very small staff of about sixty experts, most drawn from the elite administrative groups, the initial aim of the CGP was to persuade risk-adverse French industrialists that market forces could work for them and that the state would intervene in providing credit for product and market development. There was never a fixed concept of French planning, which may explain why foreigners found it so hard to understand (see Reading 4-1). As the original director, Monnet, wrote (1976, p. 306), economic modernization would emerge "by the marshalling of simple

TABLE 4-1   The Evolution of French Planning

Years	Changes	Dislocations
First Plan (1947–51)	"Monnet Plan" hidden within national budget; concentrates on heavy industry	Inflationary spiral 1951 and Pinay deflation; extend plan to 1953
Second Plan (1954–57)	Econometric design; conceive "économie concertée" and press self-financing; parliamentary review in 1955	National budget organized in current and capital expenditure; North African and S.E. Asian pressures
Third Plan (1958–65)	Start industrial sector target; linked to Min. of Finance with new economic budget	Algerian revolution; 1958 devaluation; cost of relocating 800,000 *pieds noir*
Fourth Plan (1962–65)	Contractual agreements in public sector; CGP under prime minister 1962; Min. of Finance creates Forecasting Division in 1965	Inflationary spiral 1962 and Giscard's Stabilization Plan 1963; EEC adjustments
Fifth Plan (1966–70)	"Massé Plan" introduces collective targets for regions and public works; add incomes policy; convert plan to cost figures	1968 student rebellions and strikes; 1969 devaluation
Sixth Plan (1971–75)	Introduce productivity goals; strengthen employment and incomes policy component	1973 oil crisis, Pompidou "mini-plan" 1974
Seventh Plan (1976–80)	Establish priority programs; CGP under president in 1975; create "industrial budget" in 1977	1974 Fourcade "action plans"; 1975 "recovery plan"; 1976 Barre Stabilization Program
Eighth Plan (1981–85)	Conversion of national plan to "priority plans" (PAP); control shifts to Ministry of Industry	Oil price increases; 1981 Socialist government; 1982–83 Interim Plan without estimates and projections

ideas, few in number but widely disseminated, (so) that the Plan will become a national reality."

As we shall see in the chronological account of changing economic policies under the Fifth Republic, the plan changed in concept, methods, and goals throughout the postwar period. In the framework of the politics of policymaking, the most important feature is that not only was the approach to planning and its relation to the state constantly evolving, but that the planning cycles themselves were regularly disrupted by unforeseen external events. Inflationary cycles, the Algerian revolution, the 1968 strikes, the 1973 oil crisis, and other events constantly intervened to upset planning objectives (Green, 1978a). Thus, French planning is perhaps most usefully thought of as a learning process that, with changing degrees of success, involved the entire administration, business, and labor unions, as well as top political leaders. At the peak of its activities, probably in the late 1960s, the process involved thousands of French business and labor leaders, reaching down through local and regional committees, regional government, and both semipublic economic pressure groups—such as the Chambers of Commerce—and private pressure groups—such as the CNPF. The evolution of the planning is itself an illustration of how French policymakers work to overcome uncertainty within the political and economic system.

To a greater extent than with other policy problems analyzed in this book, the Gaullists came to power with a fairly well-defined economic strategy in place from the Fourth Republic. After a decade of increased growth the Planning Commission was well-organized and experienced. Ministerial coordination and economic forecasting had improved (see Reading 4-1). In 1952, the Pinay "miracle" had demonstrated that France had the capability to weather inflationary spirals and, contrary to fiscal conservatism of the past, could use deficit spending to revive the economy. In 1955, Prime Minister Mendés-France greatly elaborated the consultation process through *comités d'expansion* of local business and labor leaders, and the strategy of growth was well established. By 1960, the French were already investing about 15 percent of the national product in fixed capital and, in the 1960s, fixed investments were to rise to 20 percent of the national product. Partly to defend itself against the growing influence of the CGP, the Ministry of Finance had developed a sophisticated forecasting division, backed up by one of the most expert statistical and economic analysis agencies of Europe (INSEE). A great deal had already been done to link French public credit institutions (the Bank of France, the Caisse des Dépôts, and so on) to industrial leaders and production priorities. By the common economic measures, the Second, Third and Fourth Plans had substantially exceeded the targets worked out by the Planning Commission (see Gruson, 1968, p. 221). Thus, by 1958, the French economy had already shed much of its historic protection and expansion was widely accepted as the main goal of French economic policy making.

Agenda

In purely economic terms, the machinery of French economic policymaking that de Gaulle inherited in 1958 might seem congenial to his aims and methods. As often happens, politics confounds the pure logic of economics. French economic power was obviously essential to de Gaulle's vision of French *grandeur* and renewed military might, but he also had deep reservations about the social and political effects of rapid industrialization (see Lauber, 1981). Several key economic decisions had been made. The Fourth Plan (1962–65), with more advanced methods of resource allocation, was near completion and de Gaulle's preoccupation with the Algerian revolution left little time to redirect its goals. Shortly after coming to power, de Gaulle pronounced planning "an ardent obligation," though several French commentators noted that once the head of state had to make such a statement, it seemed likely that planning was under a shadow.

In part, the tribulations of planning were built into the system and, in part, they were a function of changing economic conditions. The Algerian war was, of course, a tremendous drain on the French economy and its inflationary effects were soon felt. The brilliant young *inspecteur des finances* that de Gaulle chose as his minister of finance, Giscard d'Estaing, shared the fear of most financial experts over devaluation and loss of control over imports. Giscard's Stabilization Plan added to internal differences, for many Gaullists thought it crippled plans for continued economic expansion, and more than a few thought it a convenient device to reassert the Ministry's control over credit and planning at a time when the CGP was growing. As would happen a decade later, the *laissez-faire* principles of the old Radicals sat uncomfortably with Jacobin ideas. For example, an early effort by Pinay establishing a French oil distribution firm without sufficiently clear state control caused grumbling in Gaullist ranks about dismantling the state.

Contrary to the impression that might be drawn from the many critics of Gaullist Jacobinism, the Gaullists had no automatic reconciliation with French industry and commerce. The last government of the Fourth Republic, for example, had given way to the fears of French businessmen that entry into the Common Market (agreed to in 1957) should be delayed. De Gaulle's decision that entry must proceed as planned (Pilleul, ed., 1979) sent alarm throughout the business community. Indeed, in the early 1960s, de Gaulle not only had an unsuccessful encounter with the labor unions (see Chapter 5)˙ but also offended the Employers Association (CNPF). The CNPF resented the "illusion of systematic dirigisme" and the "myth of the Plan" which they blamed for exposing them to new risks (Belassa, 1981). Belassa noted that from this point specific industry targets no longer figured in the national plans. The curious effect was to confirm the Jacobin apprehensions that France would not rise to the occasion as European competition increased and as import restrictions were removed. The result was that the planners and the Gaullists were forced to rely more heavily on public sector controls and instruments in order to achieve their aims.

Many of these concerns were voiced by de Gaulle's personal economic advisor, Jacques Rueff (see Reading 4-2). Without defending Jacobin habits, it should be pointed out that many of the early policies were indeed highly conflictive and hurt many of the Gaullists' obvious allies in business and commerce. For example, industrial mergers were encouraged. By 1970, France had the highest rate of industrial mergers in Europe (Suleiman, 1975). But Gaullist encouragement to big business did not extract cooperation from the CNPF. The government had little choice but to embark, in the Fifth Plan, on its own policy of "industrial champions," a strategy of reinforcing those industries, such as electronics and computers, where France was particularly vulnerable to foreign competition. The unintended effect was to make the CGP even more important in extracting cooperation from industry and in negotiating the loans intended to preserve French expansion and competitiveness. As Hall (1981) points out, the paradoxical result was that planning tended to become "an alliance between the planners and the advanced sector of industry" which gradually politicized the private sector while also privatizing the public sector. The state had to use what public resources it had to extract marginal compliance from skeptical industrialists, while industrialists who would cooperate were increasingly drawn into contractual arrangements with the state. Not until 1969 were the internal quarrels of the CNPF resolved. The Gaullists seemed to have few reliable friends in any sector of the economy.

Unwelcome among many large firms and suspected by many vulnerable small firms, early Gaullist economic policy tended to turn inward and search for new alternatives within the public sector. In fact, the early contractual agreements were designed for nationalized industries and it is not accidental that the main advocate of contractual negotiation between state and industry, Massé, later became director of the nationalized French electricity company. A second effect was to give an even freer hand to the more technocratic forces operating through the CGP. For the Sixth Plan (1971–75) even more ambitious models and control devices were envisioned, most of which never worked (see Gruson, 1971). The more technical the plan became, the easier it became for businessmen and more pragmatic political leaders, such as Pompidou, to conclude that it exceeded the capacities of either public or private actors. Third, the sacrifices imposed on French society over the 1960s began to show. For several years, real wages actually fell while the country was enjoying 6 percent growth rates. While many of the accomplishments of French economic policy were envied abroad (for example, gold reserves actually quadrupled between 1957 and 1967), leaders were aware that the social costs would eventually have to be faced. As it turned out, the May 1968 strikes made it clear that they had already exceeded the patience of most French workers.

Process

As suggested in Chapter 1, the Pompidou period is, in many ways, the most intriguing in the transformation of the French state because many of the contradictory forces at work within French society not only came to surface by the late 1960s, but Pompidou himself understood that new compromises were needed. The early Gaullists were by no means unaware of the social costs of their expansionist policies. Debré had asked the Economic and Social Council to provide advice on sharing national income in 1961. On becoming prime minister in 1962, Pompidou asked Massé to prepare a report on possibilities of an incomes policy (Hayward, 1972). In 1963, Massé chaired a national conference of top business, labor, and government leaders to consider establishing a National Incomes Commission. Among the technocrats of the CGP itself, there was growing awareness that the plan was not fully taking into account social needs. In 1964, one of dozens of clubs reflecting on the future of France, the "1985 Group," published its *Réflexions pour 1985*, many of whose social aims were elaborated for the first time in the supporting documents for the Sixth Plan on education, health, pensions, and so on. The 1967 legislative elections reminded the Gaullists that they were still a minority party.

More visible to leaders was the fact that dependence on public sector intervention in order to build a connection to private industry was expensive, and often unsuccessful. The Nora Report (1967) pointed out that between 1961 and 1965 the deficit of nationalized industries had doubled while the state had doubled subsidies. If France were indeed to foster private entrepreneurial skills, why were so many resources going into the public sector? The subsidy for the national railways, for example, equaled the total investment in nuclear energy and was three times the subsidy allocated to an overburdened and inadequate national highway system. The highly technocratic early planning responded to Gaullist goals, but it appeared to be imposing high opportunity costs in developing other, less manageable, programs.

The period of Pompidou's presidency is also crucial in that many of the contradictions and dead-ends of early, more technocratic Gaullism in the area of economic policymaking were exposed, if not definitively resolved. An intensely political man, Pompidou had less patience with the charts and models of planners. While his early connections with Rothchild's Bank could hardly be considered typical business experience, he knew something about business and understood how industrialists think. Many of the weaknesses of the first decade of Gaullist industrial policy had been pointed out to him in the Ortoli Report (1968), which reiterated the importance of releasing market forces within the French economy. But the report also stressed many aspects of economic growth that had been neglected: manpower training, educational reform (Pompidou himself was a member of the elite educational group from the Ecole Normale Supérieur), and managerial skills. France was to be no less capitalist, but it was to nurture the human talents needed to make capitalism work.

The May 1968 strikes and demonstrations were an obvious danger signal to the strategy of unfettered expansion, although, as we have seen, it is possible to overestimate the ease with which government actually intervened in the early 1960s. But the direct impact of May 1968 on economic calculations and policies is not as great as the alarmed critics of the Right or the enthusiastic advocates of the Left often assert. As outlined in Chapter 1, the strikes were as much a threat to the unions as to government and business. The 1968 legislative elections were a huge defeat for the Left. It is more the direct experience of Pompidou that has lasting effect, for he personally negotiated the Grenelle Accords, granting wage increases to workers and expanding social benefits. Overdue as the concessions were, fiscal conservatism continued and, again under Giscard, the Ministry of Finance produced balanced budgets for four years between 1969 and 1973. By 1970, the French economy was sufficiently prosperous not only to absorb the concessions, but to restore record growth rates within a few months.

A better indicator of how the 1968 crisis was actually seen at high policy levels is provided by the Montjoie Report (1968), a special study requested by Pompidou to reassess how the Fifth Plan would continue, and how the Sixth Plan might be affected (see Reading 4-3). Montjoie summarizes the Pompidou strategy: freer operation of market forces and increased competition while keeping in close touch with the social costs of rapid growth. Pompidou's political instincts meant that he could not agree with de Gaulle's version of the May 1968 events, an "irrational crisis," but it did not prevent him from setting a new process in motion. France was to turn to a more distinctly capitalist strategy by using prosperity rather than *grandeur* to guide economic policy (Luber, 1980).

His choice of prime minister, Chaban-Delmas, was, of course, indicative of this change. The "New Society" was to be a judicious

blend of a socially responsible state with renewed industrial competition. The new formula is not as interesting for its similarity to
the one followed by most large industrial nations in the 1970s as for
its sharp break with the French past. It rejected both the more
technical, state-centered approach to planning that had developed,
perhaps inadvertently, under de Gaulle, and the old techniques for
selective intervention in the private sector. There is, of course,
more than a little irony in the fact that each time a new set of
national planners produced their work, another set of planners,
who was more politically in tune with changing leadership, was
asked to implement the plan. In fact, one of Pompidou's first
decisions on assuming the presidency was to appoint a trusted
friend, Delouvrier, to do a "prestudy" of the Sixth Plan. Delouvrier's report (1972) reiterated the obstacles to modernization of the
French economy (see Hayward, 1972). As in the Ortoli Report, the
key to the dilemma is by no means original to Western economies,
which is to rely more heavily on the profit motive, but the idea of
unfettered industrial competition is also less developed in the
French economic system. Ortoli was to become Pompidou's minister of industry. After the 1969 devaluation, the French economy
soared to new records, reaching 7 percent rates of growth.

Not the least of the contradictions of the 1968 events was that it
precipitated the gradual decline of state planning. The publication
of the Sixth Plan (1970–75) produced an outcry from the Left for its
unrestrained concessions to restore free market forces in the economy, limit the growth of the public sector, and keep wage increases
in line with productivity increases. Pompidou himself reigned in the
CGP and brought it more directly under the control of the Elysée,
in part to protect himself from overzealous efforts by his reform-
minded prime minister. Typical of the internal warfare of French
government, the Ministry of Finance saw its opportunity to curb the
influence of the CGP and tried to recover control of the industrial
commissions under the CGP (Hayward, 1972). Since Pompidou
was an experienced government infighter, the overall effect was to
bring economic and industrial policy under his influence, leaving
decentralization (see Chapter 3), labor relations (see Chapter 5),
and social security (see Chapter 6) to the prime minister and his
suspiciously progressive social advisor, Delors, later to become

Mitterrand's minister of finance. Among the political advantages for Pompidou—who was already suspicious of Chaban—was that the prime minister had all the intractible problems!

But political events rarely follow either the logic or the conditions pronounced by economists. Pompidou clearly wanted to foster less restrained capitalism. In fact, corporate mergers increased and, by 1975, eleven of the forty most profitable firms in the EEC were French. But the new president was also sensitive to the growing pressure from the Left and increased dependence on the Republicas of the Center. In open rejection of the Gaullist disdain for the small merchant and businessman that was so often associated with Gaullist analyses of French political and economic weakness, Pompidou added a prominent small businessman, Royer, to the cabinet in 1969. In 1973, the *loi Royer* was passed, testimony to renewed importance of the middle class in French politics. The law helped protect about four million small merchants throughout France who were threatened by the rapid consolidation and modernization of commerce. Indicative of the precarious nature of the departure, it was attacked by the Gaullist "baron," Debré, as a concession to traditional forces, and by the Republican leader, Giscard, as unacceptable inefficiency. Only three years later, in 1976, Giscard as president appointed the president of the small business pressure group (CGPME) to the even higher post of delegate minister. The middle class was taking its revenge on the Fifth Republic (see Berger, 1977).

The new Pompidou strategy not only made compromises with less efficient members of French society, but it risked an even greater defeat. Much as critics of the Fifth Republic might protest Jacobin designs among the early Gaullists to gain control of industrial policy, an even less desirable outcome would be for firms to gain the upper hand in negotiations with the state (see Lauber, 1981). There is no reason to assume that an enhanced Ministry of Industry would be a better bargainer in the labyrinth of economic and industrial relations than was the CGP in its heyday. Quite simply, *l'état arbitre* (arbitrating state) might become *l'état partenaire* (partner state) (Hall, 1981). Of course, the state had always provided some support for firms of all kinds in tax breaks, subsidized loans of many kinds, and trading supports (Stoffaës, 1978, p. 538; Le Pors, 1976). But the prosperity strategy made the state more dependent on industrial performance while giving it less leverage over industrial decisions.

The transformation of the state into an agent for the private sector appears dramatically in the reversal of private sector loans from government. Between 1962 and 1972, government loans to businesses actually declined from 2.3 to 1.6 billion francs (Berger, 1980). The reversal began with Pompidou's economic strategy but, as we shall see, reached its full proportions with Giscard. Oddly enough, Pompidou only lived to see the worst repercussions of renewed prosperity: the serious shocks and scandals of land speculators and developers that helped erode his reputation.

Consequences

Giscard's victory in 1974 marks a third major turning point in the political assumptions underlying French economic policy. Again the policy approach suggests that the alleged unanimity and forcefulness of French politics under a domineat party system can be easily exaggerated. Giscard had been at odds with the Gaullists over some fundamental economic issues every since he was minister of finance in 1962. His neoliberal economic principles led him to suspect high public spending even if directed at laudable national goals such as defense, and he felt that the *étatiste* tendencies of Gaullist industrial and labor policies would inhibit free competition. The old rivalry between the Ministry of Finance and the CGP, itself a spending booster, weighed heavily in his judgment. Indeed, before becoming president, Giscard noted in 1973 that "Planning is inflation" (Hall, 1981, p. 132). Though his presidency continued the coalition of Gaullists and Republicans, Giscard could hardly have differed more from the Gaullist strategy and practice of economic policymaking. These differences were basic to the open break with Chirac in 1976.

The change was most visible in the radical departure of the planning process. In 1975, Giscard created a National Planning Council with himself as chairman, an obvious tactic to permit his office to dominate the CGP (Green, 1978a). The Seventh Plan (1975–80) was prepared in five months, and the mathematical wizardry so laboriously applied to the future in earlier plans was simply cast aside. The plan was no more that twenty-five priority programs (PAP or *programmes d'action prioritaire*) which are clearly much more easily manipulated for political purposes than an intricate master plan giving the CGP and the ministries wide margins of discretion in using new credits and designing implementation. The Eighth Plan (1981–85) is, of course, under revision by the Socialist government, but Giscard could hardly have given his opponents a simpler task, for the plan barely exists. Actually published after the planning period began, it is no more that twelve new PAPs with no monetary values assigned to them. Relations with the CGP became so bad that the director of the planning commission, Michel Albert, wrote the president (later leaked to *Le Canard Enchainé*, September 10, 1980) complaining that the plan had been turned into a letter of recommendation for the government itself (Hall, 1981, p. 42).

Reacting strongly to Socialist proposals for increased public spending and unemployment relief (see Reading 4-5), Giscard chose Chirac's replacement as prime minister, Barre, largely because of his economic expertise. Anticipating the resurgence of neoliberal and monetarist economic policy in Britain and the United States, Barre produced his own "Plan" in 1976 to restore international stability of the franc and industrial competition (see Reading 4-6). For a country that imports about two-thirds of its oil and coal, the economy was among the worst hit in Europe by the 1973 oil crisis. Whatever the weaknesses of Barre's political logic, he managed to turn three years of trade deficits into a surplus by 1978 and to increase exports by 25 percent (Green, 1981). In 1978, a major step toward freeing the marketplace was taken by removing wholesale price controls.

But the political implications of fiscal conservatism provide the link between Giscard's delicate political strategy and economic policy. While hoping to avoid Gaullist state control, it proved virtually impossible to shed the official commitments to both the public and private sectors. A distinguished Senator (Bonnefous, 1980) pointed out that there were more publicy run firms in France in 1974 than in 1970. Emergency plans for steel and other badly hit companies were costing the government about 30 billion francs a year. Bonnefous charged the government with "nationalization by stealth" (1980), but there were (and are) few alternatives to heavy subsidization of declining industries and massive public services. Even more embarrassing to Giscard's political allies was the failure to move investments and credits rapidly into more competitive firms. What was hoped to be a high-powered interministerial committee to increase competition among industries with a promise for growth (Comité interministériel pour l'aménagement des structures industrielles or CIASI) soon acquired the nickname "infirmary" for the number of ailing firms supported by its subsidized loans. Its failure was admitted in 1979 when a new committee (Comité de développement des industries stratigiques or CODIS) was created in the Ministry of Industry to channel funds directly into preselected firms. Quite apart from the social costs of the neoliberal strategy, it appealed to neither the Right or the Left, and left Giscard vulnerable to a cautious and uncoordinated array of small and medium-sized firms (see Berger and Piore, 1980). The strategy connected with the persons whom Giscard hoped would reelect him in 1981, but at the price of infuriating the Gaullists and feeding political ammunition to the Socialists as the plan became mired in intergovernmental complexities and failed to produce results (see Lauber, 1981).

The Socialist plans for the economy were well worked out by the 1978 elections (see Reading 4-6) although the continued inflation and oil price increases made their strategy a more difficult one to implement. One of the more stinging compromises accepted by the Communists on entering the Mitterrand government was that the necessity of a mixed economy was clearly established. The two main prongs were increased: public spending and new nationalization. Like most governments before elections, Giscard and Barre had badly underestimated the deficit for 1981 and, in the early months of Socialist rule, the estimates steadily grew from double to triple the initial projection of 30 billion francs. Even so, if the deficit approaches 100 billion francs, a perpetually cautious France will be financing debts of about 2 percent of the national product, only half the level of West Germany in 1981. The first revised budget of July 1981 added 35 billion francs to pay for increased social benefits (see Chapter 6), inescapable increased unemployment relief, and youth job programs. In doing so, Mitterrand made clear that low interest loans to businesses, exemption for increased social security charges, and a variety of employment subsidies would help the private sector (Fabra, 1981).

Nationalization was, of course, the politically controversial reform, but both the realities of the subjected industries and the methods to acheive nationalization make the change less partisan than it might appear. In effect, the French government would control about 20 percent of the industrial investment in France, and its control over production would make a modest increase from 16 to 20 percent of the total. Nearly all banking was to be nationalized, but about half of French banking had been nationalized after World War II, and the intricate workings of public investment banks meant that policies between public and private banks in France had been interlocked for many years. In the large armament firms, Matra and Dessault, there is an obvious rationale for nationalization, as in the case of steel where 40 percent of the debts were held by the government in any event. Of the eleven industrial groups being nationalized, the most controversial were naturally the more profitable groups in chemicals and electronics. In these cases, it is well to recall that Sweden, Britain, and Germany have all experimented with devices to link private management to public interest. There is no reason to think that the French experiment of full control will be less satisfactory, especially if we take into account the continued insistence of Mauroy, the prime minister, and others that nationalization does not relieve firms of sound financial management. Renault, nationalized in 1945, is one of the leading auto producers of Europe.

Both Mitterrand and Mauroy took special care to reassure the private sector that the rapidity of nationalization was intended to remove uncertainties, and that a prolonged nationalization process was likely to be more discouraging to private investment and confidence. In the intricate world of private and public interests in France, the change is not quite as dramatic as painted by partisan interests. In 1974, nearly a third of the heads of private banks were former civil servants, as were about 40 percent of the heads of nationalized industries. Though obviously controversial, the interlocking organization of business and government is not new to France. In fact, the haste with which nationalization proceeded caused some consternation within Socialist ranks because there was little time to prepare accompanying reforms to extend worker participation and to link the transition to unions at lower levels of government (*Le Monde*, July 15, 1981). To more progressive groups within the Party, rapid nationalization looked oddly similar to the arbitrary and centralized decisions of an earlier Gaullist epoch.

As for planning, the envied French accomplishment seems to have run full circle. Like so many policy instruments, it was accepted by the Gaullists more because it was there in 1958 than because they had some special use for it. Captured by the technocrats, it was left to Pompidou to liberate private interests from its growing tentacles and to launch the policy of growth and prosperity which he thought could reconcile growing social demands with increased public spending. In the third cycle, Giscard and Barre virtually rejected planning, faltered on the immense obstacle of increased energy costs, and were defeated by the inability of private investment to respond quickly enough to their neoliberalism. In the most recent changes, the Socialist policies often seem like Keynesian economics come home to roost, but the minister of finance, Delors, is no less determined than earlier ministers to defend the franc and to control inflation. Of course, there is no worse time to start planning than in a depression and, within the Mitterrand government, Rocard, the new minister for planning, was Mitterrand's chief rival for the presidency. The two-year revision is only another of a series of abrupt changes that have derailed French planning in the past. It continues the trend toward increased politicization of the plan as changing political strategies dictate both goals and methods. Even the Socialists have given the plan a new political twist by proposing a subsequent four year plan (1984–88) because it coincides with the presidential term (*Le Monde*, July 14, 1981). Given the inflationary pressures on the French economy in 1981, it is not surprising that the Intermediate Plan adopted in early 1982 only provides a broad perspective on Socialist economic goals and has no precise economic targets or estimates (Ministry of Planning, 1982).

As one of the strongest economies in Europe in 1981, it is difficult to fault French economic policymaking for failing to acheive material success in a bewilderingly complex world economy. The politics of economic policymaking have much to do with the ability of the French to redirect both approaches and goals. Even if the French government is a dominant party coalition over most of the period considered, it was constantly reshaping the machinery of economic policymaking. Compared to many European economies and Japan (Pempel, 1981), even the government's economic objectives changed remarkably. In this respect, the political importance may well be how dramatic were the changes while working within a single political framework. As we shall explore further in the Conclusion (see Chapter 8), perhaps economic adaptation was stimulated by the institutional uncertainties about which the French so often complain. The Socialist victory in 1981 also demonstrated that economic adversity can be used to make important institutional changes. The French have not only practiced good economics in the pure sense, but they have politicized economic policymaking in ways that help relieve more fundamental political doubts about French democracy.

Readings

4-1. THE PROSPECTS IN 1958*

De Gaulle relied heavily on Jacques Rueff for economic advice, and the president constituted a special committee under Rueff shortly after taking office. While this description of the economic choices facing France sounds familiar today, in 1958 Rueff's concern about inflation's destabilizing social and economic effects contrasts sharply with the concerns of much of Europe at the time. Most important, Rueff's advice is laced with concern for France's economic capabilities and international position, a nationalist economic policy that naturally led him to reflect on Germany's highly controlled economy under Hitler. (Rueff had been advocating stabilization since first advising Poincaré in 1926.) The elements of his advice can be traced throughout the Fifth Republic and were a constant source of tension between the Ministry of Finance and other, equally nationalist, impulses of Gaullists to spend more for defense, industrial support, and urban public works.

France's Promise and Needs

France is entering a new phase of its history. Rising fertility rates will soon make it a young, forward-looking nation, once more

*From *Rapport sur la situation financière,* Paris, Imprimerie Nationale, 1958, written for the president and contained in Jacques Rueff, *Combats pour l'Ordre Financier,* Paris, Plon, 1972, pp. 171–248 (selections).

suited to its greatest destiny. Already, through its unprecedented economic expansion, France has created the instrument of its own renewal. But France's accomplishments fail to approach those which its responsibilities impose on it.

For the nation to merely maintain its present level of infrastructure, schools, housing construction, and job creation for an increased population would require enormous investments.

However, to do only this, France would fall far short of its mission. To accomplish this in the coming years, France must:

—Develop the Sahara.
—Raise the standard of living of the population who have just asked for its renewed support and confidence.
—Modernize its weapons.
—Enlarge and transform its energy capacity in order to benefit from technical progress.
—Pursue the modernization and development of its productive apparatus in agriculture, industry and commerce.
—Increase support for scientific research.
—Perfect medical and hospital services.
—Promote social mobility by all appropriate means.

At the same time, France has a primary responsibility to relieve its housing shortage which undermines the social structure, introduces barriers to the free movement of manpower—injurious to technical progress—and inflicts cruel and unjust suffering on large classes of the population, making them irreconcilable adversaries of the social order.

For many years, all France's problems will be problems of investment. The nation will only be able to seize its present chance if it solves these problems—not to the point of sluggishness or decadence, but with a liberality commensurate to the task and the magnificent benefits it will accomplish.

The "Affliction" of French Finances: Inflation

Since the Liberation, France has heard the voice of its destiny. While the nation nursed the wounds inflicted on it by World War II and carried out its generous policy to favor population growth, it also expanded infrastructure, generating an unprecedented postwar expansion. France desired and, in large measure, made the investments which these circumstances required.

But except for rare and short intervals, the nation failed to obtain the resources necessary to succeed in this effort by the direct appropriation of income. The excess of expenses over revenues resulted in numerous public or private deficits, generally resolved by recourse to the Treasury [debt].

The quasi-permanent crisis in French public finances since the Liberation is only a symptom of this disequilibrium. But its financial aspect often disguises a more profound and serious economic disequilibrium. To say that the Treasury's expenditures outweigh total resources, which it obtains through taxation or borrowing, is to say that the income which it creates through public spending puts its beneficiaries in a position to levy a proportion of the national production above the level which tax payments or public loans might have prevented. By increasing aggregate demand, the deficit creates demand for goods which do not exist.

The excess of aggregate demand over the value (calculated at market prices) of national production can be used at home or abroad. Used domestically, it provokes expansion if underemployment exists or raises prices if the contrary is the case, but in general produces both, at least if the means of production are not being utilized to the fullest extent possible. Used abroad, the surplus buying power creates a deficit in the balance of payments, thereby exhausting foreign reserves.

In fact, inflation and the depletion of foreign reserves are indissolubly linked. One could show that if only one of them occurred, it would tend to give rise to the other. French and foreign experience permits the conclusion that the loss of foreign reserves and price rises are two manifestations of the same phenomenon: the existence of a disequilibrium between purchasing power and the value of goods to buy.

France has demonstrated the ineluctable force of this process. Its experience has proven that all administrative initiatives which tend to stimulate exportation—no matter how ingenious—cannot restore a balance of payments equilibrium menaced by inflation. The French experience shows that however desirable growth may be, when it springs from inflation, it is limited by the problem of foreign payments and, therefore, only leaves a choice between import controls, which generate unemployment, and the humiliating search for new foreign support.

At the same time, because inflation differentially affects prices, it provokes grave and often irremediable distortions in the structure of production. It stimulates the production of goods whose prices adjust rapidly to increases in purchasing power and discourages the production of goods and services whose prices—due to regulation or longstanding practice—follow such increases slowly or not at all.

Although less serious, an analogous situation has been observed in other sectors, notably those with controlled or regulated prices. This points up the difficulty, if not the impossibility, of escaping from inflation under an inflationary regime.

Socially, inflation leads to intolerable inequities, despite precautions to compensate for its effects. Indeed, the essence of the inflationary process are mechanisms of taxing revenues which cannot keep pace with price levels (as with rents) or only catch up slowly (as with salaries). The enhanced buying power resulting from inflation is thus withheld from those social groups that are dependent upon rents or salaries for incomes. But when taxes are matched with exemptions based on progressive rates which tend to vary their effects by earning capacity, antiinflation measures are blind and hit hardest those who should be protected. They create a profound and legitimate resentment on the part of the victimized social classes. For them, reforms and political pressure become the only instruments to defend their standard of living.

Although experience has taught us that an excess buying capacity can be neutralized by controls, price controls depend on import controls characteristic of Dr. Schacht's policy under Hitler's economic system. To restrain massive buying power outside the market, these practices necessarily led to surgical operations, along the lines of German monetary reform and, at great damage to individuals, reserve buying power is frozen, either by price increases as in France after the war, or through temporary suppression of purchasing power to repress its effects.

Therefore, the choice offered to the government is simple: either the establishment of an equilibrium between the nation's expenditures and revenues, or recourse to methods of rationing and authoritarian controls which will inevitably lead to profound political changes.

4-2. THE POLITICAL MEANING OF THE PLAN*

Possibly the greatest error one can make in interpreting French plans is to think of them as primarily economic exercises. As noted, they have changed format, objectives, scope, and seriousness of purpose over the years. This essay by an anonymous, but clearly well-placed French commentator outlines the diverse political forces within government, between the prime minister and other ministers and, by no means least, the activity of the Planning Commission itself to preserve its influence. Although the Plan as such lost much of its importance under Giscard, he, too, continued to give it publicity and was able to shape its activity to the political aims of the president.

The French Plan is a complex institution which the foreign observer may, with good reason, find surprising in that it appears to be more a vast pedagogical venture than an accurate or efficient tool for shaping economic policy. And yet it does, all the same, play an essential part in the direction of the economy. The study of administration has, up to now, shown scant interest in the working of the Plan, and in the tensions and interplay of forces it brings out. There are, of course, various reasons for this, primarily the fact that those who have an inside knowledge of its workings are faithful disciples of the Plan: they believe in it and sing its virtues, thus making a critical analysis of the institution somewhat difficult. As for the economists, they are not greatly interested in the politics and the administration of the Plan. So I should like to make certain remarks about the nature of the Plan, the political role assigned to it, and also its administrative and political ambiguity. It is not a question of theorizing but, on the basis of my personal experience, of laying down some principal guidelines for critical thought. I shall not be concerned with the familiar procedural machinery for drawing up the Plan or the methods of French-style indicative planning.

I should perhaps first try to answer this basic, too-neglected but essential question: "What is the Plan?" It is an attempt to control development, to give it direction, to fashion, artificially, a suitable time span for action which overshadows and embraces that of the limited, small-scale plans of businessmen or consumers. In this

*Anonymous, "Letters from Across the Channel: II French Economic Planning," *Public Administration* (UK) 5 (Summer 1973): 185–92 (selections). Footnotes have been deleted.

sense, the Plan sets itself against individual calculation, for example, speculation on monetary depreciation or income anticipation; it also confronts the temporality of the unforeseen snags which necessitate a "revision" of the Plan, as well as profound psychological changes, such as shifts in consumer or wage-earner's behavior, which cannot be taken into account at the planning level; finally, it stands up against the inertia of the traditional system. The Plan attempts the substitution of clear, well-defined ideas for a highly complex reality; unfortunately, these ideas are neither clear nor well-defined. The notion of what constitutes an objective is very ambiguous; it is an imposed connection between various elements of calculation, a forecasting margin of error, and not a quantifiable objective of any real validity. The Plan makes use of convenient fictions; likely to catch the imagination, but based on working hypotheses which are, for the most part, inaccessible to the uninitiated. A percentage rate of growth is essentially a fictional notion, and the revision of the national accounting in 1968 clearly showed this to be so.

The Plan, therefore, encounters three kinds of limitation: the individual or personal; "temporality" (it has to work in a given span of time); and the obstacles presented by the functioning of the traditional system. Hence the word "plan" contains, in current usage, three quite distinct notions: "constraining objectives" to be respected, which are, in fact, theoretical; the "article of faith" (*fiducia*)—either one "believes" in the Plan or one does not; and a logical programmed vision of affairs, virtually a methodological system of thought geared to a period of ten to fifteen years ahead. Now there is considerable overlapping between these three theoretical notions and each one of them encounters its instinctive opponents, trade unions, antiplanning notables, administrators who feel threatened by the Plan. There are sharp conflicts within the Plan and, therefore it is, of necessity, a compromise. There are vested interests, the strength of the traditional system, and an arbitrary reaction against a theoretical apparatus. Some reject the constraints imposed by a consistent set of choices; others are worried by the French intellectual tendency to elaborate Cartesian patterns, whereas the realities of economic life are quite different; and others remain in the past, and readily repudiate an open, forward-looking outlook, unable to understand why they are asked to consider what will be happening in 1980 or 1985, by which time they themselves will no longer be there to see it. The planners must, therefore, use guile and their choices are, of necessity, evasive and simulated. For example, the choices between social requirements and financial limitations, between technical advance and the freedom of enterprise, between investment in leading growth industries or in the public sector, are deferred, evaded. In the very nature of things, it is the prerogative of the Plan to carry out the necessary task of interpreting this absence of choice. Therein lies its principal political function, the relevance of the element of faith it comprises.

And so thoughts about the politics of the Plan must lead to an examination not of its objectives, which are relative, subject to variation within a forecasting margin of error, and so on, but rather of the constraining factors upon which it has no power to act, where decisions have already been made, and which fall outside its terms of reference. The very useful thing about the Plan is perhaps that it stimulates thought about that which lies outside the scope of the Plan, which has not been programmed—the "nonplan." Therefore, whatever the perfectionist ambitions of the planners, the unplanned areas are extremely important. Even though the Fifth Plan tried to extend its borders into unfamiliar areas, like local authority investment, wage increases, and saving, and even though the Sixth Plan is trying to move into quite new fields like working capital, it is in the nature of the Plan that it should not be all-embracing—as Alain said, "Foreseeing everything means putting up with everything" (*Tout prévoir, c'est tout subir*). If the Plan wants to achieve anything, it should not foresee everything; guile and compromise are necessary; it should be neither explosive nor aggressive. This is a rule of political wisdom, since the Plan is evidently the reflection of a divided society, uncertain of its objectives. This attempt to control the time factor, to devise a comforting, reassuring future— thereby satisfying the element of dream inherent in all policy—is no more than a desire, expressed in signs and words. It is not a tangible desire directly applicable to reality, implying obligation, albeit indirectly. It is a brittle desire, vague and incompletely formulated, based on the fiction of an open, malleable future, providing an escape from the constraints of day-to-day administration. The Plan, the expression of a will to power, is based on a number of convenient politically motivated conventions, of which one must be clearly aware. It is not a mathematical model but an expression of society's will to survive, a means of imposing a pattern on time.

The Plan is a method, among others, of bringing to light the essential elements of choice, but it cannot alone resolve the conflicts. It lacks a political dimension, political legitimacy, and the unions are, instinctively, quick to react with a feeling that the economic theorizing which they have allowed themselves to be drawn into is directed against their political role, their basic legitimacy, their freedom to oppose (*contestation*). The political theory of the Plan does not yet exist, but its corporative quasi-feudal roots would soon be apparent—producing a kind of latent conservatism due to the combined, and often contradictory, pressure of the various social and professional groups. The Plan is also a form of refusal of the present, favoring the past, of protection of vested interests. From one Plan to another, this intellectual *immobilisme* is apparent, even within the opposition shown to it. At bottom, there is no one so conservative as an expert or a group of experts (the expert has his intellectual routine, his habits of thought, and he brings to each Plan his desire to repeat exactly what he proposed, unsuccessfully, at the previous one). Often, the administration encourages this instinctive conservatism in the name of realism.

The analysis should no doubt be developed by looking at a typical commission such as social security benefits or education, to show how, on the pretext of innovation or reform, the old familiar lines are followed, how certain problems are taboo (for example, it is better to demand more teachers and avoid the question of curricula). Resistance to change takes some unexpected forms, and the intention (*presque-vouloir*) prudently takes over from the will (*vouloir*).

Need we go further? To reflect not on the technical but on the political and psychological limits of the Plan would no doubt lead to a certain skepticism about its operation: all the conflicts and uncertainties within it make the common interest hard to ascertain. Who has the right to declare, in the name of the common interest, that the interests of this or that professional group must be sacrificed for this common good. Who knows what will, or ought probably to be, sacrificed? The art of prediction is limited in this field; to what extent, and by what right, can decisions be taken by the expert forecaster? There is also the bias of the experts who are subject to prejudice and habits of thought. Reflections on the Plan should lead to reflection about deciding the common interest, which is distinct from the sum of individual interests, and about the legitimacy of the centers of economic decision-making. There is nothing so vague as the political philosophy of the common interest.

However, it seems that the traditional ministerial departments are acutely aware of these problems of the common interest and, after all, they are responsible for the administration of the common interest. Does not the Plan partly divest them of their basic responsibility? Is not the problem, then, to reintegrate the Plan into the work of the administrative departments, to get from them an internal, continuous planning "between Plans"? It is up to the ministries to do their planning, to have their groups of experts capable of collaboration in the drawing up of policy, to evaluate limiting factors and settle priorities. It is not a good thing to have planning in isolation from the day-to-day running of departments. At one moment the ministry (or head of division) is "playing the game," is cooperating with the planners, and at another moment it is not "playing the game," is opposing the Plan, without any consistency. Only serious internal planning, with a highly qualified staff, can ensure coherent programming, with the necessary periodical review, backed up by analytical studies of the system of budgetary programming (RCB) and of national sector accounting. It is the only way to ensure that the spirit of the Plan percolates down to the basic level of the *chef de bureau*. But because of a reverential awe of the Plan, no one has yet dared to develop this policy of internal departmental planning. This is one of the courses that should, however timidly, be embarked upon during the Sixth Plan.

Fundamentally, what needs to be feared in the Plan are good intentions, and the good faith involved. The planners are often good people who know nothing about the budget, the monetary system, the importance of the unions, free enterprise (that is, the desire to make money), individual hardship (for example, in the case of expropriation)—in short, people used to juggling with abstractions and amusing themselves with nominalist fictions. This is certainly a very sophisticated sort of administration, but it can be a dangerous one. There must be a limit to the ambitions of the Plan, which cannot do everything, cannot decide everything, and, above all, is not really responsible. Whether one likes it or not, the responsibility for overall economic equilibrium lies with the minister of the economy and finance, and it is hard to see how this responsibility can be shifted. Of course, some people benefit from this confusion, perhaps even the Ministry of Finance, but it is difficult to make this confusion and conflict into rules of conduct. But the administration lives on these necessary conflicts, which are surely signs of health.

We must accept the Plan as it is, with all its faults. It is essential to be aware of its political limits if one is to avoid being taken in by an appearance of rationality, by a certain mathematical perfectionism. As an article of faith (*fiducia*), the Plan is necessary and even useful to the extent that a certain consensus is created, where society is obliged to show an act of will (*vouloir*). But it is wise to remember that the Plan represents no more than an inclination (*presque-vouloir*) and by the nature of things an element of fiction enters into it.

4-3. SHIFTING THE COURSE OF ECONOMIC POLICY*

Following the May 1968 demonstrations, the government urgently requested a report from the economic expert, Montjoie, to assess the impact of the concessions and dislocations on the French economy and, in particular, necessary changes in the Fifth Plan. As in the past, the main concern was inflation and France had to devalue in 1969. Like the report done before the demonstrations, the emphasis is on increasing industrial productivity and competition. The adjustments recommended by Montjoie signal the departure from the étatiste methods of the early Fifth Republic, and open the way for a genuinely liberal economic policy, later pressed even further by Giscard. Not unlike conservative economists in Britain and the United States a decade later, the report favors a "supply-side" strategy that will hopefully avoid inflation, encourage private investment, and maintain a stable currency. The report covers a broad range of topics, including unemployment, growth of social benefits, national debt, and trade balances, but the focus is on the need to press even harder for industrial modernization.

*Montjoie Report, *Rapport sur les problèmes posés par l'adaptation du Ve Plan*, Planning Commission, September, 1968.

The Proposed Strategy

During the next few years, contradictory policy objectives must be reconciled. The maintenance of full employment, improvement in the equality of life and the pursuit of public priorities justify the drive for economic growth. But continued expansion cannot be achieved without strengthening foreign trade—and hence, the competitiveness of our companies.

Only a policy of increasing productivity to catch up with increasing production costs will allow us to reconcile these diverse objectives. While continuing to carefully monitor wage and price levels, a greater emphasis must be placed on productivity gains.

This is why the proposed strategy aims at accelerating [the economic] transformation through growth, thus using to advantage the recent shock to the French economy in order to create a climate favorable to rapid expansion and the implementation of an energy policy. These measures would allow firms to take advantage of increasing demand and provide incentives to their modernization and restructuring while, at the same time, protecting those who may be victims of such rapid change.

This strategy is based on the following three principles:

1. Rapid economic growth based on industrial competitiveness meets certain conditions.

Three objectives can be met through development. The first is to insure full employment. To the extent that unemployment is not a structural inadaptation of the labor supply to the labor market, but rather an overall imbalance in the labor market, only a general economic expansion can absorb it.

The second objective [favoring a growth policy] is to allow the development of business competitiveness. Sustained growth during the next two or three years can, in effect, be considered as both cause and consequence of large gains in productivity: a consequence, as it reveals unutilized production capacity within existing investments; a cause, as the utilization of existing personnel and equipment creates new productivity gains. Moreover, a climate of sustained growth is necessary to revive productive investment and to guarantee subsequent competitiveness.

The third objective is to facilitate the adaptation of businesses and their personnel. It is hardly necessary to point out that accelerated change has a completely different significance depending on whether it takes place in a context of diminishing employment opportunities, or an expanding labor market. Growth cannot substitute for an active manpower policy, but it can lower such a policy's cost and increase its effectiveness.

However, certain limits to the projected growth rate must be considered. First, too rapid development can compromise productivity gains. Whereas starting from a position of underemployment allows the utilization of productivity reserves, to systematically maintain full employment would lead to the use of technically and economically outmoded equipment and be limited by the qualitative inadequacies of our manpower.

Second, economic and social ramifications must be taken into account. Along with the progressive utilization of reserve capacity and the manifestation of pressures on the labor market, inflationary pressure on wages and prices, characteristic of labor shortages (*suremploi*), will reappear. French experience in this regard is so clear that further comment is unnecessary.

The maintenance of our external balance of payments imposes another limit to rapid growth; it should not be compromised in the present to assure future competitiveness. The drain on foreign reserves temporarily provoked by increased imports, a result of accelerated growth, must remain within reasonable limits. Certainly, France still has large reserves, but given possible capital transfers, our room for manpower is very limited.

Finally, economic growth must essentially be based on the modernization, adaptation, conversion, and enhanced competitiveness of our firms. The experiences in 1962–63 and at the beginning of the Fifth Plan, demonstrate that a policy of support for, and stimulation of the economy based on demand runs the risk that the latter is satisfied by increasing imports. Given the present situation of our foreign commerce and balance of payments, a flight of capital would not only threaten the effectiveness of these measures but might also create an obstacle to their implementation by producing an unacceptable drain on foreign reserves. On the contrary, the proposed strategy aims at promoting expansion only to the extent that restored business competitiveness is consistent with other elements making up demand. Therefore we favor supply—induced rather than demand-induced growth—not merely growth for its own sake, but a policy of growth fueled by productive investment and exportation.

2. Business modernization must be the state's responsibility.

Here we will consider only two aspects of the state's role: the improvement of business [profit] margins and protection against foreign competition.

Business profit margins are the outcome of complex forces acting on the distribution of surplus value: competitive pressures on prices, wages, and so on, of which state fiscal burdens are only one element. As recently decided, action aimed at improving the profit margins of businesses directly subject to international competition may become necessary, whether through granting public investment aid or more generally by reinforcing our industry's competitiveness in foreign markets.

The choice of expansion made possible by the supply side and not "pulled" by demand does not entirely rule out the risk that the growth of internal demand may result in excessive recourse to importation. Failing the imposition of quotas or taxation on imports, it would be tempting to resort to fiscal measures more acceptable to our trading partners. Thus, the idea of lowering charges on industry, while increasing the value-added tax. In any case, the effect of such measures on prices and public finances should be carefully considered before they are adopted.

3. Workers must also be protected against the consequences of rapid change.

It is unnecessary to insist upon the fundamental importance of this condition. Measures designed to meet this condition are taken up in a special chapter devoted to employment policy and professional training.

4-4. INDUSTRIAL AND BUDGETARY PROPOSALS OF THE COMMON PROGRAM*

Although the Common Program of the Communists, Socialists, and Radical Socialists did not survive until the 1978 elections, it represents an enormous achievement in reconciling the diverse eco-

---

*Parti Socialisti, Parti Communiste et Mouvement des Radicaux de Gauche, *Programme Commune de Gouvernement,* Paris, Flammarion, 1973 (selections).

nomic objectives of the Left. The program of industrial nationalization was one of the most controversial components of the program and its implementation proved to be a major stumbling block in revising the program in 1977, eventually leading to its dissolution. In addition, the Common Program foresaw major changes in tax policies which are outlined in some detail. The combined effect was to reverse the growing strength of the parties of the Left in the legislative elections.

The Democratization and Expansion of the Public Sector

To smash the domination of large capital concentration and to institute a new social and economic policy—a break from present policy—the [Socialist—Communist] government will progressively transfer to the people the principal means of production and financial institutions now in the hands of the dominant capitalist groups.

The public sector will be extended, democratized, and restructured. Nationalized industries, granted a high degree of autonomy in management, will be obliged to act in accordance with the National Plan. Changes in property law will allow workers to acquire management responsibilities. When workers want such changes in accordance with the government, new management structures will define the conditions for worker intervention in the designation of administrative councils, the organization of work, personnel management, and relations with the Plan.

Along with nationalization, collective appropriation will assume various forms: mixed public-private firms (*sociétés d'économie mixte*), cooperatives, mutual benefit societies, local public services, and so on.

The first session of the legislature will reach a minimum level of nationalization. The transfer to public ownership must focus on the entire banking and financial sector, and those industrial and investment groups which occupy a strategic position in key economic sectors:

—Firms fulfilling essential public services.
—Companies dependent on public funds.
—The main centers of capitalist accumulation which monopolize most sectors of production, thereby reducing competition.
—Firms controlling sectors essential to the development of the nation's economy.

Crossing this minimal threshold should permit us to limit and to circumscribe monopolistic influence while leaving an important private sector.

Restructuring the productive apparatus should be progressively and flexibly accomplished, according to an industrial policy that is adapted to technical and social necessities and that takes into account the international character of economic life. Nationalization must not be bureaucratization (*étatisation*). Further nationalizations will be geared to economic development and the needs of the masses to be determined as they take larger responsibilities. When workers want their firm to be nationalized or to enter the public sector, the government will propose this to Parliament.

Nationalization will involve the entire banking and financial sector, specifically:

—All commercial and deposit banks. Foreign banks will be supervised by the Bank of France to insure they do not work against the objectives of the Plan or the new economic policy.

—All other financial establishments, such as housing finance companies.

—Large private insurance companies.

The laws for the mutual and cooperative credit banks will be democratized.

The principal credit agencies (Crédit National, Institut de Développement Industriel, financial agencies depending on industry, and parts of the Caisse des Dépôts) will be regrouped in a National Investment Bank which will be in charge of financing a large part of the Plan goals and of industrial development.

Public involvement will be structured in order to assure a dynamic management of their part of the public inheritance. In industry, a minimum extension of the public sector will achieve nationalization of the following sectors:

—In their totality, natural resources, armaments, space and aeronautics, and nuclear and pharmaceutical industries.

—The greater part of the electronics, computer, and chemical industries.

To implement these aims, the government will nationalize the following industrial groups:

—Dessault [aircraft]; Roussel-Uclaf [pharmaceuticals]; Rhône-Poulenc [chemicals].

—ITT-France [computers]; Thomson-Brandt [electrical]; Honeywell-Bull [computers]; Pechiney-Uginè-Kuhlmann [chemicals]; Saint-Gobain-Pont-à-Mousson [not labeled]; Compagnie Générale d'Electricité [electrical].

The responsibilities of public power will take the form of stockholding, possibly up to a controlling share in:

—Steel and oil (Usinor-Vallourec, Wendel-Sidélor, Schneider, Compagnie Française des Pétroles-CFOR-Total).

—Air and sea transport, the treatment and distribution of water, the finance telecommunications, and autoroute concessions.

The government will actively support the national firms of Renault, E.O.F., and the Commissariat à l'Energie Atomique in their foreign and domestic commercial activities.

The democratic government will develop measures designed to protect the interests of small stockholders. Shareholders in expropriated firms will be justly compensated according to an essential distinction between small and moderate investors living on their savings, and large capital holders.

4-5. THE FRENCH ECONOMY UNDER BARRE*

In 1976, Barre instituted a "plan" to stabilize the French economy. The turbulence of the world economy, especially soaring oil prices, meant that his plan was frequently adjusted. In many respects, his policies were a more determined effort to pursue the goals pronounced in the later 1960s: a strong franc, a favorable trade balance, and increased productivity. However, inflation remained at ten percent or more, and unemployment increased rapidly. His profound liberal convictions were displayed when he removed wholesale price controls in 1978 despite all these economic uncertainties. There were constant rumors that the president would dismiss his prime minister before the 1981 elections in order to distance himself from this checkered record, but Barre remained. The Economist *assesses his record from 1976 to 1979.*

When President Giscard d'Estaing, on August 25th three years ago, named Mr. Raymond Barre prime minister of France, in place of Mr. Jacques Chirac, he introduced the new premier as "France's

*Economist, "Three Years of Barre," August 25, 1979.

best economist." Mr. Barre's job was to restore an economy badly shaken by the 1973 oil crisis and mismanagement thereafter. His priorities were to beat inflation, close a gaping trade deficit and stabilise the franc. Mr. Barre, formerly an EEC commissioner, gave himself three years to do the job. That deadline is now here, and virtually none of the specific goals set in what became known as the Barre plan has been achieved.

Mr. Barre has failed to pull inflation appreciably below the 10% level which he inherited in 1976. Worse, the 1979 figure, which he once boasted would be 8% and falling, will jump beyond 11%. The trade balance, coaxed into a 2 billion francs ($450m) surplus last year by a creditable export effort, is sliding back into a deficit likely to reach 10 billion francs this year. Unemployment, just over 900,000 when Mr. Barre took office, has surged to 1.4 m (some 6% of the work force), and will rise further. Economic growth is dipping below the modest 3% which the government reluctantly accepted as a minimum target this year, with 2% in view for 1980. To sustain a modicum of growth, the country, which at one time regarded government deficits as original sin (though recently it has regularly had them), will accept a bonanza hole of 40 billion francs in the budget for 1980. About the only area where Mr. Barre can claim success is the currency, which has held fairly firm since 1976, apart from inevitable slippage against the D-mark.

No wonder that the unions are promising a hot rentrée—they actually held a rail strike this week, and the socialist confederation is calling for "massive" joint action with the communist one—and that one point in Mr. François Mitterrand's call for renewed unity on the left is to block the Barre plan, while Mr. Chirac and his neo-Gaullists, supposed allies of the government, are licking their chops and calling for expansion.

Mr. Barre is justified in blaming oil prices for his failure, but only up to a point. He was well off course before the latest bad news about oil landed. In the past three years, the French have not been obliged to make serious sacrifices. Real living standards have been permitted to rise by at least 2% annually even while Mr. Barre was talking tough. Only now has he finally decided to freeze them—he says.

Yet any judgment on Mr. Barre must take into account more than the unimpressive economic figures. He has presided over an extraordinary change in French economic life: its release from the smothering embrace of the state. In the past year price controls, which had wrapped the whole system in a protective but counter-dynamic cocoon since 1945, have been lifted in most business sectors. The hope was to raise profits and encourage investment, thus modernising industry and giving it competitive rein. Liberalisation also meant the restructuring of industry, the choking of lame ducks and the streamlining of sectors long padded by the state's indulgence, often granted for questionable political reasons instead of sound business ones.

The policy is right for France, putting it on the same footing as its main rival and trading partner, West Germany. But is is naturally taking time to bite. The scrapping of price controls has not opened the sluice-gates to inflation as hidebound dirigistes predicted, but it is causing uncontrollable inflationary bubbles here and there, lately in foods. The steel crisis has indeed produced the necessary slimming (40,000 jobs gone or to go out of 150,000 two years ago) but at the price of bringing the industry effectively into state hands. Restructuring is lagging in other industries. Employers have not responded to Mr. Barre's goading and incentives for new investment: private-sector productive investment has been almost stagnant for five years, not even last year's right-wing victory in the parliamentary election having restored the confidence of business. For the left, the sight of the luxury liner France gliding out of Le Havre last week for refitting in more efficient West German shipyards epitomised the price some hard-hit regions are paying for Mr. Barre's liberalisation policy.

Even without Opec's latest blows (which will add some 20 billion francs to France's oil bill this year) Mr. Barre's timetable was optimistic: liberalisation could hardly work within three years of being first announced. But he was under political pressure: Mr. Giscard d'Estaing must run for re-election in early 1981. In any event, Mr. Barre's failure is relative: France is no worse off than several other western countries. So the president might reasonably judge it unfair to dump him now—and reaction abroad, probably unfavourable, would be apt to make France's economic problems worse.

But if Mr. Barre stays, can his policies remain unchanged? So far his reply to accusations of failure has been to press for more austerity. Left-wing and Gaullist proposals that the state should plough money directly into job-creating expansion have been derided as irresponsible. But acceptance of a larger-than-ever budget deficit suggests that the president at least sees the need for some stimulus. Neither man would want to (or should) yield to those who would like the apronstrings of nanny state retied. But both may find fiscal flexibility more expedient than unyielding loyalty to a battered plan.

4-6. THE SOCIALIST ECONOMIC PROGRAM*

Shortly before the 1978 elections, the Socialist Party estimated that its program would cost about 30 billion francs, most of which would be covered by an inflation-proofed national loan. The Party intended to increase the minimum wage (SMIC) by 200 francs a month, but promised that the increase would be paid by the state, not the employers. The Party also promised to relieve unemployment by creating nearly 400,000 jobs (half in the public sector) in 1978 and another 500,000 in 1979, while keeping inflation at 10 percent. In the following article, Mathieu, Le Monde's *economic correspondent, assesses the difficulties that these proposals might encounter.*

Avoiding the Dangers of Economic Recovery

Nine months after the Communist Party's publication of its version of the Common Program [PS-PCF 1972 agreement], and the day following the televised debate between Prime Minister Barre and Socialist leader Mitterrand, the spokesman for the Socialist Party presented his party's account of 1978 and 1979. With all the cards on the table, the ways in which the PS intends to apply the Common Program can be evaluated. The Party reaffirms its intention to adhere to financial standards advocated by Mitterrand since 1974.

The process has not been easy since the Socialist Executive Committee decision last month to support the two main unions in their claim for a minimum wage raise of 200 francs, despite the risk this could pose to many firms. The formula used by the PS to

*Gilbert Mathieu, "Eviter les périls de la relance," *Le Monde*, February 15, 1978.

integrate this decision into their program is a compromise between various ways of minimizing its possible inflationary consequences.

According to the plan, firms will see their social security contributions reduced in 1978 by 200 francs per employee, that is, nearly a quarter of fringe benefit expenditure. At the same time, the projected salary increases for moderate and high income groups will be more strictly regulated to limit the "accordion effect" from raising the minimum wage. Overall salary and contribution increases are set for 18 percent while the minimum wage will rise by 37 percent, so substantial increases will affect only those in the lower or lower-middle income ranges—involving 80 to 85 percent of the wage earners. In cases where these measures fail to save threatened industries, temporary aid will be granted while awaiting a general economic recovery to put them back on their feet.

But the spiraling cost of inflation is not the whole story. To avoid demand inflation resulting from wage rises for low income groups, the PS proposes temporary control on prices, preferably by the extension of exemptions to the value-added tax, thereby depriving the treasury of revenue while obliging it to contribute to social security to compensate for lowered business contributions. At the same time, the indexed [inflation-proofed] national loan proposed by the Socialist Party will probably be increased as a means of absorbing some excess purchasing power, while financing two-thirds of the budgetary deficit. The deposit limits in the national savings banks will be raised to allow their indexed interest rates to work to greatest advantage. Finally, fifteen billion francs are expected from taxes on capital and 125,000 large estates, and from a renewed campaign against tax fraud.

Thus revised to take into account the January decision, the Socialist proposal entails an increase in public spending and consumption on the order of 10 percent and 4.3 percent, respectively. Only a 2 percent rise in tax revenues is projected (far from the doubling of taxes predicted by Prime Minister Barre) and the plan relies on a large spontaneous progression in social security and tax revenues arising from the economic recovery.

Therefore, in this program the budgetary weapon is used to stimulate the economy, as is done in most major countries during the past eighteen months on the OECD's recommendation. This translates to a large additional budgetary deficit, mostly due to a reduction in business and social security contributions. Even so, the resulting deficit is less than that of West Germany, and the PS predicts a significantly lower deficit in 1979 owing to larger tax revenues arising from the recovery.

Comparison with the Communist Party's Proposal

In two years the Socialist Party expects a progressive restimulation of the economy from its policy, including a substantial decrease in unemployment rates. Projected growth under this program is set at 4.9 percent this year (higher than the OECD figure) and 5.6 percent in 1979. Starting this year, 390,000 jobs will be created (half in the public sector, half by natural expansion); 500,000 more jobs will be created in 1979, mostly through economic expansion. The total increase in consumption for this year is projected at 5.5 percent, and growth in the business investment rate at 5 percent (0.5 percent, according to the OECD). Of course, this recovery would stimulate imports more than exports (9.8 percent and 7 percent, respectively), so that our trade deficit would reach 18 billion francs in 1978, a level between that of 1976 and that of 1977.

These figures, situating France among the leading Western countries (but no more) bear no relation to the apocalyptic descriptions given daily by the majority coalition leaders. This is evident in the figures prepared for and used by Prime Minister Barre on last nights' televised debate—figures prepared eight days before the Socialists revealed their intentions. Not only this, but the majority bases its calculations on the Left already having come to power as of January 1, and attributes a number of projects to the Socialists that they have never recommended, systematically assigning maximum negative effects to their intentions and failing to take into account the financing and compensation proposed by the PS—all the while confusing public and private finances. In the end, one has to ask whether the majority leaders are talking about the same project as that presented today.

A comparison of the Socialist plan with Communist Party figures is more meaningful. The two parties have not adopted the same basis for calculation nor have they used the same years of reference. Beyond details in evaluation, comparison shows a difference in perspective on the desired rhythm and magnitude of economic stimulation. The Communist Party aims for a significantly higher growth rate which most logically—despite good intentions—aggravates inflation and worsens the commercial deficit. This is especially true because of the PCF projects less business investment than the Socialist Party and much higher household consumption, while also hoping for a lowered rate of inflation.

Three Wagers

The Socialists' figures are much more realistic, although overly optimistic on certain points:

1) Can inflation be kept under 10 percent if, for fiscal reasons, exemption from the value-added tax are limited to certain products? This will depend on the vigilance of price control—and unions and consumers—in abiding by the temporary controls. If successful, difficulties may appear later, when controls are lifted.

2) Will firms delay reacting to the surge in popular consumption by investing? If they act as they did in 1968, the Socialists will win their bet on investment. But if, out of fear of the future, financial difficulties, or a wait-and-see attitude, firms delay in buying equipment, a production bottleneck could develop between a heightened demand and barely increased production. This would influence prices and the budgetary deficit. It is regrettable that the PS did not publish a financial overview of businesses in their global account to give a better understanding of their financial capacities and the projected slump in self-financing (*autofinancement*).

3) Finally, it is not apparent that the foreign trade deficit can be kept below its 1976 limit if rapid growth is achieved immediately. The Socialist Party has claimed that, as in the good old days, consumption in France will not rise more than twice the rate of expansion. This is an average figure; there is no guarantee it can be applied to extremes. The PS anticipates that France will explain to its Common Market partners why it must restrict certain imports, while accomplishing industrial conversion in conjunction with nationalizations to produce a commercial recovery. But we have known for many years that European negotiations are very slow and never seem to end.

Reality can thus offer many corrections to flaws in the Socialist program—without, however, invoking the bleak picture of economic disorder depicted by the majority. Economic recovery, whatever the risks, would bring enormous advantages for employment, the quality of life, stimulation of investment, and industrial restructuring. This is what the Left wants in order to finance its social projects and rejuvenate the national economy. Ten years ago, when the majority congratulated itself on its economic performance without excessive inflation, it saw a noble design. Why this sudden protest against political leaders who try again to release France from the fatality of "stagflation"?

For all that, if the program's chances for success and its risks are to be measured, it would be wrong to focus on the economic section. Reflection on the project for a new society should have a broader scope.

5 Industrial Relations: In Search of Compromise

The relations between government, business, and unions constitute one of the most intense debates about French policymaking. The intensity of the debate often obscures substantial reforms in areas of industrial and labor relations, and is fired by the multiple uncertainties confronting all three parties. Indeed, the political rhetoric reached new heights over the past two decades as many of the most important reforms were being made. Contrary to the common image of the Gaullists as the ruthless oppressors of the labor movement, there have, in fact, been more efforts to open new links between business and labor over the past twenty years than ever before. Given Gaullist economic and social objectives, it was essential that workers and employers cooperate. As we shall see, many of the most important concessions to workers are, in fact, the result of strong government pressure to extract compromises from business.

Gaullist determination to modernize the economy and to stimulate production made them inescapably vulnerable to working-class demands. As in the case of local and regional reform, they were the victims of their own ambitious programs. Historically, the labor movement had been as divided and weak as political parties, so the least conflictive course would have been simply to let unions languish. But many of the factors contributing to weak union organization also contributed to the general economic and social weaknesses of France: the patriarchal and cautious management of many businesses; the small scale of many firms; the ineffficient market structure; and the neglected industrial infrastructure. If the Gaullists and their successors hoped to modernize the economy (see Chapter 4), they could not avoid increasing the power of unions and workers generally.

While it would be misleading to suggest that the Gaullists or Giscardians wanted to increase union power, there has been an energetic effort over the past twenty years to remove the institutional uncertainties plaguing industrial relations. This exercise is crucial to the argument of the book in several ways. First, the fragility and instability of political institutions meant that government could not rely on parties and the legislature to construct new relationships. Even if French unions did not harbor deep suspicions over involvement in politics, there was little reason why any strong organization should look to the National Assembly for help. In this respect, the experience of the French labor movement is virtually opposite the British experience where the Labour Party and the Trades Union Congress have no choice but to ally forces and, when in power, can rely on statutory changes to advance the interests of the working class.

Second, a weak labor movement is, in many ways, less well-suited to the tasks of industrial modernization than a strong movement (Dubois et al., 1978). With only about a fourth of French workers organized in unions, it is an open question whether Gaullist aims were more threatened by conservative businessmen or by the weaknesses of unions. One cannot build institutions unless people are organized. There were no possibilities of pursuing the German strategy of relying on parapublic institutions to regulate labor-management relations. Except for the Communist-controlled union (CGT), the multiparty structure and the internal divisions of the Left made alignment with parties difficult.

Despite the political emotions aroused by strikes, the divisive ideology of the French working class, and the daring experiments in worker-ownership, the real threat to the Fifth Republic was that institutional ambiguities would only produce a stalemate. Harassed by reactionairies in their own ranks and rebuffed by the historic suspicion of government among workers, the most surprising result is that the Gaullists were able to make as much progress as they did. In doing so, their delicate task was to persuade both employers and workers that their well-being inextricably interlocks in the modern industrial state.

Context

The weakness of French labor unions is not simply a function of employer malevolence, but involves several critical choices of the early unions, the stormy history of the left-wing parties, and the relatively late emergence of France as an industrial power. Well before the turn of the century, the more advanced British unions were deeply involved in providing benefits for workers, while in Germany and Sweden the unions were strong supporters of a growing Social Democratic party. But the political uncertainties of the Third Republic left little room for unions, although a law of 1884 gave them the right to organize and is still regarded as the charter of the labor movement. Although militant unions developed in France in the late nineteenth century, they were confined to the relatively concentrated areas of industrialization. The political turbulence of the Third Republic inhibited the growth of unions. The CGT was only formed in 1895.

A second handicap was that like most continental unions, the CGT was deeply involved in the bitter internal rivalries of the Communist International, and generally subscribed to the view that any participation in a *bourgeois* state would only delay a proletarian revolution. The strongest formula was devised by Georges Sorel who thought that unions are the only true revolutionary vehicle and that direct action by militant workers is the only avenue to a true socialism. His ideas were echoed in any early CGT declaration. "While in theory you are acting in the name of the state of tomorrow, in practice you only act to fortify the state of today; we act outside in order to have the disappearance of the state as our general objective and progressively detach our action of all contact with the state" (Monatte, 1976, p. 127). These views were enshrined in the Charter of Amiens (1906) which looked upon worker solidarity and direct confrontation as the basis of a new social order. The main weapon was the general strike which, at the appropriate historical moment, was to crumble an enfeebled capitalist system. Lenin's decision that the party, and not the union, was to be the political weapon of the working class sparked the first of many debilitating ideological debates as the USSR shifted tactics at the expense of European Communists.

A consequence was that, in 1922, the labor movement split over its allegiance to the new doctrine enforced by the Soviet Union. Where institutions are weak, leaders must live by their wits. Between the wars, the French labor movement was dominated by Leon Jouhaux who felt that "unions have misunderstood the complexity of economic rivalries, the force of capitalism, and its effect on the state" (Branciard, 1978 p. 9). Although the anarchist strand of the French labor movement practically disappeared after the First World War, dedication to class struggle and hostility to capitalist society produced more factions. In 1919, the French Confederation of Christian Workers (CFTC) was formed and based on the doctrine of social peace as pronounced by Pope Leo XIII in the encyclical *Rerum Novarum* of 1891. Jouhaux's hopes for a united labor movement were finally realized in 1936 when the Communist, Christian, and socialist (CGT) unions united to defend the republic against a growing fascist movement. (Bron, 1970). The massive general strike of the workers in 1934, involving over 12,000 strikes and two million workers, helped save the Third Republic rather than destroy it. It was the threat to French democracy rather than the promise of a socialist utopia that brought the labor movement to the peak of its prewar membership, nearly five million workers, in 1936.

But worker solidarity was short-lived. In the euphoria of the liberation, the unions worked together immediately following the Second World War and important gains were made, in both labor organizations, in firms and in social benefits (see Chapter 6). New schisms developed after 1947. The CGT, by then under Communist control, followed Stalin's directions to resist the reconstruction of western Europe and the early efforts to build a European defense. Still imbued with the fervor of the Resistance, the CFTC continued as the main, but still confessional, arm of non-Communist socialist workers. A group of secular socialist workers split from the CGT to form the CGT-FO. The teachers formed their own union, the National Education Federation (FEN). In brief, the labor movement reflected all the internal divisions of the parties and, by doing so, could exercise little influence over policymaking. Thus, the internal politics of the French labor movement became (and remains) no less intricate and obscure than the divisions among the parties themselves.

As argued in Chapter 1, under conditions of great institutional uncertainty, political groups tend to conceal their strength. Contrary to the image of France as a highly bureaucratic society, there are no official records of union strength nor are the unions eager to document their membership. Their fears are not so much that government would use such figures to manipulate unions, but that the union rivalries would be encouraged and that the implied political associations of the unions would, in turn, threaten union autonomy. This is, of course, less so in the case of the CGT whose leaders hold office in the PCF. The CGT is thought to have about 1.8 million members, but membership fluctuates and there is high turnover. Only a quarter of the membership belongs to the PCF which creates a delicate situation for the CGT Secretary-General, Georges Séguy. The union is particularly strong in the metal industries, mining, transport, ports, and in two important public sector industries, electricity and nuclear energy production.

In 1964, the CFTC split; the largest faction, estimated now to be about a million members, became the French Democratic Confederation of Labor (CFDT). Most CFDT members are socialists, and their leader, Edmond Maire, staunchly defends the complete autonomy of the unions as an independent social force. A deeply reflective man, Maire sees the development of self-management (*autogestion*) as the key to a peaceful and constructive transformation of the capitalist state into a socialist society (Maire and Julliard, 1975). His insistence that reform must begin in the workplace and neighborhood not only aligns him in the apolitical tradition of French unions, but also creates deep differences with the centralized CGT. The CFDT is particularly strong in the tertiary sectors of insurance, banking, and public health, as well as more technical industries such as chemicals (see Reading 5-4).

The CGT-FO is the non-Communist remnant of the prewar CGT; it probably has slightly over a million members, and is particularly strong in the civil service. Its leader, André Bergeron, is a conventional Social Democrat whose frank denunciations of the idealistic aims of the CGT and CFDT is a constant source of embarrassment to militant workers. After the 1964 split, the CFTC continued as a minor union of about 200,000 members whose strength is largely confined to the traditionally strong Catholic regions of France. Also considered a union, but of a radically different nature, is the General Confederation of Cadres (CGC) of foremen, supervisors, and technicians. These persons have little sympathy with other unions, but are no less content with the CNPF. The CGC claims about 250,000 members in high technology industries, communications, and services. A large white-collar class appeared relatively late and inescapably feels uncomfortable among the militant unions. For obvious reasons, the CGC found the thinly-veiled liberalism of Giscard compatible with its views.

While one should not underestimate employer resistance to unions, the ability to organize only a fourth of the active population of over 20 million persons suggests there are deeper reasons for the weakness. A large working class was slow to appear in France and, in 1910, there were eight million employers (*patrons*) for eleven million workers. Despite the political turbulence of France, conservative economic policies plus the economic reserves of a strong agricultural economy meant that, at the height of the depression in 1936, there were under half a million unemployed compared to six million in Germany. The stagnation of French population itself meant there were fewer opportunities to mobilize workers (See Maurice and Sellier, 1979).

The French state has never excluded its "social partners" from those areas where they have a legitimate interest. Regardless of impassioned rhetoric and internal rivalries, unions are consulted in the elaborate planning procedures (see Chapter 4), have assigned places on the Economic and Social Council, are granted public funds through factory committees (*comités d'entreprise*), and are included in top advisory bodies on unemployment (ASSEDIC), the social security system (USRAAF), working conditions (ANACT), manpower training, and continuing education. As we shall see, any major piece of legislation affecting labor-management relations, and a multitude of social policies, cannot proceed without elaborate official consultation and, whenever possible, previous agreement between unions and employers. Indeed, in more than a few instances, particularly the Grenelle Accords following the 1968 strikes, government has pressed employers to make major concessions to workers. With the full protection of the state, workers participate in an almost endless sequence of elections for factory committees, conciliation boards (*prud'hommes*), and in larger firms for union committees (*sections syndicales*). Given the vulnerabilities and schisms of the labor movement, government seems to work very hard to elicit working class opinion and actively seeks reliable formulas for labor-management relations.

One might assume that employers and managers, presumably having more common aims, would more easily unite, but this is not the case. The National Employers Association (CNPF) was formed with government prodding in 1946 in hopes of having a single pressure group to represent business in the early planning exercises (see Chapter 4). But at the same time, a more conservative pressure group was also formed to represent the millions of small shopkeepers and small businesses, the Confederation of Small and Medium Enterprises (CGPME). In addition, there survived a strong industrial pressure group for steel, the Union of Metallurgic and Mining Industries (UIMM) which represented some 12,000 firms employing over two million workers in the 1970s. At the departmental and municipal level, there are also the Chambers of Commerce and Industry, whose semiofficial status as local spokesmen for business interests and partial funding from local taxes is a thorn in the side of the more ambitious, modern business groups. Businesses have even spawned their own dissident groups, such as the Council of Young Directors in the 1960s which combatted the cautious CNPF until it was reorganized under the impulse of a rapidly modernizing France (see Reading 5-5).

Given the great uncertainty that such an intricate array of organizations can reach agreement, it is perhaps natural that the French are more concerned about strikes than many countries with much worse strike records. Strikes are endemic to France but, in relation to the days lost per worker, France is much better off than the United States and has almost half the losses as strike-ridden Britain (Adam and Reynaud, 1978, p. 20). Over the longer term, the total days lost has actually declined since the turn of the century, and was lower during the Gaullist government than during the Fourth Republic (La Grange, 1979). What distinguishes France is that it has more strikes than most countries, most of them unofficial. As Adam describes strike activity in France (1968, p. 1014), the "unions are against the enterprise more than the entrepreneur." Contrary to the image of French government as overbearing and arbitrary, the right to strike is unqualified, but individual rather than collective (see Reading 5-7). The consequence for both unions and management is perplexing for there is virtually no machinery to anticipate or to moderate conflict as in the United States nor do the unions have to bear responsibility through their monopoly of strike privileges, as in Britain.

An indication of the social discontent underlying French strikes is the high strike levels of capital intensive and high productivity industries (Bernard, 1978), where one might expect more enlightened management and more secure workers. But even within the same industry strike activity varies. The vast majority of strikes last for a day or two and lost working time varies greatly from one area of the country to another (Erbes-Seguin and Cassassus, 1977). There are also severe fluctuations over fairly short periods of time. Strikes diminished dramatically following the 1968 riots, in part because the CGT had been the main supporter of the Grenelle Accords. When the CGT disapproved the sudden upsurge of wildcat strikes in 1975 and helped arrive at a settlement in a large electricity plant, 300 workers denounced the decision (Bonaffe-Schmidt, 1977). More prone to localized rivalries than Britain and Germany, unions resort to strikes at great risk, because unsuccessful strikes may provoke the workers to switch membership to a competing union.

Unlike nearly all European countries and Japan, there is virtually no reliable legal or customary procedures for mediation, conciliation, or arbitration in French labor-management disputes (see Reading 5-2). As a leading analyst of French labor relations, Reynaud (1978) points out, there are all kinds of laws and rules, none of which are used. Instead, there is an intricate network of "collective conventions" which are usually rather vague national statements of purpose between employers and workers. The conventions have no legal status, vary widely in time period, carry no penalties for strikes or lost production, state desired rates but have no power to fix salaries, and are signed by a constantly changing array of labor and business groups, sometimes on an industry-wide basis, sometimes for a particular occupational group, and sometimes for a limited region (Martin, 1974). There is perhaps no better indication of the highly informal and indirect nature of labor-management relations, and of the immense difficulties of building a reliable and durable institutional framework for one of the crucial problems of the modern industrial state.

For this reason, labor-management relations in France are both more comprehensive and less defined than in most of Europe. There is no question of the state imposing rules, and what rules exist are "negotiated law" (Reynaud, 1978, p. 116). that often require years of patient consultation. In instances where government has intervened arbitrarily, failure is almost certain. For example, in the early 1970s, a law requiring firms to provide workers with an annual report on social measures and economic conditions within the firm (*bilan social*) was secretly prepared and forced through the National Assembly. It became "an obligation which interests no one" (Adam and Reynaud, 1978, p. 71). because none of the "social partners" felt committed. In this complex relationship, the state is both protagonist and mediator. The paradoxical and largely unintended result is that serious conflicts and long-term industrial problems tend to percolate through the state machinery, and eventually await the diplomatic and cautious efforts of government to find solutions.

But French industrial relations are also more comprehensive in that they involve a much wider range of issues than found in countries with more stable patterns of collective bargaining and stronger unions. As Erbes-Seguin (1976, p. 136) notes, there is "permanent opposition over the model of society at the same time as relative agreement on the level of bargaining." Each union has its political model of society and one can easily become so involved in these intense, but abstract, concerns that accomplishments of the past twenty years go unrecognized. The rapid social and economic change of the past twenty years had enormous repercussions on workers so that the more general societal preoccupations have been stimulated rather than diminished. Between 1962 and 1975, roughly 2.5 million persons were added to the the workforce. While a million persons from agriculture sought industrial employment, hundreds of thousands of women were also seeking jobs (*Données Sociales*, 1978, p. 48). While undergoing these shocks, France enjoyed neither the politically active labor movement of Britain nor the highly organized unions of West Germany or Sweden when devising new industrial relations policy.

Agenda

When the Gaullists came to power in 1958 there was no clear agenda for the future of industrial relations, nor had any clear initiatives from the Fourth Republic pointed the direction for the future. In the 1958 elections, the Communists were severely defeated and the Party—and consequently the CGT—was going through a difficult transition. The elimination of the old Catholic Party (MRP) in the 1958 elections had left a demoralized, confessional union (CFTC) which was split and did not emerge with any clear purpose until the CFDT was formed in 1964. As happened in several of the policy areas, the main problem was within the Gaullist Party, not outside it. De Gaulle remained loyal to a left-wing splinter group in his party led by two deputies, Vallon and Capitant, who hoped that the party would expand to include worker interests. Obviously, their group also provided a base for the Gaullist strategy of driving a wedge between the parties of the Left and for directly appealing to worker votes.

Policies dealing with labor and industrial relations, though cautious, are actually a more distinct innovation of the Fifth Republic than are the problems of administrative reform, decentralization, or social security. For example, in 1958 a collective agreement was reached on unemployment policy and the first national unemployment agency (UNEDIC). In 1967, these plans were enlarged to include all wage-earners; the state itself, contrary to the long established precedent of separating social benefits from the national budget (see Chapter 4), agreed to make a direct contribution. There followed the inquiry into incomes policy (see Chapter 4) and into ways that workers might be induced to support the modernization of French industry (Masselin Report, 1961). A 1966 law strengthened factory committees and, in the interval before the 1968 strikes, over 8000 new committees were formed. In 1966, the "social partners" were also invited to participate in plans to modernize the steel industry (*Plan Acier*). A government order of 1967 made the first provision for indemnity in the case of dismissal, although a law on dismissal was not agreed upon by the "social partners" until 1973.

But two reforms in particular characterize the problems of the French state in relation to the rapidly changing structure of employment, and the Gaullist goals of rapid modernization. De Gaulle was not adverse to industrial relations reforms that might promote a more united France as he imagined it. Under the urging of the left-wing Gaullists, Vallon and Capitant, and seeing the opportunity of the breakdown of the CFTC (plus the threat that more progressive workers from the CFTC might join the CGT), a government order of 1959 instituted a plan for profit-sharing. In the confused and weakened world of labor and business politics, both the unions and the recalcitrant CNPF opposed the plan. Full commitment came in 1965 when the government accepted an amendment to the budget (Vallon amendment) directing the government to propose a law in six months that "recognized and garunteed the right of workers to increases in the value of firms due to self-financing" (Casanova, 1967, p. 97). An inquiry to organize the scheme was launched by de Gaulle's close supporter, Debré, then minister of finance.

Debré found no serious legal obstacles to the Vallon amendment but, like most initiatives in the industrial relations area, it left most interested parties confused. The CGT was reserved, but unable to dismiss the idea. The newly-created CFDT had participated in planning the scheme and was favorable. The CGT-FO came forth with the classical union response that it might handicap unions in bargaining for wages. But the Gaullists no doubt had an eye on the 1967 legislative elections, and the impending impasse was decided by de Gaulle in a press conference in late 1966. His reference to the necessity "to give workers an active association in the economic task which it can help accomplish" left no doubt that the government was committed to profit-sharing. The new law affected all firms employing over 100 workers (14,000) and, by 1976, nearly 17 billion francs had been accumulated from the profits of over 10,000 firms. As in nearly every reform, the unions sat on the boards administering the funds which paid dividends to almost three million workers in 1976 (*Bulletin Mensuel des Statistiques du Travail*, 1979).

The second major reform was much less dramatic but, in many ways, more vital for the future of French workers; it also provides an important insight into the delicate relationship between the CGT and the CFDT. The early economic planning of the Fifth Republic recognized the importance of manpower training (Bernard Report, 1965) which had been neglected by conservative employers and never before aligned with national economic objectives. The concept of "social advancement" (*promotion sociale*) figured heavily in both the Fifth and Sixth Plans. Again with an eye to the approaching 1967 elections, the president and leading Gaullists produced a law on manpower training (*formation professionelle*) in 1966, even though many of the more reactionary elements of the party were highly skeptical. In brief, the law required firms entering into manpower agreements to contribute one percent of their profits to a fund (FAF) which would be administered by an inter-ministerial committee (see Thuillier, 1967). Local decisions were to be coordinated by regional and departmental committees and, within the participating firms, the factory committees were to be consulted. As in the case of profit-sharing, the training scheme did not get unreserved official support until the 1970s. By 1974, agreements included 130,000 firms and nearly two million workers. Nearly five billion francs were spent, with average contributions slightly over 1.6 percent of profits; large firms (over 2,000 employees) contributed 2.5 percent of profits (Chéramy Report, 1976).

As happened often in the early Gaullist years, good politics made bad economics. Both the labor training and profit-sharing schemes placed new burdens on natural Gaullist allies and were not incentives for increased investment and employment. But by the mid-1960s, the politics of industrial relations were more complex than the economics. In the 1965 CGT Congress, the idea of common action with the Socialists was raised and, in early 1966 (after thirty prolonged meetings), the CFDT and the CGT signed an agreement on common union goals. With the prospect of increased representation in the 1967 legislative elections, politics was doing what economic self-interest could not. There were also important changes within the CNPF. In 1965, it issued its Charter of the Employer, a reactionary view of industrial relations that so unequivocally rejected even the tentative Gaullist efforts to bring some order and purpose to industrial relations that several major firms resigned from the CNPF. Again, one finds the curious situation of the Gaullists being unable to find any organizational foundations for their new policies. Until late 1967, the CNPF refused to encourage any agreements to advance the reforms. Only when Ceyrac, the CNPF vice president for social relations (later to become its president) forced the issue in early 1968 was the first of the agreements on improved unemployment benefits signed. The record of the first decade of Gaullist rule suggests how futile even Jacobin designs were in the complex world of French politics.

Process

The neglect that helped produce the 1968 strikes cannot be passed over; however, not until early 1968 did the Gaullist government have a reasonably well-defined and organized setting for advancing industrial relations. While the strikes are the obvious backdrop to renewed efforts to improve industrial relations, it is by no means obvious that the strikes helped define future priorities. One close observer of French labor, Pierre Dubois (1978, p. 58) writes that it was "less of an upheaval than may be thought" and that it had "no significant effect on economic affairs." For one thing, the events of May 1968 were initially a student rebellion and not a worker rebellion. As the ranks of striking workers surged to nearly nine million, the crises of leadership and control were no less for revolutionaries than for conservatives. As the country descended into chaos, the unions were just as perplexed as was the government, in particular the CGT and CFDT whose organization had long been troubled with a bewildering display of Maoist, Trotskyite, and anarchic divergencies within the labor movement. In addition, the more advanced ideas about participation and local control of the CFDT had already become a threat to the CGT whose Leninist principles left little room for spontaneity.

With the government virtually under seige and De Gaulle in seclusion, Pompidou is often credited with discreetly making contact with Séguy, the CGT leader, and arranging the withdrawal of Communist support. For a party and union built on lifelong dedication and loyalty, the flood of untested and undisciplined students into many factories throughout France was a catastrophe. When the Parisian students marched off to the Renault factory in nearby Boulogne-Billancourt, a bastion of CGT strength, they found the plant firmly locked and there were no workers to greet them. As the CGT shifted tactics, its militants could be seen carefully organizing the demonstrators and rather rudely shoving student leaders aside. In its attachment to Leninist ideas, an unruly mob did not appear to be the Communist vanguard of the working class.

In negotiating the subsequent agreements with the unions, Pompidou had an introduction to the politics of labor relations that De Gaulle never experienced. The Grenelle Accords are sometimes compared to the 1936 Matignon Accords of 1936 when the Popular

Front government, under the Socialist Blum, also agreed to major changes. However, the 1968 situation is barely comparable. In 1968, the Communists had firm control of the largest union and the political risks were much greater. Like the Fifth Republic, the Communists were fighting for their existence, and from this common ground two of the most unlikely allies in French politics joined to compel French industrialists and businessmen to make huge concessions. In one blow, the Grenelle Accords increased the minimum wage (SMIC) by 30 percent, provided a general wage increase of about 10 percent, and made plans for a 1968 law creating union committees (*sections syndicales*) in firms with over fifty employees. The risk to the CGT is suggested by the rejection of these agreements by the Renault workers on the day following their announcement. Nonetheless, when de Gaulle announced the elections of 1968, he could confidently state that "the CGT will do nothing to hamper the process of electoral consultation."

There are few calm interludes in French politics, but the disastrous losses of the Left in the 1968 elections encouraged the Gaullists to press ahead with their ideas to build industrial harmony. In the distinct tradition of French labor-management relations, the concept was not to regulate conflict, but to generate new ideas about the social responsibilities of both firms and unions. The outline for such reforms had been provided some years before by Bloch-Lainé (1963) and the main policy instrument was to be the "contractual policy" based on voluntary collective agreements among the "social partners." This is one of the fascinating ways where the often grandiose ideas of the planners of the 1960s (see Chapter 4) overlap with social and industrial reform. Their thinking is quite compatible with many of the ideas of the CFDT on invigorating worker participation at the plant-level by sharing social obligations and management responsibilities. The new strategy had obvious political appeal to the Gaullists because all these ideas were (and are) an anathema to the disciplined and centralized Communists.

Pompidou had, of course, seen the political possibilities of an "opening to the left" and was the architect of many of the reforms in the mid-1960s. Once elected president in 1969, he chose Chaban-Delmas as his prime minister, more with an eye toward building a broader appeal for the Gaullist party than for Chaban's economic ideas (see Chapter 4). The slogan of a "New Society" was nonetheless something more than electoral ballyhoo. Chaban's social adviser was Jacques Delors, a product of the "Saint Simonians" and a prolific writer on the necessity of profound structural reform of French labor relations (1965). As a social planner in the CGP, Delors had worked closely with Ceyrac, who was also persuaded that new ways must be found for business to accept social responsibilities and who became president of the CNPF in 1972 (see Reading 1-1).

Difficult as it may be to think of the Gaullists as revolutionary, the subsequent flood of collective conventions broached problems that French politics had studiously avoided since the Third Republic. While it must be remembered that the convention is a wholly informal agreement carrying no sanctions and having no legal status, the transformation of French labor relations in the early 1970s is almost dizzying, and can only be presented here in highly compressed form. An interprofessional agreement of February 1969 assured workers of previous notice in the event of industrial mergers (later agreed to by the chemical and metal industries); the monthly payment of wages replaced weekly salaries in an agreement of April 1970 (extended to chemicals, metal working, paper, steel, and construction); and the earlier manpower training agreements were reinforced to protect apprentices and young workers in July 1970. Closely following was an agreement raising maternity leave reimbursements to 90 percent of salaries and, in early 1971, progress was made in reducing working hours. But even where the state intervened to make law from collective agreements, there was still a long process of negotiation. The 1973 law on improved working conditions, for example, did not lead to an interprofessional agreement until 1975. Even so, by April 1970, over 4000 agreements had been signed improving benefits for about 2.5 million workers, and setting standards for the remaining French workers. However laborious and gradual this process may seem, there is no doubt that, for several years, Pompidou and Chaban-Delmas were forcefully pressing for new concessions.

Although the government's "strategy of encouragement" (Dubois, 1978, p. 77) did not carry the statutory force of reform efforts in other advanced industrial states, it did permit industries, unions, and local firms to adjust to new objectives as compromises

could be found. Contrary to the image of the Jacobin state, the aim
had never been to force all citizens to adhere to universal standards.
The Jacobin ideal itself meant that the state should indicate the way
to social harmony rather than compel any particular group of
citizens to conform. Possibly the best illustration of Gaullist concern for social harmony in the area of industrial relations is the long
struggle to convert weekly wages to monthly salaries (*mensualisation*). This was a promise made by Pompidou in the 1969 presidential campaign; the implications for French employees were not
symbolic, and the concessions implied by monthly salaries were
precisely those that would appeal to a pragmatic president. A
monthly salary entailed a whole array of increased benefits: more
notice of change of jobs; improved guarantee against dismissal;
larger allowances for paid holidays, paid vacations, and sick leave;
more compensation for accidents; and better maternity rights. In
the highly complex system of occupational classification and the
attached benefits, increasing the status of workers to monthly paid
employees had multiple effects (Bunel, 1973; Burnot, 1979).

   All this is not to say that acknowledgement of social responsibility was devoid of immediate political self-interest. After several
years of consolidation, in 1970 the CFTC became "officially"
socialist; in 1971, the reflective and resourceful Edmond Maire
became secretary general of the CFDT and, in 1972, the long
struggle to unify the left-wing produced the Common Program of
the Socialists and Communists. Whatever the probusiness tendencies of the Gaullists, there was no reliable spokesman for industry
until Ceyrac reorganized the CNFP in the early 1970s. In the area of
labor relations, as in most areas of social policy (Chapter 6), there
were no easy solutions for the Gaullists, and the abrupt dismissal of
Chaban-Delmas in 1972 indicates the severe tensions within the
party. It may be difficult to sympathize with a party that had ruled
for over a decade, but the Gaullists were buffeted between the
catastrophe of 1968 and the approaching legislative elections of
1973 and, even more ominously, the presidential elections of 1974.

Consequences

   By Giscard's presidency, France had developed the intricate
system of collective bargaining, labor benefits, and industrial regulations that characterizes the complex field of industrial relations

in every advanced industrial society. Unlike the pragmatic Pompidou, Giscard was more interested in abstract proposals about the distant future. For example, in what many regard as a more patriarchal approach than that of the fiercely nationalist Gaullists, Giscard's "Letter to the Prime Minister" of late 1975 outlined the president's ideas about the degrading nature of manual labor, a theme which he had acquired from his labor adviser, Stoleru. Among the president's priorities for 1975 was a reexamination of the firm, its social basis, and how social unity might be advanced within the workplace. The general idea had actually been launched by the Gaullists in their 1973 law on working conditions (Delamotte, 1976), which required employers to report annually to factory committees on plans to improve working conditions, and established a National Agency for Improving Working Conditions (ANACT).

In line with his own neoliberal thinking, Giscard looked to the firm as the unit of reform. To explore such possibilities, he appointed the Sudreau Commission (1975) whose report, in many ways, echoed the enlightened self-interest that a decade before pervaded Bloch-Lainé's report. Noting the resurgence of strike activity over 1973, Sudreau described the precarious nature of the "social dialogue" that constructive labor-management relations require. The Commission called for further strengthening of the factory committees to overcome the anonymity of the worker; extension of profit-sharing plans and organization of "surveillance committees" to work with management; modernization of the basic statutes of the firm (relatively unchanged since 1804) in order to make the firm's social obligations more explicit; and a devising of new structures to involve both workers and managers in industrial conversion and development (see Reading 5-3).

But the Sudreau Report produced little in the way of concrete results. On the one hand, it alarmed more Jacobin members of the president's Gaullist supporters because the state's role would be diminished. By this time, the energy crisis and unemployment were also pushing the CNPF toward a more conservative position so their receptivity to a rather vague proposal for sharing managerial responsibility was lukewarm. The CFDT could only be pleased with the overture to more worker involvement, while the CGT found the report a threat to the class struggle and a capitalist plot to undermine worker militancy (Weiss, 1979). If Giscard's aim had been to drive another wedge between the forces of the Left (not a difficult thing to do), his strategy could not have been better calculated, but there were also crippling divisions among his own supporters (Delmon Report, 1975).

But the institutional uncertainties of the Fifth Republic continued to hamper such ambitious reforms, and a period of economic stagnation is not a propitious moment to extract concessions from either management or unions. A long and rancorous debate in the National Assembly destroyed hopes of having a meaningful system of joint surveillance, and immediate economic problems overcame longer term reforms. As unemployment approached a million persons, the departmental unemployment committees were reinforced, an interprofessional agreement was reached on implementing the law on dismissal, and for the first time the state began to contribute heavily toward unemployment benefits. As the conflict between the Gaullists and the Giscardians intensified over 1976, it was hardly possible to launch a new initiative. In an obvious electoral ploy before resigning as prime minister, Chirac produced a vague plan to spend thirty billion francs to preserve jobs and pushed through a law providing 90 percent compensation for jobs lost for "economic" reasons. His successor, Barre, later complained that the compensation proposal had cost the state over twelve billion francs to assist a mere 100,000 workers (*Le Monde*, May 3, 1977).

Since unemployment had never been a serious problem in France, the steps taken by Giscard, Barre, and an innovative minister of labor, Boulin, over 1978 and 1979 display considerable resourcefulness, and illustrate some of the advantages of a highly diverse system based on social obligation (Baudrillart and Colin, 1979; Vinstock Report, 1977). In early 1977, an agreement of the CNPF, CGT, and CFDT enabled the government to compensate workers with shorter hours. There were additional agreed measures to encourage early retirement. In May 1977, Barre and Ceyrac worked out a scheme to encourage training and employment of young persons, and a new tough employment law was passed in early 1978. The final step was a National Employment Pact that Boulin negotiated in late 1978 (Colin and Espinasse, 1979). In included special unemployment relief for depressed regions, further reduction in working hours, more part-time work, and increased taxation on overtime wages. Much to the chagrin of the Left, one of the moderate socialists, Robert Fabre, accepted Giscard's invitation to conduct an inquiry into ways of expanding employment opportunities (Fabre Report, 1979). In 1979, the country anticipated spending twenty-eight billion francs in unemployment relief about a fourth of which was provided by the state. Total state expenditure on employment-related programs had expanded to about forty-five billion francs (*Le Monde*, December 26, 1978).

Within the established area of organized industrial relations, the political setting was not encouraging. The CNPF came out with a more harsh position (see Reading 5-5), while the rivalry of the CGT and CFDT increased following the breakdown in 1977 of the Common Program between the Socialist and Communist Parties. For example, negotiations among the "social partners" for shorter hours and work week dragged on for nearly two years. The impasse was finally dislodged when Giscard appointed a close friend, Pierre Giraudet, to head a special mission as the 1981 election approached (see *Le Monde*, January 19, 1980, and April 24, 1980). The CGT increasingly aligned itself with the bitter criticism of the Communist Party against the Socialists. The CGT secretary general, Séguy, noted as early as the 1978 legislative elections that his union would make "no sacrifices for a left-wing government" (*Le Monde*, July 24, 1980). Maire's worries that the CFDT would be plunged even further into party politics at the neglect of self-management produced new hesitation (see Reading 5-4). After several futile efforts to cooperate with the CGT, Maire bluntly stated (*Le Monde*, October 30, 1979), that "the CGT is an obstacle to union action." On the eve of the 1981 elections, Séguy's reluctance to give unqualified support to the Polish strikers brought cooperation among the unions of the Left to a nadir.

As Dupeyroux (see Reading 5-6) points out, the major unfinished task in organizing industrial relations in France remains the clear definition of right to strike, and the mutual obligations of unions and management during industrial conflicts. Oddly enough, the Socialist victory of 1981 did little to clarify whether France will develop the more highly organized procedures and sanctions common to most European countries. In some respects, the uncertainties have multiplied. While the Communists have entered into the government, the CGT as well as the Party are threatened by the wave of popularity that swept the Socialists into office. There are signs that the CGT secretary general, Séguy, is under a shadow for cooperating, however reluctantly, with the Socialists, and a more militant Leninist, Krasucki, increasingly speaks for the CGT. If the Communist union were to openly reject the new government, the Left would be as severely divided when in power as it was in opposition.

The CFDT and its secretary general, Maire, were strong supporters of the Socialists. But their distinctive approach to industrial relations leaves many issues in dispute. In his meeting with the prime minister (*Le Monde*, August 11, 1981), Maire noted the various opportunities for increased local participation in Socialist reforms that were being lost and asked that there be local unemployment committees, renewed elections to social security committees (see Chapter 6), and regional level worker committees to advise on nationalization policies. As an old friend of Rocard—Mitterrand's rival and now minister of planning—Maire's insistence on more localized consultation in the revision of the Plan might also embroil the CFDT in internal party differences.

The immediate benefits for workers were substantial. Mitterrand was true to his promise to increase the SMIC by 10 percent, and he brought great pressure on business to negotiate a thirty-nine hour week and a fifth week of paid vacation (*Le Monde*, July 19-20, 1981). But like every government in a complex welfare state, the intricacies of bargaining and industrial relations held few political rewards. Mitterrand and Mauroy were obviously preoccupied with mounting unemployment and, in the fall of 1981, Mauroy made what many regarded as a rash promise that unemployment would not be allowed to exceed two million persons (it was then 1.8 million). The Socialist Party had its own agenda for reform, including priority to nationalization (see Chapter 4) and decentralization (see Chapter 3). Both these reforms created new uncertainties for the private sector which had already been asked to share substantial increased social security charges. Thus, the Socialists appeared no more eager to enter into the complex and prolonged negotiation that any major restructuring of industrial relations would presuppose.

Given the divided unions and the political uncertainties that France had faced over the past twenty years, the accomplishments to 1981 were not negligible. By the early 1970s, nearly three-fourths of the firms covered by agreements to form factory committees (those employing over ten workers) had done so. By 1976, almost half the firms obliged to form union committees (those employing over fifty workers) had done so, while 80 percent of the large firms (over 300 employees) had union committees (Ministry of Labor, 1977). As we have seen, there were and remain strong preferences both among unions and employers for a voluntary, nonstatutory approach to industrial relations. In a system with intricate patterns of interdependence, the reforms of dismissal and the monthly wage took months and even years to complete.

The first approach in the early Gaullist years was particularly *étatiste* and did not work well. In fact, the contractual policies developed over the late 1960s were based on the public sector and were of such a highly technical character that both unions and employers distrusted them. Under Pompidou, French labor relations turned to the more pragmatic approach common in many Western democracies. In the third period, Giscard accepted the pattern of "permanent negotiation." Given the intricacies of labor and party politics, there is little reason to think this pattern will change substantially in the future. Within six months of taking office, the new Socialist government was severely criticized by the CFDT for neglecting worker participation in both the nationalization and decentralization plans.

Industrial relations are replete with institutional uncertainties in every democratic country because both business and labor distrust statutory controls. In France, these apprehensions are reinforced by the deep ideological divisions among the main unions as well as the uncertainties that the unions themselves confront at the plant level in competing for members. In the successive efforts to introduce reforms in industrial relations such as manpower training, unemployment benefits, monthly wages, shorter work weeks, and dismissal controls, the historic suspicion of both workers and business toward government has always complicated the devising of more orderly procedures to respond to industrial weaknesses. Given the difficulties of reaching agreement, it may be more surprising that the governments of the Fifth Republic kept trying to enlarge the area of understanding between business and labor than that the governments made so little progress. Each foray into the treacherous and unrewarding field of industrial relations exposed the vulnerabilities of French government and raised new doubts about the effectiveness of national political institutions.

Readings

5-1. UNION PARTICIPATION IN PLANNING*

In the mid-1960s, French planners still hoped that a system of mutual cooperation (concertation) could be organized in order to involve business, unions, and government in the planning process. These ambitious plans had a distinctly progressive orientation and were part of the general strategy of the planners to work out a new system of industrial relations, including an incomes policy, which would hopefully circumvent the weaknesses of the trade unions and overcome the cautious attitude of most French businessmen. One of the leading young planners involved in this effort was Jacques Delors who saw the Plan as an opportunity to restore harmony and confidence in French industrial planning. In this address to the Social Affairs Section of the Planning Commission, he outlines his hopes that concertation will remove the uncertainties that make both labor and business suspicious of the state, but still voices reservations should consultation obstruct the planners in achieving national objectives.

Planning and Union Responsibilities

Leaving to union leaders the task of indicating under what conditions they would accept any engagement in the preparation and execution of the Plan, and without underestimating the importance of whatever conditions they might be led to impose, we will accentuate, as concerns us, the necessity of a dialogue—which is the foundation of the Plan and of efficiency.

*Jacques Delors, "Planification et réalités syndicales," *Droit Social* 28 (March 1965): 154–60 (selections).

In my view, progress toward cooperation can only be realized if one simultaneously improves the quality of the dialogue and the efficiency of the means of planning.

Concerning the Dialogue

I cannot insist too much that the dialogue must be founded on the theme (mutual trust) found in all the presentations made since the beginning of the conference.

I would, however, like to emphasize that a dialogue can only be valuable with equal responsibility and equal knowledge, which presupposes, in the first place, equal access for all to the sources of information.

How can one imagine that a labor movement could be sensitive to the necessities of conversion or adaptation of an industry if the employer's association does not put its cards on the table and does not show the precise assumptions which affect the situation of the branch (local union) in question?

How can one hope to discuss within the modernization commissions (study groups) the problems of the branch, and questions related to regional investment, if all the partners around the table do not have knowledge of the same conditions?

Finally, the dialogue can progress with equality only with a clear consensus on the role of each partner in the consultative organizations and notably in the commissions for modernization.

Allow me to give two examples of the last idea:

The first concerns job training. It is normal that in a modernization commission—taking into account the importance of training—union members express a different point of view than the employers' group. In this area, there can be equality of competence and equality of responsibility.

Contrast when a union member, in a commission of the Plan, says to an employer in the auto industry, "You make an auto poorly; if you do not accept my point of view, this proves that the Plan is not democratic." In such a case, the unionist is poorly situated—it appears—for his intervention, since the choice of an auto model is the exclusive responsibility of the employer. Certainly, one can be attentive to suggestions from union members, but one cannot end with a vote that puts the official of the enterprise in a minority and which would make him impose a decision of this kind.

In the end, for a dialogue to exist, it is necessary to avoid overly juridical methods and to place a value on informal consultation.

Therefore it is for us, administrators of the Plan, to attach more importance to consultation with professional associations, unions, and social groups, outside our primary concerns. We go, therefore, to the Economic and Social Council, before its committees, to debate the problems which preoccupy each other. Let us suppose, for example, that we are faced with estimating consumption for 1970. Certainly, we have reliable technicians, we have statistics, but to arrive at the right point even with our techniques, and even at unknown conclusions, one fact may escape us which a member of the Council may add to our study. I think that in uncertain areas, as for example measuring needs, an informal agreement with one another is important. One cannot estimate needs uniquely by consulting statistics even if they are well made.

Finally, for a dialogue in the true sense, it is necessary to have a clear formulation of the choices and also of the procedures and institutions which give each the capacity and the means to be involved.

Thus, we arrive at the contractual policy to which I have made reference. If one wishes that more of the professional organizations and unions engage in the limited contracts in a limited time and with limits to their obligations, it would be necessary as well to modify procedures and institutions.

Take the case of (industrial) conversion and adaptation. How can one dream, given the present organization of branches and of consultation, that one could truly elaborate a policy of conversion and adaptation with the assistance of the state?

The same in matters of salary negotiation: how can one arrive at the end with a policy of *concertation* of incomes if, when one discusses a contract salary at the national level, one has no idea of its real effects?

Concerning Efficiency

The procedures should be democratic but they should not become a burden such that they paralyze efforts and compromise the necessary clarity of debate.

To multiply the consultations is to lose their seriousness and their influence.

I allude to a recent debate of the Economic Council: numerous councilors wished that in addition to the two main issues—one on the main directions of the Plan, and the other, on when the Plan should be terminated—that there should be a third debate on the hypotheses which had been redone in the previous report on the directions of the Plan.

If we proceed this way, the administrators of the Plan would be made into scribes to rewrite the Plan under the dictates of others, parliamentarians or members of the Economic Council.

There is a useful role and a useful degree of democratic influence which should not be overextended. I do not wish to say that we have attained it; I wish to say only that it is necessary to guard against excessive zeal which would make us spend all our time in consultation at the expense of the reflection and studies which constitute the prerequesite for a democratic debate.

Another condition of efficiency: The interventions of the public sector in an area related to the private sector could be built on a better organization by ameliorating the structures and constant research on economic rationality. These things should not paralyze initiative nor suppress liberties.

Put otherwise, the priority should always be given to economic means over administrative means. Administrative procedures have a constraining and sanctioning character which is incompatible with our general philosophy and our society.

That is why the Plan is linked to *concertation* procedures in the areas of reforming incomes policy. In the conference on incomes policy we are holding, neither the employers' nor the trade unions' organizations wish to return to a paralyzing central direction (*dirigisme*) which, in addition, brings to them the risk of suppressing economic and social liberties.

This said, it is necessary to admit that a society which fixes ambitious economic and social objectives for itself should accept the consequences for its daily behavior.

It is unthinkable, in my view, that the professional and union organizations should claim the privilege of consultation and, at the same time, refuse all cooperation (*concertation*).

It is impossible—and this is a profound conviction of the planners—to accomplish the ambitious objectives of the nation without prolonged *concertation* in the elaboration and execution of the Plan.

It is the driving idea, the only idea perhaps, which could be expanded from this talk which we believe deeply when we consider on the one side, the French aspiration and, on the other side, the possibilities of the French economy.

It is, justifiably, the absence of this consultation prolonged in [the Plan's] execution to which we attribute the dislocation of the economy, the increase in prices, and stabilization programs.

Professional and union organizations cannot acquire a larger role in consultation and, at the same time, refuse the restraints, which are light in relation to those that might be imposed, and which are needed to realize strong and harmonious growth.

5-2. AMBIGUITIES OF FRENCH COLLECTIVE BARGAINING*

Both unions and employers have had great difficulty in organizing themselves for collective bargaining. Like many agreements affecting professional and private interests, collective agreements (conventions collectives) have no special legal status and France is virtually without any effective labor law affecting negotiations. A leading labor law expert, Gérard Adam, writes of the many divisions within the same industry or same occupation, and of the mosaic of agreements at the plant, company, professional and national levels, that make the process of negotiation, and ultimately wage determination, almost indecipherable in France. Contrary to the image of France as a powerful centralized state, government is almost helpless in this situation and must rely on the slow process of gradual accumulation of trust and agreement between firms and unions.

Are French collective bargaining structures poorly adapted to modern industrial society? Implicitly, the law of February 11, 1950, which still provides the framework for all bargaining institutions and procedures, is based on two major principles:

—The existence of simple industrial structures: companies with only one plant and a diversified production; well defined industrial sectors.

---

*Gérard Adam, "La négotiation collective en France: Eléments de diagnostic," *Droit Social* 12 (December 1978): 420–451 (selections).

—The initiative of different professions, of the bargaining system, and the only authority recognized in negotiation with the unions. The firm, in effect, is only bound to consult the unions, which as such are excluded [from bargaining]. Interprofessional agreements are for their part either ignored or even prohibited.

In practice, the law of July 1971 corrected the original framework by at least acknowledging the multiple levels of negotiation. Essentially, important gaps continue to exist between regulations adopted prior to the postwar industrial transformation and the complexity of new business and professional organizations.

At least four series of deficiencies of maladaptations can be catalogued in French legislation:

—The absence of clearly defined industrial sectors.
—The indeterminate and compartmentalized levels of negotiation.
—The disorganization of many professions.
—The contradiction between juridical structures of representation and the actual functioning of firms.

At present, there is no satisfactory definition of an industrial sector. The economic classification of the INSEE (National Institute of Statistics and Economic Studies) hardly establishes valid bargaining units, since it often places heterogeneous activities under one rubric. For example, "Transportation" covers the subsectors of rail, air, maritime, and automobile travel, which often do not share the same technologies, organization, financial, or commercial constraints or possess common juridical regulation.

On the other hand, a categorization based on technique—insofar as this is possible—would lead to a classification that destroys the unity of companies and sectors. While poorly conceived from an economic standpoint, such a schema would not be absurd from a societal point of view: there is nothing but occupational unionism in Anglo-Saxon countries. The fragmentation of firms in a multitude of bargaining units, and the impossibility of arriving at coherent groupings at a broader level (culminating in the great power of the amalgamated unions), presents even more disadvantages in the French situation. However, this type of classification is not completely unknown in France, as in the graphic industries where collective bargaining is organized by trade, not according to industrial activity.

All in all, from the point of view of collective bargaining, sectors have been established empirically; it seems impossible to find a common logic inspiring this categorization. Indeed, it seems that this organization was simply a matter of chance.

But why are the sectors of steel, shipbuilding, and the auto, aerospace, and electronic industries grouped into one unit—that of metals? This vast grouping is best explained by the resistance of an efficient employers' association which was organized over the past seventy-five years to resist union federations based on well-defined criteria.

On the other hand, fragmentation is sometimes extreme. Oddly enough, the common interests of metal-working are divided into small groups; toy manufacture has a national collective convention, but others for children's buggies and strollers, camping equipment, and agricultural equipment. In the garment industry, dispersement is the rule. Within the two principle divisions of military/administrative and civilian clothing, there are divisions for lace, hatmaking, buttons, and belts—to name a few. And even this apparently tight organization has gaps: between leather gloves and knit gloves, nothing covers cloth gloves. Little can be said for such tiny areas whose existence, like the "geneologists'" collective agreement, is difficult to justify.

It is not surprising that establishing bargaining units, particularly in the old trades with a solid artisan's tradition and in highly dispersed trades, is done by taste and traditions. However, we must ask whether these traditions make sense today. Above all, should professional rivalries be allowed to produce organizational fragmentation? Doesn't overly dispersed bargaining undermine its effectiveness? Here again is an area where mergers and a reconstruction of the bargaining units is in order.

During the past fifteen years professional organization has slowly evolved but without resolution of major problems.

On the union side, sharing common facilities and meeting places has led some federations to merge for no other reason than the similarities of their problems (unskilled work force, low wages, structural economic difficulties). For example, the textile, leather, fur, and ready-to-wear unions began to cooperate and then united. The CFDT is the confederation that benefits most from this movement, while the CGT and FO have more reservations concerning mergers. In any case, merging unions come up against the contradiction between the members' need for a sense of community and the logic of efficiency, centered around economic functions or common problems. Moreover, while the idea of large confederations capable of formulating global economic policy initiatives is appealing in economic terms, it is unclear whether it is operational [or functional, practical] for collective bargaining.

As J. D. Reynaud suggests, "It is time to investigate more systematically what constitutes a group of employees with enough solidarity to create a union and maintain common activities. It is perhaps naive to assume that the 'best' organization is that corresponding to a market unit or product. Our goal should be how to create, maintain, and develop communities relevant to collective action."

As for employers' organizations, the movement toward unification is even slower. For example, despite the existence of a specific ministerial department, the National Council of Commerce, and numerous organizations covering all commercial professions, commerce has always displayed reservations concerning any overall collective agreements. In this area, there are approximately thirty national agreements and up to 500 departmental agreements, according to some estimates.

In the same way, despite many attempts, the unions have never been able to reduce the number of bargaining agents in the sector of "private health care," which involves nine annual agreements; nor have efforts in the metalurgical industry met with success. The case of the steel industry merits special attention because it shows an important evolution on the part of the employers' organization. Since the 1967 agreement for the Lorraine steel industry, economic developments and state initiatives led the industry to define a social policy to deal with dismissal.

These diverse examples permit two conclusions:

1. The risks of defining industrial sectors are obvious—no objective criterion allows clear definition of the various professions. Moreover, the efforts of unions and employers to influence these developments rarely converge, nor are they part of a coherent strategy. If the steel industry is an exception, this is

due to external factors (the economic situation and the state administration's pressure) which served to correct former practices.

Without relying on authoritative intervention by the administration, only a rationalization by the involved parties themselves, not at the level of professions, could arrive at more rational structures. Why not consider the establishment of a commission of collective agreements to embark in this direction? In place of total restructuring, a special procedure could authorize unions or employer associations to appeal to the commission to decide the area of application of an agreement.

2. The definition of coherent sectors, accepted by the partners involved, does not suffice to establish satisfactory bargaining structures. A plan to achieve this cannot be considered without taking into account two other factors which, in practice, can either correct or accentuate the anamolies of the present system:

   a) The articulation of the levels of negotiation: for a decade, the development of interprofessional agreements and, to a lesser extent, company agreements have drawn attention to the problems of liaison among professions and between professions and firms. But even within professions, the multiple combinations of national and decentralized bargaining increase the complexity of the structures of negotiation. Finally, can the distinction between bargaining systems for the public and the private sectors by maintained?

   b) The organizational capacity of the professional skills must also be taken into account: the geographic dispersal of collective bargaining in metals is not comparable to that of building or commerce. In these three cases, the employers' associations have neither the same goals, nor the same organization—and therefore have different degrees of authority over their members. The decentralization of bargaining varies in significance according to whether it corresponds to a deficiency in organization or to a deliberate strategy on the part of the profession.

5-3. PROPOSALS TO REFORM INDUSTRIAL RELATIONS*

The French policymakers have always been sensitive to the inability of industry and unions to build a more stable and progressive framework for industrial relations. Following the various efforts in the 1960s and the severe setback of the May 1968 strikes, Pompidou asked for a new strategy for industrial reform which was prepared by Pierre Sudreau. Some of his more radical proposals, such as a more elaborate system of joint management and labor committees (comités de cosurveillance) to discuss the decisions of owners and employers were unacceptable, but the report nonetheless was the bench mark for industrial reform in recent years. In this section, Sudreau discusses the reasons why French industry and labor have had such difficulties coming to grips with the new social and economic issues confronting the French economy.

Difficulties in Social Dialogue

The French situation [industrial relations] is often contrasted to certain foreign countries, notably West Germany, the Scandanavian countries, and the United States, where cooperative social dialogue is facilitated due to consensus on fundamental social principles—a consensus lacking here. From this viewpoint, how can the terms of the debate on French industrial relations in 1975 be seen?

Two main factors explain the problems of the social dialogue in France.

In the first place, the multiplicity of parties and unions makes social life more complex. Undoubtedly, it also offers a greater choice for the democratic expression of opinion but, at the same time, it complicates negotiations.

Positions taken in the name of workers are inevitably unstable. The representative unions do not always sign collective agreements. Each is free to participate in negotiations or not, to sign agreements or not, and to eventually accept or renounce the negotiated agreement.

A certain grass-roots spontaneity aggravates the effects of the unions' pluralism. This tendency has always existed in the French

*Pierre Sudreau, *Rapport du comité d'étude pour le réforme de l'entreprise*, (Prepared for the president and prime minister), Paris Documentation Française, 1975 (selections).

labor movement and has recently taken on a new vigor with the influx of younger workers into the work force.

On the employers' side, the general practice has been that each employer unilaterally conducted his own labor policy. Rarely did an initiative come from the employers' organizations. Whether in reaction to organized labor or the consequence of an instinctive attachment to liberal principles, employers failed to demand a social project for the future from the French Employers' Association (CNPF). Hence, a defensive strategy is adopted by employers; if cooperation has developed or negotiations have progressed, it is most often at the unions' instigation.

However, in the course of the last few years, industrial policy-making has been shared to a greater degree in the framework of a more active contractual policy. Unfortunately, there are still too many areas where this policy is not applied.

In addition, ideological differences divide labor and management. Socialist thought has often dominated in the labor movement, whereas employers' actions are generally inspired by economic liberalism.

Certain union confederations reject the capitalist system completely and place their hopes in a transformation of the economic system. Thus, individual or collective claims are sometimes presented as part of an overall societal critique, often muddled with ideology and occasionally put forth in a fighting spirit. However, not all unions oppose their firm's interest as defined by management, even if based on the dictates of profit and competition.

For their part, employers are ill-disposed to accept the presence of unions when they act without regard for the firms' objectives. For a number of employers, union demands are *a priori* suspect since they originate in organizations whose objective is the overthrow of the social and economic order. This quasi-permanent intent to destroy the present system naturally undermines the mutual confidence necessary to fruitful negotiation. The absence of a reformist majority tendency within many unions leads some employers to reject their firms' unions as privileged representatives of labor.

New characteristics of post-1968 labor conflicts accentuate the ideological differences which divide labor and management. Although the total number of strike days in the last five years is similar to the average for the period between 1960 to 1967, recent strikes differ in character from earlier conflicts. Strikes in the private sector, which usually involve limited numbers of workers and often are limited to one firm, nonetheless made a great impression on public opinion due to their long duration and the dramatization of their claims. The mass media served to magnify this effect. The upshot is that strikers were encouraged to seek publicity and to use the pressure of public opinion to support their cause. From then on, even in localized conflicts, labor and management have found it difficult to reach an understanding based on economic data from the single firm involved; instead, the unions usually seek to advance broader objectives in each local conflict, while employers naturally try to limit the effects.

These recent developments result in longer and more bitter confrontations, especially since labor demands have changed. In addition to the traditional claim for higher wages, several new aspirations have appeared. These concern job security—workers' major preoccupation—but also working conditions, quality of life, and the constraints of rigid hierarchical organization. These new demands are often expressed by young workers who refuse a life without prospect for personal development. Their radicalization is difficult to reconcile with the collective discipline necessary to union organization. Because of this, control over the course of events during strikes has become more difficult, and the approval of negotiated settlements less certain.

All of these new practices—which enter a tradition already unfavorable to confidence between labor and management—make it harder to find solutions to the inherent problem of industrial relations. From now on, the debate centers not only on the distribution of company profits, but also on work relations on the shop floor, organizational constraints, and the delegation of authority by management. Some [people] even seek the response to these aspirations in a conception of self-management—for the firm and for the larger society.

5-4. MAIRE ON RELATIONS BETWEEN THE CGT AND CFDT*

Although the French trade unions are weak compared to those in Britain and Germany, the two major confederations are politically influential and articulate. Edmond Maire, the secretary general of the

*Edmond Maire, "Nous ne changeons pas de stratégie," Le Monde, April 25, 1978.

CFDT, has always been worried that strong commitments to parties would divert the union movement from its social objectives. This has disrupted relations with the Communist confederation (CGT) and complicated relations between the CFDT and the Socialist Party. Following Prime Minister Barre's new economic policy, Maire spoke to the Press Club. He reviews the progress of the labor movement since 1968 and expresses his reservations over excessive commitment to political parties.

Invited to speak to the Press Club, Edmond Maire explained at length that neither a reversal of the CFDT's position, nor a coalition with the *Force Ouvrière*, is under consideration. The CFDT's general secretary based his conclusions on a critical analysis of the 1974–78 period:

"The intransigence of the employers' association [CNPF] and the government led us to place our hopes in an overall policy change. Moreover, the fact that our partners on the Left presented the Common Program as a miracle cure—as if one favorable vote would satisfy our most pressing demands—led us to adopt a wait-and-see attitude and caused us to lose some of the substance and richness of our union activities."

"What we propose is not a profound change in strategy but merely a change in our methods. We want the labor movement to be the reflection—in a richer and more permanent fashion—of all that workers feel and experience in their daily lives."

For M. Maire, "The important lesson of the last ten years for the workers' movement—both for the union movement and for the politics of the Left—is that we went from *social* mobilization, without political alternatives, in 1968, to the other extreme. Everything through political change, everything through elections without social mobilization; that is the analysis in March 1978."

"The lesson drawn by the CFDT from May of 1968 has not changed in 1978. This lesson is that profound, fundamental change in response to workers' aspirations will occur in our country only if political and social action are carried on at the same time; if the political struggle is not confined to electioneering; if the parties of the Left speak honestly; if all the forces of the Left discuss with workers the real problems faced by our country, the difficulties and means of overcoming the [economic] crisis—not offering curealls which make individual reflection and difficulties unnecessary."

Analyzing the government's policy projects, M. Maire concluded that the upshot of Prime Minister Barre's speech [new economic program] was clearly "that there will be no major improvements in the unemployment problem." Nevertheless, the CFDT's initiative to meet with the president and prime minister was not without effect: The program [the Blois program] totally excluded workers and their representatives from the future. There was no mention of even a single negotiation. The new development is that negotiations will be possible in the next two months. We have already started something moving and we are convinced that this is only the beginning, as pressure from organized labor grows."

After having stated that for now, there could be no united action with *Force Ouvrière*, which "because of its anti-Communist stand excludes itself from action," M. Maire mentioned relations between the CGT and the CFDT.

While he feels that during the past few months there was a "phase of CGT regression" and that "the disastrous tactic of undermining labor unity was as much the fault of the CGT as of the Communist party," M. Maire claims the principle of united action between the two labor confederations is not in question. Recalling the polemical exchange following the elections, M. Maire declared: "We will not provide a 'shooting match' between national leaders of one confederation or the other. We believe that, in the end, unity is achieved through workers' direct participation in the inter-union debates. If no agreement exists on a demand or a strike action, the solution is not to barricade oneself in one's certitudes and to level a series of virulent tracts at one's partner; instead, it is to provoke discussion among workers, to hold meetings of worker groups or of entire firms, so that the debate transcends differences and difficulties. And what is true for short-term demands must also apply for longer-term changes."

5-5. THE FUTURE STRATEGY OF THE CNPF*

Over the 1970s, the French Employers Association (CNPF) played an important role in persuading industry to accept many social reforms such as monthly salaries, more assistance for the

*Jacqueline Grapin, "Le patronat en quête d'avenir," *Le Monde*, June 10, 1978 (selections).

disabled, and fairer dismissal practices. Despite the dispersed and complex structure of French industry, by 1980 the employers appeared more united than the workers, but there were and remain many divisions among businessmen. The CNPF president, M. Ceyrac, broadened the perspective of employers and rebuilt the CNPF. His speech to the Council of Young Directors (CJD) shows the difficulties of creating a broad-based organization and the limitations on the CNPF. The reporter also raises the question of how well the CNPF can continue to perform this role in a period of economic adversity.

Never has the employers' association appeared more united; yet perhaps it has never been more divided. Owing to the electoral battle, the chapels were sacrificed for the Church without ceasing to exist. Often the faithful remain outside if they have something to say.

The growing power of the employers' organizations grouped together in the CNPF makes sense in a society as structured and centralized as our own. But this growing strength coincides with the recognition that there are really two employers' associations increasingly estranged from each other: on the one hand, the CNPF with its headquarters at Avenue Pierre-1er-de-Serbie; on the other, the real employers' organization, dispersed throughout France and not existing as a collectivity because nothing is more marked among employers than their individualism. The first evades the real issues; the second defends itself. The one "causes," the other acts. This, then, is the division of labor among industry's leaders, resulting in certain advantages but also much discordance.

Attacked, vilified, sometimes bankrupt in the course of the last few years, this powerful social group has regained confidence since the March [1978] elections. It knows that so much depends on it: employment, the quality of life in France, the future of the government, even the survival of liberalism. What vision of the future does this important group hold? Is it that of a rearguard, attempting to defend its privileges by claiming to pursue the public interest? Or the vision of a rearguard proving its worth by marching ahead rather than following, even if this sometimes is costly? Or perhaps that of an avant-garde elite makng an assault with originality, marching towards the unknown? That depends on the specific case and level.

What the official employers' association calls its "base" has several different faces, whose interests are opposed on many points. What do the heads of large corporations and small-and medium-sized businesses have in common? These owners have so little contact with one another that it is doubtful whether they can understand each other's problems. The directors of the big Parisian businesses are former high state civil servants who have entered the private sector, "business civil servants" who do not really run their companies, professional managers who put at stake only their careers in the company's development. Farther down in the ranks or in the provinces, managers also risk their personal fortunes and most of their income in their firms. Nine-tenths of company headquarters are located in Paris, but the majority of small-and medium-sized industries are in the provinces.

This disconnection is not new, but increases in the present economic and political context, a fact which does not escape leaders of the CNPF. The Enterprise Institute, which they consider their "center for reflection," is preparing to examine a "spring report" which analyzes these opposing tendencies in a systematic study. Notably, small-and medium-sized firms believe they are at an unfair disadvantage in competing in the "administrative bazaar,"—as one small employer put it—in their relations with the state, especially in access to state markets: limited because large firms maintain their dominant positions and, in recent industrial policy, they centered almost exclusively on larger concentrations of "development poles" that leave smaller firms to their own devices. Moreover, they accuse the employers' professional associations of a nearly exclusive preoccupation with the "giants."

The character of the small entrepreneur, creater, and builder of industrial empires is, in fact, poorly understood, though he is important. He is, in general, utopian, often idealistic, and anti-establishment while, at the same time, he demands obedience to his own authority; he is easily irritated by others but claims his sociability. He is everything but serene, and fatally maladjusted. Jean Mantet, who revolutionized the world of household products, Marcel Fournier who pushed ahead in opening large stores in France, and Antoine Riboud, who expanded BSN from its base in Lyon, were first of all protesters against the established order. Don't you have to be a little crazy to enter nowadays into such adventures?

It remains true that the "employers' machine" which now excels in bringing together men and ideas, balks at integrating them. Thus, the stabilizing role of the CNPF is confirmed, though it cannot escape the distortions which threatens executives (in the private as well as public realms). Within the association itself, most experiments of the past ten years—including those of M. Ceyrac—which tried to breathe new life into the organization failed. The same faces are found in in leadership as in 1967.

Thus, the various "schools of thought" have become, according to the CNPF itself, its schools. This is one reason for M. Ceyrac's presence at the National Conference of Young Directors—unthinkable a decade ago in the era when the "young bosses" passed for "young Turcs." In fact, the CNPF has become less mobile—rendering it less easily offended—and its partners are assuaged.

The Council of Young Directors today presents itself as a collector of practical experience more than as a force for innovation. It has become a supplier of young managers at the regional level and a springboard which allows them to "move up" to Paris. For its part, enterprise and progress has lost its claws. And the Christian employers' organization is too busy finding itself to have time for anything else.

"Yes, our side [parti] is on that of the firm," wrote M. Jean Chénevier in the May Newsletter of the Enterprise Institute, an agency established by the CNPF. But this is far from a clarification of options, undoubtedly because the employers' world is, like the administration, a hydra with a thousand heads, not all of which want to follow the sweep of history. However, in the words of Gaston Berger (who likes to cite M. Jacques Delors): "To examine the future is already to change it."

5-6. THE RIGHT TO STRIKE IN QUESTION*

A principle of French labor law is that the right to strike is a fundamental individual right. On the one hand, this has meant that the law has not been used to enforce closed shops and settle jurisdictional disputes as much as in Anglo-Saxon democracies, but it has

---

*Jean-Jacques Dupeyroux, "Le droit de grève en Pologne . . . mais en France?," *Le Monde*, September 17, 1980.

also made workers more vulnerable during periods of economic decline. Using the Polish strikes to illustrate the relative weakness of the French unions to protect their members, a leading expert on social and labor law, Dupeyroux, surveys recent attempts to punish strikers with dismssal. Dupeyroux speculates that even though the CNPF has recognized the injustice of using economic adversity to punish strikers, the temptation to further disrupt unions and discipline workers may lead to even more stormy industrial relations in France.

Have Polish workers really won recognition of the right to strike? France is fascinated by this question while simply forgetting that, in fact, this right is not yet completely recognized here—sometimes this gives a comical aspect to certain [French] commentaries.

But it is hardly a joke. According to its proper meaning, a right is not truly recognized unless its exercise does not lead to the imposition of any sanction. In principle, this is the case for the right to strike, as indicated in our constitution. Moreover, its exercise must not expose the worker to "any sanction, either juridical or practical," affirmed the president of the CNPF, Mr. François Ceyrac, before the Civil Rights Commission of the National Assembly. On the other hand, if going on strike can result in permanent loss of employment, even with some compensation for unfair dismissal (*rupture abusive*), this means that the right to strike is not really recognized as legitimate. Even children would understand this principle—particularly, the children of workers fired in these conditions. What could be worse for a worker than to lose his job and again find himself unemployed?

What exactly is the situation in France? While it should have been long accepted that firing someone for going on strike is not allowed if the strike action presents no irregularities, there is still unlimited debate—as only jurists can pursue it—as to whether the judge— that is, the judge for interim proceedings—can order the immediate reinstatement of workers dismissed because of a work stoppage. The relentlessness of this debate is explained by the fact that the very existence of this right is at stake.

This matter is much too important to be left to the competence of judges; the preparatory work on the 1950 law, according to which a strike does not break a labor contract, reveals the legislator's resistance to the full recognition of the right to strike; the 1973 law on dismissals failed to include reinstatement in its measures on unfair dismissal practices. And, moreover, whatever the situation, wouldn't any reinstatement measure run counter to certain general principles of our law? And so the debate continues.

Nothing, in this hodgepodge, is worth a kopek because the real juridical problem arises prior to it: does or does not our constitution recognize the existence of the right to strike? This is the only question. If the answer is negative, if it gives a purely symbolic nod to this right, the [proceedural] "conveyor belt" runs this way: the interim judge is not competent to decide, and the reinstatement of striking workers is excluded. If, on the contrary, it is decided that our basic charter guarantees the right to strike (not merely symbolically), President Ceyrac is right—the exercise of this right should not be penalized and dismissals are not unfair, but null and void. In this case, the conveyor belt runs in the other direction; the Law of 1973 has nothing to do with the debate, and the continuation of a contract can certainly be decided by an interim judge.

The problem may soon be presented to the Supreme Court of Appeals over a May incident at Chrysler-Talbot, where about twenty workers went on strike and were first expelled and then fired by the company. Among them were several immigrants who undoubtedly imagined that the right to strike was recognized in France.

In a courageous judgement rendered July [1980], the Magistrate's Court at Poissy—in interim proceedings—declared that, unless devoid of all meaning, "the exercise of the right to strike presupposes that job security by assured by a direct contractual relationship and not merely through the indirect means of guaranteeing responsibility and the paying of damages which this may entail—the latter are incompatible with the constitutional recognition of the right to strike." It also ordered the reinstatement of dismissed workers, a decision with which Chrysler-Talbot refused to comply; they await an appeals court decision.

All that appears certain to us is that, in 1980, it is time to leave behind equivocations and pretexts. One can be for the right to strike while at the same time favorable to a more precise ruling in this area. At the risk of shocking the Left, we believe the moment has come for a general rethinking of the conditions under which this right can be exercised, if we wish to avoid the adverse consequences

England is now experiencing! One can, on the other hand, be against the right to strike, if one has the courage to frankly admit it.

But rhetoric is no longer tolerable, in a period of crisis and underemployment—that is, rhetoric consisting of warmly congratulating workers for living in a liberal democracy which grants them the right to strike, while at the same time warning them in a heartbroken tone, that the exercise of this right could cause them to lose their jobs.

The president of the CNPF knew how to shoulder his responsibilities in categorical terms. It would be difficult to understand if our courts long allowed the free run of rearguard guerillas—even more so, after the events at Gdansk.

6 Social Security: Success by Default

One of the more astute critics of the French social security system has called it an "unfinished cathedral" (Dumont, 1978). The metaphor might be applied to any modern welfare state, but it is particularly apt in conveying the intricacy and patchwork that constitutes the French system. The edifice itself is of magnificent proportions and provides a wide variety of protection for nearly the entire population. But within the church there are numerous altars, each collecting funds for different purposes and dispensing earthly benefits in different ways. Within the cathedral grounds, an almost endless sprawl of cloistered groups obtain special comforts and privileges. As in the medieval societies who spent centuries building cathedrals, the church is supposed to be above politics, but it is now obvious that its good works depend on the subsidies and protection provided by the state. The political controversies that swirl about the system have all the fervor of theological disputes, yet the system has thrived throughout the Fifth Republic and has developed an institutional network that rivals the state itself.

For many of the same reasons that retarded the development of a well-defined pattern of labor relations (see Chapter 5), both the need and the demand for social security was slow to emerge in France. The primarily agrarian population of the nineteenth century was less vulnerable to the economic and social disasters that imposed heavy and the unexpected costs on more urban societies. A self-reliant and proud middle-class looked after itself and was both politically and socially insulated from the poor. The curious result was that as the need for social security grew, it was considered a "national obligation," not a response to growing labor conflict, as in Germany, or to a growing socialist party, as in Britain. Just as industrial relations in France are imbedded in a particular concept of society which prizes social solidarity, so also the idea of social welfare, if slow to appear, was in many ways more readily accepted as a natural obligation of a civilized society and a necessary function of the state. Indeed, one of the more intriguing paradoxes of the conservative Fifth Republic, including the more recent neoliberal reconstruction under Giscard, has been that the social security system grew at unprecedented rates and was extended to a broad array of services and needs that were neglected in earlier republics.

There is perhaps no better illustration of how France deals with institutional uncertainty than the intricate proliferation of the social security system over the past twenty years. When the major commitments to a modern social security system were made immediately following World War II, disillusion with the Third Republic was strong and the shape of the new republic remained uncertain. Neither the founders nor the prospective beneficiaries wanted to entrust social security to government, and so the ubiquitous device of a public establishment was used to create an autonomous organization. While the Left was quick to accuse the government of undermining the autonomy of the system, it would have been virtually impossible for such a huge amount of public funds to remain unsupervised in any modern government. As we shall see, there were no fewer complexities and constraints once the Socialists came to power in 1981 and, in some ways, the Left is even less able to defend itself from new demands. In any event, the interpenetration of the state and the social security system is now virtually undecipherable. With very little guidance from political institutions, France has built one of the most comprehensive social security systems in Europe, except for the massive systems of the Scandanavian countries.

Context

To understand both partisan politics and policy differences as they arise in the French social security system, it is essential to grasp the comprehensive meaning attached to "social." In Britain and North America, access to social benefits is often seen in the framework of pluralist politics with various client groups, political parties, and government competing for support. But the case of

France suggests that social spending can increase at high rates even with less effective political competition (see Reading 6-4). The Gaullists and Giscardians were competing for middle class votes, while both feared the rise of united Left. Beyond the political battles, there is a distinct nationalist strain, with all the parties subscribing to an intimate relation between society and state. Indeed, the sense of national obligation and mutual dependence derived from the French political tradition is so strong that the common Anglo-Saxon phrase, "the welfare state," is rarely used in French politics.

The presumption that society and government are ideally united in their aims also means that properly speaking all social programs are part of the French concept of social security. As we have seen in Chapter 5, the French are more accustomed to labor conflict than are Anglo-Saxon countries; they see labor conflict as a sign of social weakness rather than as a natural sequence in resolving labor-management differences. Once unemployment became a major problem (which rarely was the case until 1975), the government assumed financial responsibility and created new agencies with much less resistance than one might expect from a conservative regime. These attitudes meant that delimiting "social" policies in France was necessarily an arbitrary decision (see Reading 6-3).

French social policy includes *all* policies relating to society, including unemployment, sickness, old age, children, general public health (*aide sanitaire et sociale*), poverty relief (*aide sociale*), adult education (*promotion sociale*), continuing education (*education permanente*), assistance for the handicapped and disabled, accident prevention, manpower training, youth programs, recreation, and even cultural activity. Understanding the comprehensive nature of French thinking about social policy makes the Gaullist concessions to new social needs less perplexing and, of course, also makes it more difficult for the Left to construct a critique of the Right based on the inadequacy of social programs and activities (see Reading 6-1). Like the Left in nearly every modern democracy, the Socialists and Communists would like to see more assistance provided in more distinctly redistributive ways, but it is probably harder to find neglected social needs in France than in most modern industrial states.

As in the case of many social policies, there was a distinct bipartisan quality induced by rapid industrialization and urbanization. No party could ignore the costs of rapid social change while the victims of rapid change were increasingly visible. From 1946 to 1973, the French population increased by twelve million persons (more than over the entire nineteenth century), including 8.5 million persons from increased birthrates, 1.3 repatriated the Algeria, and 2.5 million net increase from immigration (see Chapter 7). Nor could any government ignore the demographic vise of total population increase while active population decreased (*Données Sociales*, 1978, p. 44). The problem of fewer people contributing to support more people is not likely to disappear in the near future (Sullerot Report, 1979). Even so, the rate of growth of social benefits diminished very little under the economic blows of the late 1970s while, in Britain and West Germany, the rate of growth was drastically reduced (Lagrange and Launay, 1980, p. 1142.

Living in a society that remained more agrarian and self-reliant over the nineteenth century and that escaped the worst ravages of unemployment in the twentieth century meant there was less pressure to expand social services and benefits. Although millions placed their savings in mutual savings associations, there were only 100,000 persons in private pension plans in 1900 (see Ashford, 1981). In 1930, the government provided some public support for mutual retirement schemes, but state assistance was largely confined to the public sector (civil servants, military) or more hazardous occupations (mining, railroads). Much of this early help was justified by the national priority of the various occupations and, as we shall see, the early privileges later returned to complicate the development of a comprehensive social security system.

Indicative of the strong sense of national obligation that permeated social security, proposals to strengthen the family and to protect children were more welcome. Because of the early surge of opinion favoring more assistance, the first law to subsidize large families was passed in 1913. The introduction of family allowances anticipated the severe divisions that were later to develop among the various beneficiaries of a growing social security "pie." The Popular League of Large Families, organized by a Capt. Maire who was himself the father of ten children, soon spawned its own organization of 1500 affiliates throughout France (Bonnet, 1978). In 1932, family allowances became the first nationally sponsored benefit. By 1978, there were nineteen groups organized around the Family Allocation Fund (CNAF) with every conceivable group from Communist workers to the Bank of France having its own client group (Chauvière, 1978). Thus, the future problems of social security were due, not only to the relatively late development of many services, but to the organizational alliances that were created to defend particular benefits.

The reformist euphoria that gripped France after World War II, the Council of Liberation (an interim government under the liberation) passed a decree (*ordonnance*) which created the first comprehensive system. The first article of the order reads, "An organization of Social Security is instituted to guarantee workers and their families against risks of whatever nature that might reduce or diminish their capacity to earn, and to cover the costs of maternity and the family." The emphasis on the family reasserts the sense of national obligation that differentiates France from countries where social security demands were more clearly a product of class conflict. As in most social security systems, the initial intent was to protect contributors. As the new system took shape, there emerged a maze of diverse benefits for similar risks which covered many occupational groups, each defending its special interests. Such demands often crossed partisan political lines. For example, an authority on the early growth of special claims described how the Communist-dominated railroad workers threatened to withdraw from the CGT if the main union did not support their privileged benefits.

Contrary to the image of a highly centralized state, the goal of the 1945 decree was to establish an independent and self-governed machinery. The aim was, first to unify the several organizations (*régimes*) that had been set up during the piecemeal accumulation of social benefits before the war and, second, to see that the new organization was run entirely by the beneficiaries (see Reading 6-1). Although the French experts who designed the system were impressed by the Beveridge Plan in Britain, they had neither British confidence in central administration nor British intent (soon abandoned) that the system should be run on an actuarial basis. The new organization was based on contributions from employees and employers that were, presumably, to meet each year's expenditures. The administrative committees for each of the three main benefits—family allowances, old age pensions, and sickness—were elected by the supporting "social partners," including all the unions, business, agricultural, and professional groups.

But the intricate pattern of political compromise and bargaining found throughout the French policy process quickly superimposed itself on the new system. The first inroad was that the prewar beneficiaries would not give way to the single agency (*régime génér-ale*), so the system remained an unwieldly and fiercely defensive conglomerate of four different organizations. Within limited space, these complications are best illustrated in the following diagram. In effect, the general regime was never able to encompass all the social groups within the system nor all the kinds of benefits provided. The additional benefits that employees (including both more privileged groups and workers in several nationalized industries) had extracted were conceded by creating special regimes. Unemployment and large portions of old age benefits for employees were enhanced with additional payments organized in "complementary regimes"; agriculture and the self-employed had autonomous regimes for sickeness and pensions (Eustache, 1978). Contrary to the common charge that French administration generates bureaucratic tangles, government spent most of the next thirty years trying to bring some coherence and uniformity to the social security system (see Reading 6-2).

French Social Security Organizations

	Employed		Agriculture	Self-Employed
Family Allocations	Spec.		General Regime	
Health and Sickness	Reg.		Autonomous	Autonomous
Old Age	Complementary		Regimes	Regimes
Unemployment	Regimes		No Regime	No Regime

The general regime is by far the largest; it received contributions from nearly seventeen million persons in 1975, while those who pay into the special agricultural regime steadily diminished from over a million in 1960 to about 800,000 in 1975. Roughly another three million contribute to the separate regimes for agricultural proprietors and the self-employed. In principle, the various regimes are supposed to be self-supporting and in equilibrium. In fact, only the general regime and complementary regimes for additional benefits (mostly pensions) to a specific social groups and occupations have come close to this fiscal ideal.

Overall, the state provides subsidies which account for about a tenth of social security contributions but these, too, are distributed in varying proportions from negligible subsidies to the general regime to a third or more of the receipts of regimes supporting agriculture and the multitude of special regimes. Within the various categories of benefits, the ratio of contributors to beneficiaries can vary wildly. For example, pension contributors to special regimes for miners and farmers must support three persons, which is clearly impossible, while under the general regime there may be three contributors for one beneficiary, which is a workable proportion.

The visibility of increased social spending has been maintained in France because the initial plan called for a "Social Budget" which would be submitted for parliamentary approval. In 1979, social security expenditures were 464 billion francs compared with central government expenditure of 902 billion. If one deducts transfers in the state budget, since 1974 the social budget has been larger than that of government itself (Rustant, 1977). Whatever its faults, the system generates awareness of its costs. Unlike much of the rest of Europe, where government makes huge transfers to social security from general taxation (mostly income tax), contributions flow directly into the various regimes and represent over 40 percent of total French taxation. (The idea that the French pay few taxes is a myth; they simply pay taxes in a different way.)

Possibly the most important reason that the system generates controversy is that about 60 percent of the overall range of welfare contributions of all kinds are paid by employers as a payroll or salary tax. Only about half this sum goes into the social security system but, even so, social security tax rates on employers are roughly three times the rates paid by employees (Rustant, 1977, p. 62). In 1977, employers paid just under 11 percent of their payrolls toward health, maternity, and invalidity benefits while employees paid 3 percent; they paid twice the employees' rate of contribution toward general pensions and complementary pension funds as well as for accident compensation; and they carried the total contribution toward family allowances (another 9 percent). The charges on employers for unemployment benefits were four times those paid by employees (1.7 and .4 percent).

The important result is that balancing social benefits against economic costs is a much more explicit process in French politics than in countries where social security is supported by large direct transfers from the national budget, such as in Britain, or where giant pressure groups of labor and business can work out their preferred solutions, which—until recently—was the case for Germany and Sweden (see Reading 6-5). The payroll tax also has built-in inequities because high technology, profitable firms with small payrolls, often pay less to the system than do more labor-intensive, less profitable industries (Boutbien Report, 1974). The system is also a disincentive to increase employment because each additional worker brings large increments in overhead of roughly half the additional salary. But awareness of these economic disadvantages did not appear to restrict the growth of social spending under the dominant Right in recent years. Paradoxically, in a period of severe economic dislocation and increased unemployment, it was the new Socialist government of 1981 that has been compelled to make concessions to employers as it expanded benefits.

Agenda

Although de Gaulle initated the 1945 reforms as the liberator of France, when he returned to power in 1958 he had neither the time nor the disposition to turn to social problems. As one of his advisers has written, "De Gaulle was not spontaneously attracted to social questions" (Ducamin, 1979, p. 211). Lest this quickly dismissed as simple Jacobin superiority, it is important to note that the importance of improving social benefits figured in the advice of his closest confident on the economic modernization of France (see Reading 6-2). Though the Gaullists sadly underestimated the social costs of rapid economic growth over the 1960s, they were by no means insensitive to social needs.

A more plausible explanation may well be that the accumulated experience of the Fourth Republic was hardly encouraging as the state made efforts to expand coverage and to equalize benefits. After long negotiation, supervisory and technical workers (*cadres*) agreed to form a pension plan (AGIRC) in 1947, but on different assumptions than the general pension plan. In other instances, there were long negotiations with industrial groups, such as steel, to include higher status occupations. Each improvement brought new inequities and more dispersion of control. Even within the government, the "Social Budget" became a source of interministerial rivalries, and its format could not be agreed upon until 1956 (Doublet, 1971)! Nonetheless, the Constitution of the Fifth Republic reiterated the state's obligation: "The nation assures the individual and the family the necessary conditions for their development. . . . It is only human that whomever for reason of age, physcial or mental condition, or economic situation, find themselves unable to work have the right to obtain a suitable living from the collectivity."

In 1958, the social system was not yet in deep financial trouble, but the confusing organization of contributions and benefits outside the state distressed hard line Gaullists who felt that the role of the state should be well defined and well established. But those who thought that simple forms of centralization and control, so often attributed to the Gaullist barons, might solve such intricate problems were soon disabused. More accurately perhaps, the Gaullists were about to take on a controversial and thankless job that had accumulated over the previous decade. With the technocratic simplicity that characterizes many initial Gaullist policy initiatives, they first tried to attack the system globally (see Reading 6-2).

A Coordination Committee for Social Security was formed to see whether the special regimes could be brought into the system, and to search for ways of extending coverage to groups outside the umbrella of industrial and commerical employees. An important first step in 1961 was the creation of a sickness and health protection for agricultural workers (AMEX) and, the next year, nearly all benefits unavailable to agricultural workers (proprietors had their own system) were extended. A second major reform was the creation of a new agency (ARRCO) to unify the various complementary regimes affecting *cadres*, the highly skilled and lower-level managerial occupations that had so successfully resisted merger with the general regime; this agency was intended to bring some order and more equality to pensions. The commonly held idea that the French bureaucracy stealthily aggrandizes control is contradicted by the fact by 1966, ARRCO had more pension funds than those held under the general regime, and the state had no more supervisory power than before (Barjot, 1971, p. 70).

In total, nearly four million additional persons were added; sickness and health benefits were added for noncontributors and the self-employed. Pensions, a favorite political plum in every country, doubled between 1960 and 1966. Family allocations were increased for older children and, for the first time in French history, special education was provided for handicapped children. Even these early reforms strained social security funds. Sensitive to fiscal deficits, the Bordaz Report estimated that benefits might increase by fifty percent by 1970 and, more alarming, the Dobler Report predicted an 8 billion franc deficit by 1970 and advised a totally rethinking of the assumptions underlying the social security system. Gaullist good intentions seemed to generate even worse problems.

As a result, in 1967 a trusted Gaullist technocrat, Jeanneney, was appointed minister of social affairs, a newly created superministry to bring together governmental responsibilities in the field of social security. As sensitive—perhaps more sensitive—to electoral pressures as most democracies, action was delayed in 1965 because of the presidential elections and again in 1966 because of the approaching legislative elections. During this time, Pompidou,—who resisted the idea of reducing benefits—talked with the CGT, CFDT and CNPF to uncover alternatives. To further increase political uncertainties for the Gaullists, their natural allies in the CNPF published an extremely hostile report in 1965 (Piquetty Report), recommending that risks be more sharply differentiated, that limits be placed on benefits and contributions, and that the administrative committees of various components of the system be reorganized along stricter lines.

The guidelines for reform were provided for Jeanneney by a presidential commission, the Friedel Report (1966). The commission dealt rather brutally with the old assumptions of French social security. It claimed that "national solidarity" no longer characterized a system where contributions were collected much like taxes, and where neither contributions nor benefits were understood by beneficiaries. Anticipating the massive social security programs of today, the report wrote that the beneficiaries are "strangers who do not feel the least solidarity in the world" (p. 7). Perhaps to discredit criticism from the Left, the report rejected the idea of using incomes as a basis for calculating benefits because they are difficult, if not impossible, to define. Even if this was done, there would remain serious problems of how to differentiate need. The division between social security and social assistance or welfare was criticized for duplicating the same effort, and the state was criticized for providing subsidies for unclear and sometimes inconsistent reasons.

In the meantime, the state had resorted to a variety of expedient solutions for new needs by attaching additional benefits such as prenatal care, maternity leave, supplements for single parents, and housing for large families to the family benefit system. Pensions were described as a "paroxism" of complexity (p. 5) where the efforts to unify the system had, in fact, increased inequities. The report suggested that pension support which came from the general regime should be diminished if the union had ample private support for old age or was enlisted in a more advantageous complementary scheme. To begin to unravel this confusion, the report recommended that the system be reorganized to more clearly distinguish the "risks" that were covered. It is worth noting that, by 1980, the realization that the public cannot guarantee unlimited risks was more widely accepted, though this was harder to subtantiate at the time. An advantage of the French system was that it made the shortcomings of the unlimited risk assumption explicit.

It has become fashionable to accuse French techocrats of creating French problems: but, in truth, Jeanneny's task was one of converting an unpleasant truth into an institutional reality. Given the frailty of French political institutions this was (and remains) no simple task. The failure to more arbitrarily reform the system over 1966–67 had already required Treasury payments of nearly five billion francs (Guillaume, 1971, p. 85). Like many technocratic solutions in France and elsewhere, the reform made more sense in the abstract than in reality. The basic idea was to separate the three major risks (excluding unemployment, which was not serious at the time nor did it come under the social security regimes). Accordingly, three depository agencies (*caisses*) were set up for health and sickness (CNAM), family allocations (CNAF), and old age pensions (CNAF). In an attempt to equalize and to control contributions, another central agency was created to collect all contributions (URSSAF).

Although probably not the most critical changes made in 1967, the political debate centered on two issues. First, instead of being elected, the administrative councils were to be nominated by the various social partners. The CGT made this the spearhead of its attack on the reforms, even though in 1945 it had favored nomination until the Communists had control of the union. The second change was equal representation of employees and employers: nine nominated by the unions including three by the CGT and two by the CFDT, and nine by the CNPF. A direct voice in the administration of the system was too important for the larger unions to ignore. They refused offices in the new system, but attended and voted regularly. One expert felt that the most significant way to begin reforms was to diminish the powers of the National Federation of Social Security Organizations (FNOSS) made up of social security employees who fought every change in the system.

The more important changes were, first, the beginning of a control over soaring health and sickness charges. Two devices were introduced: a variable ceiling on contributions to obtain more from higher wage groups, and a complex system of allocating a portion of medical charges to the consumer (*ticket modérateur*) for medicines and prolonged illness. The reform took several years to implement, not because of administrative inefficiency, but because the ultimately redistributive effect of increasing payments from mutual insurance companies brought stiff resistance.

Perhaps the best indicator of the rapid advance of French social security over the 1960s was that increased benefits did not play a major part in the Grenelle Accords following the May 1968 strikes. In his meetings with the "social partners," Pompidou agreed to submit the 1967 order to parliament, which had to be done in any event, and where it passed into law with little resistance. Some of the powers of the "social partners" overseeing the new agencies were reinforced, and a fund for those unable to pay the individual health charges was established. Were these early efforts the reform social security a success or failure? If we assume that the government's intention was to diminish social benefits, for which there is little evidence, the late 1960s were hardly a "success." Benefits increased by 40 percent over the Fifth Plan period and at the rate of nearly 7 percent per year. Although the new charges avoided social security deficits until 1970, the administration clearly found it easier to broaden coverage than to limit benefits or to increase contributions. Indeed, there were few changes in the direction of more equality without the state itself paying a premium to privileged groups or accepting responsibility for costs that had haphazardly been added to the regimes over the years.

Process

In the second stage of the transformation of policy and politics, President Pompidou introduced an approach that is very similar to the one found in most Western democracies. Increased benefits are no longer stiffly resisted, but made contingent on increased productivity and national wealth. The growth strategy has obvious pitfall because most social benefits cannot be reduced in periods of economic adversity, while many other social costs, such as unemployment benefits and manpower training programs, may rapidly increase. The growth strategy presupposes a close coordination of social security and economic policy and depends on voluntary cooperation from the private sector.

As a pragmatic politician with an intimate knowledge of business, Pompidou's new strategy seemed a natural choice, even though he abandoned the French tradition of a parsimonious, self-financed social security system. His prime minister, Chaban-Delmas, enthusiastically subscribed to the new policy, enshrined in the electoral slogan "New Society." In fact, Chaban was made the vehicle of a new social era in French social policy. From 1970 to 1975, benefits grew at the spectacular rate of 17.4 percent per year, while contributions increased at only 8 percent a year. By 1975, the social budget exceeded the state budget. While the Gaullists certainly felt the pressure of the growing unity of the left-wing parties, the increases are large enough to suggest something more than a partisan response. France was responding to the shock of the May 1968 demonstrations, and was well on the way to developing one of the most complete social security systems in Europe.

To the alarm of many hard line Gaullists, Chaban appointed advisers with strong socialist tendencies, such as Jacques Delors, later to become Mitterrand's minister of finance. The documents of the period reflect the renewed hope of expanding the social responsibilities of government. Although preparations for the Sixth Plan

(1970–75) were well underway when Pompidou became president, a high-powered Commission on Social Benefits reported in early 1971, and there were a plethora of reports on sickness and health insurance, family policy, poverty relief, the handicapped, and an excellent study by an "Intergroup" on aging (a planning study cutting across functional policy lines), largely written by Nicole Questiaux, later head of Mitterrand's superministry for social policy (Fournier and Questiaux, 1979).

As the Intergroup pointed out, France had managed to devise a social security system which operated under three different principles. Family allowances are a "pure" transfer, affected only by the rules of distrubtion and are clearly redistributive (see Boissières and Bougain, 1979). Sickness and health benefits are obviously based on individual need so that neither costs nor demand can be controlled. Pensions are a product of group politics for numerous occupational categories, each working to maximize its return (Planning Commission, 1971). For the first time, France was squarely faced with the problems of maintaining equity and fiscal autonomy in a highly diverse system. While Pompidou did not subscribe to the socialist overtone of the reports of this period, many recommendations for specific changes became official policy (Meric, 1972).

In a system that claimed to be responsive to government's "social partners," the diverse responses to the Planning Commission's progressive stance was hardly encouraging. The CGT saw no important changes and the CFDT unhappily found the "spirit of 1967" prevailing (meaning that it wanted more local involvement and decentralization of the system). The CGC was alarmed that more flexible ceilings might increase charges on the highly skilled. The CNPF responded as it always had that increased charges cannot be separated from their "economic context," while the CGPME wanted an annual review to enhance possibilities of reversing charges on small employers. Despite the divisions of the "social partners", France was one of the few welfare states in Europe and North America where the idea of embarking on a massively funded social security system was thoroughly debated.

During Pompidou's presidency a number of major reforms expanded coverage and increased benefits. In 1971, nearly a billion francs were added to maternity benefits, including near full-pay for working mothers during prenatal and postnatal care. In 1970, a pioneering law extended more benefits to the handicapped and, in 1972, a law promised the self-employed benefits equal to those of the more fully covered employees. Pensions increased rapidly and France reached it goal of having pensions equal to one-half the minimum wage (SMIC) by 1975. By means of an agreement with the medical associations in 1970, and a law in 1972 regulating private hospitals and their care, and there were renewed efforts to bring medical costs under control.

Bringing financial order to the system was not easy, but rapid growth—and hence growing contributions over the early 1970s—relieved some of the urgency of the 1960s. The finance law of 1974 authorized moving funds for surplus regimes (most often CNAF) to deficit funds (most often CNAM), though it had sometimes been done earlier in circuitous ways. Another step toward vertical redistribution was to make health contribution ceilings adjustable from 1974. There were also new efforts to unify the financing of benefits for agricultural workers—largely subsidized by the state—by creating a single budgetary scheme (BAPSO) (See Cahiers Français, 1975). In 1970, a "solidarity charge" was placed on large firms; this indicated the more progressive policies undertaken by the CNPF under Ceyrac, but it was still only temporary relief. The results were disappointing.

Although the French have never been insensitive to the costs of social security, one is again struck by how radical a transformation of the politics of social policy took place under Pompidou. The decision was inadvertent, but the future of the welfare state was firmly attached to economic growth and the national social responsibility was accepted. Difficult as it was for the "social partners" to accept the role of the state in welfare, the initial system of autonomous and self-financing social security was, in effect, simply abandoned in favor of increasing benefits to be negotiated between government and its clients. In a remarkably short period of time, France created a self-propelled system similar to most modern welfare states. Though perhaps inadvertent, Pompidou's growth strategy effectively politicized social security at the national level. So long as economic growth increased the size of the pie, the pluralist structure worked reasonably well and brought about huge increases in total benefits. No sooner had the new strategy been accepted than it was plunged into new crisis by the pressures of the 1973 oil crisis.

Consequences

By the presidential elections of 1974, the system had grown so large and complex that only marginal change was possible. In the third stage of the transformation there were essentially two political issues: what small improvements could be made to include those small groups (no more than 2 percent of the population) still not covered by some form of benefits, and how should the growing dependence on state transfers into the social security system be handled? While Giscard distinguished himself by several initiatives to remove some of the more general social inequities from French life, such as the rigid divorce and abortion laws, the social security agenda was fairly well fixed.

The 1974 presidential campaign signifies the turning point for the full politicization of social policy. The Left's Common Program of 1972 and the Socialist and Communist programs of 1974 included large increases in the SMIC, making redistribution politics a reality in France. Significantly, the Left also promised that increased benefits would not be achieved at the cost of the special privileges given certain occupational groups in the system. Giscard enlarged on Pompidou's plans to increase pensions and promised that the minimum pension (AVTS) would reach 80 percent of the SMIC by 1980. The curious political situation was that, squeezed between determined efforts of the Right to outdo the Left's promises and the lavish increments promised by the Left, the new centrist coalition was just as profligate a social welfare spender as was the Pompidou presidency.

The limited scope for changes within the system is perhaps best illustrated by the debate over "unjustified charges" (*charges indues*). To avoid deficits and to meet special demands, each of the funds had accumulated a strange mixture of alternative uses. The estimate was that about twenty-two billion francs (Masnago, 1978) were being diverted from their intended use. First, some of the special regimes drew funds from the general regime to benefit special interests such as subsidizing public housing, contributing to the poverty fund (FNS), and meeting the costs of new benefits for mothers and single parents (see Dayan, 1976). Another source of distortions was adding taxes to free benefits such as drugs, one of the few ways a presumably strong administration could compel the powerfully organized pharmacists to share the soaring costs of medicine. A third problem was loss of contributions from delinquent employers, estimated at four billion francs in 1974. Given the size of the social security budget (about 400 billion francs in 1974), the debate tells us more about French pecuniary habits than about social security. Nonetheless, these efforts to curb costs at the margins failed and, in 1974, Giscard was greeted with a social security deficit of about a billion francs.

Possibly less cosmetic was Giscard's effort to broaden the system to the few remaining categories of excluded persons, most often the noncontributors who had no fixed or recorded income that enabled them to become regular participants. Thus, such unlikely groups as priests and prostitutes were attached to the system to fully establish the principle of universal coverage (Floreal, 1978). But the search for a compromise between the inequities of the burden of social spending and the economic interests of the country was the main preoccupation of the Giscardian regime. First, as outlined in the Boutbien Report (1974) and the Calvez Report (1978), the economic inequities of the payroll tax were reviewed. For example, it was shown that the thriving oil industry contributed 15 percent of the added value of its product to social security revenues, while a hard-pressed but labor-intensive textile industry was contributing 26 percent of the added value of its product. In effect, the payroll tax meant that less profitable firms were underwriting the social costs of more profitable firms, a contradiction even in Giscardian neoliberal economics.

There was a major study of the system by the Economic and Social Council, the de Vernejoul Report (1974) (see Reading 6-3), and another on the unjustified charges, the Grégoire Report (1975). In the tidal wave of new inquiries, possibly the Granger Report (1975) was the most important because it examined and discarded most of the alternatives for increasing contributions, thereby eliminating what might seem the simplest solution to renewed social security deficits. The Granger Report tackled one of the most controversial problems of adjusting social security contributions to salary levels which was eventually accepted in part when President Giscard's energetic minister of health, Mme. Veil, persuaded the "social partners" to have higher ceilings on higher incomes for purposes of medical and sickness benefits. But the laborious process of negotiation did not forestall new social security deficits. In 1978, the deficit reached the astronomical (in French eyes) total of five billion francs and soared to ten billion in 1979.

By the end of Giscard's presidency, the central political issue over French social security was not the universalization of coverage or the equalization of benefits, but the problem of paying for large and usually inflation-indexed benefits. Giscard's imperturbable prime minister, Barre, had promised in the 1978 legislative election campaign that the system of contributions and benefits would remain unchanged (see Reading 6-4). In fact, this was an enormous financial commitment from a government also committed to restoring a free market economy. As the Berger Report (1977) pointed out, health benefits were doubling every four years and pensions every three. Added to these burdens were the increased cost of unemployment benefits. Without increased unemployment costs, the system would actually have shown a surplus of eleven billion francs in 1976. The paradoxical result is that a government committed to reducing the role of the state had little choice but to increase the national transfer to social security. By 1980, the state contribution approached 20 percent of the social budget (see Reading 6-5).

The Socialists were well aware of the complexity and inequities built into the French social security system (Uri, 1979; Socialist Party, 1980), but were somewhat less clear about what might be done to remove them (Blum-Girardeau, 1981). As in other modern welfare states, the system could not be dismantled without enormous controversy, and the Socialists had higher priority projects in the early months of their rule. Of course, there are no problems increasing benefits. In addition to raising the SMIC 10 percent, minimum pensions were increased 20 percent (to 1,700 francs per month), and housing subsidies were increased 25 percent (*Le Monde*, June 4, 1981). These measures were also good electoral tactics and came prior to the new legislative elections. The package cost about eight billion francs and, a few months later, another six billion francs was required to pay for increased unemployment benefits. A Socialist concept of the unity of social services was implemented by creating a superministry, the Ministry of National Solidarity, under a well-known authority on the French system, Mme. Questiaux. With the 1981 budget deficit already more than doubled and new social spending estimated at fifty billion francs for the next two years, it seemed unlikely that more could be done in the immediate future (see Reading 6-6).

Perhaps the French social security system is the best illustration of the peculiar way that institutionalized uncertainties affect policymaking in France. While every effort was made to organize the system outside the reach of the state, the political appeal of increased benefits led to more state subsidies and to more state intervention. In this respect, France is no different from most modern welfare states where politicians are often quick to raise benefits and slow to find ways to pay for them. But as Laroque wrote (1971, p. 15), the basic problem was that no group would sacrifice its vested interest in order to build a unified system. Thus, the political uncertainties are compounded because the state must fight on two fronts. The intricate and partially autonomous procedures for calculating benefits and contributions creates deficits the state must pay while also trying to develop a more coherent organization. Additional uncertainty is its dependence on other legislation for miniumum wages and unemployment. Contrary to the image of forceful, centralized control, it is virutally impossible to grasp the levers of power regulating the French social security system.

If the modern welfare state was slow to appear in France, it lost little time in catching up with the major European powers and, by 1981, the 44 percent of public spending directed to social needs was not all that far behind the Scandinavian countries. Turbulent and uncertain politics did for France what consensus and corporate agreement did for much of the rest of Europe. The politics of social security were constantly shifting under the Fifth Republic, from De Gaulle's more technocratic approach to Pompidou's distinctly laissez-faire view of growth blended with increased benefits and, finally, to the full and irresistable momentum of the welfare state under Giscard and Mitterrand (Oheix Report, 1981). By default more than intent, France built one of the most complete social security structures in Europe.

Readings

6-1. THE EARLY OBJECTIVES OF FRENCH SOCIAL SECURITY*

In the enthusiasm for rebuilding France immediately after World War II, political parties were able to cooperate in organizing the first comprehensive social security system. The initial aim was to have a single fund paying for a variety of risks: old age, family allowance, and sickness and disability. Like most early social security systems, it was to cover only wage earners, but unlike most other systems, employers were to provide roughly two-thirds of the contributions, employees, one third, and the state, nothing. The reason for this was that both beneficiaries and officials, then as now distrusted state intervention and wanted a wholly autonomous social security system. Pierre Laroque, a distinguished member of the Council of State, had a major role in designing the new system. In these extracts for his recollections on founding the system, he outlines the basic objectives of French social security as it was first organized.

Until now all these [social security] efforts were dispersed. In the course of the past decade, the essential unity of the social security system has been recognized—that is, the impossibility of treating different problems in isolation, the necessity of approaching the problem as a whole in order to arrive at a coordinated solution. Indeed, this is the essential condition guaranteeing the success of such programs.

The goal which we must aim for is to give to all groups of the population (especially those whose livelihood depends on their employment) a feeling of complete security for tomorrow-the feeling that nothing will threaten their security, the feeling that whatever happens, they will always have available the minimum necessary to survival. The dispersal of the various [social security] institutions, and the conflicting principles of their legislative charters, undermines the establishment of a feeling of security. The insecur-

*Pierre Laroque, *Revue de l'Action Popularie*, September–October 1965 (selections).

ities which threaten a family must be examined as a whole, and they cannot be treated in isolation if an effective solution is to be found.

Therefore, the social security organization must be responsible for all families and cover all possible risks facing them. No social security system worthy of its name can exist if it is not backed up by a single organization.

This refers, first of all, to the financial mechanism of social security, which is based on a redistribution of income. A tax is levied on certain sectors of the population which is then redistributed to those sectors lacking adequate means. But this tax levy can be achieved in various ways. The first is a direct levy of taxpayers— under the British system's Beveridge Plan, the state supplies half of the social security fund. The French system totally rejects this solution. Starting from the principle that social security should be an achievement of the beneficiaries based on workers' effort, the French plan stipulates that beneficiaries' contributions provide the financial basis. Undoubtedly, employers' contributions will be added to those of employees; but in the end, there is no profound difference between the two, since the employers' contribution is in reality the *firm's* contribution—and today's economic and social evolution tends to associate workers with management, making them aware that the firm's money is theirs too, so that what is paid by the firm is, in reality, paid by them.

In France, as abroad, the first efforts to institute a social security system were aimed at wage earners. It is for them that lack of security was most acute. But today it seems increasingly apparent that the social security problem cannot be compartmentalized and, to be completely effective, must encompass the entire population. Experience shows that no one can claim to be protected from the risks of insecurity; no one can be certain of tomorrow; no isolated individual can be sure to be able to cover all of life's unforeseen misfortune. Perhaps most important, social security as conceived today could be assured of a solid foundation only if strongly supported by public opinion. Whether examined from the viewpoint of technique, or as a morally and socially justified system of mutual aid, social security always calls for a united effort—an effort which no one has the right to undermine.

The policy of social security is really based on the conjunction of three different policies:

First of all, it is an economic policy, dictated by the objective of full employment.

Second, this is a policy of health and medical care allowing improved prevention and treatment of illnesses—a policy whose natural counterpart is the prevention of on-the-job accidents and job-related health problems.

Third, social security is a policy of income redistribution, as it modifies incomes under the free play of economic forces. This results in a better adaptation of resources to fulfill the needs of each individual and each family, and takes into account all the circumstances affecting their incomes.

From the moment that social security is considered in the framework of a general policy endowed with standard procedures, it matters relatively little whether the resources to apply these procedures—to cover the health care costs, the compensate for injuries—originates in direct contributions or in fiscal resources. In effect, the nation's economy as a whole always supports these costs, and deciding between one method of finance or another is only a matter of considering economic or psychological possibilities. In each case, the result is the same: on the one hand, a public service works to benefit the whole collectivity, and for which it assumes the expenses; and on the other hand, there is an authoritative redistribution of a portion of national income.

The effort at standardization has not been pushed as far in the area of unemployment compensation. Important differences between rules governing allocations and pensions granted to a worker deprived of income have been retained—moreover, this is intentional. In effect, there are at least two conceptions to determine allocation levels. A simple formula (as adopted by the British legislature) can be used, whereby a basic minimum is guaranteed to all, based on the idea that all those deprived of their work are in an identical situation and need the same wage to survive. This conception has not prevailed in France which, here again, favored individualizing benefits to the highest degree possible.

The social security funds [caisses] are autonomous organizations, ruled by private law, and each endowed with an administrative council primarily composed of elected representatives of the beneficiaries. This formula is required by traditional principles of union democracy. It tends to give social security beneficiaries the feeling that their benefits are not distributed by an impersonal, anonymous administration, but by institutions controlled by their representatives and acting in their interest; moreover, that these benefits are the product of their own efforts in the framework of national solidarity. According to the French conception, social security should not only give to employees a feeling of security, but also make them aware that this security is their own doing—for which they share the credit and the responsibility. The plan for social security should favor the liberation of workers and the maximization of democracy.

6-2. EARLY RECOMMENDATIONS FOR SOCIAL SECURITY REFORM*

Unlike most Anglo-Saxon welfare sytems, the French are less prone to compartmentalize welfare programs from other government problems. In 1958, President de Gaulle convoked a Committee of Experts under Jacques Rueff—who was basically a financial adviser to the government—to review the economy, but attention was also paid to aligning fiscal and financial aspects of social security with the stabilization of economy as a whole. These ideas inspired the early, and not too successful, reforms of 1967, but in an unforeseen way these concerns have regained prominence as all the modern welfare states struggle with the fiscal burden of expanded social security systems.

The administrative statute of the various social security programs is the main problem. The annual transactions of these programs exceeds 3000 billion (old) francs. The services which they offer both in collecting and dispensing funds, however well-intentioned, do not have the quality of true public services and are not subject to the same controls as the latter.

It is for this reason that the Committee of Experts which I had the honor of presiding favored their "fiscalization"—e.g., the collection of social security by the Treasury. At the same time, the structure of these social security funds, which are entrusted to

---

*Jacques Rueff *Combats pour l'ordre financier*, Paris, Plon, 1972, pp. 271–72 (selections).

deliver an essential public service, often through elected authorities, must be studied and reformed.

It would appear desirable that the financial equilibrium of the consolidated system by secured not globally, through transfers from one system to another—for example, from family allocations to sickness insurance—but rather system by system, so that the contributions of each cover expenses. Only through such a rigorous financial compartmentalization can the link between contributions and services be maintained, in accordance with the principles of good management.

6-3. THE FRENCH CONCEPT OF SOCIAL SOLIDARITY*

Despite the diverse and often conflicting practices within the French social security system, the principle of social solidarity remains basic to the system and has been used to justify many increases in benefits under both Giscard and more recently Mitterrand. Much like the notion of equality in Anglo-Saxon social systems, social solidarity is not an undifferentiated concept. The growing complications were well outlined in the de Vernejoul Report. The author of the report shows how there are at least three distinct meanings: equality within any particular group in relation to the range of benefits for sickness, retirement, and families; equality among contributions from numerous professional groups; and equality in the distribution of the national transfer within the entire social security system. Given the well institutionalized advantages that certain beneficiaries have, and their organization around numerous régimes for occupational groups, working out a way to use state transfers more fairly is an intricate and highly controversial problem.

Solidarity [or Social Cohesion?]

In the area of social security, solidarity can be defined as the institution of a system of mutal aid allowing those without work to receive financial assistance from the employed.

This transfer can take place either within the same socio-professional category, or between distinct categories; or it can

*De Vernejoul Report, "Les Problèmes posés par la securité sociale," *Avis et Rapports du Conseil Economique et Social*, January 19, 1974.

distribute the contributions of the whole community to the benefit of certain groups or categories.

In the spirit of the 1945 legislation, solidarity—or social cohesion—provided compensation for the costs of health care, old age, and raising families, along with taxation contributed to the redistribution of income between the better-off and poorer classes. In effect, the correction of social inequalities constitutes one of the most original elements of our social security legislation.

The preamble of the April 1946 Law, establishing the generalization of social security, is particularly clear in this regard: "The implementation of the social security plan results in economic terms in income redistribution."

Even more precise are the terms of the December 22, 1950, letter from the director of Social Security to the president of the UNCAF (Family Allocation Agency): "French social security institutions have no other object than to provide mutual aid and solidarity among individuals, families, and social groups." Whether they increase family income, assist workers in meeting expenses related to illness or accident, or grant resources to the aged, these institutions establish—always in a partial and still imperfect form—an effort to introduce a degree of equality in income distribution.

Has the evolution of social security since 1945 responded to the legislative intent in this regard?

Given the state of economic research there is no precise answer to this question.

In effect, if it is relatively easy to determine the beneficiaries of social security benefits (the unemployed, the retired, the ill and families), it is, at the same time, very difficult to know to what extent each social category or each citizen had been aided by social security.

The redistributive effect of social security is expressed in the ratio between contributions and benefits. Its measure is difficult and even impossible for two reasons: one is the complexity of our social security system; the other is the lack of information on amounts of contributions.

Some studies have been undertaken; however all are fragmentary and dated. Some authors tried to compare household resources by socioprofessional category in 1950 and 1956. Their study draws two conclusions:

1) The unemployed and retired have the highest ratio of benefits to contributions. Next come wage earners and those who receive the lowest direct wages: agricultural workers, and salaried nonprofessionals.

2) Social benefits have progressed faster than income in three groups: farm owners, agricultural workers, and owners of businesses and commercial enterprises.

Studies of household income and consumption directed by IN-SEE [National Institute of Statistical Studies], have tried to establish the actual overall fiscal contribution of the various socioprofessional categories and the benefits they obtained from state and social security spending.

Such exprimental studies, whose results—even in the opinion of their authors—are highly debatable, indicate little income transfer between socioprofessional groups.

Finally, a study of the effects of family allocations and social security benefits to workers should be mentioned. According to the author, redistribution is a function of household composition and operates to benefit households with dependent children and those with only one breadwinner to the detriment of childless households and those with two employed persons. More generally, redistribution operates to the disadvantage of middle-income households, benefitting those with either a lower or higher income level.

Those studies, though of interest because of their methodology, cannot give us adequate information on income transfers due to social security. In the absence of more precise and recent data, transfers can hardly be evaluated except through analyzing different aspects of solidarity at the professional, interprofessional, or national levels.

Professional Solidarity

In addition to the general social security system for the employed, numerous special or autonomous systems exist, to the extent that contributions and benefits differ from one program to another.

Most programs function as closed systems. Sickness insurance for nonsalaried, nonagricultural workers' functions like a mutal aid society, balancing income and benefits. Thus, transfers among its members are limited; the same can be said of the retirement plans for artisans and merchants.

Certain systems (agriculture, mining, merchant marine, railways) receive large external contributions [state aid], but the majority of special systems balance their budgets and do not generate transfers. Only the general social security system contributes to sectors which are in deficit for economic or demographic reasons.

Within each separate system, social cohesion encounters a double limitation.

The first is a legal limit on maximum contribution rates, whether by salaried contributors to the general system or by nonsalaried contributors. While progressive up to a certain income level, the required contributions are digressive after this limit. In this way, the contributory effort is relatively more burdensome for lower-income groups than for those with higher incomes. In addition, the contributory limit can produce shocking inequalities: for a family whose members receive salaries below the limit, the contribution is greater than for a family with a identical income for one earner and above the limit.

The second obstacle to social cohesion is the distribution of benefits among beneficiaries. To see the effect, benefits in kind and cash benefits must be distinguished.

Benefits in kind (essentially health care) are not linked to household resources, at least beyond a certain level.

On the other hand, cash benefits, except for family allowances, increase proportionately to income, which negates any income transfer to the neediest social classes.

Interprofessional Solidarity

Limited by the compartmentalization of systems, interprofessional solidarity appears only accidentally and seemingly without well-defined political or philosophical aim.

Varying with changing circumstances, different compensation formulas have been applied to the general system and specific systems. Thus, the general system has progessively taken over the agricultural and mining sector deficits. These transfers are better explained by movements of the active population between system than by differences in benefits or contributions. Economic development has left behind once-flourishing sectors which are now in decline. Demographically, the proportion of employed to unemployed deteriorates and, in economic terms, it becomes impossible to match increased costs of services. Hence, the problem of financing social security systems rests on the general economy.

Another manifestation of interprofessional solidarity (though limited in its effects) is the common sharing of risks in the area of family benefits, which covers all social security programs.

Do these various compensation measures result in a redistribution of income among the professional categories concerned? In other terms, has a transfer been effected to benefit agricultural workers and miners at the expense of those covered by the general system? The complexity of the measure is such that it is difficult to determine who benefits: salaried employees themselves, their firms, or consumers of the products of these firms.

The only certainty is that a certain cohesion is established between expanding and declining economic sectors.

National Solidarity

Transfers can also arise from national support through subsidies, treasury advances, or designated taxes.

The state budget's role in the overall financing of the social security system is now relatively modest [about 20 percent of costs], at least in comparison with neighboring nations.

In addition to local social aid, which is a complementary but distinct part of social security, the state rarely intervenes except to finance the BAPSA (agricultural benefits). A deliberate policy of social transfers favors farmers, and responds to the economic and demographic disadvantages of the agricultural sector.

The expression of national solidarity [social cohesion] is limited by the development of complementary professional and interprofessional systems which account for almost 10 percent of social security contributions [half the total state contribution].

In effect, in relation to an overall levy on national income for social transfers, sums granted to private pension funds are a deduction from funds for the general system. Thus, there is a certain disequilibrium between the general social security system, whose financing becomes increasingly difficult, while others continue to obtain benefits from complementary systems which generally have less financial difficulty.

6-4. POLITICAL PARTIES AND SOCIAL BENEFITS*

There are few political issues more sensitive than pensions. Older voters go to the polls and they are aware of how government handles their pensions rights. An important indication of the advance of the French welfare state over the past decade is the similarity of the proposals of the Right and Left in the 1978 legislative elections. In this article, Le Monde's social security expert, Jean-Pierre Dumont, assesses the party proposals put forward in 1978. Even before the legislative elections of 1981, the Socialist Party had implemented many of their proposals. In addition, he shows why French parties, like parties in many other welfare states, are reluctant to confront the long-term implications of decisions to increase pensions. He outlines some of the complex choices which confront pension systems in every country as policymakers weigh retirement age against contributions, changing age structure and diverse occupational structures, as well as other programs that are proposed to help the aged.

The problem of larger pensions and early retirement is being widely discussed by all political parties. It will certainly receive priority in parliamentary debate as well as in union-employer meetings. A general consensus is emerging on the idea of changing to a monthly pension system, improving widows' pensions and aid for the elderly in their homes and, above all, minimum pension levels and the age to which the elderly would have a right to this minimum.

The Communist and Socialist Parties go quite far in their proposals: they intend to raise minimum allocations by approximately 40 percent as of 1978, that is, 53 percent of the new minimum monthly wage (SMIC), and bring it to 80 percent of the minimum wage within five years. But the Gaullist and the Giscardian parties advocated similar improvements when they proposed to arrive, by stages, at a pension level of 70 percent of the minimum wage. While the majority parties do not favor the systematic lowering of the retirement age to sixty years for all, they do, however, advocate the granting of the 70 percent level at retirement age.

On the other hand, differences between the parties do appear concerning the future of contributory pension systems. The Com-

*Jean-Pierre Dumont, La sécurité sociale et les projets des partis," *Le Monde*, February 21, 1978.

munist and Socialist parties, faithful to their program, intend to grant to all French citizens, beginning in 1978, the possibility of leaving the work force five years earlier: fifty-five years of age for women and those in dangerous occupations, and sixty for others. Further, they propose raising the pension levels of sixty-year-olds to 75 percent of their average earnings for their ten best years (presently 25 percent, plus an eventual complementary 20 percent for sixty-year-old retirees; 70 percent for sixty-five-year-olds).

The majority parties refuse to commit themselves in this direction. However, they propose to give concrete substance to the idea of retirement "à la carte." Up until now, the low pension rate for retirement at sixty presented little incentive to retire at this age, because five more years of work doubles the pension level to 50 percent of average income. The Gaullist party's objective, then, is to raise this rate (to 35 percent at sixty compared to 25 percent today). The present majority adds another suggestion to this—to allow the combination of pension with earned remuneration as a means of avoiding the "guillotine" of retirement which plunges retirees into idleness and boredom. While the other center parties are joined by the Socialist Party in calling for a reform of laws governing employment during retirement, both the Socialists and Communists favor limiting retirees' pursuit of gainful employment. One thing seems certain: legislators and the "social partners" will have to deal with this delicate problem within the next five years.

In general, the majority parties favor a progressive amelioration of retirement benefits, whereas the opposition favors a "big step forward." Is this long-demanded call for retirement at age sixty realistic?

The cost of the moderately ambitious program of the Gaullists is already high: at least twelve billion francs and probably more. That of the Left's Common Program seems explosive: 13.5 billion francs from 1978, according to the Socialists; 59 billion francs in 1980, according to Communist estimates.

Reform of the retirement system poses both financial and qualitative problems.

The first problem with the Left's suggestions is this: French workers are increasingly hesitant to retire at age sixty. While it is true that the present generation—especially workers who have suffered from poor conditions from 1930 to 1970—aspire to a well-deserved rest, it is dangerous and even wrong to expect the same attitude on the part of future generations. A life expectancy of seventy-five or even eighty years will cause today's adults to demand the continuation of employment past the age of sixty.

The second problem with the Left's proposition is this: a new retirement system for five years cannot be instituted without regard for its long-term consequences. The present budget deficit, legal obligations, the Pension Fund, and, above all, the demographic evolution from now through the year 2000 must be taken into account. In effect, is it irresponsible to promise retirement at sixty or fifty-five when demographers are well aware that such a system runs the risk of leading pension funds to catastrophe after 1985? It is relatively easy to promise medium-term improvements, because from now to 1985 a dwindling number of workers will arrive at age sixty-five (those born in the 1920s), decreasing the burden on the active population. But after 1985, the demographic situation will reverse to the detriment of the working population. This is of great concern since all retirees will receive full pensions, having contributed for a full 37.5 years, in contrast to the present pool of retirees. A further cost: the increasing burden of those over sixty-five years of age.

The Left can defend its program, on the condition that it greatly increases the contribution rates or taxes, and facilitates gainful employment for women to raise the number of contributors. Another solution, suggested by the CGT, is to provisionally lower the retirement age while accepting a gradual retreat over twelve years.

A third solution—more coherent, less costly, and more just, although rarely discussed—would be to abolish the age limit entirely, substituting the criterion of length of employment. After 37.5 or forty years in the work force, full retirement benefits would be conferred whatever the age of the retiree. This formula would grant retirement to manual workers at the age of 55 or 57, because they often began to work at fifteen or seventeen, and to white collar professionals (*cadres*) at the age of sixty-five if their active careers began at twenty-five. Such a formula would safeguard the future; it would restrict pension rights in the 1985–95 period as young people enter the work force at a later age. But whatever options are put forward and decisions taken to favor the elderly, promises made to the sick and their families must still be taken into account.

6-5. THE GROWTH OF SOCIAL SPENDING*

By 1980 it was clear that the Giscard government had increased social benefits at rates exceeding by far the increases in most of Europe since the oil crisis of 1974. Unlike democracies where the social security system is part of the political process or brought more directly under governmental supervision, France had difficulty curtailing social security benefits. The 1978 legislative election platform of Barre also pledged the government to make increases, especially for the aged and handicapped, while medical benefits still had no control on either the demand for services or on the prices charged by doctors. In 1981 President Mitterrand came to power and pledged to increase pensions and other social benefits, many of which were made under decree powers before the ensuing legislative elections. In this reading, a leading social planner and president of the eighth Plan's Commission on Social Protection and the Family analyzes why France has been unable to restrict welfare spending.

The degree of budgetary socialization of a country can be measured by the percentage of national wealth which is given to state and local governments and to the social security system. Today the past decade's evolution can be understood. From 1970 to 1979, this obligation went from 35.6 percent to 40.8 percent of the gross national product (GNP).

This increase of over five percentage points is for the most part (4–1/2 percent) due to social security obligations. Transfers are distributed in the form of cash benefits (family allocations, pensions, unemployment or accident compensation), or in kind (health care, home services). Today these transfers represent approximately 30 percent of disposable household income compared to 23 percent in 1962. Their rapid increase over the past few years has several causes:

—Social policy: increasing the minimum pension age and aid to the handicapped.

—An increase in the size of old age pensions far more rapidly than inflation (four to five percentage points above this rate from 1974 to 1979).

*René Lenoir, "Les voies de la socialisation," *Le Monde*, March 11, 1980 (selections).

—The cost of health care, whose rate of increase surpassed that of the GNP by seven to eight percentage points.

—The appearance of a significant unemployment which entails increased unemployment compensation (thirty billion francs in 1979) and a drop in social security contributions.

In proportion to the GNP, the national tax burden has decreased by one percentage point, from 18.9 percent to 17.9 percent. But two reservations must be made concerning this apparent moderation. The first is that the rapidly growing social budget is less "fiscalized" in our country than in our neighbors: 20 percent of [social security] revenues as compared to 27 percent in West Germany and 42 percent in Great Britain. If it were more heavily financed by taxes, it would have increased even more rapidly (or the slowdown in spending would have started sooner!).

The second point is that the national budget deficit has reached 100 billion francs in four years. This deficit is financed by borrowing. Loans do not appear as part of the "obligatory contribution." But it is clear that state borrowing directly competes with society's other financial needs. In good years and bad years, this deficit represented 1.5 percent of the GNP, which raises the levy for [social security] expenditure to 19.4 percent of the GNP in 1979.

The third means of socialization, the local fiscal [tax] levy, increased by 1 percent in ten years. Its growth was more rapid than the GNP growth rate from 1970 to 1976; since then, it has slowed down somewhat. Local governments are big investors; they construct nearly two-thirds of all public works. These expenditures are financed easily—perhaps too easily in France: state subsidies and loans from powerful lending institutions (the *Caisse des Dépôts*, *Crédit Agricole*) channel savings toward the public sector. For ten years, investments have increased on the average by 15 percent and debt service charges by over 20 percent. But when deciding to invest, municipal and departmental councils do not always take into account the consequent operating expenses. The user rarely pays for public services at their actual cost—this is true of highways, swimming pools, and day-care centers alike. Local taxpayers make up the difference.

Departmental taxes have increased appreciably and at the same rate as communal taxes (except in some departments where they have risen faster). Departmental taxes, like state taxes, could have increased at a slower pace. Their relatively fast expansion is explained by the growth of social assistance expenditures which make up nearly a quarter of net departmental spending, but also by the departmental councils' wish to build public works, especially by granting subsidies to local governments. One would hope for enhanced choice at the local [communal] level with increasing assistance for local initiative. But is this possible as long as France contains 36,000 communes?

The fourth means of socialization—outside of tax obligations—would be the nationalization of economic activities under a monopoly. In effect, a national firm in a competitive sector affects individual choices only by the quality of its products. No one is forced to by a Renault. But we can only buy energy at the EDF (the nationalized French electricity company).

This fourth means has not been pursued. Certainly, a notable increase of the share of monopolistic nationalized industries in national production would have the same result. The figures necessary to measure this are lacking.

Thus, without new nationalizations, socialization has increased slightly in ten years through means of the tax obligations. Too much or not enough? With a 41 percent levy on the national product, French social spending is a percentage more than West Germany (led by a social democratic party, moreover), far behind Sweden at 53 percent, but far ahead of the United States at 30 percent.

Liberals will find this excessive; Communists will say we must go much farther. Independently of all ideology, common sense indicates that our assessment of such a percentage depends on the size and growth of national wealth: 40 percent of little is too much; 40 percent of an abundance is acceptable.

Moreover, the revolt against the local tax burden has begun in the United States—psychological factors are of major import. This is why increasing tax burdens are more easily accepted in periods of growth—when citizens' disposable income is also rising—than in periods of stagnation.

Rather than debating an illusive figure, an attempt can be made to appreciate the social and economic impact of the tax levy. In social terms, the transfers permit the reinforcement of social solidarity: this includes single individuals, childless couples and families (family allowances); the employed and unemployed (old age pensions, unemployment compensation); and, above all, the healthy and very ill (3 percent of the sick account for 50 percent of expenses). But contrary to an accepted notion, the redistributive effect of transfers is minimal, except vis-à-vis certain individuals who work little or not at all. The level of social security contributions, the effect of family size (greater for higher income families), and the larger tax burden for working couples keep the social budget from playing a redistributive role.

An appreciation of the economic impact of social services made possible by public taxes entails a reevaluation of the effectiveness of any monopolistic institution or company. The question is twofold: are the services adapted to the fulfilling of society's objectives and could they be offered at a lower cost?

To ask the first question is to assess the overall policy which is to examine the definition of means and ends. The debate is, therefore, limitless and a solution is often not possible: only on the day of combat is an army's value tested—in the same way, increasing life expectancy no longer measures the effectiveness of a health care system, and an educational reform bears its fruits a generation later.

There remains the question of implementing public objectives at a lower cost. Accounting experts occupy themselves in denouncing too costly methods and procedures. But the managers themselves should utilize the measurement instruments developed through experience: the nationalization of budgetary choices and comparison of cost ratios. If budgetary analysts concentrate only on social security, hospital mismanagement may be denounced. But it should not stop here—useless tourist routes, exorbitant trade advantages granted to public enterprises, and the tax administration of a department all have the same effect. Resources that rely on national wealth are not employed in the best way; they uselessly constrain individual freedom of choice and drain resources from more worthy uses.

The socialization [of the budget] can be a positive thing, but badly controlled socialization puts the society in jeopardy and even makes the notion of public services suspect. Two centuries ago, social claims were directly inscribed in the grievances books (*Cahiers de doléances*) to ensure the moderate and honest use of money taken from citizens. If they had to draw up such notebooks, our contemporaries might be more moderate.

6-6. SOCIAL SECURITY DILEMMAS
UNDER MITTERRAND*

President Mitterrand came to power in 1981 committed to substantial improvement in social security benefits, but also at a time when the country had nearly two million unemployed as well as heavy financial obligations for other major reforms. After the initial round of benefit increases before the 1981 legislative elections, the Socialist realized that the growing deficit of the social security programs placed severe limits on how much more could be done in the near future. The deficit under existing obligations plus anticipated unemployment benefits through 1982 was expected to be fifty billion francs. In this article the Le Monde *social policy expert, Jean-Pierre Dumont, discusses the dilemma of future policy under conditions of severe economic constraint.*

A financial plan is necessary! Nearly fifty billion francs must be found for social security for 1981 and 1982.

The moment of reconciliation has come even if the government takes time to reflect and to coordinate before announcing the financial measures for social security and UNEDIC, the regime for unemployment benefits.

It is a rude awakening. Did not the previous government of M. Barre announce only a year ago that M. Barrot and M. Farge had to rescue social security from disaster? The French government must now admit that the "deficits," so swiftly minimized by manipulation when the Socialists were in opposition, unhappily remain real and always arouse surprise and incredulity. But the figures are there with all their meagerness and brutality.

It is urgent to intervene on behalf of UNEDIC. The economic crisis that has continued since 1974 has revived with new shocks, either political or from oil problems, with the success of the Socialists and the wave of resignation or torpor of the employers.

Unemployment has not ceased rising since the beginning of the year. As M. Bergeron (FO) explained, unemployment compensation has progressed to impressive proportions: in one year the total number of compensated days of work by UNEDIC has grown 34 percent and by the end of 1981 the annual rate of growth will be 36

*Jean-Pierre Dumont, "L'heure des comptes," *Le Monde*, August 30–31, 1981, (selections).

percent. In order to assure the payment of about fifty-four billion francs in 1981 rather than the thirty-five billion in 1980, UNEDIC needs five or six billion francs this year and, according to forecasts, must find twice these additional resources for 1982, ten to fifteen billion francs. The total is eighteen billion francs as the Matignon has indicated. Therefore, it is impossible to call on temporary measures even for the 1981 deficit. Because of economic difficulties and the pressure of young workers arriving on the labor market to 1983–84, new resources will be needed for some years.

The new government does not wish to penalize enterprises in hopes of respecting its objective of social solidarity. As a result, the remaining possibilities consist of an appeal to various categories of the French population: each must contribute. But such an exercise of social solidarity is far from being unanimous within the government and, after three hours of debate, M. Brunhes, the Matignon spokesman for social affairs, announced, "The interministerial committee has not made a decision."

This is only a diplomatic expression to translate opposition from ministers over a special effort from civil servants and others (a special civil service contribution had been suggested). M. Le Pors (minister for the civil service) is hostile to this solution and limited his response to a laconic "One must reflect." All the same, M. Burnhes says such a special contribution is "seriously" being studied.

If one recalls the special "drought tax" (after the 1976 drought), one can only approve a tax or loan for unemployment. Another interministerial committee meeting is planned and M. Mauroy, more truly the Elysée, will rapidly arbitrate since the decision must be before the UNEDIC Administrative Council by September 29. The Matignon promises that in no case will funds be cut off: the unemployed will continue to get their normal payments.

For social security there is less urgency, but there is an undeniable problem that is still grave. The financial need is, in effect, about seven billion francs by the end of 1981. It is estimated at about twenty-two billion for 1982.

How does one explain such a parallel decline? Less than a year ago, M. Farge, secretary of state for Social Security, declared, "M. Barrot and I have saved health insurance from disaster and can say we have opened the way for a reliable equilibrium." At the moment we seriously doubted such a preelectoral declaration. At that time, the Barre government remained silent during the preparatory work on the Eighth Plan concerning any redistribution of an important deficit.

Social security is very sick. A cyclical crisis (unemployment) adds to a structural crisis: the inadequate revenues and the poor division of contributions among the French at the expense of lower salaries and firms using manual labor. . . . M. Mauroy has asked Mme. Questiaux to prepare a "financial" plan. The prime minister has indicated that the priority will remain employment and that, consequently, measure to safeguard social security "should protect employment." M. Brunhes elaborated that it is a question "of not charging firms."

Swallowing the pill promises to be as bitter as the financial problems of limiting other Socialist projects. It is obvious that reform of pensions (reducing retirement age to sixty years) must be postponed for many years. In certain government circles one does not conceal that there will be "deceptions." A single consolation: our European neighbors are equally confronted with the same crisis and their solutions are even more draconian; for them it is a matter of reducing benefits.

7 Immigration Policy: Social and Economic Uncertainties

Of all the issues discussed in this volume, immigration policy poses the most difficult problem in terms of fixing objectives and defining policy. It is perhaps the most dramatic illustration of both the weakness and the confusion within an administrative system that has often been criticized for being too rigid. It also demonstrates the elusive, diffuse nature of many policy problems, in both socioeconomic and political terms. In neither respect were any of the three formulations of policymaking considered in this book certain of how to respond or even how to define the problem.

A wide variety of policy considerations come to bear on immigration. There are, first, changing international conditions such as the creation of the Common Market and the breakdown of Franco-Algerian relations which led to abrupt changes in policy. Second, immigration did not totally elude the Gaullist vision of a French Union embracing a hundred million Frenchmen and, at least in the early stages of immigration policy in the 1960s, relatively candid admission that the rapid economic modernization of France needed a larger labor force to withstand European competition. But in terms of the policy process itself, perhaps the most confusing circumstance was that the composition, qualifications, and needs of the immigrant workers and their families constantly change. From this perspective, the institutional and political uncertainties of French policymaking were a decided advantage. There was neither the temptation to attempt isolation of the issue from government as in West Germany, nor the illusion of a permanent solution (often tinged with racial feeling) as in Britain. Not having any good answers can sometimes be the best policy.

From a policy perspective, the entire issue of immigration policy is further confounded by the broad concept of social security discussed in Chapter 6. While the French have always been demanding in granting citizenship, their country has been a refuge for political dissidents, and social justice is freely distributed. Unlike countries where the combination of a variety of policies to meet special needs is difficult for administrative reasons, the interdependence of education, housing, and welfare is familiar to French policymakers. If the amount of assistance needed was not immediately forthcoming, the idea of meeting diverse needs was not strange or difficult within the French system. For all the prejudice and occasional violence that immigration has triggered in France, French nationalist pride has made its citizens aware of the problem. Although further immigration was barred after 1974, the permanent foreign worker population had reached 1.7 million by 1976, and the total foreign population, about 4.1 million. These persons represented 7.7 percent of the total population and 8.5 percent of the work force (Couralt and Villey, 1979; Lebon, 1978).

In analyzing the French experience, it is important to understand that France, in this case as in others, does not readily fit the standard explanations very well. The Marxist view of foreign workers as a "reserve army" for a depleted capitalist system does not square with the many political and economic uncertainties that, in fact, characterize the French response. As Piore (1979) has pointed out, France and several other European countries do not have the homogeneous labor market or the strong identification with increased productivity assumed by the more determinist, socio-economic model. Similarly, the liberal view of the world cannot explain the national self-interest that influenced both the providers of foreign labor as well as France. A more accurate version of French immigration policy from a political perspective might well be that France never knew what policy to follow.

Context

Although France is most often thought of as a culturally homogeneous country, it is worth remembering that the cultural reverence of most French people was constructed with great effort over the nineteenth century. Moreover, France has had foreign minorities for some years. In the 1911 census, 3 percent of the

French population was foreign, and, by 1931, dislocations and upheavals in Europe brought the foreign population to over 6 percent of the total (heavily Polish and Italian). Then, as now, the French took a pragmatic view toward the flow of foreigners to their country. With the depression of the 1930s, stricter conditions gradually reduced foreigners to about two million persons.

As in the case of Britain, the colonial empire was the second confounding circumstance. Although French colonial rule was harsher and more brutal than the British model, the French held out the promise of full equality for those who could achieve French cultural and educational standards, the well-known *mission civilisatrice*. As Fanon (1961) and others have pointed out, the ultimate effect on individuals was profoundly destructive, but the idea of a "French nation" reaching around the world appealed to the French no less than to the British. Indeed, the French went farther than the British by making the French Union (an assembly of colonial representatives) part of the Constitution of the Fourth Republic (see Marshall, 1973). Declining birthrates and huge losses in European wars fed these ideas. Immediately following World War II, a population expert, Alfred Sauvy, persuaded de Gaulle that France needed over five million permanent migrants. Thus, well before the flood of migrant workers to Germany, Switzerland, and Scandinavia in the 1960s, the French had thought about immigration in a nationalist, rather than an economic, framework.

The confusion over the correct policy course can easily be traced to the immediate postwar period (see Reading 7-1). The Ministry of Labor, then under a Communist minister, favored temporary rather than permanent entry which was advocated by those hoping to stabilize the population. The planners, still in an embryonic stage of development, claimed that France did not need more labor (Tapinos, 1975, p. 16). An interministerial commission on immigration, under the short-lived Ministry of Population, pushed the demographic argument. In the midst of this triangular struggle the National Office of Immigration (ONI), formed in 1945, was supposed to supervise immigration and work permits, although the Ministry of Interior retained control of residence and entry permits. As Freeman (1979, p. 77) points out in a good account of the period, the result was chaos. In effect, France had no policy at all. Until 1962, persons from Algeria and the overseas departments could enter with no restriction whatsoever, and most immigrants from all countries came as tourists, sought work, and then entered the labor force. Until 1968, hardly a fifth of the immigrant workers came through official channels, and the main task of ONI was to rather ineffectually catch up (the French speak of *regularisation*) with thousands of new foreign workers.

The permissive attitude of national government toward immigration under the Fourth Republic meant that the country had no very good record of the entry, departure, or utilization of foreign labor. There are three main sources of statistics, none of them wholly reliable. The census is considered the most reliable, but provides no information on many problems such as illiteracy, mobility, training, and housing (Lebon, 1978). The record of entry permits kept by the Ministry of the Interior tends to overestimate immigrants because many leave without taking the trouble to cancel permits, and many persons possess permits who are not in France. The best records are probably the annual surveys of employment by INSEE and an irregularly administered survey of foreign labor by the Ministry of Labor, although the latter omits public sector employment, and excludes firms with less than ten employees. Because it is confined to the active population, it is not useful in assessing the social and family needs of immigrants. In countries where entry is more strictly controlled, such as Germany and Switzerland, there are much better records, while in Britain, which has consistently refused to have racial or ethnic identification in its census, records are much worse.

As we shall see, relieving the appalling social conditions of most immigrant workers became one of the major issues under the Fifth Republic, but compared to many European countries the French took many, if not always effective, steps to meet the social, housing, and educational needs of foreign laborers. In 1945, a Social Action Fund (FAS) was created, drawing in part on the payroll taxes paid by employers and in part on ministerial budgets, but the expansion of immigrant social services received relatively little attention until 1958. The diverse origins of the workers, as well as the shifting composition of the foreign work force over time, meant that voluntary organizations to defend immigrant interests are nearly as confusing as the diverse responses of ministries and official agencies. The Center for Information and Study of Mediterranean Migrants

(CIEMM), for example, lists eleven groups primarily concerned with defending migrant rights. There are at least seven public and semipublic agencies concerned with immigrant housing (Granotier, 1970, pp. 104–105). There are three literacy organizations, although the Benevolent Society for the Education of Foreigners (AEE) is probably the leading agency. In a pattern that is common in French government, voluntary, semipublic, and public organizations receive varying subsidies and privileges from government.

As in most countries, the differing legal status of immigrant workers also complicated the shaping of a coherent policy. The overseas French departments are treated as French. The Algerians negotiated their own agreements with France, and these negotiations have changed radically as regimes change in Algeria and, more recently, in response to French needs for Algerian oil and gas. Given France's longstanding interest in North Africa, both Morocco and Tunisia receive certain privileges under special agreements. For most ex-colonies in Africa, there are bilateral agreements. Since the free migration requirements of the Common Market came into effect in 1968, workers from member states can enter and leave freely. The large numbers of Spanish and Portugese workers (now the largest nationality groups) also have their own agreements. No other European country has as diverse and evolving sources of immigrant labor.

There are similar spatial and occupational complications. About a third of the total immigrant population lives in the Paris region, where the total population in 1975 was nearly 12 percent foreign. The two additional areas of concentration are the Rhone Valley surrounding Lyon and in the Provence-Cote d'Azur region in the southeast. In seven of the twenty-one French regions, foreign population is approaching 10 percent (Ministry of Labor, 1977). By far the largest occupation of immigrant workers is construction (27 percent of all employees in 1976) and auto assembly (20 percent of all employees in 1976). They also provide roughly a sixth of the workers in mining, steel, foundries, plastics, hotels, and restaurants. Because France has been relatively liberal in permitting families to join workers, there are thousands of domestic servants who elude the official surveys. Immigrant workers are also critically important in the menial tasks of refuse collection and public transport. When the Paris metro workers went on strike in 1980, Parisians were soon wading knee-deep in trash in the subways, where practically the entire janitorial workforce is foreign.

As we have seen with several other problems, immigration is another issue that reached alarming proportions just as the Gaullists came to power. Until 1956, only about 50,000 permanent workers arrived each year, and the number was actually declining in the early 1950s. By an odd historical coincidence, the Algerian revolution that brought de Gaulle to power also rapidly increased the arrival of Algerians in France. Indeed, one of the events that made the French aware of the brutal costs of the revolution was the terrorism of rival Algerian factions in the rapidly growing shanty-towns (*bidonvilles*) as they extracted money from immigrant Algerians. At the same time, the French economy was growing rapidly and demand for labor exceeded French capacities. After 1956, over 100,000 workers came to France each year and, by 1962, there were over 200,000 entering each year. Although many North Africans came alone (which creates another serious social problem for families left behind and lonely workers in French cities), families also arrived in greater numbers so that, by 1962, France was increasing its foreign population by over a quarter million persons per year. Among the many problems de Gaulle inherited from the Fourth Republic, immigrant labor was one of the most difficult to resolve.

Agenda

The Fifth Republic was slow to develop any clear policy on immigration. Part of the reason was the diverse nature of immigrant problems, but part of the reason is also that government received misleading advice. The Third Plan (1958–61) was cautious about increased dependence on foreign labor supplies. The Fourth Plan (1962–65) was simply wrong. The forecast net increase was 290,000 workers and the actual number was 718,000 (Tapinos, 1975 p. 57). Given the powers often attributed to top French civil servants, their total ignorance of the effects of the Algerian war is further evidence that French administration may not be as effective as often presumed by its critics. In addition, de Gaulle's successful efforts to terminate the war meant that, after 1962, over a million additional Algerian French, many of them no more familiar with France than were the Algerian workers, also arrived. They tended to settle in the south of France which provided both a familiar climate and familiar occupations. They were bitterly hostile to the Algerians, and their concentration created an inflammatory social mix with the many Algerian workers in the area and, in a few years, led to racial violence. As part of the Evian Accords (the Franco-Algerian liberation agreement) in 1962, the French agreed to accept as many Algerians as wished to come. Roughly a fourth of the Algerian work force was in France. If this mass of unemployed had added to the problems of wartorn Algeria, the burden—plus the loss of millions of francs sent home by Algerians in France—would have severely threatened the new country. In fact, the first Algerian government of Ben Bella encouraged Algerian workers to remain in France and the nationalist party (FLN) newspaper wrote that their presence in France "serves the reciprocal interests of our two countries" (Adler, 1977, p. 72). Contrary to more ideological interpretations of labor migration, the situation was agreeable to both countries.

To further complicate the decision on a coherent policy, the composition of the foreign labor force began to shift significantly after the early 1960s. As Italian industrial prosperity attracted the early influx of Italian workers home, more Spanish and Portugese arrived, most often through unofficial channels that were later "regularized." Though never a major portion of the immigrants, the numbers of black African workers also increased as de Gaulle sought to cement relations with the ex-colonies through bilateral agreements. The growing numbers of Africans and their appalling living conditions, often even worse than the overcrowded slums where North African workers congregated, was noted as early as 1964 in the Esperet Report (1964). Most important, perhaps, was the fact that France was anticipating the effects of unrestricted labor mobility once Common Market regulations came into effect in 1968. Although the government still had no clear policy in the early 1960s, the Fifth Plan (1966–70) anticipated a net annual increase of only 65,000 immigrant workers (Tapinos, 1975, p. 73).

Though largely ineffective in the 1960s, the French reaction to increased foreign labor contrasts with that of Britain's and some other European countries. From relatively early stages in the increase of immigrant workers, the French concept of social security (see Chapter 6) sharpened awareness of social conditions. In part to pave the way for an Algerian peace settlement, the FAS was set up in 1958. Initially it was directed only at Muslim workers, but conditions had become so deplorable that the fund was extended to all foreign workers in 1964. Two initiatives were taken at this time to cope with the growing problem. The Ministry of the Interior used the territorial administration to organize regional and departmental studies of the needs of foreign workers, and the Ministry of Labor was directed to prepare a general evaluation of immigration policy. The study outspokenly condemned the disjointed efforts to shape an immigration policy and, in particular, the ineffective efforts of ONI to assure that immigrants had jobs. Foreseeing the racial conflict that might occur, the report also warned that failure to meet the social needs of immigrants and their families might well feed xenophobic reactions among the French. Polls taken at the time already showed that the French estimated the foreign population at roughly twice its actual size (Tapinos, 1975, p. 66).

In a pattern that can be traced through a number of French policy problems, the initial effort was to mobilize groups among the workers who could work with the administration to ameliorate squalid conditions. Among the early organizations formed at the time were the Movement to Assist Overseas Workers (ATOM), the Federation of Associations to Support Immigrant Workers (FASTI), and the Association for the Support and Aid of African Workers (SOUNDIATA). Within government, a single Direction of Population and Migration was formed within the Ministry of Social Affairs (later split again into two ministries). The intention was to keep closer count of the movement and occupations of foreign workers. Between 1962 and 1965, the percentage of registered immigrant workers with permanent work permits nearly doubled.

Because the Algerians were the bulk of new workers in the early 1960s, the 1962 agreement was renegotiated (the Nekkache-Grandval Accord), and the influx of new Algerian workers was limited to 12,000 a year. The agreement was considered highly unfavorable to Algeria which depended on the French labor market, and it became an important factor in the overthrow of Ben Bella later in 1964. Once the Boumediene government was in place, the agreement was again negotiated, with Algeria asking for 45,000 admissions and France finally agreeing to 35,000 a year. As in earlier agreements, the selection of the workers was handled by an Algerian agency (ONAMO) and medical certification by French authorities. Under these conditions, Algerian workers were given nine months to locate employment in France, which was less than the French preference that workers arrive with specific employment agreements. Unlike West Germany, the French bureaucracy never seemed able to assemble such an efficient operation, nor was it ever favored by employers. These uncertainties meant, of course, that it was also easier for French employers to evade social security taxes and other benefits for immigrant workers.

Although the French knew by 1970 that they had a major problem on their hands, they still did not have a coherent or consistent policy. The restraints organized in the mid-1960s were not particularly effective, although the number of new arrivals, including families, dropped to about 275,000 (down from over 300,000 per year since 1964)) in 1967 and 1968, possibly because both employers and workers were temporarily discouraged by signs of inflation and the diminishing value of the franc. But in 1969 the influx of immigrant workers and families soared to the unparalleled level of nearly 360,000 persons and, in 1970, even higher to 390,000 persons. There were many influences at work, but the basic explanation is probably that provided by Tapinos (1975, p. 89): French employers simply "refused to play the game" of regularizing immigrant labor under the voluntary plans of 1964. This was much like the difficulties of structuring labor relations in the 1960s (see Chapter 3). Though the explanations differ widely, France, like Britain and the United States, allowed an explosive social problem to develop over the late 1960s, and only the violence of the early 1970s finally persuaded government that France must shape a real immigration policy.

Process

If the futility of French policy toward immigrants had not become unmistakable during Pompidou's presidency, it would be possible to link the socioeconomic explanation to the second period in the transformation of immigration policy. Pompidou was clearly sympathetic to big business and built his economic policy on growth principles, but, however unhappily, he subscribed to the labor policies and social reforms that hopefully would make growth possible. Even within the unions there were divergent views over immigrant workers that might threaten the labor peace so essential to a growth strategy. But the relative ease with which French employers could acquire less skilled and often cheaper foreign workers was also a threat to French economic development. It discouraged business from investing in new technology and new products and probably preserved labor intensive firms that would not be able to compete with more efficient European and less costly Third World producers. Labor intensive firms had the lowest priority of French industrial targets. Tapinos (1975, p. 87) hazards a guess that the rapidly increased productivity from 1970 to 1972 can be attributed to steps to curtail immigrant labor. Thus, Pompidou's support for industrial and commercial strength, in many ways, was more comprehensive and less circumscribed by nationalist aims than was de Gaulle's economic policy (see Reading 7-1).

In any event, one of the unforeseen consequences of the 1968 strikes and demonstrations was that the franc was devalued and new economic stabilization measures were imposed. Employment in France was less attractive to foreigners, particularly where the economies of countries supplying labor, such as Spain and Algeria, were growing. Thus, for a variety of reasons, the numbers of permanent workers added to the work force steadily declined from over 200,000 in 1970 to 177,000 in 1971 and 119,000 in 1972 (Villey, 1980, p. 87). What had changed was that France, like West Germany, had acquired a large, permanent foreign work force so that the total number of foreigners in the population was growing even though entry was curtailed. It is difficult to weigh the options, but the social costs gradually became greater than the economic advantages. The choice was dramatized as scandals over immigrant housing cast a shadow over the "New Society" that Pompidou and Chaban-Delmas hoped to build in the early 1970s. The direction of change was anticipated in the Calvez Report (1969) which suggested that all non-Europeans be issued only temporary work permits and that ONI be strengthened to enforce immigration restrictions. For different reasons, the CGT agreed with these ideas because more careful control would prevent employer abuses and would strengthen immigrant worker organizations (CGT, 1971, p. 26).

As in most countries, the misery of immigrant workers was hidden from the eyes of most French. Their plight became a national scandal in 1970 when five workers were asphyxiated in a Paris suburb, Aubervilliers, where it later appeared that a slum landlord was extracting exorbitant rents from forty-five workers who were sleeping in shifts in five rooms. The prime minister, Chaban-Delmas, visited the scene and was visibly shaken, vowing "to take measures tomorrow, and I mean as of tomorrow, to begin the elimination of these housing units" (Freeman, 1979, p. 92). His immediate response was to form an Interministerial Group on Unsanitary Housing (GIP) which would direct a share of the employers' housing contribution (amounting to 600 million francs in 1975) to relieve immigrant housing problems. Although dating from the mid-1960s, the program to demolish the sprawling shantytowns adjacent to many cities was intensified, often with the unfortunate effect of simply forcing immigrant workers into abandoned and substandard apartments. But the primary responsibility for immigrant worker housing remained with the National Society for the Construction of Housing for Workers (SONACOTRA) whose efforts were divided between building apartments for single workers and low-cost immigrant family housing.

More indicative of the transformation of the immigrant worker issue into a social problem were growing demands from the unions—and gradually from immigrants themselves—that they be given full political rights. Oddly enough, the demand reflects the comprehensiveness of French social security which provides immigrants with most of the benefits given the French, although family allowances may vary where bilateral agreements provide that a portion of the allowance be remitted to families still in the country of origin. After 1964, the CGT took a more active interest in organizing immigrants. The CGT, CFDT and CGT-FO have often cooperated in petitions on behalf of immigrants, but the CGT and CFDT are as divided on how best to mobilize immigrants as they are on the mobilization of French workers (see Chapter 5). Under the liberal impulse of the "New Society," in 1972 immigrant workers were given the right to sit on factory and union committees (see Reading 7-2).

Membership in political parties is legally forbidden, but all the parties of the Left have immigrant worker sections and representation of immigrant groups at high levels of the party organization. Many were surprised when an immigrant member announced at the twenty-first PCF Congress of 1974 that half the new members in his department (a Parisian suburb, Hauts-de-Seine) were immigrants (Miller, 1979, p. 36). But full acceptance of immigrants is a delicate issue for the parties of the Left. The Communists resisted the granting of voting rights to immigrants, but the Socialists favored voting rights for local elections. Given the hostile feelings of many French, particularly in the constituencies where the parties of the Left are competing for votes, neither party can easily take a more radical position.

As the social costs of immigrant labor became more explicit, the French government tried to curtail entry more severely. Although immigration problems are, in many ways, intractible issues, the results of the two circulars limiting entry are another illustration that French administration may not be infallible. One circular came from the Ministry of Interior (Marcellin circular) directing that all illegal entrants could be "regularized," but would need a work contract of one year and proof of adequate housing. The circular from the Ministry of Labor (Fontanet circular) was intended to improve housing and to simplify its administration. As Freeman points out (1979, p. 93), the effect was to increase the insecurity of immigrant workers because they were responsible for finding housing and, therefore, feared moving to new jobs. Neither employers nor workers were pleased with the directives, and the deadline was repeatedly extended. In 1975, the Council of State struck down both circulars for complex reasons involving the deprivation of workers' legal rights.

The unfortunate effect was the spread of alarm among immigrant workers and, quite possibly, the mobilization of racial hostility. There was a resurgence of neofascist activity in France over 1973 that, in part, fed on growing racial fear in France. Perhaps an even more threatening consequence for the Pompidou government, already embarrassed by real estate scandals and handicapped by the illness of the president, was that it provided another rallying cry for the unification of the Left in the approaching legislative elections. Although relations between the CGT and CFDT were strained, it also enabled the two parties to find a common cause in defense of immigrants. Oddly enough, in rejecting the injustice of the circulars, the unions also favored halting all new immigration until existing foreign workers had been properly registered. Because many immigrant workers from North Africa and Portugal arrived from villages where jobs and contacts in France were shared in order to spread the loneliness and the risks of leaving home, the unions' position was not necessarily reassuring. As Minces (1973, pp. 329–55) found in her interviews with immigrant workers, many regard unions as a "vain and dangerous" activity which may only make them more vulnerable to the changing demands of employers and politicians (see Reading 7–3).

While any government order appears arbitrary, the intent of the Marcellin and Fontanet circulars was to deal with the confusion of immigration policy within government as much as to impose new restrictions. With little success, the French administration had been trying to integrate population and labor policies ever since the formation of the Direction of Population and Migration in 1967. As often happens when indecision and confusion delay action on ex-plosive social issues, violence helped achieve what government seemed unable to do. The human cost appeared dramatically in August 1973 when a mentally disturbed Algerian worker stabbed a bus driver to death in Marseille. No doubt breeding on the resent-ment of the ex-colonial French in the south of France, terrorist gangs subsequently killed four Algerians and wounded two in re-venge attacks. A strike of 30,000 Arab workers in Marseille was followed by a strike of 20,000 in Toulon. Already skeptical about its agreement with France, the Algerian government totally suspended emigration to France in September 1973.

Although the French were not as immune to the social effects of immigration and racial discrimination as some European countries, the issue had almost changed faster than government could produce a new policy. Though no more an initiator of policy than most European parliamentary systems, the National Assembly success-fully pressed for an antidiscrimination law in 1972 which provided new penalties for inciting racial hatred. But the important change was that, by 1975, Portugese workers soon exceeded Algerian (23 and 21 percent of the foreign workforce respectively). Moreover, Portugese and Spanish workers brought their families to France more frequently than North Africans. The Iberian foreign popula-tion is half female and the North African foreign population only a fourth female (Ministry of Labor, 1977). The changing composition is another reason why a simple economic calculus tells us little about the overall policy which, by 1975, was extended from problems in the job market and housing to education, training, the family, and even womens' rights. The consequences were not what anyone anticipated, and the burden fell on the new president, Giscard d'Estaing, who—for obvious reasons—had said very little about immigration policies during the 1974 election.

Consequences

Few policy problems have simple, rational solutions, and Giscard's rapid and deverse response to growing racial tensions was welcome to most French. Though Giscard had said little about immigration, the growing violence and the deplorable social conditions of many immigrant workers were an obvious blot on his program to bring social harmony and liberal reform to France. When he took office, one of his first acts was to create a secretary of state for immigration, which raised the issue to cabinet-level significance for the first time. On the recommendation of the new official, Postel-Vinay, all immigration was suspended in June 1974. After recommending a crash housing program of 15,000 units at a cost of a billion francs, which was quite possibly more than the troubled French economy could bear in 1974, Postel-Vinay resigned. In a presidential style that was to eventually arouse suspicion among many French, Giscard chose one of his own Republican party disciples, Paul Dijoud, to be the new secretary of state.

With remarkable speed, Dijoud assembled an elaborate program which responded to a range of social, economic, educational, and industrial issues involving immigrants (Secretary of State for Immigrant Workers, 1977). In a candid introduction to the "New Immigration Policy" that must have disarmed the Left, Dijoud admitted that immigrant labor was an integral part of the labor force, essential in some sectors that French people avoid (1975, pp. 13–14). Having faced economic realities, he then proceeded to the more subtle social changes: the growing proportion of families among immigrant workers, the trend toward more intermarriage with immigrants (nearly 7 percent of all marriages in 1974), and the diverse national origins of the then virtually permanent foreign population of 3.4 million persons. Quite simply, the message was that having accepted the economic advantages of immigrant labor, France must now provide the social and financial support to give them equal opportunity in French society.

In rapid order, a number of decrees set out the social and economic reforms that would hopefully subdue the grievances of the immigrant worker population. An amendment to the 1974 finance law directed that a portion of the employers' salary tax (see Chapter 6) for housing be channeled into immigrant housing programs. In 1980, this source provided 1.5 billion francs. Although steps had been taken by the Ministry of Education in 1970 to provide orientation classes for children of foreign workers, decrees over 1975 provided that primary school children could have a third of their instruction in their own language, if requested. Negotiations were begun to obtain teachers from the students' countries of origin and FAS funds were shifted to support cultural activities of the immigrant groups. The rights of immigrant children to university scholarships were to be protected and, in 1976–77, there were 160,000 scholarships given to youngsters from immigrant families.

Unlike the stringent and often humiliating steps taken in Britain to exclude non-British families, the relative ease of entry for families was further protected and clarified. Where the head of the family had resided in France for one year and had suitable lodging, families could move to France if they were not seeking jobs. For this reason, foreign population continued to climb after the 1974 ban on immigration and, over the late 1970s, about 25,000 family members arrived each year. In 1975, the conditions which limited immigrant worker participation on union committees were rescinded. Though still inadequate, steps were also taken to enlarge professional training programs for immigrant workers, some of them in the language of origin. In 1974, 93,000 immigrant workers took part in such classes at a cost of over 100 million francs, but most agree the effort is still much too small.

Simultaneously with the reassurance of more social benefits for those in France, there were tougher measures to stop illegal entry. In late 1974, the restrictions on non-EEC entry were extended to the African ex-colonies. Although the CNPF and the CGT agreed that entry should be more carefully regulated and limited to temporary work permits, many small employers still took advantage of illegal entrance. Over 1975, the conditions for the renewal of permits were narrowed and efforts were made to increase the confidence of permanent workers who were upset by more stringent police surveillance of the foreign population. In November 1975, a decree terminated the use of permanent work permits. The finance law of the same year increased penalties on firms employing illegal entrants and placed a charge on employers for the services of ONI. In a decade, immigration had fallen from 288,000 in 1970 to 56,000 in 1979. Of the 56,000 entries in 1979, over 39,000 were families, most often of Spanish and Portugese workers who made up the majority of new workers (Villey, 1980, p. 87).

Most of the targets of the Seventh Plan (1976–80) (Lebon, 1979) were reached but, as in most European countries with large immigrant populations, the social problems of immigrants became more inflammatory in unexpected ways. For one thing, by 1980 the immigrant workers were better organized, partly because of more energetic efforts by government itself to regularize foreign labor. By the late 1970s, the immigrant workers in various cities were effectively linked through the Federation of Associations of Solidarity with Immigrant Workers (FASTI). There was a much more effective information system to explain to foreign workers their rights and to assist in legal appeals: the Group for Information and Support of Immigrant Workers (GISTI), and an antidiscrimination organization, the Movement Against Racism (MRAP) that was in turn linked to a number of French civil rights groups. In part, a more vigorous effort to voluntarily repatriate foreign workers from mid–1977 (Lebon, 1979) also contributed to their militancy. The curious effect of growing racial tension was that Giscard and his advisers badly mishandled the renewed effort to control immigrant labor.

Giscard worked increasingly with a narrow group of trusted officials of his own party which may explain why he so seriously underestimated the controversial character of the new proposals (see Reading 7-5). In the spring of 1979 two new bills were unveiled: the Bonnet project on restricting entry (named after the same minister of the interior who bungled local reform (see Chapter 3), and the Stoleru project under the Ministry of Labor on restricting work permits. The intent of the laws was actually quite simple, namely, to restore effective control of foreign labor to ONI as had been initially planned in 1945. With the rapid decline in labor immigration, one might think this a fairly simple decision, but the new rules were phrased in such threatening language that they mobilized opposition which ranged from the predictable resistance of the PCF to the Paris bar association. For a president already under suspicion of arbitrarily extending his powers and facing a presidential election in 1981, drafting bad laws was both poor political judgment and another example of rather clumsy administration (see Reading 7-4).

The Bonnet proposal of 1979 tightened police powers of expulsion and authorized the police to hold suspected illegal immigrants for seven days. The Stoleru proposal would have discontinued all permanent labor permits, and as old permits ran out they would be renewed for only three years where jobs existed. (The EEC workers and Algerian workers came under separate rules and are not included.) The proposals were so heatedly debated in parliament for their excessive police powers that an embarrassed government decided to hold them over to 1980. To add to the confusion, the Stoleru bill was actually withdrawn by his colleague, Bonnet, who thought the rules on residence permits still too liberal (*Le Monde*, November 30, 1979). In addition, a normally compliant Constitutional Council rose to the occasion and rejected the powers of detainment, and the Council of State declared that the government had no right to forbid a certain class of persons entry on tourist permits. The Socialist government promised to repeal the oppressive sections of the new legislation and did so in the fall of 1981. But even the Socialists ran afoul of the strong emotions that immigrant labor issues create and was strongly criticized by its own left wing for not completely dismantling the regulations and rules affecting the immigrant population.

The irony of the embarrassment was that what the French were laboriously pushing through parliament was common practice in many European countries, as the frustrated ministers often said in the debates. Indeed, the secretary of the Joint Council for the Welfare of Immigrants in Britain noted that the British Home Office had all these powers with even less right of appeal (*Guardian*, June 1, 1979). The black mark against Giscard was made more visible by ill-timed increases in immigrant housing rents. It appears that the acrimonious battle that followed was unnecessary. In fact, the increased rents were nearly equaled by increased subsidies for lower paid workers and one close observer felt the entire manipulation was simply to encourage single workers to return home (*Le Monde*, June 17, 1978). By late 1979, about twenty of the sixty-five hostels for single workers in Paris were closed because the occupants refused to sign new rental agreements with SONACOTRA, the immigrant housing agency (*Le Monde*, September 29, 1979). The controversy was fired by the periodic expulsion of foreign workers, often thought to be ringleaders in the rent strikes. Compared to most European countries, France had, in fact, made a substantial effort to house immigrant workers. In 1979, over 200,000 immigrant families were housed by the government housing agency (HLM) and 170,000 by the special housing credits directed to SONACOTRA and other special housing agencies. In its haste to solve the immigrant worker problem, the Giscard government seemed unable to capitalize on what France had done relatively well.

If Giscard was squeezed between his policies of harsher control on entry and the mounting costs of social benefits for immigrants (see Le Pors, 1976), the Left was equally confused by the issue. The Socialists and the CFDT had always championed the civil and social rights of immigrants, but the voluntaristic dimension of CFDT policy and the decentralized structure of the Socialist Party made decisive action awkward. The brunt of the immigrant issue actually fell on the PCF and CGT; the first ran most of the working class suburbs surrounding Paris, and the second was strong in the automotive, mining, and municipal unions where there are numerous immigrants. The Communists defunded immigrants since the competition with the CFDT developed in the 1960s, but their efforts to increase their power through local government created a conflict. Communist mayors began to encounter racial hostility, and the mounting costs of social services for immigrants limited what they could do for their own voters. The compulsory demolition of most shanty-towns was that the left-wing mayors, most often Communist in the working class Parisian suburbs, squeezed the Communists between their wish to represent working class immigrants and working class French. Many schools in Communist communes were one-half immigrant children (there were about a million school-age immigrant children in France in 1980), while the sagging "social budget" had to divert several billion francs to social benefits for immigrants (the total estimated cost to the state was about four billion francs per year).

A typical example is the Communist-run commune of Ivry-sur-Seine, north of Paris, where the immigrant population approaches a fourth of the population (*Le Monde*, November 4, 1980). Amid the protests of local residents, the mayor was caught between allocating more public housing to immigrants and the French residents' growing alarm that they would become a "foreign" commune. In some northern Parisian suburbs in Yvelines, racist incidents and crime multiplied to serious proportions. Cafés refused to serve African immigrants and, in one incident, the mayor's wife was threatened by racist groups because of the mayor's defense of immigrants (*Le Monde*, April 22, 1980). To many immigrants, the PCF battle against new African ghettos was only part of a familiar struggle for survival at the national level against hostile police and more stringent work permit rules. The PCF plea that immigration be planned "in relation to the needs of the French economy" (*Le Monde*, November 8, 1980) was barely distinguishable from the increasingly harsh restrictions imposed by Giscard's government. In the 1980 election campaign, the PCF leader, Marchais, echoed early Communist demands to limit immigration, but he also led a demonstration of 10,000 people through the Parisian suburb of Vitry to shouts of "No to ghettos." The real question was, of course, where they would live if they left the Communist communes.

The Socialists were not under as severe cross-pressures. After Mitterrand's victory it was a foregone conclusion that the Bonnet law would be amended to replace administrative discretion on conditions of entry and residence with a normal judicial procedure (*Le Monde*, September 11, 1981). A law was also passed protecting immigrant associations. The question of foreign workers voting in local elections (permitted in Sweden since 1976) which the Socialists favored was conveniently postponed so as to avoid offending Communists in the government. As it turned out, the Socialist government itself was surprised to find its own group in the National Assembly very unhappy that the new legislation was not more liberal (*Le Monde*, October 1, 1981).

By 1981, the problem of immigrant workers in France, as in most of Europe, had become an issue of how to reconcile a multicultural society with a more homogeneous tradition. At no time over the past twenty years has the French government appeared certain of its immigration policies and, as often as not, administrative advice has been misleading. The technocratic solution of the early Gaullist years was grossly miscalculated. The more competitive orientation of Pompidou was met with reservations from unions, business, and ex-French colonies. Giscard's good intentions were soon qualified with harsh police and administrative actions. Even the Socialists were snared in the political cross-pressures generated of immigration policies.

The true dimensions of the immigration issue for France goes well beyond the social and economic costs simply because France herself made such a fundamental contribution to the creation of the modern democratic state. The perplexity and confusion of the foreign worker is not to be neglected (see Reading 7-3), but an even greater cost would be to sacrifice the humanist principles written into law for the first time in the French Charter of Human Rights in 1789. The draconian solution of simply expatriating foreigners has never appealed to the French though it has been seriously proposed by the CNPF (see Reading 7-5). French confusion, often masking more arbitrary treatment in recent years, can easily give way to unmistakable racism (see Reading 7-6). Fortunately, the precautions taken by the Socialist government indicate that the worst possible political result will not occur.

Readings

7-1. THE SEARCH FOR AN IMMIGRATION POLICY*

The inability of the French state to persuade employers to cooperate in fashioning a new immigration policy became a major embarrassment after immigration was barred in 1974. As part of the search for a new policy, the Economic and Social Council conducted its own study under M. Calvez, a representative of the employers' associations. His conclusions outline the failure of the National Office of Immigration (ONI) to extract compliance from employers. While the Calvez Report favors simplification of procedures and better information for immigrants, it does not respond to the growing problems of racial tension and unrest within the country.

*Economic and Social Council, "La Politique d'Immigration" (Calvez Report), *Journal Officiel (Avis et Rapports du Conseil Economique et Social)*, 1975 session, 23, May 1975, pp. 349–375 (selections).

Proposed Measures: Principles

The experience of the last thirty years has led to several conclusions:

1) The system created under the 1945 decree which created the ONI (National Office of Immigration) and the so-called "foreigners' charter," never functioned satisfactorily. "Clandestine" or "spontaneous" immigration has consistently represented a large proportion of all immigration: 53 percent of permanent foreign workers used the regular procedures in 1960, 69 percent in 1964, 79 percent in 1967, and 87 percent in 1968. In spite of efforts to end it, the minister of labor estimates that 40 percent of foreign workers enter France under irregular (illegal) conditions.

2) The long-term aims at the time of the ONI's creation were soon abandoned. Within the framework of changing plans, foreign manpower needs were calculated by simply subtracting demands from offers and projecting the recent trends for each nationality.

3) The practical problem which influenced immigration in the 1960s was the difficult living conditions which many foreigners residing in France found. The capacity of the social aid agencies was thus constantly overwhelmed by the rapid growth of needs arising from the controlled influx of migrants. The efforts undertaken in the last few years have not absorbed the accumulated influx.

4) A new awareness of immigrant problems has arisen in both the countries furnishing manpower and in the "host" countries. The necessity to adapt the number of migrants to existing possibilities—not only for employment but also for housing, education, promotion, and so on—is increasingly felt in the host countries. The "furnishing" countries, on their side, not only view the emigration of their inhabitants as a safety valve to soak up their surplus population and to benefit their economy in income transfers from migrants, but also see emigration as an important element in their policy of cooperation with the developed countries.

5) Finally, the changes in the composition of the migratory flows and the relative decline in immigration by those of European origin were important factors in aggravating immigrant problems.

Only by taking into account these various factors can we define the needs of possible resumption of immigration. These policies should be at the same time programmed, negotiated, and selective:

Programmed, because a large migratory influx has repurcussions for the economy and society as a whole and presupposes the establishment of appropriate structures of accommodation. In this area, the public authorities cannot limit themselves to reacting only to employers' needs. The public interest, in all its aspects, should guide their decisions.

Negotiated, in order that the interests of the "supplying" countries are taken into account, and the rights of those directly involved are better assured. Only close international cooperation can permit us to avoid migratory flows created by economic fluctuations, as well as unfair differences in the treatment of immigrants according to ethnicity. In order to avoid the appearance and development of racial discrimination, it is desirable to take into account the problems of the adaption of migrants.

Implementation

1) It is impossible to make *a priori* decisions concerning either the size and composition of immigration or the importance of familial immigration. In this regard, it is appropriate to proceed to an examination of precise studies and projections concerning the development of accommodation, manpower needs in the various economic sectors, and the possibility of relieving manpower shortages by other means than recourse to foreign manpower.

2) When the suspension of immigration is enforced from July 1974, it would be appropriate to reinforce the coordination and collaboration between countries of emigration and France in view of four objectives:

—To better prepare candidates for emigration, necessary information on employment and French society should be given to them in their native language; an introduction to the French language and professional training should be assured. This, of course, presupposes that the responsibility of the National Office of Immigration be expanded.

—To achieve a better balance in the types of employment offered to migrants.

—To facilitate the arrival of families and particularly of spouses.

3) The official procedures of admission for foreigners should be simplified in order not to discourage interested workers or potential

employers. This should be accomplished (a) by reference to studies detailing the French economy's manpower needs in the medium term, and (b) through agreements concluded with the countries of emigration.

The procedure of regularization should, on the other hand, become exceptional.

Measures for the repression of illegal traffic in foreign manpower should be strictly applied.

4) The problem of seasonal laborers should be the object of specific measures, especially in regard to working conditions in agriculture, to avoid recourse to seasonal workers in industry, and to facilitate the return of migrants to their native lands.

The implementation of a genuine immigration policy will necessarily lead to the end of uncontrolled immigration.

In any case, France must remain a host country and provide to immigrants living conditions appropriate to our era.

7-2. UNIONS AND IMMIGRANTS*

As in several other European countries, the labor unions have conflicting interests when confronted with immigrant issues. The more radical nature of French unions means that they wish to mobilize any discontent among immigrant members, but their weakness creates difficult choices in sharing jobs, benefits, and even control over plant-level organizations. On the whole, immigrants have been discouraged with the response of the unions whose efforts are, in turn, complicated by the intricacy and diversity of industrial relations in France. These ambivalent feelings come to surface in a study of immigrants conducted by Juliette Minces. In this selection, she discusses the mixed reactions of immigrants to unions.

Immigrants and Unionization

For many immigrants, union activity is "useless and dangerous." Lack of information leads them to equate union action with political activity. They know the latter is outlawed and are afraid to participate in the former. To belong to a union—particularly in the early

*Juliette Minces, *Les travailleurs étrangers en France*, Paris, 1973, Seuil, pp. 329–331.

days of their residence in France—is, for them, to interfere in French affairs. To be involved in politics is too risky. Pressure from all quarters reinforces their fears. It is sufficient for them to be "advised" not to unionize, or told that a certain union is "Communist." The official company interpreters, the priests of their communities, embassy agents, and the foreign police who infiltrate their companies and neighborhoods all add to the pressures by the employers and the police to make them abandon any vague desire to join a union. They fear dismissal, loss of residence, and expulsion. Blackmail—principally involving the work card and residence visa—is frequent. And these fears are well justified since, for several years, and particularly since the 1968 disturbances, a certain number of immigrants have been reprimanded for their participation in union activities. The French state and the employers' association (CNPF) have every reason to "provide examples" to maintain this attitude—as do their countries of origin, who do not want returning citizens to acquire union training and an antiestablishment or protesting attitude. The more reactionary the country (Greece, Turkey, Morocco, Spain, Portugal), the more it seems to receive the understanding of the French government. All immigrants are subjected to this type of pressure to a greater or lesser degree, but it appears that the most restricted are the Portuguese, Moroccan, Turkish and, since the military *Putsch*, Greek communities.

Most foreign workers are not inclined to unionize, because they feel neither the need nor the support, and because they are subject to such pressures. Most prefer to adopt the attitude of curious and uninvolved spectators. Above all, during the first years, they scarcely believe that their participation in workers' struggles could benefit them as foreigners. There is little to be gained by obtaining a union membership card, getting involved, contributing financially, and risking retribution by the employer for mediocre results.

The influence of union militants is, in any case, weakened by the rapid rotation of migrants in a firm and, in general, by the shortness of their residence in France. (Even if their stay is prolonged, they always live as if here provisionally.) This attitude does not lead to their full integration. Immigrants cannot acquire a taste for participation in the factory's internal life and are less likely to be considered by the unions as full-fledged participants in the company's life. Also, foreign workers are difficult to mobilize except for specific initiatives which directly concern them and which sometimes explode with an alarming violence.

When the foreign worker decides in spite of all this to unionize, why and on what criteria does he make his choice?

From the outset, it can be affirmed that migrants rarely decide according to ideological criteria. Those who are exceptions to this rule were already familiar with French unions in their home countries and, generally, were politically active there. In general, they join the CGT which is considered the most active in the defense of workers. Their information is too sketchy for them to know the differences between the two main unions (the FO is not well-represented in sectors with a high percentage of immigrants). Union literature hardly reaches the immigrant, since he is often unable to read in French—or even in his native language. He can only imperfectly understand speeches, at the level of slogans and catchwords. All the unions seem to say the same things. Moreover, he does not understand why there should be several unions, since they all share the same goal: the defense of workers. The migrant thus chooses his union as a function of its importance in his firm, according to what his friends say. If he decides to join, it is because he hopes to find solutions to various problems he encounters. He will sign up with the union that seems to him the most efficient, the most "for the workers," the "only union which stands up for foreigners" (it is with the last slogan that the CGT was able to attract immigrants, through their interpreters, in certain companies like Simca-Chrysler), or the apolitical union (FO). The importance of a union determines the migrant's decision to join it; above all, he is concerned with results—for example, when a foreign delegate can be forced on management. In any case, it is always by the daily routine in the workplace that he judges the value of a workers' organization. In general, the immigrant expects that the union be a mutual aid society, capable of solving immediate individual problems, and able to offer him protection and assistance in exchange for his vote and his contribution. Thus, there is a big difference between what he expects and what the unions can obtain for him. This is one reason for his frequent disillusionment with unions.

7-3. AN IMMIGRANT SPEAKS TO THE ISSUE*

The response of immigrants and their organizations to discrimination and abuse are divided and uncertain. The constant threat of police repression leaves them vulnerable, and many immigrants feel subjected and lost under French culture and French practices. In this particularly sensitive account in Le Monde, Tahar Ben Jelloun reflects on the uncertainties that feed psychological fears from a colonial past and, in turn, the colonial feelings that influence the French response to the needs and feelings of immigrants.

At the same time as France decided with a flourish of generosity to welcome five thousand Asian refugees (chosen according to specific skills; ability to speak French; the existence of relatives in France; or having rendered services to France), the antiriot squads and regular police decided with a similar flourish to expel the immigrant workers who were conducting a rent strike against the SONOCOTRA [public housing agency for immigrants] residences.

An immigrant's daily life is riddled with uncertainty, emptiness, and fear. Forced to leave his native country and his family and expelled from his own land by misery and underdevelopment, he knows what it is to be exiled, to sell his labor. His body is his only capital, and the markets of rich countries inflict a violence and an injury which often ruins an individual life forever.

To be suspected; to be questioned and searched, hands against the wall, in the corridors of the subway; to be everywhere wearing a guilty look, guilty of everything and of nothing; to have the look of an undesirable alien, held responsible for the crisis and, above all, for unemployment—these are humiliations which hurt deeply and profoundly undermine the soul.

It is true that the parties of the Left support the cause of immigrant workers in its general principles. However, they remain prudent and measured in their support. Even in serious crises when immigrants' lives were in danger, as during the anti-Arab violence of the summer of 1973, the Left, while denouncing racist murders, failed to mobilize real help. A great deal of progress has been made

*Tahar Ben Jelloun, "Les lois de l'hospitalité," *Le Monde*, October 3–4, 1979 (selections).

in the past three or four years, but this cannot be attributed to a mobilization of the Left, which remains lukewarm and slow to respond.

In fact, the Left doesn't know how to reconcile its duty with self-interest, or how to control the racism of the part of the working class which is convinced that immigrants are the cause of unemployment.

Here lies one of the Left's contradictions. The slogan "same boss, same struggle" is fine, but it is only a slogan. Of course, French labor militants often side with the immigrants. These are generally militants of the extreme Left, leftist Christian organizations, or simply individuals fighting racism and injustice in various associations.

As for the unions, their relationship to immigrants is more complex. Solidarity often trails in the wake of the competition between the two largest unions. But many immigrants want nothing to do with these political rivalries. What they want is the unreserved support from the whole working class for their demands, particularly the most basic ones. Other immigrants, especially young workers, side with militant unionism. They are combative and never lose hope of returning to their native lands.

A Menace to Democracy

The Right has a clear position on this subject: send back the surplus manpower, kick out the "agitators," and pass strict laws to regulate immigrant movement within France.

If only immigrant workers were voters! They would be treated very differently, if only during the few weeks of the electoral campaign. (The Socialist party last year sponsored a law which would have granted immigrants the right to vote. The Communist party is more reticent in this regard. In any case, it is a "point of disagreement" between the parties, according to the Socialists.) Unfortunately, they are only workers. They have only their labor to offer. In any case, the low point of the crisis is that Giscard's government is going to pass restrictive laws. Is it the present crisis or the Left's inherent contradictions which have kept the opposition from mobilizing major segments of the population against the proposed Stoleru-Bonnet law? Surely, there were protests and reactions in parliament; but it is a question which should concern all liberal and democratic Frenchmen whether of the majority or the opposition. What is today affecting immigrants could one day be applied to the French in the spirit of the law. Those capable of passing exceptional laws for a foreign population who give service to France are also capable of proposing laws to restrict French liberties. This threat to French democracy is revealed in the current crisis. The malaise discussed around the world has not only economic causes, but also arises from the deterioration of individual rights.

Perhaps one refuses to see and accept the image of the immigrant community in France: a mirror reflecting a bad conscience. Immigration is, first of all, a problem of French society. The official France of bureaucracy and political parties underlines not only the weaknesses of a dominant system, but also the vague impulse of a society which has failed to establish just and equal relations with the Third World. Humanistic discourses on aid and support for under developed societies become noble sentiments, but are not followed up with concrete measures. If France as well as other European nations are sincere in their desire to come to the aid of these countries, they should provide a good example, starting with the members of the Third World in their suburbs. It is time to abandon illusions. The hypocrisy of the dialogue is only one facet of the cold and cynical rationality of the capitalist system.

In such a France, immigrant workers have only a single set of images expressed by discrimination and usury. Immigrants are marginal to this society; they must stay on the fringes while remaining always available. The implicit contract presupposes complete availability. The worker becomes an interchangeable element, easy to relocate, and easily (preferably without a family) sent home.

7-4. PROBLEMS OF A MULTICULTURAL SOCIETY*

In 1979, the Giscardian government proposed two laws to clarify French immigration policy. As in Britain and other European countries, the problems of immigrants tend to be broken into segments that conveniently fit national procedures. In effect, the first proposed

*Paul Teitgen, "L'engrenage discret de l'arbitraire," Le Monde, October 18, 1979 (selections).

law tightens immigration procedures under the Ministry of the Interior in order to facilitate expulsion, while the second law, under the Ministry of Labor, would make it easier to withdraw work permits for a variety of infractions. Paul Teitgen, a progressive Catholic, describes the confusion and injustice the new laws will create for immigrants and, in particular, how they will remove nearly all legal and administrative protection.

Since 1974, several governments have suspended immigration, although reuniting families was not outlawed. A policy of "return aid" was tried, without success. Public protest against the regulation by administrative tribunals and the Council of State increased the insecurity of the immigrant population, whatever the social costs, such as the brutality of their treatment and repercussions on the national interest. These last two concerns are at the heart of the laws [1979 legislation] under consideration.

The first, proposed by the Ministry of Interior, has already been thoroughly treated in these columns. Expulsion becomes the automatic sanction for any foreigner in an illegal situation—due to falsified papers, illegal entry, maintenance of "fake tourist" status after three months, no residence permit, or failure to renew the residence permit. No procedural guarantee exists, unless the foreigner entered France legally and obtained a residence permit. Expulsion can be exercised *manu militari*. And to top it off: administrative internment will be instituted in France for the first time since 1957, for the foreigner turned back at entry as well as for the deportee whom the administration judges unable to leave the country on his own. Adopted in two readings by the National Assembly, and improved by the amendments at the Senate Commission on Laws, this text will be discussed October 18 in a public session in the senate. This body refused to consider it in May and June of 1979.

The second bill, proposed by the Ministry of Labor, provides for the withdrawal of work permits, not only if the foreigner is unemployed for more than six months, but also if a work contract is broken following a late return from vacation. Firing results in the withdrawal of the work permit, which leads to loss of the residence permit and, therefore, to the possibility of expulsion. Henceforth, the immigrant worker will be at the mercy of his employer!

Also, the renewal of work permits will be done by each department, according to quotas set by the Ministry of Labor; it will take into account the local employment situation. For the residence permit, which remains distinct from the work permit, two categories will exist: the ordinary resident permit with a three-year validity, and the permit for privileged residents granted after twenty years' residence in France. In any case, the residence permit will automatically be withdrawn if the work permit is "unless the foreigner has proof of stable and sufficient resources not resulting from the exercise of a salaried occupation." The rich can sleep well!

The two bills, closely related in content, will prove to have closely related effects. Why, despite parliamentary mistrust, was it decided to consider the two separately? The intention is clear—the nationals of the European Economic Community are protected by a special statute unlike those originating in North Africa or Black Africa. In other words, foreigners will be placed under these special rules, while the "common law" will be reserved for Europeans. This would be to forever renounce our privileged ties and reciprocal obligations which history—even violent—has created and maintained between our country and African nations. Consider tomorrow: why will one continue to learn French in Algiers, Rabat, or Dakar? English will offer them broader and more secure advantages.

The seriousness of the propositions is extreme—institutionalized administrative internment; administrative discretionary powers; the judicial supervision avoided or rendered inoperative; immigrants placed in a constant state of legal insecurity; xenophobia and racism sanctioned and legitimated at high levels. All this throws into gear new dangers of the arbitrary powers which, against their wishes, the police will be required to exercise.

One would have hoped that the churches would give a straightforward opinion on these proposed laws. Let us remind those who have a duty not to remain silent, what Mgr. Chaptal, assistant bishop of Paris, wrote in 1931 regarding a massive effort to repatriate foreigners: "We needed them to insure the proper functioning of our economy. Are we morally in the right to throw back into the international street after having used them and cooperated in their uprooting?"

7-5. CONSIDERING REPATRIATION*

As economic decline in the late 1970s hurt the job market, there were growing pressures in France and other European countries to force immigrant workers to go home. The government rejected such a policy, but a report by M. Ambroise Roux of the CNPF raised new fears among immigrants that a draconian and unfair solution might be imposed on them. Because many immigrants work in menial jobs that French would not perform, it is doubtful that more than a few thousand jobs would be created, even if immigrants were forced to return to their homes. The social costs would be immense because several million immigrants and their families are, in effect, permanently located in France. In any event, such a policy could only be applied to immigrants outside Common Market countries and would be highly discriminatory as well as ineffective in solving the long-term problem.

What is eating at Ambroise Roux? Author of a report on energy presented at the Employers' Association (CNPF) general meeting, the vice-president declared himself in favor of reducing by half the number of foreign workers in France, in other words, to reduce the number of immigrant workers from two million to one million by 1985 by means of a "prudent and progressive, but continual policy."

Certainly, as M. Roux pointed out later, such a reduction would be much smaller in magnitude and slower in implementation than the Swiss and German policies of the last few years and there is no question of performing unacceptable deportations. One would content oneself with "losing"—this is the word used—some 100,000 immigrants yearly.

A Malthusian solution? M. Roux simply takes up the theme of Jacques Chirac in 1976, then prime minister, as he compared the number of unemployed Frenchmen to that of immigrant workers. Since then, M. Chirac has retracted his statement in order to play the scandalized virgin in response to the restrictive measures recently adopted by Lionel Stoleru, undersecretary of labor. But the coals were lit.

*Jean Benoit, "La 'bombe' de M. Ambroise Roux," *Le Monde*, January 20, 1978.

Curiously, the Roux report was not taken up in M. Chortad's (vice president, CNPF) general statement concerning social problems facing the CNPF. François Ceyrac, the president, even explained that foreigners had rendered an important service to the French economy, and that no "brutal or authoritarian measures, such as putting the status of these men and women in jeopardy," were being considered. M. Ceyrac, like M. Roux, believes that the developing countries should progressively improve their economies to permit them to "recuperate" their citizens, as do Italy and Spain.

But isn't it first essential to assure the countries who lend us their manpower—and those who help provide our work force—the best chances of survival? And is it reasonable to think that we can do so without immigration for many years to come?

The leaders of the CNPF are not unaware that, despite unemployment, French youth—due to the difference between their education and employment opportunities—continue to leave unhealthy, dangerous, or generally poorly paid jobs, which foreign workers willingly accept. Hasn't the widespread nonnative employment become a structural feature of our economic structure in the past ten years? Even with an accompanying effort to promote the value of manual labor, it is doubtful that a policy which focuses on hiring French citizens in the sectors "reserved" for immigrants can lead to a large immigrant exodus without provoking serious industrial disruptions.

Above all, the CNPF seems to ignore the fact that a very serious interministerial report by Le Pors calculated by simulation that if 150,000 foreign workers were sent home each year, it would only open up 13,000 jobs in France.

These, then, are the simple positions of the CNPF, known for its "realism." Their psychological consequences risk producing more uneasiness for immigrants and feeding racist and xenophobic reactions by Frenchmen, always exacerbated in times of crisis.

In point of fact, what does M. Stoleru think of this? The undersecretary declared, during his press conference on Wednesday, that he "disapproved" of the CNPF suggestions, "because one cannot carry out a policy of voluntary departure and, at the same time, propose a detailed plan, specifying numbers and dates."

Isn't M. Roux's bomb only a wet firecracker?

7-6. REACTIONS TO INCREASED RACIAL TENSION*

In early 1981, racial incidents in the crowded immigrant areas surrounding Paris began to multiply, and Communist mayors were caught between defending their voters or the immigrants. In two particularly bad incidents, a Communist mayor led a public demonstration against a Moroccan accused of peddling drugs, and another joined Communist militants in forcefully expelling fifty Mali workers from their quarters. Over the spring of 1981, there were also several terrorist anti-Semitic acts; the most serious was the bombing of a synagogue. Quick to see the link to discrimination against Jews in Russia, an organization to defend Jewish rights, Le Renouveau, came to the rescue of the offended immigrants and capitalized on the embarrassment of the Communist Party. In this interview with L'Express, the president of the group exposes the contradictions of Communist policies and behavior, and joins the struggle to defend immigrant civil rights.

Henri Hajdenberg: What is surprising is that no party, no union, none of the antiracist organizations or those defending human rights have mounted a broad counterattack against the antiimmigrant campaign of the Communist Party, which rests on the basest of instincts: racism. The infiltration of the MRAP—the ex-Movement Against Racism, Anti-Semitism and for Peace—which became, under the pressure of its Communist leaders, the Movement Against Racism and for Friendship Among Peoples—explains its lack of reaction. Its absence was already noted in the defense of Soviet Jews. As for the political parties, they give the impression of being afraid of going against the current during this electoral period, not daring to arouse public solidarity with the immigrants.

L'Express: It is more common to see the Jewish community demonstrating regarding Israel or anti-Semitism . . .

HH: —Actually, the Jewish community has not been involved enough up to now in support of immigrants who are the victims of discrimination, intolerable rules and regulations, and racist campaigns. *Le Renouveau* wants to give another dimension to the Jewish community's political expression, especially in the area of defending human rights. Our collective memory, sensitized by a long past of persecutions is impregnated by a Biblical memory:

*Henri Hajdenberg (interview), "Les juifs et les immigrés," *L'Express*, March 7, 1981.

"You are enslaved among nations." Individually, Jews are always found in the middle of the war waged by men of good will against all forms of discrimination.

L'Express: After the attack on the rue Copernic synagogue, it was nonetheless the MRAP that organized a long march through Paris, and the CGT and the Communist Party that provided the big batallions of marchers.

HH: The Communist organization wanted to regain the antifacist reflex for political reasons, accordingly it preferred to attribute the attack to the extreme right rather than that nearly established since, an act of Palestinian terrorism. Today, the mobilization against immigration is destabilizing our democratic society. In these two cases, the Communist Party demonstrates its electoral opportunism—French Jews vote, but immigrant workers do not.

L'Express: Why do you, a Jewish elector, attach so much importance to an action that is also electoral?

HH: Although it is not responsible for the Government's bankruptcy of power in the area of immigration policy (from the laxness of the prosperous years where drug dealers and the "ghettoization" of the suburbs, the government has passed to a repressive policy of expulsions), the Communist Party has taken a serious initiative: it has taken up facist slogans (which it formerly denounced) in its current offensive against immigration.

This antiimmigrant campaign of the *"Parti des Fusillés"* [party of violence] tends to legitimate rampant racism in the depths of our country, a racism rejected as shameful after Nazism and Vichy. While it was possible to make neo-Nazi cliques impotent, such as the ex-Fane, it is practically impossible to be able to do so against a party which, in France, has the strongest structure, the largest grass-roots organization, the most effective territorial implantation throughout the country—means unequalled by those who pursued nazification.

Today it is necessary to be completely aware of the danger of explosive racist violence which the Communist actions imply, even if their policy has only electoral motivations. Faced with a climate of unprecedented tension between communities, this is cause for great alarm. So we have taken the initiative of assembling leaders of all persuasions who are engaged in the struggle for human rights, in order to arouse a sense of dignity and to create a national mobilization against these attacks.

8 Conclusion: A French Secret or Putting Politicians to Work

The economic pressures and social unrest of recent years have produced a growing literature on the "crisis" of Western democracy (Crozier and Huntingdon, P. 1975). The general argument of this book is that France defies such classification along exogenous factors and, in many respects, has always been a highly politicized, possibly an "overloaded" (Rose, ed., 1980) government. Institutional uncertainty has been perpetuated because France never made well-institutionalized demarcations about the use of collective authority. For very different historical reasons, most modern democracies entered the era of the advanced welfare state with fairly clear ideas about the use of political influence as it relates to the politics of policymaking. On the other hand, France did not develop a stable two-party system which managed to bring some coherence to even a highly pluralist and internally divided United States. Nor did France turn to the bureaucracy to find substitutes for stable political institutions as happened in Sweden and Germany. The use of administrative power preoccupied nearly every regime throughout French history. Though bureaucracy had great influence, the issue of how it should be used was never settled. In a word, making a virtue of uncertainty is critically important in the French policy process because institutions are poorly defined.

As I have argued in this and the British book (Ashford, 1981b), the politics of policy should be grounded in the fundamentals of democratic theory rather than in externally defined measures of "success" and "failure." Democratic values have often thrived under conditions of great social and economic stress and they have often been abused under conditions of social and economic affluence. Obviously, democracies are threatened when they cannot meet some minimal level of performance, but such levels are defined differently in every political system and, even if carefully measured, would show highly varying institutional and political characteristics. For this reason, the promise of studying democratic politics through the policy process must focus on a narrower question: how the working out of the compromises and agreements which surround real choices relates to collective authority through institutionalized behavior. I would not exclude the idea that institutions might actually be too stable to link values to performance as appeared to be the case in local reforms in Britain (Ashford, 1981b). In any event, the basic idea is that institutions do not have singular functions as often assumed in more abstract political science models. They must provide definitions of how collective authority may be used, relate collective authority to a wide range of issues, and, in turn, provide accountability for those decisions that are made and implemented through other processes and agencies of government.

Under these conditions, as suggested in Chapter 1, France inescapably becomes an anomaly when comparing modern democracies. The erratic institutional development of the nineteenth century, the crises of the Third Republic and the relapse into Vichy facism all make France seem a failure as democracy. Another way of viewing the same problem is to say that electoral politics and party competition had great difficulty in defining institutional norms. While social and economic change was slow, this was not a major institutional problem. But once social and economic change accelerated under the Fourth and Fifth Republics, the institutional weaknesses (how to link democratic values to collective authority) reappeared. As the policy analyses demonstrate, France displayed a remarkable capacity to direct its energies and resources to meet new social and economic challenges, but in doing so it also had to compensate for the missing institutional links. The evolution of modern democratic institutions occurred simultaneously with the urgent need to formulate many new policies and solve some highly intricate problems brought upon France, and other democracies, by the rapid development of the modern welfare state.

The aim of the book has been to show how the politics of policymaking has in some respects compensated for the uncertainties caused by party realignment and intense political competition of the past twenty years. The policy materials show how France passed through distinct phases of institutional development as the Gaullist supremacy was challenged and, in many ways, proved incapable of dealing with some fundamental issues. The Pompidou period is a critically important transition for, not only were party politics and electoral pressures more directly linked to the policy process, but an attempt was made to adjust de Gaulle's vision of France to the realities of an affluent society. Giscard's claim that neoliberal principles could be superimposed on an already intricate policy process proved overly ambitious and gradually deteriorated into what appeared to many French people to be an even more alarming denial of basic democratic processes and accountability. For very different reasons, both his supporters on the Right in the Gaullist Party and his opponents on the Left in the Socialist and Communist Parties agreed that basic rights and procedures were being suspended. While the uncertainty surrounding French institutions alarmed both the Left and Right, it was the Socialist victory in 1981 that once again, as so often has happened in French history, demonstrated that the mediating institutional structure was not as ineffective as feared.

Thus, the politics of policy involve three problems: the definition of democratic rights and obligations or, simply, how to apply democratic values; the construction of mediating institutions to relate democracy to collective authority and, ultimately, to performance; and assurance that the level of performance is both quantitatively and qualitatively adequate to assure the process of compromise within the institutional framework. There is no simple or unilinear relationship among these problems. While the frenetic pace of elections in France hardly allows us to suggest that popular commitment to democracy was weak, the imbalance introduced by the Fifth Republic undertook a major experiment in institution-building while it also tried to reach ambitious levels of performance. The causal links among these problems is much tidier in most modern democracies largely because the chronological sequence can be more readily demarcated. Among democracies, Britain is probably the most orderly as the analysis of democratic development by T. H. Marshall (1950) suggests. He suggests that democracy goes through three phases of defining legal, political and, eventually, social rights. Such a formal sequence could only be imagined in a country with remarkable, possibly unique, ways of preserving institutional stability through periods of dramatic social and economic change.

Relying on the policy process to help build institutions is, of course, a risky process. If the French people were not so deeply persuaded of the virtues of self-government, the Gaullist experiment might have failed in more profound ways than to simply fall short of its social and economic goals. Whatever the inadequacies of the Jacobin ideal, de Gaulle put the institution-building process on the French political agenda. There is more than a little irony that de Gaulle's determination and occasional excesses in trying to build institutions provided the groundwork for the Socialist victory of 1981. De Gaulle's commitment to French democracy was fulfilled by Mitterrand.

The Demise of the "Two Frances"

As I have suggested in comparing the study of policy and politics to political science more generally, a conventional approach to the politics of policymaking tends to assume that the links between participation and performance are well organized and are readily harmonized with democratic control of government. While this more abstract view works reasonably well for more general comparative purposes, it does not allow us to specify the reverse causality, that is, how policy affects politics, nor does it come to grips with the highly diverse institutional frameworks that every modern democracy has created to transform demands and preferences into performance. Working with a country framework, the second problem—the unique characteristics of each institutional framework—bears more heavily on this study. A complete analysis of the politics of policy involves the peculiar historical experience of each democracy. Historians are more sensitive to these qualities of democratic life. As Zeldin (1979, p 21) notes in his superb nineteenth-century history of France, the problem is to see "the history of Frenchmen not in terms of what divides them but of what unites them."

As we saw in Chapter 1, France does not lack for outspoken critics. But their criticisms tend to repeat the problem rather than to point to possible solutions of reconciling stable institutions with a more complex policy process in contemporary France. One of the

values of comparative analysis is to show how many of the controversies facing contemporary France and firing the many criticisms of French institutions are by no means unique to France and,
therefore, do not necessarily allow us to locate the particular characteristics of the French institutional problem. For example, every
European democracy went through exercises to reduce bureaucratic influence as the state expanded over the 1960s and 1970s.
Both Labour party leaders and German Social Democrats worried
that a civil service geared to a more conservative regime would not
be able to pursue their goals. There was a pitched debate (with little
consequence) in Britain over the growing powers of the prime
minister in the 1960s, as well as a continued attack by both Labour
and Conservatives on the administration. Sweden's dependence on
administratively organized consensus and conflict resolution is so
extreme that one American analyst, Anton (1980), coined the
phrase "administered politics" to describe the system. Thus, the
power of the civil service by itself does not distinguish France
although it has been the most frequently selected target of critics of
French political life.

A result of the controversy over French politics as phrased in
more general political terms, and also by many French critics, is that
the many options facing France are posed in polar terms. As Douglas Johnson (1978, p. 4) points out, the constant threat to the
manifestation of democratic values gave a certain validity to the
"two Frances" argument. There were crises of clerical against
anticlerical France; Bonapartists against republicans; Dreyfusards
against aristocratic remnants at the turn of the century; Vichy
France against the Resistance; and, most recently, a spatial polarization of Paris against the "French desert." Johnson also observes
(p. 5) that these dichotomies are unrealistic "for in each period of
history the contending forces were themselves internally divided
and, over time, the polarization of French politics gave way to
periods of complacency and stability." Because much of early political science in France was built on electoral sociology, the dichot-
omy was echoed in academic circles. While France has clearly
passed through critical elections (1877, 1936, 1946), it is a large
inference to suggest that only such polarized elections are relevant
to understanding more profound changes in French institutions and
in the policy process as it shapes French institutions.

The concept of "two Frances" relies, of course, on more conventional political science models and may be more nearly a creature of social science than a reality of French politics. In the past two decades, the deep social cleavages of urban and rural society, of religious differences and of regional differences have been moderated. While perhaps not an intended consequence of de Gaulle's forced pace for social and economic development of France, a highly commercialized society subject to mass communication has helped homogenize the French people. Mendras (1979) underscores the changes in family structure, age, relationships, and urban life that have helped subdue the historic divisions within French society. Although de Gaulle perceived these issues largely in terms of French military and economic power, he contributed to the solution of even deeper social differences. In this respect, Mitterrand follows in de Gaulle's footsteps because the new president also saw that the historic divisions within the Left must be overcome for French institutions to work. Both men saw the problems of institutional development in very different ways, and both rejected the idea of "two Frances."

As appears in most of the volumes in this series, the politics of policymaking tends to elude the more simplified polarizations that are used for electoral and partisan purposes. The chronological structure of the policy analyses for France helps in seeing how the political considerations were constantly weighed against the other requirements of responding to French policy problems. As Decaumont (1979, p. 15) notes, the period of "unanimous Gaullism" was relatively short. De Gaulle's more arbitrary policy decisions and his unconstitutional display of presidential power in forcing a referendum on the direct election of the president in 1962 only helped to underscore the critical problem of linking the policy process to institutional forms. The changing content of policy issues from the mid-1960s indicates the beginning of a search for institutional stability. Pompidou may be easily underestimated in French political development because he became the vehicle for the transition to "normal" politics. The restoration of party politics, the "search for an opening to the left," and the "New Society" itself were steps toward institutional stabilization. In contrast, the more strident Gaullism of Chirac as the party began to lose power displayed "the sterile side of Gaullism" (Frears, 1977, p. 19) and, by

1974, was no longer persuasive. Giscard certainly did not lack an image of a new France, but it was a bland sequel to the Gaullist act. Giscard's plea to calm (*décrisper*) political controversies may actually have touched French political sensitivities, but there was also a self-serving dimension to the argument. His assurance that "only the political class is in a state of fever" could not help but create suspicion that he hoped to preserve his own presidency.

But building the institutional bridges between a socially transformed France and more complex policy machinery was not easy. For one thing, institutional uncertainty helped perpetuate weak political parties. Not knowing how, if at all, parties might influence policy in the National Assembly and Senate exacerbated anxieties within parties and made it more difficult to subdue personal rivalries in order to be a credible alternative government. The early practice of delaying the presentation of Gaullist government programs to parliament, and the parties' difficulties in using the amorphous parliamentary committees as a check on policymaking all contributed to the aloofness of government. De Gaulle could speak in derisory tones about the "regime of parties" because the parties had their own problems finding a place in a poorly defined institutional framework. Not until parties perform the most essential of political acts, producing an alternative governments as in 1981, is the role of parties in both institutions and policymaking made clear. De Gaulle's more arbitrary decisions were, of course, a stimulus for the opposition though it is important to recall on the eve of a Socialist victory that, until the 1968 legislative elections, the Left often appeared more rigid and less innovative than the Right (Wilson, 1969). For much of the 1960s, not only was the social basis of "two Frances" less apparent, but the party structure that might in fact respond to a homogeneous society was by no means clear.

As described in Chapter 1, the divided executive made the solution to institutional problems even more obscure. The fears generated in the 1974 presidential elections and the 1978 legislative elections, compounded by the uncertainties of the breakdown of the Common Front on the Left in 1978, further distracted attention from the problems of building more stable institutions. Throughout this delicate process of electoral and party change, the policy process kept attention on the even greater damage that might be done to French democracy if institutional constraints were not recognized. The Constitution of the Fifth Republic accentuated the threat of "two Frances" reappearing, but did little to work out the more intricate relationships within government that enable modern democracies to convert competitive politics into effective decisionmaking. The worst outcome in terms of institutional development would have been an Assembly controlled by the Left under a president aligned with the Right. While the dilemma surfaced during the Pompidou presidency, his solution was to avoid direct confrontation only late in his term of office and when his influence was waning. France had built a modern decisionmaking process out of necessities forced on the society by de Gaulle. The independent effect of policymaking on France was, therefore, more significant than the particular disputes over specific decisions and future policies as such because the policy process accentuated past institutional weaknesses. For this reason, policy itself was constantly complicated by direct partisan manipulation, making a more stable and institutionalized compromise more difficult. The unintended effect was to make the policymaking process itself a surrogate for the use of collective authority in ways that are seldom necessary in countries where mediating institutions are well established.

Using Policies to Build Institutions

Many of the weaknesses of the enlarged role of policymakers in the Fifth Republic were apparent before the 1968 strikes. Many of the studies being done within government on incomes policy, the enlargment of social benefits and the reform of local government, though poorly designed, acknowledged the risk that Gaullist accomplishments would fail because there was no broader basis for consensus and agreement on future priorities. Even Pompidou's strategy of rapid growth coupled with more generous social measures was expedient in terms of the gravity of the French institutional problem in relation to democratic governance itself. But neither an unfettered policy of prosperity nor the refurbished pluralism of Giscard were consistent with French political or administrative traditions. By 1970, French government had become too crucial in a wide range of negotiations, regulations, and support for policy goals to depend on withdrawal from policy responsibilities and commitments as a means of building more stable institutions. In this indirect sense, the policy process propelled France into considering its institutional options.

The paradoxes of Pompidou's administration help us separate the political dilemmas of institutional change from the relatively simple and determinist judgment of success by nonpolitical criteria. First, the "New Society" itself was a celebration of affluence, but it also raised the dilemma of prime minister whose popularity and political acumen threatened the prestige of the president. Chaban-Delmas was removed shortly after receiving a massive vote of confidence. Second, Pompidou's efforts to build a strong party organization provided younger Gaullists with clearer institutional objectives. The old Gaullist "barons" were badly divided over the 1969 referendum, itself an intricate device to clarify institutional relationships in France, and the younger party leaders, such as Chirac, realized that a simple Jacobin solution would no longer work. Third, the effort to build new links between government and industry was never abandoned even though it never worked very well. The new contractual policies between government and private firms were few and the major experiments were actually conducted on nationalized firms and public services. Though a master in daily political conflicts, Pompidou's solution was to depoliticize the policy process by protecting it from institutional control.

Giscard's approach was in many ways similar, but rested on a more pronounced pluralist philosophy. The liberal reforms of abortion, the voting for eighteen-year-olds, and protection for women carried the message of new institutional direction, but were not accompanied with reliable institutional definitions. Thus, institutional uncertainty was in many respects heightened under Giscard and itself based on political changes that the French were slow to accept. As Frears points out (1977, p. 20), Giscard shared Mitterrand's conviction that party politics would only work if the Communists left their political ghetto to become respectable republicans. The breakdown of this possibility with the destruction of the Common Front by the Communists renewed fears of institutional risk, while simultaneously reaffirming the worst apprehensions of Giscard's Gaullist supporters. Though Giscard did appoint several prominent Socialists to important offices, the process of institutional reconstruction stagnated. Welcoming disgruntled members of the painfully-built Socialist alliance into the Elysée, which Giscard did by appointing Fabre, leader of small party faction of the Common Front, increasingly appeared to be no more than symbolic acts unable to change institutional realities. Cerny (Cerny and Schain, 1980, p. 32) suggests that appointing a nonpolitical prime minister was itself a cynical device to foment party discord.

Each president of France has struggled with the problems of institutional instability and, for various political reasons, has found himself checkmated as critically important steps were about to be made to clarify the nature of democratically governed institutions. The more intricate and far-reaching the role of government became, the more ominous became the institutional vacuum. With varying degrees of success, all the modern democracies have sought solutions to the gap between democratic participation and the complexities of government. The French problem is only more visible and more acute. As government grew, the possibilities of executive power abuse increased but so also did fears that any new institutional compromise would not work. As the problems of guiding the policy process and adjusting policies to new preferences and demands increased, the institutional void was more frightening, while at the same time the French people and French democracy rested more and more heavily on a policy process that might work independently of the normal institutional checks. Unchecked, the development of an intricate and effective policy process unhampered by institutions can become an authoritarian and arbitrary process. The policy analyses have tried to show how the politicization of policymaking took place in France even though the institutional framework was weak and uncertain. Clearly, the French approach to policymaking is laden with risk to democratic governance.

First, there is simply the possibility of governmental stagnation as rival forces conflict with no institutionalized framework for compromise over the use of collective authority. Whatever the shortcomings of Gaullist and Giscardian policymaking, the determination to preserve an influential role for France prevented deadlock. In this fundamental sense, the policy process became a stimulus for institutional development because leaders were repeatedly confronted with rivals and competitors working through the policy machinery itself or with situations where their policy objectives could only be accomplished by making judicious concessions to political competitors. Nor could the issue of institutional development ever be put aside as in totalitarian societies. De Gaulle, Pompidou, and Giscard all had ideas about institutional reform and these proposals were constantly interacting with immediate policy problems.

A second risk is that policy control will gravitate irretrievably into the hands of the bureaucracy. Without underestimating the influence of the *grands corps*, the broad nature of the policy problems facing France, as well as the complex organization of clients and beneficiaries that had been inherited from earlier republics, precluded this from happening. As Suleiman argues (1974), the possibility of politically (as opposed to an administratively complex) dominant bureaucracy could not evolve for several reasons. Higher civil servants were so occupied with Gaullist programs in the early 1960s that their abilities were fully absorbed in rebuilding France. The politicization of the higher civil service, though resisted by some highly influential civil servants (Bloch-Lainé, 1976), foreclosed the possibility of a state within the state effectively institutionalizing itself. High civil servants certainly enjoyed the privileges and access found in every modern welfare state, but there is no evidence that they sought to turn institutions to their advantage. Both the Swedish and German bureaucracies have much longer and more controversial histories involving their institutionalized roles in decisionmaking.

The third and most serious threat to forging new institutions is an inability to breach the gap of succession. A democracy unable to select leaders by democratic means is paralyzed. While the transfer of power from de Gaulle to Pompidou, from Pompidou to Giscard, and most recently from Giscard to Mitterrand is hardly the orderly process found in Britain and America, the executive must still yield to electoral forces. The paradox is that although electoral participation was stimulated by political and ideological rivalries, interest was in no small degree generated by institutional uncertainties. Of course, every democratic leader likes to create an image of himself or herself as critical to the nation's future well-being, but in few other European countries has succession been more clearly a test of the viability of democratic institutions.

As still continues in Japan (Pempel, 1981), a dominant party structure raises serious doubts about democratic institutions. The periodization of the policy analyses is, in part, to underscore how great were the transformations of the executive even within a governing majority that was fundamentally unchanged from 1958 to 1974 and only partially modified from 1974 to 1981. While no substitute for democratic alternation, the impact on the policy process as France was successively governed by a proud general, a crafty man of affairs, and a brilliant product of the elite administrative schools had a dislocating effect which kept institutional issues alive. In this respect, Mitterrand's election is more significant as an affirmation of democratic institutions in France than for the more obvious ways in which it may or may not affect the actual performance of government.

While more stable and institutional relationships between demands and performance were slow to appear, we have already seen in Chapter 1 how sensitive French leaders were to electoral and party problems. Even in simple quantitative terms, the sheer vitality of democratic participation in France is impressive and is expressed not only in hotly contested formal electoral procedures, but in numerous elections for union committees of several kinds, for governing bodies of many policy agencies such as social security, and for an endless variety of semipublic institutions. As Hayward (1976) has argued, conflict itself has a legitimation effect in French politics. The policy process itself has been organized intentionally to absorb dissent, no doubt partly because the stable institutions which help forge compromises in other democracies are less developed. Even the election of 65,000 representatives to savings and loan societies generates a heated dispute among contending political groups and trade unions (*Le Monde*, March 23–24, 1980). The intensity of participation makes the institutional vacuum in French political life more visible, but it also prevents those who might deny democratic rights from filling the vacuum.

The Politics of Policymaking:
Filling or Creating the Institutional Void?

Relying on the policy process to build more stable relationships between democratic participation and the performance of government, particularly given the complexity of the modern welfare state, is a risk-laden endeavor. To some extent, all the modern democracies have experienced problems of adjusting political institutions that were designed for a simpler age to the policymaking requirements of intricate and controversial decisions. As I have argued thus far in the Conclusion, the hope that a simple polarization of French attitudes and interests will somehow provide spontaneous guidance to such a difficult process seems exaggerated and, very likely, no longer corresponds to the realities of French society. Institutions are a device to aggregate conflicting views and expectations, but even the stability of democratic opinion is reduced with the cross-pressures and changing preferences of a public responding to the intricacy of the welfare state. In a somewhat perverse way, France is a particularly instructive example because institutional uncertainties made French politics and policy even more vulnerable to such conflicts and uncertainties than happened in many European countries.

If my inference is reasonable, one would expect to see the politics of policymaking in France reflecting the inability of French institutions to provide overall guidance and to aggregate popular views in ways that permit institutions to direct the executive and administrative activities of government. This is not to say that French policymaking is necessarily less "democratic" in its ultimate formulation, but only that it is much harder to trace through the relationship of demands to performance. A more highly institutionalized relationship might well have arrived at the same decisions. The "country argument" of the book is rather that, in the absence of reliable instruments for aggregating democratic views and balancing institutional needs against more short-term policy needs, the politics of policymaking takes on special significance. It is not the specific policy "failures" or "successes" that are important, as they might be in a more conventional policy evaluation of a single country, but how the politicization of policymaking must also provide institutional guidance that would most often be more stable and more organized in countries with agreement on the use of collective authority. The *dual* function of policymaking is perhaps the most distinctive feature of the French policy process. It bears both institutional and decisional importance because the rules of aggregation are uncertain.

The argument is not that the French policy process did not perform well over the past twenty years or that it did not fulfill the preferences and expectations of a majority of the French people. On the contrary, the performance compares favorably with most modern democracies and, in some areas, is superior. But from a comparative perspective on the politics of policymaking, it is possible to ask broader questions of more fundamental importance to democratic governance. The question for this study has been how does France bring the larger issue of institutional adaptation and innovation into balance with the growing complexity of the welfare state. The logic of the analysis should be clear. The performance of a government's policymaking chores does not allow us to make inferences about the democratic quality of its institutions. But under conditions of high institutional instability, the policy process may still be examined in terms of the democratic norms that would normally be expected to operate in more institutionalized ways.

The politicization of French administration, outlined in Chapter 2, has most often been attacked as the most serious inadequacy of French politics (Crozier, 1970; Birnbaum, 1977). Putting aside the many social and economic changes that may well have prevented French bureaucracy from becoming a more fundamental threat to French democracy, the pattern of mutual dependence between elected and administrative actors continues throughout the Fifth Republic. The surprising result is not that they pursued their administrative self-interest so assiduously (and what bureaucrats do not?), but that they did not make more serious inroads into political life. France might easily have had a more entrenched administrative state in 1980 than we find evidence for. Only in the earliest moments of Gaullist rule did they have something like unrestrained power and, as we have seen, they made enough errors to cast doubts on their efficiency. The expanding role of government required new talent and new methods, but the top civil servants were often brought directly into political life and, in doing so, were subjected to the same electoral and party checks that operate throughout French politics. Their opportunity to pursue political careers may have been created by the weakness of political institutions, but the simple presence of numerous civil servants in elected office is by no means unique to France.

The effective political mobilization of local and regional political leaders to frustrate national plans for consolidation of communes and to use the localities as instruments for parochial objectives, described in Chapter 3, was only possible because strong national institutions could not overcome their claim to legitimacy and help overrule their influence in the policy process. The laborious, multiple attack on local reform is a function of having no easy way to exclude local political actors from the design and implementation of the sorely needed urban programs and investments. Britain, Sweden, and even a federalized Germany have had fewer problems reorganizing local government. For the Left, the communes and departments became the training ground for new political leaders and a proving ground for their electoral cooperation while, for the Right, the localities provided the legitimation denied by weak national political institutions. Perhaps more clearly than in any other case, the communes, departments, and regions provided a substitute for nationally institutionalized politics.

Economic policymaking, outlined in Chapter 4, was no less subject to the uncertainties of French politics, though it is a more difficult set of relationships to trace because of the mixture of private and public interests. As we have seen, the political assumptions underlying the growth of the economy changed dramatically from Gaullist *étatisme* to Pompidou's growth strategy and finally to Giscardian neoliberalism. The ambiguities of these changes are greater because economic policy could not acquire the blessing of a strong parliament and stable party system. Indeed, it is the political importance of the small businessman and merchant that returned to haunt the technocrats and politicians by the end of the 1960s. Even the planning process is subjected to major political redirection as successive presidents change their judgment of its political and economic role. The economic dislocations of the Plan were probably the most important factor preventing it from becoming an even more effective substitute for reliable institutions. Oddly enough, one of the unintended consequences of institutional ambiguities was to perpetuate the intricate interlocking relationship of public and private economic interests so that Mitterrand's nationalization policies appeared much less threatening to the French people than they would in countries where stronger institutions have succeeded in drawing clearer boundaries between economic interests.

Institutional stability also helps define the conditions and concerns of the labor force in relation to parties and parliaments. In some cases, as in Britain, this takes the form of an alliance between a huge union organizatin and the leading party of the Left; in other cases, an institutionalized relationship may emerge from complex organizational links to policymaking bodies less closely aligned with government, as in West Germany. As we saw in Chapter 5, none of the diverse formulas to link workers to policymaking have developed in France. The curious effect is that the two major unions, the CGT and the CFDT, are virtually alternative institutional models for France. The Communists have not yet produced an alternative to the command economy and the CGT remains their instrument. Under Maire, the CFDT has another vision of French society built on decentralized authority and direct participation. One effect is the state of "permanent crisis" in French industrial relations which is only another way of expressing that there are almost no agreed principles and guidelines for collective bargaining. The ambiguities of industrial relations are as embarrassing to the new Socialist government as they were to the coalitions of the Right, in some ways more so because the Socialists are committed to working in close cooperation with the unions.

As we saw in Chapter 6, the social security system was intentionally organized around institutional and organizational principles that excluded government. Social security was to be a self-financed and self-managed program. But, as in every welfare state, government became indispensable in extracting the additional contributions required as demand for social assistance increased and, in more recent years, the system has become increasingly dependent on direct transfers from general taxation. In dealing with the vested interests within the system, the political controversies over its administration, and the intricacies of equalizing benefits, the government by no means appeared to be the powerful agent that is so often alleged. The curious result has been that almost without the guidance of strong national institutions to redefine the meaning of "social solidarity," the system has grown immensely and has expanded to protect most noncontributors. When the Socialists came to power in 1981, there was little more to be done although they will certainly be under pressure to increase benefits and to remove the inequities among contributors.

French indecision about immigrant workers, outlined in Chapter 7, is of course conditioned by economic self-interest although it is by no means clear that cheap labor enhanced Gaullist economic goals.

In terms of the politics of policymaking, it would be more accurate to describe the French situation as one where government never had very much control because of illegal entry, and where the diverse composition of foreign labor made it difficult to construct any single policy. Put differently, even if there were clear channels for the use of collective authority in France, it is hard to imagine what might have emerged. The confused and contradictory efforts of the much stronger British Parliament, for example, suggest that responding to the conflicting values and interests involved in migrant labor issues may be no more successful than French muddling through. Neither unions nor business were much clearer than the French government. In the expression of democratic values, perhaps the Socialist effort to guarantee the political rights of immigrants, including permission to vote in local elections, has been the most important step in clearly redefining the problem.

Institutional Development:
Stimulus or Deterrent to Policymaking?

Political institutions are the recognized means of bringing democratic forces into balance with the policy process. While the performance of the Fifth Republic, measured by the normal external standards of success and failure, has been impressive, a last question might be how has the problem of institutional uncertainty in France changed or not changed the French political system. More specifically, will the uncertain relationship between a strong executive and the widely dispersed politics of participation change under a Socialist-led Republic?

In reply to the first question, the argument of the book has been that many characteristics of the policy process have operated as substitutes for the fragility of national institutions. There is first the intricate pattern of interdependence found in central-local relations, industrial relations, social security, and economic policymaking. The complexity of intergovernmental or intersectoral decisions is, in part, the result of there being no stable institutional framework within which interested parties and clients might organize. There are good reasons why those critics of French policymaking, and particularly those with understandable concern that the bureaucracy might exercise excessive influence in the policy process, find such ambiguity threatening. But one must also recognize, as may be more apparent in a policy-based approach to politics, that the ambiugities are often no less in the intricate policy processes of other advanced welfare states. What the critics omit is that in the absence of such an intricate process of bargaining and such diffuse, but effective, forms of resistance to executive decisions, democracy in France might well have been much more seriously threatened over the past twenty years than the excesses of executive and administrative power suggest.

While policy changes have come about slowly and laboriously, the intricate and interlocking policy process provided the aggregation of interests and the critical negotiating arena that is more often found in linking electoral and party politics in Western legislative processes. Contrary to the view of excessive administrative power, the administration has had to work very hard to extract even minimal agreement from the diffuse relationships impinging on policy decisions. Major legislation on reforms in industrial relations, local and regional government, and social policy has taken several years and sometimes longer. A more appropriate question on the politics of policymaking in France might be how did democratic values manage to survive in such an unwelcome environment? As I have suggested, the answer is the irrepressible demand of French citizens for full participation even at the cost of imposing great uncertainties on both institutions and policymakers. At the level of partisan politics, none of the leaders have been able to ignore the sometimes incoherent and often strident form of party politics in France. From a policy perspective on French politics, it is the remarkable ability of the French people to insist on their democratic rights *without* institutional stability that constantly kept presidents and prime ministers off balance. There is no evidence that leaders ever intended to threaten the democratic foundations of French politics and much evidence that they were constantly distracted by the problems of organizing parties and fighting elections.

Will the ambiguities in the exercise of collective authority change under the Socialists? First, it should be recognized that Mitterrand has much in common with his predecessors. He has often been considered a "mystery man" of French politics (Criddle, 1978). He has not been adverse to playing the more conventional socialists against the more radical socialists in his climb to power (see R. W. Johnson, 1981). Without detracting from the enormous task of uniting the Socialists over the past decade, the Socialist Party remains divided internally as the composition of the first cabinet reveals (see Chapter 1). His Communist supporters are under severe pressure to justify their participation in his government and the Communist labor union, the CGT, under pressure to maintain its strength.

Given the long and exhausting struggle of the Left to come to power, it is perhaps expecting too much to think that they might forego the advantages of executive office. But the first months of Mitterrand's rule were hardly a change from earlier use of executive power. The familiar "waltz of the prefects" continued and about thirty-five prefects changed assignments, with three senior prefectoral officers from the Marseilles region joining the mayor of Marseilles, the minister of interior, in key prefectoral and advisory positions in Paris. There was a shuffle of university rectors, criminal court judges, and intelligence service heads, as well as the dismissal of a number of directors of public television and radio services, a perenially politicized issue in France. Mitterrand understands the immense significance of the alternation of power, but is no less willing to use presidential powers. When asked how he felt about the institutions inherited from earlier versions of the Fifth Republic, he replied "They were made for me (*Le Monde*, August 11, 1981). In responding to a question about relations between the president and the prime minister, Mitterrand did not suggest that presidential powers within the cabinet were about to be compromised. "Under the Fifth Republic it is understood between the President of the Republic and a Prime Minister that the Prime Minister should step aside the day it is necessary; if he endures seven years so much the better" (*Le Monde*, September 9, 1981). While there has been a clear division of labor between Mitterrand and Mauroy, the president, as those before him, takes his status seriously.

Any party in opposition for decades would be likely to come to power determined to make important changes while the euphoria of victory lingered on, but this natural urge conflicts with Socialist principles in several ways that became apparent in the first reforms pressed on parliament. The forced pace of nationalization was reasonable to minimize business uncertainties, but drew skeptical reactions from the left wing of the Party and from the CFDT because more time had not been taken to involve regional commit-tees in the process. In 1972, Mitterrand said that were Richelieu alive today he would nationalize industry to preserve the power of government, and some of Mitterrand's supporters saw the shadow of absolutist methods in the 1981 nationalization program (*Le Monde*, September 1, 1981). The rapid approach to decentraliza-tion also brought reservations from Socialists who thought there should be more local involvement in the reform (see Chapter 3). Adverse economic conditions also made it difficult for the govern-ment to restore widespread consultation in the planning process although Mitterrand's rival, Rocard, the minister for planning, promised that regional committees would be given a larger role.

More important, perhaps, are the institutional reforms that Mit-terrand has discussed in the past. As is almost inevitable in a system where the policy process has so often eluded clear institutional control, most of them would impose limits on the exercise of execu-tive power. The new president has promised that parliament would "recover its institutional rights," but the modality for such a redis-tribution of powers had not been announced in late 1981. Mitter-rand has also spoken favorably of making the president's term of office coincide with the Assembly's five-year term, similar to the reform planned by Pompidou. The most radical institutional reform would be the introduction of proportional representation which was included in the 1981 election manifesto. Moving toward a more accurate system of representation is a two-edged sword for the Socialists. Roland Cayrol and his colleagues (*Le Monde*, August 18, 1981) have calculated that the most common form of pro-portional representation would have cost the Socialists about 100 seats of their majority of 289 in the 1981 legislative elections, while the other major parties (including the Communists) would have each gained about thirty seats each. For the Socialists as for the coalitions that preceded them, institutional change is extremely risky.

As Maurice Duverger has suggested (*Le Monde*, June 19, 1981), perhaps France has only changed "from one domination to another." But in terms of the underlying balance of political forces as they affect the policy process, the change is momentus. He writes, "The regime of a dominant party has ended the regime of the dominant state which can progress toward a more realistic pluralism because it is better balanced." A balancing of electoral, party, and institutional politics did not emerge from the last over-whelming victory, the 1968 legislative elections, where the Gaullists had an absolute majority of 358 seats, because the state still took priority in the politics of policymaking. But the Socialists have a more awesome burden. They have brought about the first true alternation of power in the Fifth Republic. The sheet size of the victory makes them sensitive to the historical strength of demo-cratic values in French society. Two decades of institutional uncer-tainty make them intensely aware of potential abuse and weak-nesses of the French policy process as it tries to aggregate opinions and define new ways to use collective authority. The magnitude of the social and economic changes they hope to make mean that the institutional fragility of the French Republic cannot escape their attention.

The lesson from the first two decades of the Fifth Republic for other Western democracies may be that highly structured, partisan politics cannot solve problems of redefining and redirecting institu-tionalized authority. Without the stability of other European pow-ers and Japan, France has managed to build a policy process that has worked remarkably well and has preserved the essentials of democratic governance. As all democracies enter a period of unpre-cedented complexity in policymaking, France may demonstrate how democracy can be preserved in the modern welfare state, much as France inspired democratic movements throughout the world two centuries ago. But a close examination of the French policy process suggests that it served as a surrogate for institutionalized authority, even though such effects were not foreseen by its leaders. Indeed, the reconstructed French *état* may have stimulated a search for new compromises between collective authority and democracy because the state had to forge new policy solutions if democracy were to survive.

References

General

Agnès, Yves. 1980. "L'Etat-Giscard," *Le Monde Dimanche*, March 2.
Andrews, William, and Stanley Hoffman, eds. 1981. *The Fifth Republic at Twenty*. Albany, N.Y.: SUNY Press.
L'Année Politique. Paris: Presses Universitaires de France. Annual chronology and commentary on French politics and society since 1944.
Anton, Tom. 1980. *Administered Politics: Elite Political Culture in Sweden*. Hague and Boston: Martinus Nijoff Publishing.
Ashford, Douglas E. 1982. *British Dogmatism and French Pragmatism: Central-Local Relations in the Welfare State*. London and Boston: Allen & Unwin.
————. 1981. *Policy and Politics in Britain: The Limits of Consensus*. Philadelphia: Temple University Press, and Oxford: Blackwells.
Berger, Suzanne, and Michael Piore. 1980. *Dualism and Discontinuity in Industrial Societies*. Cambridge: Cambridge University Press.
Birch, Anthony. 1980. *The British System of Government*. London: Allen & Unwin.
Birnbaum, Pierre. 1977. *Les Sommets de l'Etat*. Paris: Seuil.
Bon, F. 1978. *Les Elections en France: Histoire et Sociologie*. Paris: Seuil.
Borricaud, Francois. 1970. "Michel Crozier at le Syndrome de Blocage." *Critique*, pp. 960–76.
Bunel, Jean, and Paul Meunier. 1972. *Chaban-Delmas . . . .* Paris: Stock.
Cerny, P. G. 1972. "Cleavage, Aggregation, and Change in French Politics." *British Journal of Political Science* 2:443–56.
Cerny, P. G. and M. A. Schain, eds. 1980. *French Politics and Public Policy*. New York: St. Martin's Press.
Chapman, Brian. 1955. *The Prefects and Provincial France*. London: Allen & Unwin.
Chapsal, J., and A. Lancelot. 1975. *La Vie Politique en France depuis 1940*. Paris: Presses Universitaires de France.

Cohen, Samy. 1980. *Les Conseillers du Président: De Charles de Gaulle à Valéry Giscard d'Estaing*. Paris: Presses Universitaires de France.

Collective Work. 1977. *De Gaulle et le Service de l'Etat*. Paris: Plon.

Cotteret, J. M. et. al. 1960. *Lois Electorales et Inéqualitiés de Representation en France 1936–1960*. Paris: Colin.

Criddle, Byron. 1978. "The French Socialists." *West European Studies* 1:157–62.

Criddle, Byron. 1975. "Distorted Representation in France." *Parliamentary Affairs* 28:154–79.

Crozier, Michel. 1970. *La sociéte Bloquée*. Paris: Seuil. Translated as the *Stalled Society*. New York: Viking, 1973.

―――. 1964. *The Bureaucratic Phenomenon*. Chicago: University of Chicago Press.

Crozier, Michel, S. Huntingdon, and J. Wanatuki. 1975. *The Crisis of Democracy*. New York: New York University Press.

de Baecque, Francis. 1976. *Qui Gouverne la France?* Paris: Presses Universitaires de France.

Debré, J. L. 1974. *Les Idées Constitutitionelles du Général de Gaulle*. Paris: Librairie Générale de Droit et de Jurisprudence.

Decaumont, F. 1979. *Le Présidence de Georges Pompidou: Essai sur le Régime Présidentialiste Français*. Paris: Economica.

Dogan, Mattei. 1979. "How to Become a Cabinet Minister in France: Career Pathways, 1870–1978." *Comparative Politics* 12:1–26.

Données Sociales. 1978 and other years. Paris: Documentation Française. Annual series of social, economic, and demographic statistics.

Dumont, Jean. 1979. *Erreurs sur le Mal Français ou le Trompe-l'oeil de M. Peyrefitte*. Paris: Vernoy.

Dyson, Kenneth. 1980. *The State Tradition in Western Europe*. New York and London: Oxford University Press.

Easton, David. 1965. *Systems Analysis of Political Life*. New York: Wiley.

Frears, John. 1972. "Conflict in France: The Decline and Fall of a Sterotype." *Political Studies* 5:31–41.

Frears, J. R. 1981. *France in the Giscard Presidency*. London and Boston: Allen and Unwin.

―――. 1977. *Political Parties and Elections in the French Fifth Republic*. New York: St. Martin's.

Gagnon, Paul. 1981. "The Fifth Republic and Education: Modernity, Democracy and Culture." In Andrews and Hoffman, eds., *The Fifth Republic at Twenty*, pp. 367–81.

Giroud, Françoise. 1970. *La Comédie du Pouvoir*. Paris: Fayard.

Giscard d'Estaing, Valéry. 1978. *Le Projet Républicain*. Paris: Flammarion.

Godechot, Jacques. 1968. *Les Institutions de la France sous la Révolution et l'Empire*. Paris: Presses Universitaires de France.

Grémion, Catherine. 1979. *Profession: Décideurs*. Paris: Gauthier-Villars.

Hayward, Jack. 1976. "Institutional Inertia and Political Impetus in France and Britain." *European Journal of Political Research* 4:341–59.

————. 1973. *The One and Indivisible French Republic*. London: Weidenfeld and Nicolson.

Hoffman, Stanley. 1974. "De Gaulle as a Political Artist." In *Decline and Renewal: France since the 1930s*, pp. 202–53. New York: Viking.

Hoffman, Stanley, et al. 1963. *In Search of France*. Cambridge: Harvard University Press.

Johnson, Douglas. 1978. "The Two Frances: The Historical Debate." *West European Politics* 1:3–11.

Johnson, R. W. 1981. *The Long March of the French Left*. New York: St. Martin's Press.

Keeler, John T. S. 1981. "The Corporate Dynamic of Agricultural Modernization in the Fifth Republic." In Andrews and Hoffman, eds., *The Fifth Republic at Twenty*, pp. 271–91.

Kesselman, Mark. 1970. "Over Institutionalization and Political Constraint: The Case of France." *Comparative Politics* 3:21–44.

Kreigel, Anna. 1972. *The French Communists: Profile of a People*. Chicago: University of Chicago Press.

Lagroye, Jacques. 1976. *Chaban-Delmas à Bordeaux*. Paris: Pédone.

Langrod, G., ed. 1972. *La Consultation dans l'Administration Contemporaine*. Paris: Cujas.

Laroque, Pierre. 1953. "Problèmes Posés par les Elections Sociales." *Revue Française de Science Politique* 3:222–30.

Marceau, Jean. 1977. *Class and Status in France*. Oxford: Clarendon.

Marshall, T. H. 1950. *Citizenship and Social Class*. Cambridge: Cambridge University Press.

Massot, Jean. 1979. *Le Chef du Gouvernement en France*. Paris: Documentation Française, Notes et Etudes Documentaires. No. 4537–4538, December.

————. 1977. *La Présidence de la République en France*. Paris, Documentation Française.

Mayntz, R., and F. W. Scharpf. 1975. *Policy-Making in the German Federal Bureaucracy*. Amsterdam and New York: Elsevier.

McHale, V. E., and S. Shaber. 1976. "From Aggressive to Defensive Gaullism: The Electoral Dynamics of a 'Catch-All' Party." *Comparative Politics* 8:272–90.

Mendras, Henri. 1980. *La Sagesse et le Désordre, France 1980*. Paris: Gallimard.

———. 1979. "An Optimistic View of France." *Tocqueville Review* 1:24–63.

Pempel, T. J. 1981. *Policy and Poitics in Japan: Creative Conservatism.* Philadelphia: Temple University Press.

Peyrefitte, Alain. 1976. *Le Mal Français.* Paris: Plon.

Pilleul, Gilbert, ed. 1979. *"L'Entourage" et de Gaulle.* Paris: Plon.

Rose, Richard, ed. 1980. *Challenge to Governance.* Beverly Hills, CA.: Sage Publications.

Sokoloff, Sally. 1980. "Rural Change and Farming Policies: A Terminal Peasantry." In Cerny and Schain, eds., *French Politics and Public Policy,* pp. 218–42.

Suleiman, Ezra. 1978. *Elites in French Society: The Politics of Survival.* Princeton: Princeton University Press.

———, ed. 1977. Special Issue, "Politics and Society in France." *Comparative Politics* 10 (October).

———. 1974. *Politics, Power, and Bureaucracy in France: The Administrative Elite.* Princeton: Princeton University Press.

Tavernier, Yves. 1967. "Une Nouvelle Administration pour l'Agriculture: La Réforme du Ministère." *Revue Française de Science Politique* 17:889–917.

Thoenig, J. C. 1974. *L'Ere des Technocrates.* Paris: Editions d'Organisation.

Thomson, David. 1958. *Democracy in France.* Oxford: Oxford University Press.

Tocqueville, Alexis de. 1951. *Democracy in America.* New York: Knopf.

Vaughan, Michalina, Martin Kolinsky, and Peta Sheriff. 1980. *Social Change in France.* New York: St. Martin's Press.

Waterman, Harvey. 1969. *Political Change in Contemporary France: The Politics of an Industrial Democracy.* Columbus, Ohio: Merrill.

Wilson, Frank L. 1979. "The Revitalization of French Parties." *Comparative Political Studies* 12:82–103.

———. 1971. *The French Democratic Left 1963–1969: Toward a Modern Party System.* Stanford: Stanford University Press.

———. 1969. "The French Left and the Elections of 1968." *World Politics* 21:539–74.

Wright, Vincent. 1978a. *The Government and Politics of France.* London: Hutchinson.

———, ed. 1978b. Special Issue, "Conflict and Consensus in France." *West European Politics* 1 (October).

Wylie, Laurence. 1966. *Chanzeau: A Village in Anjou.* Cambridge: Harvard University Press.

———. 1957. *Village in the Vaucluse.* Cambridge: Harvard University Press.

Zeldin, Theodore. 1979. *France 1848–1945: Politics and Anger*. Oxford: Oxford University Press.

Administrative Reform

Anonymous. 1975. "Letter from Across the Channel: III. The Ecole Nationale d'Administration." *Public Administration* (UK) 53:153–58.

Ashford, Douglas E. 1977. "The Wonderful World of French Administration." *Administrative Science Quarterly* 22:140–50.

Birnbaum, Pierre. 1977. *Les Sommets de l'Etat*. Paris: Seuil.

Bloch-Lainé, François. 1976. *Profession: Fonctionnaire*. Paris: Seuil.

Bodiguel, J.-L. 1978. *Les Anciens Elèves de l'ENA*. Paris: Fondation Nationale des Sciences Politiques.

Bouvard Report. 1973. "Fonction Publique et Réformes Administratives." *Journel Officiel*, Avis présenté au nom de la commission des lois constitutionelles, loi de finances pour 1974 (no. 646), 1973–1974 session. pp. 1–52. Imprimerie National.

Cahiers Français. 1980. *La Fonction Publique*. Paris: Documentation Française, nos. 194 and 197.

Collection Sociologie des Organisations. 1974. *Ou Va l'Administration Française?* Paris: Editions d'organisation.

Crozier, Michel. 1979. *On ne Change pas la Société par Décret*. Paris: Grasset.

———. 1964. *The Bureaucratic Phenomenon*. Chicago: Univeristy of Chicago Press.

Debbasch, Charles, ed. 1976. *La Décentralisation pour la Rénovation de l'Etat*. Paris: Presses Universitaires de France.

———. 1969. *L'Administration au Pouvoir*. Paris: Calmann-Lèvy.

Grémion, Catherine. 1979. "De Gaulle et la Réforme Administrative." In Pilleul, ed., *"L'Entourage" et de Gaulle*, pp. 200–209.

———. 1979. *Profession: Décideurs*. Paris: Gauthier-Villars.

Institut Charles de Gaulle. 1977. *De Gaulle et le Service de l'Etat*. Paris: Plon.

Institut Français des Sciences Administratives. 1973. *Les Superstructures des Administrations Centrales*. Paris: Cujas.

Jobert, Michel. 1974. *Mémoires d'Avenir*. Paris: Grasset.

Kessler, M.-C. 1978. *La Politique de la Haute Fonction Publique*. Paris: Fondation Nationale des Sciences Politiques.

Luchaire, François, and Gèrard Conac. 1979. *La Constitution de la République Française*. Paris: Economica.

Martinet, Giles. 1973. *Le Système Pompidou*. Paris: Seiul.

Pilleul, Gilbert, ed. 1979. *"L'Entourage" et de Gaulle*. Paris: Plon.

Stevens, Anne. 1978. "Politicisation and Cohesion in the French Administration." *West European Politics* 1:68–80.

Suleiman, Ezra. 1978. *Elites in French Society: The Politics of Survival*. Princeton: Princeton University Press.

———. 1974. *Politics, Power and Bureaucracy in France*. Princeton: Princeton University Press.

Thoenig, J.-C. 1973. *L'Ere des Technocrates*. Paris: Editions d'Organisation.

Local and Regional Policy

Ashford, Douglas E. 1982. *British Dogmatism and French Pragmatism: Central-Local Relations in the Welfare State*. Boston and London: Allen & Unwin.

Ashford, Douglas E. 1980. "*La Tutelle Financière*: New Wine in Old Bottles?" In Ashford, ed., *National Resources and Urban Development*, pp. 95–114. New York: Methuen, and London: Croom Helm.

Aubert Report. 1978. *La Réponse des Maires de France*. Paris: Documentation Française.

Basdevant-Gaudemet, B. 1973. *La Commission de Décentralisation de 1870*. Paris: Presses Universitaires de France.

Becquart-Leclercq, J. 1976. *Paradoxes du Pouvoir Local*. Paris: Fondation Nationale des Sciences Politiques.

Bodiguel, J.-L., et al. 1970. *La Réforme Régionale et le Référendum du 27 Avril 1969*. Paris: Cujas.

Bourjol, Maurice. 1975. *La Réforme Municipale*. Paris: Berger-Levrault.

Chapman, Brian. 1953. *Introduction to French Local Government*. London: Allen & Unwin.

Collective work. 1975. "Les Nouvellés Institutions Régionales." *Bulletin de l'Institut International d'Administration Publique*, April-June.

Delorme, André. 1981. *La Réforme de la Fiscalité Locale 1959–1980*. Paris: Documentation Française, Notes et Etudes Documentaires, no. 4615–16, 14 April.

Deneux Report. 1979. "L'Evolution de Rôle des Etablissements Publics Régionaux dans le Domaine Economique et Social." *Avis et Rapports du Conseil Economique et Social*, pp. 1073–1107. 1979 session, July 31.

Fort, Henri, and Dominique Flecher. 1977. *Les Finances locales*. Paris: Masson.

France. 1976. Direction de l'Aménagement Foncier et de l'Urbanisme, Ministry of Infrastructure. *Recueil d'Informations Statistiques sur l'Urbanisme* (annual publication).

Giraud Report. 1981. *Rapport*. Paris: Journel Officiel, October 22. (Annexe au procés-verbal de la séance du 22 octobre 1981, 3 vols.)

Gourevitch, Peter. 1981. *Paris and the Provinces*. Berkeley: University of California Press.

Grémion, Catherine. 1979. *Profession: Décideurs*. Paris: Gauthier-Villars.

Grémion, Pierre. 1976. *Le Pouvoir Périphérique*. Paris: Seuil.

Grossman Report. 1973. "Les Possibilités Offertes aux Collectivités Locales en Matière de Ressources Financières Externes (Subventions et Emprunts)." *Avis et Rapports du Conseil Economique et Social*, July 13.

Guichard Report. 1976. *Vivre Ensemble*. Paris: Documentation Française.

Hayward, Jack, and Vincent Wright. 1971. "The 37,708 Microcosms of an Indivisible Republic: The French Local Elections of March 1971." *Parliamentary Affairs* 24:284–311.

———. 1977. "Governing from the Centre: the 1977 French Local Elections." *Government and Opposition* 12:433–54.

Institut Français des Sciences Administratives. 1977. *L'Administration des Grandes Villes*. Paris: Cujas.

———. 1977. *Vers la Réforme des Collectivités Locales*. Paris: Cujas.

Kesselman, Mark. 1967. *The Ambiguous Consensus: A Study of Local Government in France*. New York: Knopf.

Lagroye, Jacques. 1973. *Chaban-Delmas à Bordeaux*. Paris: Pedone.

Lagroye, Jacques, and Vincent Wright. 1979. *Local Government in Britain and France*. New York and London: Allen and Unwin.

Léotard Report. 1979. "Faut-Il Limiter le Cumul des Mandats?" *Revue Politique et Parliamentaire*, November, pp. 18–37.

Machin, Howard. 1978. "All Jacobins Now?: The Growing Hostility to Local Government Reform." *West European Politics* 1:133–50.

———. 1978. *Prefects of the Fifth Republic*. London: Croom Helm.

Mény, Yves. 1980. "Financial Transfers and the Local Government in France: National Policy Despite 36,000 Communes." In Douglas E. Ashford, ed., *Financing Cities in the Welfare State*, pp. 142–57. London: Croom Helm, and New York: St. Martins Press.

———. 1974. *Centralisation et Décentralisation dans le Débat Politique Français (1945–69)*. Paris: Librairie Générale de Droit et de Jurisprudence.

Ministry of Infrastructure. 1976. *Etudes d'Urbanisme*. Paris: Documentation Française. (Annual series of urban statistics.)

Peyrefitte Report. 1974. *Décentraliser les responsabilités*. Paris: Documentation Française.

Richard Report. 1981. *Rapport*. Paris: Journel Officiel, December 4. (Annexe au procés-verbal de la séance du 4 décembre 1981, 3 vols.)

Socialist Party. 1980. "Les Propositions Socialistes pour la Décentralisation de l'Etat et la Réforme des Collectivités Locales." *Communes de France*, November. (Also *Proposition de Loi*, no. 3406, First Session 1977–78, National Assembly. *Journal Officiel*, December 20, 1977.)

Thoenig, J.-C. 1980. "Local Subsidies in the Third Republic: The Political

Marketplace and Bureaucratic Allocation." In Douglas E. Ashford, ed., *Financing Cities in the Welfare State*, pp. 119–41. London: Croom Helm, and New York: St. Martins Press.

―――. 1978. "State Bureaucracies and Local Government in France." In Kenneth Hanpf and Fritz W. Scharpf, eds., *Interorganizational Policy Making: Limits to Coordination and Control*, pp. 167–97. Beverly Hills, Ca.: Sage Publications.

―――. 1975. "La relation entre le Centre et la Périphérie en France." *Bulletin de l'Institut International d'Administration Publique* 36:77–123.

Thoenig, J.-C., and F. Dupuy. 1980. *Réformer ou déformer: La Formation Permanente des Administrateurs Locaux*. Paris: Cujas.

Vasseur Report. 1979. "Les Orientations de la Politique d'Aménagement du Territoire." *Avis et Rapports du Conseil Economique et Social*, pp. 1–48. January 12.

Wylie, Laurence. 1974. *Village in the Vaucluse*. 3rd ed. Cambridge: Harvard University Press.

Economic Policy

André, Christine, and Robert Delorme. 1978. "The Long-Run Growth of Public Expenditure in France." *Finances Publiques* 33:41–67.

Barrou, Y., et al. 1979. *Les Performances Comparées de l'Economie en France, en RFA et au Royaume-Uni*. Paris: INSEE (Series E-69). November.

Belassa, Bela. 1981. "The French Economy under the Fifth Republic, 1958–1978." In William Andrews and Stanley Hoffman, eds., *The Fifth Republic at Twenty*. pp. 204–26. Albany, N.Y.: SUNY Press.

Berger, Suzanne. 1981. "Lame Ducks and National Champions: Industrial Policy in the Fifth Republic." In William Andrews and Stanley Hoffman, eds.,*The Fifth Republic at Twenty*, pp. 292–310. Albany, N.Y.: SUNY Press.

―――. 1977. "D'une botique à l'autre: Changes in the Organization of Traditional Middle Classes from the Fourth to the Fifth Republics." *Comparative Politics* 1:121–36.

Berger, Suzanne, and Michael Piore, eds. 1980. *Dualism and Discontinuity in Industrial Societies*. Cambridge: Cambridge University Press.

Bloch-Lainé, François. 1963. *Pour une Réforme de l'Entreprise*. Paris: Seuil.

Bonnefous, Edouard. 1980. *A la Recherche des Milliards Perdus*. Paris: Presses Universitaires de France.

Cahiers Français. 1977. *L'Entreprise: Structure et Pouvoir*. Paris: Documentation Française, no. 180.

CERC. 1979. *Deuxième Rapport sur les Revenus des Français*. Paris: Documents de Centre d'Etude des Revenus et des Couts.

Chevallier, François. 1978. *Les Entreprises Publiques en France.* Paris: Documentation Française. Notes et Etudes Documentaires, nos. 4507–8. March 9.

Cohen, Stephen. 1977. *Modern Capitalist Planning: The French Model.* Berkeley: University of California Press.

Division Etudes des Entreprises. 1974. *Fresque Historique du Système Productif.* Paris: INSEE (Series E-27). October.

Dubois, Pierre. 1974. *Mort de l'Etat-patron.* Paris: Editions Ouvrières.

Fabra, Paul. 1981. "Une Politique d'Exceptions." *Le Monde,* July 19.

Gaudin Report. 1979. *Premières Eléments pour une Programme Nationale d'Innovation.* Paris: Ministry of Industry.

Green, Diane. 1980. "The Budget and the Plan." In P. Cerny and M. Schain, eds., *French Politics and Public Policy,* pp. 99–124. New York: St. Martin's Press.

————. 1978a. "The Seventh Plan—the Demise of French Planning?" *West European Politics* 1:60–76.

————. 1978b. "Individualism versus Collectivism: Economic Choices in France." *West European Politics* 1:81–96.

Gruson, Claude. 1968. *Origine et Espoirs de la Planification Française.* Paris: Dunod.

Hall, Peter A. 1981. "Economic Planning and the State: The Evolution of Economic Challenge and Political Response in France." In G. Esping-Anderson and R. Friedland, eds., *Political Power and Social Theory.* Greenwich, Conn.: Jai Press (forthcoming).

Hayward, Jack. 1975. "The Politics of Planning in France and Britain." *Comparative Politics* 7:285–98.

Hayward, Jack, and Michael Watson. 1975. *Planning, Politics and Public Policy: The British, French and Italian Experience.* Cambridge: Cambridge University Press.

Hayward, J. E. S. 1972. "State Intervention in France: The Changing Style of Government-Industry Relations." *Political Studies* 20:287–98.

————. 1966. "Interest Groups and Incomes Policy in France." *British Journal of Industrial Relations* 4:165–200.

Kinsel, Richard F. 1980. *Capitalism and the State in Modern France.* Cambridge: Cambridge University Press.

Lauber, Volkmar. 1981. "The Gaullist Model of Economic Modernization." In William Andrews and Stanley Hoffman, eds., *The Fifth Republic at Twenty,* pp. 227–39. Albany, N.Y.: SUNY Press.

Lelong, Pierre. 1979. "Le Général de Gaulle et les Industries de Pointe." In Gilbert Pilleul, ed., *"L'Entourage" et de Gaulle,* pp. 177–98. Paris: Plon.

Le Pors, Anicet. 1977. *Les Béquilles du capital.* Paris: Seuil.

————. 1976. *Les Transferts Etat-Industrie en France et dans les Pays*

Occidentaux. Paris: Documentation Française (Notes et Etudes Documentaires, nos. 4303–4–5). July 12.

McArthur, John, and Bruce Scott. 1969. *Industrial Planning in France*. Cambridge: Harvard University Press.

Ministry of Planning. 1982. *Plan Intérimaire: Stratégie pour Deux Ans 1982–1983*. Paris: Documentation Française.

Nora Report. 1967. Groupe de Travail du Comité Interministériel des Entreprises Publiques, *Rapport au Premier Ministre*. Paris: Documentation Française. April.

Organization for Economic Cooperation and Development. 1979. *France*. February.

Ortoli Report. 1968. *Rapport du Groupe d'Experts*. Comité de developpement Industriel, Planning Commission. April.

Rueff, Jacques. 1972. *Combats pour l'ordre financier*. Paris: Plon.

Servan-Schreiber, J.-J. 1969. *The American Challenge*. New York: Atheneum.

Shonfield, Andrew. 1965. *Modern Capitalism*. London: Oxford University Press.

Stoffaës, Christian. 1978. *La Grande Menace Industrielle*. Paris: Calmann-Lévy.

Stoleru, Lionel. 1969. *L'Imperatif Industriel*. Paris: Seuil.

Suleiman, Ezra. 1975. "Industrial Policy Formation in France." In S. Warnecke and E. Suleiman, eds., *Industrial Policies in Western Europe*, pp. 23–42. New York: Praeger.

Vedel Report. 1976. "Le Financement des Entreprises Publiques." *Avis et Rapports du Conseil Economique et Social*, pp. 1129–59. 1976 session, December 3.

Zysman, John. 1977. *Political Strategies for Industrial Order*. Berkeley: University of California Press.

Industrial Relations

Adam, G. 1968. "Ou en Est le Débat sur la 'Nouvelle Classe Ouvrière'?" *Revue Française de Science Politique* 18:1003–21.

Adam, G., and J. D. Reynaud. 1978. *Conflits du Travail at Changement Social*. Paris: Presses Universitaires de France.

Baudelot, Christian, and Anne Lebeaupin. 1979. "Les Salaires de 1950 à 1975." *Economie et Statistiques* no. 113, July-August, pp. 15–23.

Baudrillart, W., and J. F. Colin. 1979. "Le Nouveau Régime de l'Indemnisation du Chômage: Les Prémisses de la Vraie Réforme." *Droit Social*, no. 12, December, pp. 495–504.

Bernard, J.-P. 1978. "Conflits Sociaux et Economie Industrielle." *Revue d'Economie Industrielle* 4:5–29.

Bienaymé, A. 1978. "Incomes Policy in France." *Lloyd's Bank Review*, April, pp. 33–48.

⸺. 1967. "La Loi du 3 Décembre 1966 sur la Formation Profession-elle." *Droit Social*, no. 7-8, July-August, pp. 405–21.

Birien, Jean Louis. 1978. *Le Fait Syndical en France*, Paris: Publi-Union.

Bonaffé-Schmidt, J.-P. 1977. "Malaise Syndical et Comité de Grève." *Economie et Humanisme* no. 237, pp. 60–72.

Branciard, Michel. 1978. "De F. Pelloutier à L. Jouhaux," *CFDT Aujour-d'hui* (special number: "Sydicalisme et Pouvoirs") no. 34, November-December, pp. 3–16.

Bron, Jean. 1970. *Histoire du Mouvement Ouvrier Français*, (Vols. 1, 2, and 3). Paris: Editions Ouvrières.

Bulletin Mensuel des Statistiques du Travail. No. 70, 1979 Supplement. "Participation."

Bunel, J. 1973. *La Mensualisation, une Réforme Tranquille?* Paris: Editions Ouvrières.

Burnot, R. 1979. "Bilan de la Mensualisation." *Droit Social* No. 11, November, pp. 396–413.

Cahiers Français. 1980. *Chômage et politique*. Paris: Documentation Française, no. 195.

Casanova, J.-C. 1967. "L'Amendement Vallon." *Revue Française de Science Politique* 17:97–109.

CFDT. 1980. "Le Syndicalisme dans la Crise." *CFDT Aujourd'hui* (special number) no. 43, May-June.

Chéramy Report. 1976. "La Formation Professionelle Continue." *Avis et Rapports du Conseil Economique et Social*, November 10, pp. 1075–127.

Colin, J.-F., and J. M. Espinasse. 1979. "Subventions à l'Emploi, un Essai d'Analyse." *Travail et Emploi* no. 1, June, pp. 37–50.

Delamotte, Y. 1976. *L'Approache Française envers l'Humanisation du Travail*. Geneva: Institut International d'Etudes Sociales.

Delmon Report. 1975. "La Réforme de l'Entreprise." *Avis et Rapports du Conseil Economique et Social*, August 5, pp. 497–520.

Dubois, Pierre, 1976. "French Employment Policy during 1974–1976." In National Commission for Manpower Policy, *Reexamining European Manpower Policies*, Special Report No. 10, pp. 101–20. Washington, D.C.

Dubois, Pierre, Claude Durand, and Sabine Erbès-Seguin. 1978. "The Contradictions of French Trade Unionism." In C. Crouch and A. Pizzorno, eds., *The Resurgence of Class Conflict in Western Europe since 1968*, pp. 53–100. New York: Holmes and Meier.

Dubois, Pierre, et al. 1971. *Grèves Revendicatives ou Grèves Politiques?* Paris: Anthropos.

Durand, M. 1979. "La Grève: Conflit Structurel, Système de Relations

Industrielles ou Facteur de Changement Social." *Sociologie du Travail* 21:274–96.

Erbès-Seguin, S. 1976. "Les Deux Champs de l'Affrontement Professional." *Sociologie du Travail* 18:121–38.

Erbès-Seguin, S., and C. Casassus. 1977. "Structures Revendicatives: Les Lieux d'Arbitrage du Conflit Industriel." *Revue Française des Affaires Sociales* 31:101–18.

Fabre Report. 1979. *Une Politique pour l'Emploi au Service de l'Homme.* Paris: Documentation Française.

Hayward, Jack. 1975. "Employers Associations and the State in France." In S. Warnecke and E. Suleiman, eds., *Industrial Policies in Western Europe*, pp. 118–51. New York: Praeger.

Hayward, J. E. S. 1972. "State Intervention in France: The Changing Style of Government-Industry Relations." *Political Studies* 20:285–98.

La Grange, H. 1979. "La Dynamique de Grèves." *Revue Française de Science Politique* 29:665–92.

Landier, Hubert. 1980. "La Crise du Syndicalisme et l'Evolution des Comportements Patronaux." *The Tocqueville Review* 2:110–22.

Maire, Edmond, and Jacques Julliard. 1975. *La CFDT d'Aujourd'hui.* Paris: Seuil.

Martin, D. 1974. "Le Contenu des Accords d'Entreprise." *Revue Française des Affaires Sociales* 28:45–75.

Maurice, Marc, and François Sellier. 1979. "Societal Analysis of Industrial Relations: A Comparison between France and Germany." *British Journal of Industrial Relations* 17:322–36.

Ministry of Labor. 1977. "Les Sections Syndicales: Etude Statistique de l'Institution au 1er Juillet." *Revue Française des Affaires Sociales* 31:59–76.

Monatte, P. 1976. *La Lutte Syndicale.* Paris: Maspero.

Reynaud, J.-D. 1979. "Conflict and Social Regulation." *British Journal of Industrial Relations* 17:314–21.

———. 1978. *Les Syndicats, les Patrons et l'Etat.* Paris: Editions Ouvrières.

———. 1975. "France: Elitist Society Inhibits Articulated Bargaining." In S. Barkin, ed., *Worker Militancy and Its Consequences, 1965–75.* New York: Praeger.

———. 1975. "Trade Unions and Political Parties in France: Some Recent Trends." *Industrial and Labor Relations Review* 28:208–25.

Saposs, David J. 1931. *The Labor Movement in Post-War France.* New York: Columbia University Press.

Schain, Martin A. 1980. "The Dynamics of Labor Policy in France: Industrial Relations and the French Trade Union Movement." *The Tocqueville Review* 2:77–109.

Smith, W. Rand. 1981. "Paradoxes of Plural Unionism: CGT-CFDT Relations in France." *West European Politics* 4:38–53.

Sudreau Report. 1975. *La Reforme de l'Entreprise*. Paris: Documentation Française.

Suleiman, Ezra. 1975. "Industrial Policy Formation in France." In S. Warnecke and E. Suleiman, eds., *Industrial Policies in Western Europe*, pp. 23–42. New York: Praeger.

Thuillier, G. 1967. "Les Incertitudes de la Planification en Matière de Formation Professionelle." *Droit Social* no. 11, November, pp. 537–46.

Vinstock Report. 1977. "Le Dispositif Actuel de Prévision en Matière d'Emploi." *Avis et Rapports du Conseil Economique et Social*, pp. 487–507.

Weiss, D. 1979. "Syndicats et Crise Economique." *Revue des Affaires Sociales* 33:65–79.

Social Security

Ashford, Douglas E. 1981. "The British and French Social Security Systems: Welfare by Intent and by Default." Unpublished.

Barjot, Alain. 1971. "L'Evolution de la Sccurité Sociale (Juin 1960–Juin 1966)." *Revue Française des Affaires Sociales* 25:61–79.

Beattie, R. A. 1974. "France." In T. Wilson, ed., *Pensions, Inflation and Growth*, pp. 253–304. London: Heinemann.

Berger Report. 1977. Assemblée Nationale, Commission on Cultural, Family and Social Affairs. "Rapport d'Information sur la Réforme de la Securité Sociale." *Journel Officiel*, Documents parlementaires, no. 3,000, pp. 1–604. June 16.

Blum-Girardeau, Catherine. 1981. *Les Tableaux de la Solidarité*. Paris: Documentation Française.

Boissières, Catherine, and Gerard Bougain. 1978. "Importance des Prestations selon la Situation Familiale." *Bulletin CAF*, no. 10-11, pp. 6–30.

Bonnet, Charles. 1978. "Cents Ans d'Histoire." *Informations Sociales*, nos. 6–7, pp. 13–31.

Boutbien Report. 1974. "Problèmes Posés par le Mode de Calcul des Cotisations Sociales Notamment au Régard des Industries de Main-d'Oeuvre." *Avis et Rapports du Conseil Economique et Social*, pp. 663–80, March 27. And "Les Problèmes Posés par la Securité Sociale," pp. 1315–26. September 26.

Bughin, Evelyne. 1980. "L'Evolution des Rémunerations Minimales Garanties et du SMIC depuis le Janvier 1976." *Travail et Emploi* no. 4, April, pp. 69–82.

Cahiers Français. 1975. *Sécurité sociale*. Paris: Documentation Française, no. 172, September-October.

Calvez Report. 1978. "L'Assiette des Charges Sociales et les Industries de Main-d'Oeuvre." *Avis et Rapports du Conseil Economique et Social*, pp. 225–55. December 5–6.

Chauvière, Michel. 1978. "La Galaxie des Associations Familiales." *Informations Sociales* no. 6–7, pp. 53–66.

Cohen, S. S., and C. Goldfinger. 1975. "From Permacrisis to Real Crisis in French Social Security: The Limits to Normal Politics." In Leon Lindberg, Robert Alford, Colin Crouch, and Clause Offe, eds., *Stress and Contradiction in Modern Capitalism*, pp. 57–98. Lexington: Heath.

Dayan, Paulette. 1976. "Sécurité Sociale: Son Evolution depuis les Ordonnances de 1967." *Economie et Politique* no. 262, May, pp. 44–52.

de Vernejoul Report. 1974. "Les Problèmes Posés par la Securité Sociale." *Avis et Rapports du Conseil Economique et Social*, pp. 1–110. January 19.

Doublet, Jacques. 1971. "La Securité Sociale et son Evolution (Octobre 1951–Juin 1960)." *Revue Française des Affaires Sociales* 25:27–60.

Ducamin, Bernard. 1979. "Les Obstacles à la Politique Sociale du Générale de Gaulle." In G. Pilleul, ed., *"L'Entourage" et de Gaulle*, pp. 210–18. Paris: Plon.

Dumont, Jean-Pierre. 1981. *La Securité Sociale: Toujours en Chantier*. Paris: Editions Ouvrières.

———. 1978. "Une Cathédrale Inachevée." *Le Monde*, May 23.

Dupeyroux, J.-J., ed. 1972. "Aspects Sociaux du Vie Plan." *Droit Social* (special issue) No. 4-5. April-May.

ENA Study. 1976. "Perspectives de la Securité Sociale." *Revue Française des Affaires Sociales* (special issue) vol. 30, July–September.

Eustache, Jeanne. 1978. "Une Exigence Collective: La Protection Sociale." *Informations Sociales* no. 5, pp. 9–22.

Euzeby, Alain. 1979. "Financement de la Securité Sociale et Emploi." *Droit Social* no. 11, November, pp. 384–95.

———. 1978. "Faut-il Fiscaliser la Securité Sociale?"

Ferny, Antoine. 1972. "La Securité Sociale depuis les Ordonnances de 1967." *Revue d'Economie Politique* 82:983–97.

Floreal, Nicolas. 1978. "Peut-on Généraliser la Généralisation?" *Droit Social* no. 9-10, September–October, pp. 5–13.

Foulon, Alain. 1981. "Vingt Ans de Politique Sociale." *Le Monde*, September 25.

Fourastie, J. 1981. *Le Jardin du Voisin*. Paris: Livres de Poche.

Fournier, J., and N. Questiaux. 1979. *Le Pouvoir du Social*. Paris: Presses Universitaires de France.

Friedel Report. 1966. *Rapport Preliminaire* (Commission d'Etude des Structures de la Securité Sociale), May. Paris: Prime Minister's Office. Mimeographed.

Galant, Henry C. 1955. *Histoire Politique de la Securité Sociale Française 1945–1952*. Paris: Colin. (Cahiers de la Fondation Nationale des Sciences Politiques, no. 76.)

Granger Report. 1975. Ministry of Social Security, Commission Chargée d'Etudier un Aménagement de l'Assiette des Cotisations de Securité Social. *Rapport.* Mimeographed.

Grégoire Report. 1975. Ministry of Social Security, Commission Chargée d'Etudier les Charges Supportées par les Régimes de Protection Sociale et par l'Etat. *Rapport.* Mimeographed.

Guillaume, Michel. 1971. "L'Evolution de la Securité Sociale Période 1966–1970." *Revue Française des Affaires Sociales* 25:81–97.

Hatzfeld, Henri. 1971. *Du Paupérisme à la Securité Sociale: Essai sur les Origines de la Securité Sociale en France 1850–1940.* Paris: Colin.

INSEE. 1978. *Données Sociales*, 3rd ed. Paris.

Lagrange, François, and Jean Pierre Launay. 1980. "Les Comptes Sociaux de la Nation." *Les Institutions Sociales*, pp. 1121 63. Paris: Documentation Française.

Laroque, Pierre, ed. 1980. *Les Institutions Sociales en France.* Paris: Documentation Française.

———. 1971. "La Securité Sociale de 1944 à 1951." *Revue des Affaires Sociales* 25:11–26.

Lenoir Report. 1979. *Rapport de la Commission Protection Sociale et Famille.* Paris: Documentation Française (Eighth Plan).

Masnago, Franz. 1978. "Les Charges Indues." *Droit Social* no. 9-10, September-October, pp. 116–27

Meraud Report. 1976. Planning Commission (CGP), Commission des Inégalités Sociales. *Rapport.* Paris: Documentation Française.

Meric, Jean. 1972. "Le Vie Plan et la Securité Sociale." In Dupeyroux, ed., *Droit Social* (special issue), pp. 156–69.

Oheix Report. 1981. *Contre la Précarité et la Pauvreté.* Paris: Prime Minister's Office.

Planning Commission (CGP). 1971. *Rapport de la Commission: Prestations Sociales.* Paris: Documentation Française.

Revue Française des Affaires Sociales (special number). 1980. "60e Anniversaire de Ministère de la Santé et de la Securité Sociale." Vol. 34, no. 4, October-December.

Rollet, Christian. 1978. "Pourquoi Modifier l'Assiette des Cotisations Sociales?" *Droit Social* no. 9-10, September-October, pp. 128–33.

Rose, Richard, and Guy Peters. 1978. *Can Government Go Bankrupt?* New York: Basic Books.

Roson, Henri. 1976. "Les Grandes Tendances de l'Evolution de la Securité Sociale en France." *Bulletin International de l'Institut d'Administration Publique* 37:7–20.

Rustant, Maurice. 1977. "Le Financement de la Securité Sociale." *Economie et Humanisme* no. 235, March, pp. 56–78.

Socialist Party. 1980. "Proposition de Loi Relative à la Protection Sociale." Paris: Assemblée Nationale (Documents), Second Session 1979–80, June 25.

Sullerot Report. 1979. "La Situation Démographiques de la France et les Implications Economiques et Sociales." *Droit Social* no. 3, March, pp. 129–39.

Uri, Pierre. 1979. "Taillables et Corveables." *Le Monde*, July 27.

Immigration Policy

Adler, Stephen. 1977. *International Migration and Dependence*. Westmead, England: Saxon House.

Allal, Tewfik, et al. 1977. *Situations Migratoires: La Fonction-Miroir*. Paris: Galilée.

ben Jalloun, Tahar. 1979. "Les Lois de l'Hopitalité." *Le Monde*, October 4.

Benoit, Jean. 1980. "La bombe de M. Ambroise Roux." *Le Monde*, January 20.

Calvez Report. 1975. "La Politique de l'Immigration." *Avis et Rapports du Conseil Economique et Social*, pp. 349–75. May 23.

———. 1969. "Le problème des Travailleurs Etrangers." *Avis et Rapports du Conseil Economique et Social*, pp. 307–23. March 27.

CGT. 1971. *Pur une Politique de l'Immigration Conforme aux Intérêts des Travailleurs Français et Immigrés*. Paris.

CIEMM. 1979. (Committee to Protect Migrant Associations). Statement on control of immigrant organizations.

Courault, Brune. 1980. *Contribution à la Théorie de l'Offre du Travail: Le Case de l'Immigration en France 1946–1978*. Thèse doctorale, Paris.

Courault, Bruno, and Oliver Villey. 1979. "1,640,000 Travailleurs Etrangers en Octobre 1976." *Economie et Statistiques* no. 113, July-August, pp. 29–35.

Dijoud statement on new policy. Introduction to special issue of *Droit Social*, 1975.

Dupeyroux, Jean-Jacques, ed. 1976. "Les Travailleurs Immigrés." *Droit Social* (special issue) no. 5.

Esperet Report. 1964. "Problèmes Posés par l'Immigration des Travailleurs Africains en France." *Avis et Rapports du Conseil Economique et Social*, pp. 545–66. June 23.

Fanon, Franz. 1961. *Les Damnés de la Terre*. Paris: Maspero.

Freeman, Gary. 1979. *Immigrant Labor and Racial Conflict in Industrial Societies: The French and British Experience 1945–1975*. Princeton: Princeton University Press.

Granotier, Bernard. 1970. *Les Travailleurs Immigrés en France*. Paris: Maspero.

Gremy, François. 1980. Letter to *Le Monde*, June 24.

Lebon, Andre. 1979. "L'Aide au Retour des Travailleurs Etrangers." *Economie et Statistique* no. 113, July-August, pp. 37–46.

————, ed. 1978. "Les Immigrations Externes." *Revue Française des Affaires Sociales* 32 (special issue).

LePors, Anicet. 1976. *Immigration et Développement Economique et Social*. Paris: Documentation Française.

Lesire-Ogrel, Hubert. 1978. "Prise en Charge des Problèmes des Travailleurs immigrés." *CFDT Aujourd'hui* no. 31, May-June, pp. 66–95.

Marshall, D. Bruce. 1973. *The French Colonial Myth and Constitution-Making in the Fourth Republic*. New Haven: Yale University Press.

Miller, Mark. 1979. "Foreign Workers in France: The Case of the Sonacotra Strike." Mimeographed.

————. 1979. "Reluctant Partnership: Foreign Workers in Franco-Algerian Relations 1962–1979." *Journal of International Affairs* 33:219–37.

Minces, Juliette. 1973. *Les Travailleurs Etrangers en France*. Paris: Seuil.

————. 1967. *Les Travailleurs Etrangers en France*. Paris: Seuil.

Ministry of Labor. 1977. *Immigration et 7e Plan*. Paris: Documentation Française.

————. 1977. *Les Etrangers au Recensement de 1975*. Paris: Documentation Française.

Piore, Michael. 1979. *Birds of Passage: Migrant Labor and Industrial Societies*. Cambridge: Cambridge University Press.

Secretary of State for Immigrant Workers. 1977. *La Nouvelle Politique de l'Immigration*. Paris: Documentation Française.

Tapinos, Georges. 1975. *L'Immigration Etrangère en France*. Paris: Presses Universitaires de France (Cahier no. 71, Institut National d'Etudes Démographiques).

Teitgen, Paul. (Council of State). 1979. "L'Engrenage Discret de l'Arbitraire." *Le Monde*, October 18.

Villey, Olivier. 1980. "Le Main-d'Oeuvre Etrangère et la Crise en France." *Travail et Emploi* no. 4, April, pp. 83–92.

Index

Adam, Gérard, 193, 195, 212
Administration and politics, 14, 69–73, 80–83, 98–100, 139–42, 233, 310–14; detached service, 69–70; in Fourth Republic, 45–48; and Socialists, 45. *See also* Grands corps; National School of Administration; Prefects
Administrative reform, 65–80, 84–88, 96–98, 100–104; and de Gaulle, 70–73; and Giscard, 77–80; and Mitterrand, 104–6; and Pompidou, 73–74
Africa, 270
Agnès, Yves, 98
Agricultural policy, 58
Algeria and France, 15, 21, 29, 32, 70–71, 151, 152, 268, 270, 275
Algerian workers, 272–74, 278. *See also* Immigration policy
ANACT, 203
André, Christiane, 147
Anton, Tom, 46, 55, 304
Ashford, Douglas E., 46, 48, 62, 109, 111, 300, 301
Autogestion (self-management), 78, 104, 191

Bank of France, 148, 152, 178, 232
Barjot, Alain, 237
Barre, Raymond, 24, 40, 52, 123, 140, 160, 179–82, 204, 245, 263
Belassa, Bela, 153
Ben Bella, Farhat, 272

Benoit, Jean, 296–97
Berger Report, 245
Bergeron, André, 191
Berger, Suzanne, 158, 159, 161
Bernard, J.-P., 194
Bernard Report, 197
Birch, Anthony, 56
Birnbaum, Pierre, 47, 73, 313
Blanc, Louis, 41
Bloch-Lainé, François, 25, 73, 75–76, 84, 200, 310
Blum-Giradeau, Catherine, 245
Blum, Leon, 41, 148, 200
Bonaffé-Schmidt, J.-P., 194
Bonnefous, Edouard, 62
Bonnet, Charles, 231, 281–82, 284
Bordaz Report, 237
Borricaud, François, 17, 45
Bourrel Report, 120
Boutbien Report, 235, 244
Bouvard Report, 76–77, 94–98
Britain, 3, 7, 14, 25, 30, 31, 34, 48, 52, 56–57, 59, 60, 62, 70, 74, 107, 189, 194, 195, 227, 228, 231, 232, 235, 248, 268, 282, 304, 314, 316
Bron, Jean, 190
Budget, 74, 75, 147, 172, 256; budgetary deficit, 183; budgetary powers in Parliament, 20
Bureaucracy. *See* Administration and politics; Grands corps
Business pressure groups, 29, 193, 221–24, 225–27. *See also* CNPF

339